D0907154

Review of Marketing Research

Review of Marketing Research

VOLUME 1

Naresh K. Malhotra

Editor

M.E. Sharpe
Armonk, New York
London, England

Library of Congress ISSN: 1548-6435
ISBN 0-7656-1304-2 (hardcover)

Printed in the United States of America

The paper used in this publication meets the minimum requirements of
American National Standard for Information Sciences
Permanence of Paper for Printed Library Materials,
ANSI Z 39.48-1984.

MV (c)   10   9   8   7   6   5   4   3   2   1

REVIEW OF MARKETING RESEARCH

EDITOR: NARESH K. MALHOTRA, GEORGIA INSTITUTE OF TECHNOLOGY

AD HOC REVIEWERS

Dennis B. Arnett, Texas Tech University
Julie Baker, University of Texas, Arlington
Sharon Beatty, University of Alabama
Sundar Bharadwaj, Emory University
Michael J. Greenacre, University of Pompeu Fabra, Spain
Satish Jayachandran, University of South Carolina
Fred W. Morgan, University of Kentucky
Nancy Ridgway, University of Richmond
John Schouten, University of Portland
Barbara Stern, Rutgers University
J. Chris White, University of Central Florida

CONTENTS

REVIEW OF MARKETING RESEARCH

Introduction

Naresh K. Malhotra

Overview

Review of Marketing Research is a new annual publication covering the important areas of marketing research with a more comprehensive state-of-the-art orientation. Articles in this publication will review the literature in a particular area, offer a critical commentary, develop an innovative framework, and discuss the future developments in addition to containing specific empirical studies.

Publication Mission

The purpose of this series is to provide current, comprehensive, state-of-the-art articles in review of marketing research. A wide range of paradigmatic or theoretical substantive agenda are appropriate for this series. This includes a wide range of theoretical perspectives, paradigms, data (qualitative, survey, experimental, ethnographic, secondary, etc.), and topics related to the study and explanation of marketing-related phenomena. We hope to reflect an eclectic mixture of data and research methods that is indicative of a series driven by important theoretical and substantive problems (Iacobucci 2002; Stewart 2002). The series seeks papers that make important theoretical, substantive, empirical, methodological, measurement, and modeling contributions. Any topic that fits under the broad area of "marketing research" is relevant. In short, our mission is to publish the best reviews in the discipline.

Thus, this publication will bridge the gap left by current marketing research publications. Current marketing research publications such as the *Journal of Marketing Research* (USA), *Journal of Marketing Research Society* (UK), and *International Journal of Research in Marketing* (Europe) publish academic articles with a major constraint on the length. In contrast, *Review of Marketing Research* will publish much longer articles that are not only theoretically rigorous but are more expository and also focus on implementing new marketing research concepts and procedures. This will also serve to distinguish the proposed publication from the *Marketing Research* magazine published by the American Marketing Association (AMA).

Articles in *Review of Marketing Research* should:

- Critically review the existing literature.
- Summarize what we know about the subject—key findings.

- Present the main theories and frameworks.
- Review and provide an exposition of key methodologies.
- Identify the gaps in literature.
- Present empirical studies (for empirical papers only).
- Discuss emerging trends and issues.
- Focus on international developments.
- Suggest directions for future theory development and testing.
- Recommend guidelines for implementing new procedures and concepts.

Articles in This Volume

This inaugural volume exemplifies the broad scope of the *Review of Marketing Research*. It contains a diverse set of review articles covering such areas as emotions, beauty, information search, business and marketing strategy, organizational performance, reference scales, and correspondence analysis.

Johnson and Stewart provide a review of traditional approaches to the analysis of emotion in the context of consumer behavior. They argue that appraisal theory provides an especially relevant approach for understanding the emotional responses of consumers in the marketplace. They review appraisal theory and provide examples of its application in the contexts of advertising, customer satisfaction, product design, and retail shopping. Appraisal theory is the leading contemporary framework in emotion theory. The authors also briefly mention other approaches, such as dimensional theories. Appraisal theories can be applied in a variety of areas in marketing to incorporate appraisals and the concepts of emotional and behavioral coping, and research along these lines should be fruitful.

Beauty is in the eye of the beholder. Holbrook explores the concept of beauty as experienced by ordinary consumers in their everyday lives. He considers the definitions of beauty typically supplied by philosophers of art from the perspective of aesthetic experience. Such definitions operate in the realm of *langue*—semantics, language use, or linguistic competence. Thus, these definitions operate in a form of language that exists according to certain semantic and syntactic rules but that does not necessarily reflect how the language is generally spoken in the vernacular. The latter concern belongs to the realm of *parole*—pragmatics, usage, or psycholinguistic performance. Here the words are deployed by actual speakers of the language in ways that shape the common, culturally shared meaning. He applies the method of the *collective photographic essay* to explore the concept of beauty as it appears in *parole*. In this method, ordinary consumers take photographs intended to elucidate the concept of "What Beauty Means to Me" and explain their photographic intentions by means of short paragraphs or vignettes. These vignettes and photos are analyzed semiologically by means of hermeneutic interpretation. The application of this *hermeneutic circle* produces a *Typology of Beauty in Ordinary Discourse*. This typology conceptualizes everyday usage of the term "beauty" as falling into *eight categories* distinguished on the basis of *three dichotomies*: (1) Extrinsically/Intrinsically Motivated, (2) Thing(s)-/Person(s)-Based, and (3) Concrete/Abstract. Detailed examples, drawn from the texts of the informants' vignettes and photographs, illustrate each of the eight types of beauty. His major conclusion is that the philosophically grounded definition of aesthetic beauty (*langue*) fails to capture the diverse ways in which the concept of beauty appears in everyday discourse among ordinary consumers (*parole*). Though distinct conceptually, these eight types of beauty tend to commingle in consumption experiences. The concept of beauty deserves more attention and other approaches to the study of beauty should be explored in the domestic as well as cross-cultural settings.

Consumer information search has been an area of research interest in consumer behavior and marketing for over three decades. Xia and Monroe first review the literature on consumer information search, and then the literature on browsing. Because literature on browsing in marketing is scant, their review of browsing integrates literature from library science and information systems. Based on their reviews of these streams, they propose an extended consumer information acquisition framework and outline relevant substantive and methodological issues for future research. Beyond passive browsing, the notion of passive acquisition of information needs to be examined in a broader light.

Hunt and Morgan review the progress and prospects of the "resource-advantage" (R-A) theory. They provide a brief overview of R-A theory and discuss the progress made in developing the theory's research program. They examine in detail the theory's foundational premises, show how R-A theory provides a theoretical foundation for business and marketing strategy, and discuss the theory's future prospects. Future research should not only critically examine the R-A theory to further refine it, but also focus on how R-A theory and its premises can be *applied* to the practice of business and marketing strategy.

The resource-based view of the firm has had a considerable impact on strategy research in marketing that focuses on performance-related issues at the business, product-market, and brand levels. Bharadwaj and Varadarajan provide an interdisciplinary review and perspective on the determinants of organizational performance. They examine the classical industrial organization school, the efficiency/revisionist school, the strategic groups school, the business policy school and the Profit Impact of Market Strategy (PIMS) paradigm, the Austrian school, and the resource-based view of the firm. They propose an integrative model of business performance that models firm-specific intangibles, industry structure, and competitive strategy variables as the major determinants of business performance. There is a dearth of research that incorporates the structure-conduct-performance (SCP), competitive strategy, and resource-based perspectives and investigates firm-specific variables in performance models. More research along these lines is encouraged.

Vargo and Lusch focus attention on consumer reference scales, the psychological scales used to make evaluations of marketing-related stimuli, in consumer satisfaction/dissatisfaction (CS/D) and service quality (SQ) research. They question the disconfirmation of the expectations paradigm in relation to (1) whether standards other than or in addition to expectations influence evaluations, and (2) whether the standards are associated with vector attributes, as implied by the disconfirmation model, or serve as ideal points. They review the disconfirmation model, its related issues, and the latitude models found in the CS/D and SQ research literatures. They propose social judgment-involvement (SJI) theory, a latitude-based theory from social psychology, as a potential theoretical framework to augment, replace, and/or elaborate the disconfirmation model and latitude models associated with CS/D and SQ research. They also advocate SJI theory for potential adaptation of its research methods for further inquiry into the nature of consumer reference scales. They report a preliminary exploratory study using a modified research method from SJI and offer a research agenda. The issues of relevant standards of comparison and the role of these standards, the boundary conditions, and the impact of situational and personal variables deserve more attention.

Finally, Malhotra, Charles, and Uslay review the literature focusing on the methodological perspectives, issues, and applications related to correspondence analysis (CA). Starting with a historical note, they describe the key features of CA and the principles and requirements governing CA. They also discuss the equivalent approaches to CA and the methods for scaling of points along the principal axes. They examine the various diagnostic tools and give special attention to interpretation of solutions. The appropriateness of homogeneity analysis is discussed. They conclude with a list of the creative applications and the technique's limitations.

References

Iacobucci, Dawn (2002), "From the Editor-Elect," *Journal of Consumer Research*, 29 (June), 1–3.
Stewart, David W. (2002), "Getting Published: Reflections of an Old Editor," *Journal of Marketing*, 66 (October), 1–6.

Review of Marketing Research

CHAPTER 1

A REAPPRAISAL OF THE ROLE OF EMOTION IN CONSUMER BEHAVIOR

Traditional and Contemporary Approaches

ALLISON R. JOHNSON AND DAVID W. STEWART

Abstract

This article provides a review of traditional approaches to the analysis of emotion in the context of consumer behavior. The authors argue that appraisal theory provides an especially relevant approach for understanding the emotional responses of consumers in the marketplace. A review of appraisal theory is provided as well as examples of its application in the contexts of advertising, customer satisfaction, product design, and retail shopping.

A considerable body of research has recognized emotion as one of the more important factors in specific consumer responses to marketing stimuli and consumer behavior in general. For example, consumers' emotional responses have been a central focus of research on the impact of advertising (e.g., Holbrook and Batra 1987), the formation of satisfaction judgments (e.g., Westbrook and Oliver 1991), and the processes of consumer decisionmaking (e.g., Luce, Payne, and Bettman 1999). As Richins (1997) notes, "the importance of emotions in the sphere of consumer behavior has been firmly established" (p. 127).

Although emotion is widely recognized in the study of consumer behavior, systematic inquiry into the determinants of emotion and its effects on consumer response has been hindered by the lack of a general theory capable of explaining the complex nature of the process and the phenomenology of emotional response (Bagozzi, Gopinath, and Nyer 1999). Though several theories of emotion have been influential in marketing research, no single theory has captured the complexity of emotional response and its role in consumer behavior. It is well established that consumers' emotional reactions differ as a function of their consumption experiences, but it is less clear *how* the purchase or consumption experience influences the nature of emotional response. Indeed, the same consumption experience can produce quite different emotional responses across consumers and even within the same consumer over time. Emotional response also seems at times to be at odds with rational or objective thought. This latter phenomenon raises questions about the relationship between cognition and emotion and the way(s) in which cognitive and emotional processes interact in consumers' decisionmaking.

Within the discipline of psychology, the study of emotion has sought to answer similar types of questions about the fundamental nature of emotion, while also seeking to parsimoniously represent the complex phenomenology of emotion across many different situations. In recent years, research in psychology has tended to converge on a group of related theories of emotion, known as appraisal theories, as a unifying approach to the study of emotion, because appraisal theories have provided the most convincing and comprehensive answers to date for key theoretical and practical questions about the nature of emotion (Ekman and Davidson 1994; Scherer, Schorr, and Johnstone 2001).

Appraisal theories define emotion as a mental state that results from processing, or appraising, personally relevant information (e.g., Frijda 1993; Frijda, Kuipers, and ter Schure 1989; Lazarus and Smith 1988; Ortony, Clore, and Collins 1988; Roseman, Spindel, and Jose 1990; Scherer 1988; Smith and Ellsworth 1985). Appraisals are defined as the results of those information-processing tasks that indicate the implications of the situation for the interests and goals of the individual, and thereby determine the form that emotional reaction takes in a given situation. Thus, appraising is the processing of information that leads to emotional response, while appraisals are the "conclusions" that are reached through processing, which define the tenor of the emotion experienced (Lazarus 2001). For example, the most basic task of appraising is to determine whether a situation is "good" or "bad" for the individual in terms of his or her goals, and the resulting appraisals are part of either a positive or a negative emotion. Appraisal theories specify a number of dimensions of the appraisal process that further differentiate emotional reactions—in addition to simply feeling "good" or "bad"—based on an individual's unique construction of the situation, and identify the process(es) by which emotional responses occur and are experienced by the individual.

Appraisal theories address many of the reasons for the variations in the ways that emotions are produced and experienced and in the functions that emotions serve. Although appraisal would seem to imply a conscious cognitive mechanism, the process of appraising personally relevant information is not necessarily conscious, and may occur automatically upon perception (Lazarus 1991b). In addition, situations that are appraised and emotionally responded to may be "real" in the sense that they are defined by physical dimensions present in the external world or they may be "imagined" in the sense that they exist only in the form of memory or projective imagery (Boninger, Gleicher, and Strathman 1994; Hetts et al. 2000; MacInnis and Price 1987; Perugini and Bagozzi 2001; Plutchik 1984). Appraisal theory also suggests that emotions are functional in that they often, though not always, serve to motivate actions that serve the goals of the individual, and motivate other types of coping responses (Frijda, Kuipers, and ter Schure 1989; Lazarus 1991b; Plutchik 1982).

Research in basic psychology has provided considerable evidence to support the conceptualization of emotion that is inherent to appraisal theories. There are, however, several formulations of appraisal theory and each approach contributes to an overall picture of emotion that portrays the complexity and nuance of emotional phenomena. In addition, appraisal theories provide fertile ground for the development of hypotheses related to diverse situations in which consumers' emotional responses are involved.

The purpose of this article is to first provide a brief review of prior work on emotion in the context of consumer behavior, then to advance an integrated conceptual model of emotional response-based appraisal theories. Finally, the article offers several areas of marketing practice to which appraisal theories can be applied and directions for future research.

Review of Emotion Theory in Consumer Behavior

A Matter of Definition: Emotion, Affect, and Mood

A fundamental problem that has long plagued research on emotion, both in psychology and in the context of consumer behavior, is the definition of terms. Various terms have been used in the literature to describe phenomena that may or may not be the same, though they may be related. Such terms as "emotion," "affect," and "mood," have frequently been used interchangeably in the literature, and the same term may be used to refer to different phenomena. It is not the purpose of this article to debate the relative merits of various definitions of the extant terms in the literature. However, it is necessary to clearly define the meaning of terms as they will be used throughout this article. For purposes of the present exposition, "affect" is not considered synonymous with "emotion." Rather, emotion is defined here as a mental state with a specific referent (i.e., emotion is tied to a target such as a person, object, or event). In other words, emotions are "about something" (Clore and Ortony 2000; Lazarus 1994; Spielman, Pratto, and Bargh 1988) as opposed to being a more generalized feeling or state. In addition, emotions are experienced in relation to situations or targets that have implications for the individual's goals or well-being (e.g., Lazarus 1991b).

"Affect" is commonly understood as a blanket term that includes emotion as well as mood and attitude. While attitudes and moods are related to emotions, they are conceptually distinct. Attitudes can be antecedent to emotion and form part of the knowledge structure of beliefs that inform and shape emotional reactions. Emotions may also influence attitudes, in that emotional reactions may be used as input in forming an evaluative judgment (e.g., Batra and Ray 1986). However, attitudes are distinct from emotions because attitudes tend to be primarily evaluative in nature and are generally assumed to include cognitive and behavioral intention components as well as a general affective component. Emotion is distinct from mood because mood states are generally dissociated from any particular object or event. It is certainly the case that a mood or general affective state of being may be triggered by an emotional response to a specific target, but, in the present context, the focus is on the process by which the emotion is triggered and the influence of the emotion in a specific circumstance rather than how such an emotional trigger may create an ongoing, generalized affective state or mood.

A common distinction between emotion and mood involves the duration and intensity of the affective episode; that is, moods are longer and less intense than emotions (Bagozzi, Gopinath, and Nyer 1999). However, this is not always true, and conflicting examples are easy to find. For example, one person may feel extremely negative toward everyone and everything after experiencing a very frustrating situation, but he or she may recover quickly if the situation is resolved. Another person may feel somewhat hopeful about a particular situation in which it seems that he or she has a good chance of achieving a goal, and, if it is a long-term goal, this hopeful emotion may last for a considerable time. The first person is in a very intense negative mood for a short period of time, and the second person experiences a mildly positive emotion for a long period of time.

Another possible distinction between mood and emotion may be the intensity of the physiological reactions that accompany the affective episode. Emotions can be related with intense autonomic arousal, while moods are rarely associated with similarly intense physiological arousal (Russell and Barrett 1999). Emotions may be accompanied by strong physiological reactions such as those associated with "fight or flight," that is, the experience of anger or fear, respectively. Intense physiological arousal is not typically associated with mood, but some moods may be accompanied by physiological changes and arousal, as in the cases of severe depressive moods or extremely euphoric moods.

Although these distinctions may be useful in the context of some inquiries, the key distinction among the various definitions of mood and emotion as they are used here is whether the affect is an integral part of the response to a specific target in a particular, personally relevant situation or is merely incidental or part of a more generalized response. While attitude and mood are interesting areas of inquiry, for the present purposes they are conceptually distinct from emotion because they are likely to have different causes and effects. It is important to make this distinction clear because some research on affect in consumer behavior has not clearly distinguished among attitude, mood, and emotion.

Theoretical Approaches to the Study of Emotion

Dimensional Theories

Several of the more influential approaches to the study of emotion in the context of consumer behavior fall within a general class of theories that are often referred to as dimensional theories. Although there are differences among the various theories within this general class, all dimensional theories attempt to simplify the representation of affective responses by identifying a set of common dimensions of affect that can be used to distinguish specific emotions from one another. Among the exemplars of dimensional theories of emotion that have been applied to the consumer behavior context are Russell and Mehrabian's (1977) PAD[1] model and Watson and Tellegen's (1985) circumplex model. Within the context of consumer behavior, dimensional theories have proven especially useful in predicting consumers' responses to store atmosphere (Donovan et al. 1994), to service experiences (Hui and Bateson 1991), and to advertising (e.g., Holbrook and Batra 1987; Olney, Holbrook, and Batra 1991), among others.

Dimensional approaches to emotion typically distinguish between a dimension of affective valence (i.e., direction) and a dimension of affective arousal (i.e., intensity) (Bagozzi, Baumgartner, and Pieters 1998). Generally, these two dimensions are used in place of longer lists of affective terms to simplify the measurement of affect, or to simplify the predictive role of affective measures, by descriptively classifying emotions along these two dimensions. However, the use of only two dimensions tends to miss the nuances of emotions that are a part of common experience— very different emotions may be characterized in the same way using only valence and intensity. In contrast, circumplex models have been developed to capture the nuances of the experience of emotion. Circumplex models propose a variety of dimensions of affective response based on the relative similarity of emotions and their applicability to a particular target setting or object.

Work on the relationship of affect to satisfaction judgments by Mano and Oliver (1993) is characteristic of consumer research that has employed a dimensional approach. These authors use a circumplex model of affect with valence and arousal as two orthogonal dimensions. These two dimensions yield eight affective terms representing the main points of the circular representation (see Figure 1.1). "Pleasant" and "unpleasant" represent the two poles of the valence dimension, and "arousal" and "quietness" anchor the continuum of the arousal dimension. The combination of the two dimensions yields "elation" and "distress" as the high-arousal valenced affects. "Calmness" and "boredom" are used to represent the low-arousal affective states.

Though useful in establishing a foundation for the study of emotion in consumer behavior, dimensional approaches offer only a simplifying description of emotional response without offering a theoretical account of the causes and consequences of emotion. Dimensional approaches have also been criticized for their failure to capture the full range of emotions that consumers experience (Lazarus 1991c). While there is no doubt that the dimensions of valence and arousal are important, it is clear that these two dimensions do not explain all of the nuances of emotions. Even when various combinations of the two basic dimensions are used to classify emotions, as is the case with circumplex models, the full range of emotions and the subjective feelings associated with them may not be captured. In recognition of the shortcomings of dimensional approaches to

Figure 1.1   **Circumplex Model of Affect**

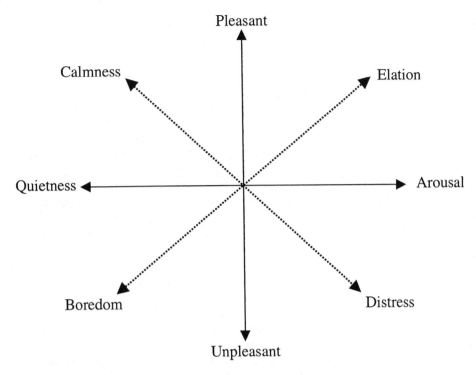

emotion, the need to capture greater specificity of emotional response, and the need to account for finer distinctions among emotions, researchers have proposed alternative theories to account for more of the richness of the subjective experience of emotion.

Basic Emotions Approaches

In an effort to overcome the limitations of dimensional theories, several scholars have attempted to identify a set of basic emotions that define all subjective emotional experiences. These approaches are based on cross-cultural and developmental research that suggests the existence of a finite set of discrete emotions—such as joy, anger, sadness, and fear—that are innate to all human beings (e.g., Izard 1992; Plutchik 1982). The subjective experience of emotion is the result of the particular pattern of responses across these various basic emotions. Thus, in any given situation it is possible to describe emotional response by measuring the extent to which each of the basic emotions is experienced (Richins 1997). In consumer research, work on hedonic experiences has provided the impetus for moving away from simple dimensional approaches to approaches that provide a means for describing more differentiated and subtle emotional states (Hirschman and Holbrook 1982; Holbrook and Batra 1987; Holbrook and Hirschman 1982; Westbrook 1987).

The basic emotions approaches have been criticized as merely labeling without a sound theoretical foundation that explains the experience of emotion (Roseman 1984). Taken to the extreme, there could be a basic emotion for every emotional response resulting in literally thousands of such basic emotions. The parsimony of the dimensional approaches is lost in an effort to capture all of the nuances of subjective emotional response. On the other hand, identifying a discrete finite set of emotions may also unnecessarily limit the range of descriptors for subjective emotional experiences and miss important distinctions among these experiences. Consistent with this criticism is the fact that much of the research on the theory of basic emotion has focused on the communication of emotion rather than on predicting the occurrence and consequences of emotions. Early work on basic emotions was based on facial expressions associated with emotion that are universally displayed and understood across cultures (Izard 1971). It is not necessarily the case that all emotions are communicated through nonverbal articulation, and some emotional experiences may not be communicated at all (Ekman and Davidson 1994). For example, hope does not have a universal facial expression, and is therefore not generally included within the set of basic emotions, though it is widely accepted as an emotion with important consequences (MacInnis and de Mello 2002). It may also be the case that some of the subjective experiences of emotion are culturally bound and therefore not easily defined by a combination of universal basic emotions.

The reliance of basic emotion approaches on labels of the subjective emotional experience is especially problematic. Because the composition of the basic emotion set is derived from evidence that certain emotions are expressed and labeled similarly across cultures, basic emotion approaches cannot account for emotional reactions that are not readily labeled in some cultures or for emotional expressions (e.g., facial expressions) that may be similar across a wide range of emotional experiences. The requirement that the basic emotions be common to a wide range of cultures excludes emotional experiences that have been labeled in some cultures but not in others. For example, there is a word in some cultures for the experience of pleasure in response to another's misfortune—*schadenfreude* in German (*Merriam-Webster Dictionary* 2003)—that is not commonly labeled with an emotional term by other cultures and is therefore excluded from consideration by basic emotion theorists. In addition, the expression related to experiencing pleasure in response to another person's misfortune is likely to be similar to the experience of other positive emotions, and so cannot be distinguished based on expression alone.

Though the basic emotion approaches have afforded some valuable insights regarding the role of emotions in consumer behavior, they were not designed to address the process and consequences of emotions. To fill this void, other theories, which more specifically focus on the causes and consequences of emotion, have been proposed and applied in the context of research on consumer behavior. One theoretical approach in particular, attribution theory, has been used to explain consumer behavior and has also addressed, to some extent, the causes and consequences of emotional responses.

Attribution Theory

Although developed for a different purpose and not originally intended as a theory of emotion, attribution theory has frequently been used to predict differentiated emotional responses arising from the distinctions that people make about the cause(s) of an event (Weiner 1985). Consumers' emotional reactions often vary depending on the perceived cause of a particular outcome. For example, the same product failure may produce anger or regret depending on whether the consumer attributes the failure to the manufacturer or to his or her failure to follow the directions for use (e.g., Folkes 1984; Maxham and Netemeyer 2002). In one specific illustration of this type of research, Folkes (1984) found that consumers were more likely to be angry and to complain when the cause of a product failure was perceived to be the producer of the product rather than the consumers' own actions.

Attribution theory was developed to explain and predict behavior that arises from perceptions of causal factors (Weiner 1985; Weiner, Russell, and Lerman 1979). Three distinct dimensions of causal attributions have been identified: (1) the locus of the cause (internal versus external to the individual), (2) the stability of the cause (likely versus unlikely to recur), and (3) the controllability of the cause of the outcome of the relevant situation (controllable or not). These dimensions of attribution have been shown to be associated with different patterns of behavior and emotional reactions. For example, as Weiner observes (1985), if an individual attributes the cause of a negative outcome for another person to his or her own actions (i.e., internal, controllable attribution of cause), the person making the attribution of personal responsibility for another's misfortune is likely to feel guilty. In addition, the person may be likely to take actions to repair or to make up for the transgression. This behavior is especially likely if the person attributes the behavior to unstable factors, like a mistake due to insufficient information, rather than to factors that are perceived to be stable, like personality, which may lead the person to conclude that he or she is just a bad person, and to feel shame instead of guilt. If the cause is stable, there may be little to be gained from trying to repair the harm done, because the cause is likely to create similar situations in the future. Thus, attributions are focused on explaining causes and may also influence perceived emotion as a result.

As this example demonstrates, attribution theory is more properly a theory of the process of identifying and coping with causal factors and outcomes. Although the literature on attribution theory has addressed potential emotional reactions, it is not a theory of emotion per se. The empirical research validating attribution theory does provide evidence of a link between cognitive distinctions and differentiated emotional reactions, however, and it suggests a need to more fully consider the relationship between cognitive processing and emotion.

The view that an attribution process plays a role in the subjective experience of emotion also finds support in research outside of attribution theory. For example, the classic work of Schachter and Singer (1962) on the misattribution of emotion describes a process by which people label arousal using situational cues as the basis for attributing generalized arousal to specific subjectively experienced emotional reactions. Schachter and Singer demonstrated that people experiencing undifferentiated arousal created by the administration of a drug tended to label their arousal as either positive or negative depending on the cues present in their environment. The occurrence of undifferentiated arousal that requires explanation is relatively rare, however. In most cases, arousal occurs with emotion after the implications of the situation have been determined.

Attribution theories are the most immediate and closely related predecessors of appraisal theories, and they are similar in that they focus on the role of cognitive processes in shaping emotional response. However, research comparing attributions and appraisals suggests that appraisals are better predictors of emotional response than are attributions (Smith et al. 1993). In addition, appraisal theories specifically focus on explaining the causes and consequences of emotion, building on attribution theory by considering the full range of possible situations rather than focusing only on situations in which ambiguous information about causality must be interpreted. Attribution theories tend to assume that the process of examining and explaining the situation in which an emotional reaction may occur is conscious and deliberate, because these theories focus on ambiguous situations that require interpretation. However, there are often very clear implications of a situation for an individual, causality is often very obvious, and evidence suggests that emotional reactions can and do frequently occur automatically and without conscious effort to interpret the situation. Appraisal theory is very much a functional theory of emotion because it focuses on the role emotion plays in coping with the environment by examining the antecedents and consequences of emotional response in a specific, goal-relevant circumstance.

Theories of the Automatic Versus Controlled Nature of Emotion

In recognition of the fact that emotion often occurs in the absence of effortful interpretative process, Zajonc suggested that affective responses do not require cognitive interpretation (e.g., Zajonc 1980; Zajonc and Markus 1985). Based on evidence that affective evaluations can be immune to cognitive manipulations and can precede identification judgments, Zajonc claimed that affective responses could occur without any cognitive mediation. However, Zajonc did not account for the possibility of automatic, unconscious appraising of perceived stimuli. Automatic cognitive processes can occur quickly, without effort or awareness, and can be much more difficult to disrupt or change through cognitive manipulations than conscious, deliberate processes (Bargh 1982; Clore and Ketelaar 1997).

At a minimum, the work of Zajonc and others (Clore and Ketelaar 1997; Lazarus 1991a; Spielman, Pratto, and Bargh 1988; Wyer 1997) provides evidence that emotion can occur without conscious processing of perceptual information. The affective responses examined in studies like those conducted by Zajonc are similar to emotions because they have a specific object as their referent. However, the responses studied may often have been attitudinal rather than emotional, at least as defined in the present article. Nonetheless, these studies suggest that emotional processes can also occur either as a result of conscious processing or as a result of automatic processing.

The Advent of Appraisal Theories

Appraisal theories arose in psychology in response to the limitations of earlier theories of emotion. For example, prior theories could not easily explain the reasons for the variability of emotional reactions of different individuals in identical situations. Past research, using both attribution theory and the cognitive dimensions of emotional response, has clearly demonstrated that different interpretations, or appraisals, of a given situation routinely occur. Appraisal theory builds on this prior work by identifying the types of appraisals that are important in differentiating emotional reactions across situations and individuals. Appraisal theory also provides a framework for the study of the process and evolution of emotional response over time. Although appraisal theory is not unknown to consumer researchers (see, e.g., Luce 1998; Luce, Payne, and Bettman 1999; Luce, Bettman, and Payne 2000), its full potential as a means for examining emotional response among consumers has yet to be realized.

Appraisal Theories

Appraisal theory suggests that emotional response unfolds as a multistage process consisting of (1) the antecedents of the appraisal process, (2) the process of appraising personally relevant information, and (3) the consequences of appraisal and emotions. Figure 1.2 provides a pictorial representation of these states.

Antecedents

Emotion does not occur in a vacuum, and individuals do not enter an emotional experience as a blank slate. Although individuals may influence the situations in which they find themselves, and often quite consciously place themselves in specific situations, the situation exists outside of the individual and provides both a context for emotion as well as a guide to the meaning and

11

Figure 1.2   Appraisal Model of Emotion

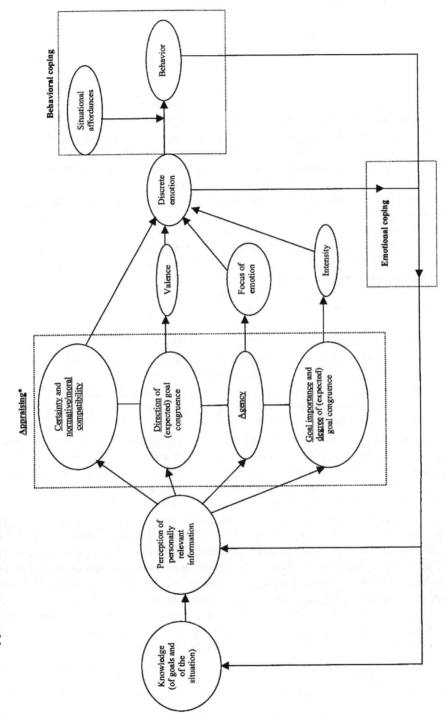

*Underlined terms are separate appraisal dimensions, though they may be contained within the same node for illustrative simplicity.

consequences of an emotional response. Though appraising the situation based on the individual's unique perspective is the ultimate determinant of his or her emotional response, situations typically place constraints on the conclusions any given individual is likely to reach. For example, if a person dies in the middle of a desert, it is unlikely that most individuals would reach the conclusion that the cause of death was drowning, based on the constraints of the situation. In addition, the situation constrains the potential behaviors that the individual may engage in as a result of an emotional reaction. These constraints have been called situational affordances, because the behavior of the individual is likely to be influenced by the opportunities afforded in the situation. Thus, if a person finds that they have bought a defective item at a flea market or swap meet, the situation does not present the opportunity to return the item, because there are no receipts involved and the seller may have been anonymous and not easily located.

Individuals also enter every situation with their own idiosyncratic perspectives based on their unique experiences, expectations, and goals. Everyone has goals and expectations, no matter how broad or vague. The goals of a particular individual in a specific situation are the most important determinant of emotional reactions. If the person who purchased the defective item at the flea market had the goal of using it as decoration rather than for whatever function it was designed, he or she will probably not have a negative reaction upon finding that it does not work. However, a person who expected the item to function in order to achieve a particular outcome would be likely to be disappointed or angry. Though these two people encounter the same situation, their differing goals in the situation lead to quite different emotional reactions.

Thus, the individual's knowledge—which includes expectations and beliefs about the situation and relevant goals in that situation—and the perception of personally relevant information are antecedent to the process of appraising. Knowledge influences perception in that expectations and beliefs about goals, and about the situation, guide the attention of the individual to those aspects of the situation that are likely to be personally relevant (e.g., Cohen and Areni 1991; Groeger 2000). The perception of personal relevance is dependent on the individual's own goals and beliefs. Specifically, the perception of personal relevance involves the process of comparing and relating knowledge to the elements of the individual's situation in order to determine the significance of the situation for the pursuit of the individual's unique and specific goals in that situation.

The specific interpretation of the meaning of a situation and its elements, the process of appraising, depends on the knowledge possessed by the individual about the situation, as well as the particular goals that are relevant to the specific individual in this situation (Lazarus 1991a; Lazarus and Smith 1988). Knowledge about the situation includes expectations and beliefs about the opportunities and resources present in the situation. Such knowledge may be based on prior experience in similar situations, vicarious learning about the situation obtained from others, or other sources. Knowledge about goals also includes a representation or belief about what achieving the goals would mean, or "look like," in the context of the situation (Austin and Vancouver 1996; see also Boulding et al. 1993). Both of these types of knowledge provide the basis for appraisals in any given situation. Without expectations or beliefs about the situation, and without a representation of the desired state in the context of the situation, there can be no basis for evaluating or inferring the personal relevance of information that is perceived in the situation. Thus, the knowledge that an individual brings to the situation is an important antecedent of emotional processing.

Knowledge about goals includes information regarding the outcome desired and about whether that outcome involves avoiding an aversive situation or seeking an attractive situation (Gollwitzer and Moskowitz 1996). For example, goals may focus on completing tasks, on achieving outcomes related to social relationships, or on achieving particular experiential outcomes. Goals may also focus on avoiding a task, particular social relationships or experiential outcomes.

Motivational orientation is a concept used in appraisal theories to describe whether a goal is focused on achieving a positive outcome or on avoiding a negative outcome (e.g., Higgins 1997). Both desired goal outcomes and motivational orientation have been found to impact the experience of emotion (e.g., Lazarus 1999; Roseman, Antoniou, and Jose 1996), but their influence is generally regarded as indirect in that goals tend to exist before personally relevant information is perceived in a given situation. Goals will, however, influence those features of the situation to which attention is directed and even the situations in which individuals try to place themselves. Thus, goals indirectly influence the appraisal process and emotional response by focusing attention, but they do not directly enter into the process of appraising.

Attention to personally relevant information may be consciously controlled or it may be automatically directed without consciousness, even when the individual is otherwise under cognitive load or even actively trying to ignore the source of stimulation (Bargh 1982). An individual's specific knowledge structures associated with the situation and relevant goals in the situation, as well as general knowledge such as language, allow this automatic perception to proceed. For example, if people speak in a foreign tongue about a topic relevant to a personal goal, the information will not be perceived because there is no knowledge structure to allow the translation of the information. However, if someone hears a voice talking about a matter that is important to achieving a goal, the information is likely to be automatically registered, even if the person is engaged in another task such as a conversation (Bargh and Ferguson 2000).

Once information is perceived to have relevance to an individual's goals, it must be analyzed for its specific implications within the particular situational context. The individual must infer the meaning of the information and its implications for goal pursuit.

Appraisal

As noted earlier, appraisal is the process whereby an individual gives meaning to a situation and its associated elements. There are several dimensions of the appraisal process. These dimensions are associated with the specific information-processing tasks that must be performed on personally relevant information in appraising the implications of the situation (Lazarus 2001; Reisenzein and Spielhofer 1994; Roseman, Spindel, and Jose 1990; Scherer 2001). These information-processing tasks involve inferences, evaluations, and judgments about the nature of personally relevant information. An important tenet of appraisal theories is that the subjective construal of personally relevant information (i.e., appraisal) determines emotions, as opposed to any "objective" truth regarding the situation (Lazarus 1995). The variability of subjective construals in response to the same objective situations explains the variability in emotional reactions that occur among individuals, as well as within individuals on different occasions. These variations in appraisals are primarily, but not exclusively, the result of different or changing goals or different expectations of the situation.

Dimensions of Appraisal

The process of appraising includes six dimensions that serve to differentiate discrete emotional reactions that may occur in response to the perception of personally relevant information. The phrase "discrete emotion" refers to an emotional reaction consisting of any combination of appraisals on the given dimensions. To avoid the problem of restricting emotional reactions to those that can be readily labeled, as in the basic emotion approaches, discrete emotions may or may not correspond to an easily identified emotion label. This definition of the range of emotional reactions accounts for the well-known experience of emotional states that are not easily described; the lack of a label does not necessarily preclude the experience of a subjectively experienced emotional state.

The dimensions of appraising information that differentiate and inform the experience of discrete emotions are associated with specific assessments and inferences regarding: (1) the direction of goal congruence, (2) agency, (3) certainty, (4) normative/moral compatibility, (5) goal importance, and (6) the degree of goal congruence. These dimensions of the appraisal process, the tasks of appraising, are defined in Table 1.1. All of these dimensions have been identified and empirically supported in prior research and this research is discussed below. Appraisals associated with these dimensions give definition and form to emotional response. Once the process of appraising personally relevant information along these dimensions has taken place, the appraisals that result become part of a particular discrete emotional reaction.

Direction of Goal Congruence. An individual's appraisal of goal congruence involves the most basic interpretation of personally relevant information. Appraising goal congruence, sometimes referred to as motive consistency (Roseman, Spindel, and Jose 1990), results in an assessment of whether achievement of personally relevant goals is facilitated or hindered in the current situation. This appraisal involves determination of the *direction* of goal congruence because it is defined by whether the situation is perceived to move the individual closer to, or away from, desired goals (Clore and Ortony 2000; Lazarus 1991b; Ortony, Clore, and Collins 1988; Roseman 1984; Roseman and Smith 2001; Roseman, Spindel, and Jose 1990; Scherer 1982; Scherer and Ceschi 1997; Smith and Ellsworth 1985, 1987; Smith et al. 1993). The appraised direction of goal congruence determines the valence of emotional response and differentiates positive and negative emotions.

Emotional reactions are not necessarily bipolar, in the sense of being exclusively positive or negative (e.g., Smith and Ellsworth 1985) even though the appraisal of the direction of goal congruence itself is bipolar. Different elements of a situation (i.e., different pieces of information) may be appraised separately as having different implications for goal pursuit, leading simultaneously to both positive and negative emotional responses. In addition, the same situation and individual pieces of information within the situation may be appraised with respect to different goals, and may have different implications for the individual's different goals, such as moving the person toward one goal while moving him or her away from another. Thus, appraisal theories can account for mixed or ambivalent reactions that individuals may experience in any given situation (Ellsworth and Smith 1988; Scherer and Ceschi 1997).

Agency. Appraising agency involves the assessment of the various entities (people, objects, products, etc.) involved in a situation and the role each has played, or might play, in the outcome of the situation. The agency dimension differentiates between emotions that are directed at the self, at other people, or at objects. The appraisal of agency involves a process that determines the focus or target of an emotion (Lazarus 1991b; Ortony, Clore, and Collins 1988; Roseman 1984; Smith and Ellsworth 1985; Smith et al. 1993; Tesser 1990; Weiner 1985). Appraisal of agency is similar to the process of attribution of the locus of cause in Weiner's attribution theory (e.g., Weiner 1985) and has also been referred to as appraisal of responsibility (e.g., Manstead and Tetlock 1989). However, a person or object can be the focus of an emotional reaction without being judged to be causal in or responsible for a situation or particular outcome. When appraisal of a situation indicates that another entity is the cause or bears responsibility for the situation, people or objects may still be the focus of an emotional response because they were impacted by the situation or because they were unable to change the outcome of the situation.

Table 1.1

Appraisals

Appraisal	Definition of the appraisal task	Emotion differentiation	Related terms	Conceptual and empirical support
Goal congruance *Illustrative emotions*: happy, sad, disappointed, pleasant surprise	Evaluating the situation in terms of (expected) goal success vs. failure, or whether it is consistent vs. inconsistent with values or ideals	Differentiates between positive and negative emotions (valence)	• intrinsicpleasantness • goal conduciveness • motive consistency • goal-path obstacle • difficulty	(Clore and Ortony 2000; Lazarus 1991b; Ortony et al. 1988; Roseman 1984; Roseman and Smith 2001; Roseman et al.1990; Scherer 1982; Scherer and Ceschi 1997; Smith and Ellsworth 1987; Ellsworth 1987; Smith and Ellsworth 1985; Smith et al 1993)
Agency *Illustrative emotions*: proud, angry, ashamed	Inferring whether there is a person (self or other) oir object that is responsible for, or in control of, the situation	Differentiates emotions that focus on the self, another person, or an object from emotions that do not reference an agent	• locus of causality • responsibility • attribution • blame/credit • intentionality	(Lazarus 1991b; Ortony et al. 1988; Roseman 1984; Smith and Ellsworth 1985; Smith et al. 1993; Tesser 1990; Weiner 1985)
Certainty *Illustrative emotions* hopeful, joyous, anxious, sad	Determining whether the outcome is known or certain	Differentiates between outcome-related emotions and anticipatory emotions	• time of event • temporal orientation • probability • likelihood	(Fridja et al. 1989; Ortony et al. 1988; Roseman 1984; Roseman et al. 1994; Scherer 1982, Smith and Ellsworth 1985; Tesser 1990)
Normative/moral comparability *Illustrative emotions*: proud, guilty, ashamed, embarrassed, evaluation,contemptuous admiring,	Evaluation of morality and the probable evaluation of the situation by significant others	Differentiates emotions that reflect concern with moral values and the evaluations of others (versus emotions that do not reflect these concerns)	• legitimacy • fairness • consistency with others' standards • internalized social standards • self-evaluation, self-esteem • object evaluation • problem source	(Ellsworth and Smith 1988; Lazarus 1991b; Manstead and Tetlock 1989; Roseman et al. 1996; Roseman et al. 1990; Scherer 2001; Scherer and Ceschi 1997; Smith and Ellsworth 1987; Smith and Ellsworth 1985)
Goal importance	Evaluate the importance and value of the desired state in the current situation	Differentiate emotion intensity	• concern relevance/urgency • seriousness	(Fridja 1993; Fridja et al. 1989; Lazarus 1991b; Scherer 1982; Scherer 1988)
Degree of goal congruence	Evaluate the extent to which the situation meets (or is likely to meet) expectations or approximates the desired state	*Illustrative emotions*: happy, joyous, anxious, afraid, irritated, angry, hopeful, expectant	• expectedness • predictability • perceived likelihood	(Clore and Ortony 2000; Fridja et al. 1989; Ortony et al. 1988; Scherer 1997)

The process of appraising agency does involve assessing whether the person or object is causal or responsible for outcomes in the situation, and emotional reactions will vary depending on the appraisal of the target's role in the situation. To illustrate, consider a situation in which one witnesses a person viciously punch another person, with no provocation. The situation is likely to be personally relevant because most people have a goal of predictability and safety in their social world. The aggressor is identified as responsible for the situation and would likely be the focus of the emotions of anger and fear, while the victim would likely be the focus of pity and empathy, based on the fact that that person is not responsible for the situation. Another example of an emotional reaction to a target that is not judged to be a causal agent in a situation would be a case where a product is purchased to solve a problem but fails to prevent a negative outcome. A bandage might be purchased for a scrape that has already become infected, in the hope that it would help heal the wound. The consumer may be disappointed that the bandage failed to solve the problem, but she is unlikely to conclude that the bandage was responsible for the infection.

In some circumstances, appraising may indicate that no person or object is responsible for or involved in a particular outcome in a situation, which results in judgments of indeterminate agency in the situation. Indeterminacy judgments are sometimes called circumstance-caused agency appraisals (e.g., Roseman, Antoniou, and Jose 1996). Judgments of indeterminate agency are related to emotions that do not specifically reference a cause (though they do reference an outcome or event), such as joy or relief, in contrast to emotions like pride or contempt that reference a specific agent. Emotions that reference a specific agent are typically related to an assessment of responsibility for the situation (or the lack thereof), whereas emotions with an indeterminate appraisal of agency focus on the event or situation itself. In other words, some emotions reference the agency of a particular target (e.g., anger or pity), and other emotions can be experienced regardless of agency in the situation (e.g., hope and anxiety).

Certainty. The appraisal of certainty involves the assessment of the extent to which the situation implies an outcome that is known with confidence (Frijda, Kuipers, and ter Schure 1989; Ortony, Clore, and Collins 1988; Roseman 1984; Roseman, Wiest, and Swartz 1994; Scherer 1982; Smith and Ellsworth 1985; Tesser 1990). Certainty is important in the determination of emotional reactions. The certainty dimension differentiates among emotions that reference an outcome that is known with some degree of certainty (e.g., joy, anger, and relief) and anticipatory emotions that reference an outcome that is unknown or uncertain, such as hope, anxiety, and dread. Certainty appraisals are informed by goal achievement, that is, whether a goal has been obtained or is perceived as likely to be obtained. The emotions that arise from appraisals of uncertainty serve a motivational function in that they inform the individual about the likely success of continuing to pursue a goal or the need to pursue another goal, either because the current goal is unlikely to be achieved or has been achieved already (Bagozzi, Baumgartner, and Pieters 1998).

Certainty with respect to goal outcomes can arise either from the outcome having come to pass in the current situation or from experience or knowledge about having achieved the goal in similar contexts. Conversely, uncertainty may be due to a lack of experience or knowledge about the goal when the achievement of the goal is still in the future. The appraisal of certainty includes a temporal dimension that has been recognized in a number of prior works (e.g., Fleeson and Cantor 1995; Roseman and Smith 2001). The critical issue is not whether an outcome has or has not occurred in similar circumstances but rather whether there is conviction or confidence that the outcome will occur in a given situation. When an outcome has not yet occurred, appraisals of certainty may lead to confidence that the desired outcome will be achieved in the future.

Anticipatory emotions arise when appraisal leads to some degree of uncertainty and indicates that the probability of the achievement of a relevant goal has the potential to change. Anticipatory emotions are valenced—they can be positive like hope, or negative like dread and anxiety—depending on the expectations that the individual has about the likelihood of achieving the desired state of the goal. The valence of anticipatory emotions is due to the appraisal of the direction of *expected* goal congruence. In addition, the degree of uncertainty that is present can impact the quality of the emotional experience. For example, if knowledge of the likelihood of achieving a pleasant outcome indicates that achievement of the outcome is highly probable, a positive anticipatory emotion is likely to be experienced, or, if it seems likely that a negative outcome will occur, one would experience a negative anticipatory emotion, like dread. (Note that there does not seem to be an appropriate label in English for relatively certain positive anticipation, which emphasizes the value of appraisal approaches over basic emotion approaches.) Outcomes that seem less likely might result in experiencing hopeful or anxious emotions.

Normative/Moral Compatibility. Appraising normative/moral compatibility involves an assessment of the situation in terms of what is deemed to be normal and right by the individual and within the specific social context (Ellsworth and Smith 1988; Lazarus 1991b; Manstead and Tetlock 1989; Roseman, Antoniou, and Jose 1996; Roseman, Spindel, and Jose 1990; Scherer 1999, 2001; Scherer and Ceschi 1997; Smith and Ellsworth 1985, 1987). This appraisal is linked to emotions that indicate the relevance of norms and moral issues in the situation. It cues emotions like shame, which is associated with violation of a social norm or a moral conviction, or like pride, which is associated with the achievement of normative or moral ideals. The appraisal of the compatibility of a situation that includes moral and normative standards reflects the importance of the social and cultural context in interpretations of the implications of specific information related to goals.

For example, certain cultural values are more conducive to appraisals related to shame than to appraisals related to guilt (Creighton 1990; Stipek 1998). In Japan, the experience of shame is more common than that of guilt, because Japanese culture places a higher value on collectivist ideals than individualist ideals. Individualist ideals are more conducive to the experience of guilt, which is more strongly related to the responsibility of the individual for his or her behavior than to the individual's responsibility to the community, which is more likely to produce the experience of shame.

Appraisals Affecting Emotional Intensity. Two types of appraisals have been linked to the intensity of emotion: goal importance and the degree of goal congruence. The appraised importance of a goal increases the intensity of emotion because it is associated with the value or desirability of the state that is sought, or the severity of potential consequences of failure (Perugini and Bagozzi 2001; Sonnemans and Frijda 1995). Emotional reactions are more intense in reaction to the estimation and expectation of more valuable gains and more painful losses.

Emotional intensity is related to goal congruence with respect to the *degree* to which the situation meets expectations or approximates the desired state (Clore and Ortony 2000; Ortony, Clore, and Collins 1988). If the situation exceeds expectations, the resulting positive emotion is likely to be more intense than if the situation merely met expectations or matched the desired state. If the situation is extremely divergent from expectations in a negative direction, the resulting negative emotion is likely to be more intense than if the situation merely fell slightly short of the desired state or met pessimistic expectations.

Emotional intensity within the context of appraisal theory is somewhat similar to the concept of arousal used in dimensional theories of emotion. However, dimensional theories do not speak to the factors that affect the intensity of emotions, whereas appraisal theories specifically address and make predictions about the degree of arousal ·and emotional intensity that is likely to be experienced. In addition, Scherer (1997; Scherer and Ceschi 1997) provided evidence that the appraisal of intensity is independent of other appraisals. Table 1.2 illustrates the distinctions between levels of emotional intensity in combination with the appraisals that differentiate the type of emotional experience. The inclusion of appraisals that differentiate emotional intensity provides a means for predicting discrete emotions that are likely to have different consequences based on the level of intensity of the emotional experience. For example, experiencing joy as a more intense version of happiness (all other appraisals can be held constant) may be more likely to motivate future behaviors similar to those that led to the positive outcome in the current situation.

The Overall Process of Appraising. Figure 1.2 provides a visual illustration of the process of emotional appraisals, beginning with the preexisting knowledge of the individual and the perception of personally relevant information. Following the perception of personally relevant information, the situation is appraised for its implications for the individual, using the dimensions of appraisal that are relevant in the particular situation. Appraisals of each of the six dimensions defined above may operate in parallel, and the results of one appraisal may influence other appraisals. Figure 1.2 depicts the six dimensions of appraisal as connected by nondirectional links, to indicate that each appraisal has the potential to impact the results of the appraisal on the other dimensions. For example, negative, goal-incongruent outcomes may be more likely than positive outcomes to be attributed to agents other than the self, all else being equal (Klein 2001). The appraisals of certainty and normative/moral compatibility contribute directly to the differentiation of discrete emotions, while the goal congruence and agency dimensions influence discrete emotions through their effects on the valence of the emotional reaction and the focus of the emotional reaction, respectively. Emotional intensity is determined by the degree of goal congruence of the situation, and by the importance of the goal to the individual. The valence, intensity, and focus of the emotion in turn contribute to the discrete emotional reaction. Table 1.2 describes how appraisals along different dimensions may combine to differentiate emotional responses.

Consequences of Emotion. Once the discrete emotional reaction is distilled through the process of appraising the personally relevant information, emotions may provide feedback to the the individual (see Figure 1.2). As an emotion is experienced, entering awareness, it may be perceived as additional information about the situation (e.g., "I'm feeling angry about standing in line for an hour at the bank because they don't have enough tellers"), and behaviors contemplated or performed in response to the emotion may also provide feedback to the individual about goals and about the situation (e.g., "I tried asking the bank manager to open another window, but all the other tellers are at lunch"). Both the emotion and the behavioral tendencies inspired by the emotion may contribute to the knowledge of the individual about goals and about the situation. Emotional reactions and the judgments resulting from appraisal become part of the individual's knowledge structure about his or her goals in the context of the situation that instigated the emotional processing. In addition, emotional responses and behavioral tendencies or urges can result in additional information that may prompt further appraisal (e.g., "I want to shout at the bank manager, but I know I would feel embarrassed afterward").

The consequences of emotion are defined by the process(es) of coping with the implications of appraisal for the individual's goals. Behavioral tendencies (also called action tendencies, c.f. Frijda, Kuipers, and ter Schure 1989; Oatley and Johnson-Laird 1987; Plutchik 1982) associated with discrete emotions are generally adaptive responses to the situation, that is, attempts to bring the situation in line with the desired state of the goal. These behavioral tendencies can be trans-

Table 1.2

Appraisal Combinations

	Goal congruence				Normative/ moral compatibility
	Positive		Negative		
	Certainty				
Agency	Certain	Uncertain	Certain	Uncertain	
Moderate Intensity[a]					
Self	Proud	Hope	Guilt, shame	Anxiety	Relevant
	Happy	Hope	Distress	Anxiety	Irrelevant
Other person	Admiration	Hope	Contempt	Anxiety	Relevant
	Grateful	Hope	Anger	Anxiety	Irrelevant
Object or circumstances	Satisfied	Hope	Disappointed	Anxiety	Relevant
	Pleased	Hope	Sad	Anxiety	Irrelevant
Indeterminate or irrelevant	Glad	Hope	Pity	Anxiety	Relevant
	Happy	Hope	Sad	Anxiety	Irrelevant
High Intensity[a]					
Self	Proud	Anticipatory	Humiliated	Afraid	Relevant
	Joyous	Excited	Depressed	Afraid	Irrelevant
Other person	Love	Anticipatory	Disgust	Afraid	Relevant
	Love	Excited	Enraged	Afraid	Irrelevant
Object or circumstances	Delighted	Anticipatory	Frustrated	Afraid	Relevant
	Delighted	Excited	Miserable	Afraid	Irrelevant
Indeterminate or irrelevant	Delighted	Anticipatory	Commiserate	Afraid	Relevant
	Joyous	Excited	Miserable	Afraid	Irrelevant

Notes: The emotions in the table are included as examples for illustrative purposes and have not all been empirically validated. Other emotion labels may be found to be relevant to any of the combinations of the appraisal dimensions listed. In addition, different emotion labels may be found to be more appropriate depending on the context under study.

[a]Emotion intensity is moderate in the upper level of the table and extreme in the lower level of the table. In the upper level of the table, goal importance is moderate, and the situation is appraised as relatively close to the degree of goal congruence expected. In the lower level of the table, goal importance is high, and the (expected) situation far exceeds or falls short of the goal.

lated into actual behavior only if the situation affords resources and opportunities for the behavior to be performed. Situational affordances are defined as the conditions present in the environment that allow the individual to take action to advance goal pursuit.

If the conditions present in the environment do not allow the individual to take action to align the situation with goals, the individual must incorporate that information into knowledge structures, and such information may inspire further emotional processing (Folkman and Lazarus 1988; Lazarus 1999; Scherer 2001). The process of assessing the opportunities present in the situation and the potential for behavioral responses is one aspect of assessing the potential for constructively coping with the situation. However, assessment of the potential for coping also involves examining opportunities to reinterpret information in the context of the individual's other goals, or revising goals to be more consistent with the affordances in the current situation.

Emotion Regulation

Emotion regulation is aimed at coping with the implications of a given situation for the individual and his or her goals and well-being. "Coping" is simply the means by which an individual identifies and assesses the adaptive potential and significance of various actions or strategies. Coping can focus either on changing the emotional response to the situation or on taking action within the situation. Lazarus (1991b; 1999) describes these two types of coping responses as emotion-focused coping and problem-focused coping. Emotion-focused coping involves behaviors or strategies aimed at moderating the emotional reaction; problem-focused coping is associated with identifying and implementing behaviors and strategies that solve the problem (e.g., removing or avoiding obstacles) or otherwise advance the goals of the individual.

Emotional coping involves an attempt to alter one's perspective regarding the situation. Such coping involves reappraising the situation by shifting the focus of the appraisal process to a different or revised goal. Revising the goal with respect to the object or situation changes the perspective and approach to the situation by guiding attention and information search to other aspects of the situation. Such reappraisal, in turn, is likely to alter the emotional reaction. Behavioral (or problem-focused) coping involves taking some action in an attempt to bring the situation in line with one's goals. Through feedback to perception and knowledge, the appraisal process can contemplate the likely emotional outcomes of actions that are being considered as well as reappraising the situation based on the results of actions that are actually taken. As opposed to emotional coping, which involves changing some aspect of the goal, behavioral coping is likely to be aimed at completing the original goal, by taking action either to overcome problems or to continue to reap the rewards of a positive experience with that type of goal.

Though the word "coping" may seem to have a negative connotation, both positive and negative emotions may inspire the revision of goals as well as behavioral tendencies aimed at furthering goal pursuits. Work by Barbara Fredrickson addresses the behavioral tendencies that are associated with positive emotions, advancing a theory that emphasizes the role of positive emotions in motivating the continued pursuit of successful goals and in broadening the range of potential goals that are considered (Fredrickson 1998, 2001). Thus, coping includes both striving to achieve positive goals and associated emotions as well as efforts to escape or alter negative situations or to revise thought processes to diminish negative emotion.

Coping is relevant to consumer behavior because consumers must cope with their emotional reactions to consumption experiences and service encounters and because coping with the results of other goals may motivate goals related to consumption behavior. As Folkes (1984) observes, consumers reacted to product failure by complaining when their appraisal of the consumption situation inspires anger and indicates that the manufacturer was at fault. This is an example of behavioral coping aimed at solving the problem of a dysfunctional product. In addition, when a consumer is frustrated in the pursuit of goals in other areas of life, consumption may offer an opportunity for emotional or behavioral coping. Consumers who use consumption goals as an alternative to other frustrated goals are engaging in emotional coping, as when a person attends a movie to take his or her mind off an unsuccessful day at work. Consumption behavior can also offer opportunities for behavioral coping such as using a product or service to solve a problem encountered in goal pursuit. For example, a consumer of an accounting service may decide to consume those services to solve the problem of being confused by the tax code.

Coping may motivate a variety of consumption behaviors, and marketers would do well to consider appealing to the types of emotions that might motivate consumers to use their products or services for emotional or behavioral coping. In addition, companies should consider the possible coping behaviors that might result from both positive and negative consumption outcomes associated with their own products and services. Work on service recovery has begun to address this problem (Maxham and Netemeyer 2002; Smith and Bolton 2002).

Multiple and Mixed Emotions

In natural settings, people often experience multiple discrete emotions simultaneously (e.g., Scherer and Ceschi 1997; Smith and Ellsworth 1987). The experience of multiple emotions has frequently been observed in naturalistic studies, such as a study of emotions experienced by students in the context of an exam (Smith and Ellsworth 1987). Longitudinal studies also indicate that multiple or mixed emotions occur at the same point in time as well as at different points in time. Empirical evidence suggests that the appraisal process operates in much the same way regardless of whether a single emotion or multiple and mixed emotions are involved. Recognition of the fact that multiple, simultaneous appraisals of different aspects of a situation may occur is likely to provide a more complete picture of all the emotions that are experienced in a given situation and be more likely to reveal the probable causes and consequences of these emotions. Scherer and Ceschi (1997) suggest that mixed positive and negative emotional reactions may occur as a result of emotion-focused coping, where an initial negative emotional response is modified by attempts to find a "silver lining" and to focus on goals that are more likely to be achieved.

One consequence of the experience of emotion is a continuation of emotional processing, which leads to changes in emotional reaction over time. One emotion may feed the appraisal of a situation and lead to new or altered emotional response. Thus, anger and associated behavior may give rise to a sense of guilt if behavior is subsequently judged to be inappropriate, or a sense of relief and pride if the behavior produces a positive outcome consistent with goals. In addition, because multiple goals may be relevant in any situation, and because any situation may contain information with different implications for a single goal, different emotions may be experienced depending on the goal(s) and facet(s) of the situation to which attention is directed. In situations that implicate many goals, especially goals that conflict with one another, multiple and conflicting emotions may be experienced. In situations with conflicting implications for any given goal, mixed emotions are likely to occur. Such situations may make behavior and other responses difficult to predict and manage, because it may be difficult to determine to which aspects of the situation attention will be directed and how this attention might affect coping responses. However, compared to any other available theories, appraisal theories provide the richest and most comprehensive understanding of emotion and its consequences.

Application of Appraisal Theories to Research on Consumer Behavior

Appraisal theories offer a more complete description of the emotion process than do other theories that have been used in consumer behavior research involving emotion, because appraisal theories address the causes and consequences of emotions and more completely describe the range of possible emotional reactions through combinations of all the appraisal dimensions. Such detailed and rich descriptions allow researchers who are studying emotion in the context of consumer behavior, or who are studying another area of consumer behavior that involves emotional response, to identify and examine emotion at the level of detail most appropriate in the context under study. Researchers can also focus on the stage of the emotion process that is most relevant to the phenomenon of interest.

Appraisal theories offer ways to address some of the challenges inherent in research on emotion. Methodological issues related to measuring emotions often complicate research on emotion. The most common approaches to the study of emotion do not provide guidance for reliable measurement of differentiated emotional experiences. Basic emotion approaches to the study of emotion lack a theoretical basis for linking emotional terms, though statistical analyses of lists of emotion terms have yielded conceptual groupings (e.g., Richins 1997). Dimensional approaches group emotions based on valence and intensity while ignoring the additional distinctions that exist in emotional experiences (e.g., Holbrook and Batra 1987; Westbrook and Oliver 1991). In addition, these approaches do not recognize the importance of assessing consumers' goals and perceptions of the situation in the study of emotion.

Basic emotion measures often rely on single-item ratings of emotion terms, which limits the power of statistical tests in discovering consequences and antecedents of emotions. In addition, relying on the labels available in the common vocabulary for emotional experiences limits the range of the emotions studied to those that have a clear definition in the native language. Though not limited by single-item measures, dimensional measures of emotion neglect variation in emotional experiences. Dimensional approaches typically use multi-item measures of the valence and intensity of emotional reactions, without distinguishing emotions within those dimensions. Appraisal theories allow for the measurement of differentiated emotional states and for the development of multi-item scales of those emotions.

Various physiological measures of emotional response have been proposed and employed in research on the emotional response of consumers (Klebba 1985; Weinstein, Drozdenko, and Weinstein 1984). However, such methods are cumbersome, very intrusive, and do not differentiate many of the emotions that are experienced as subjectively different (Stewart 1984, 1985; see also Cacioppo and Petty 1985). Such measures also provide little insight into the causes or consequences of emotional response.

In contrast to other approaches to the measurement and study of emotion, appraisal theories provide guidance for the development of multi-item measures of differentiated emotional reactions. Appraisal theories suggest that emotion can be measured using measures of the relevant appraisals, using terms consistent with the appraisals of interest (e.g., Smith et al. 1993). For example, guilt can be measured with items assessing the extent to which the situation is appraised as a violation of a moral standard or norm that has been committed by the individual, resulting in a negative outcome for another person. Thus, a measure of guilt could be developed using items that assess the extent to which the consumer feels "sorry," "regretful," and "remorseful," as well as "guilty." Guilt could also be measured using appraisals of the extent to which the person feels bad based on a recognition that he or she did something wrong or did something that resulted in a negative outcome for another person.

The literature on appraisal theories also provides methodological guidance on techniques to measure perceptions of situations in which emotions occur. Research on appraisals often uses the critical incident methodology, which prompts participants to recall and describe a situation in which they experienced the emotional state of interest (e.g., Tesser and Collins 1988). For example, if the researcher is interested in studying consumers' experiences of guilt, participants could be asked to describe in detail a situation in which they felt guilty for purchasing or using a product or service. These descriptions are then coded and analyzed to assess the appraisals that are relevant in situations where the emotion occurs as well as for emotion regulation attempts and other emotions that were experienced in the same situations. The critical incident methodology can be used in conjunction with more controlled measures of the phenomena of interest to provide insight into the occurrence of emotions in consumption situations.

Though the techniques suggested by appraisal theories improve on approaches commonly used in the past, there remain methodological issues in the study of emotion using the appraisal paradigm. Appraisals can occur unconsciously or automatically, which means an individual may not be aware of, or have conscious access to, the process by which they came to have an emotional reaction (Lazarus 1995). Thus, measuring appraisals may elicit reconstruction of a reasonable account of an emotional situation, rather than measuring the actual processing that gave rise to the emotion.

In addition, measuring emotion can lead to demand and reactivity effects. Measuring emotion with questions or rating scales may indicate to participants that they are expected to have an emotional reaction, leading them to report emotions they are not actually experiencing in an effort to please the experimenter (Lazarus 1995). Emotional experiences may also be reactive to being examined (e.g., Tangney et al. 1998). Emotions may change when an individual makes an experimenter-directed effort to examine his or her own emotional state. For example, emotional coping processes may augment a negative emotional reaction when the experimenter makes an intervention that leads the person to examine his or her emotional response.

Though research on emotion is complicated by the lack of direct access to the phenomena of interest, this dilemma is not unique to emotion research. As in other research on processes internal to the consumer, research methods used to triangulate the phenomena are the best solution to the problems of indirect study (e.g., Bargh and Ferguson 2000). Appraisal theories offer the theoretical grounding to guide research on emotion in selecting appropriate methods and measures of the emotional constructs of interest. Research on consumer behavior can benefit from the application of appraisal theories to the study of consumers' emotion and of other processes and behaviors that affect or are affected by consumer emotions.

Future Research

Some areas in consumer behavior research offer obvious opportunities for appraisal theories to offer a more complete picture of the role of emotion. Though any area in which emotion plays a role can potentially benefit from the application of appraisal theories, these areas offer immediate opportunities for appraisal theories to provide insight. For example, research on the role of affect in advertising, and on consumers' judgments of satisfaction, can use the framework presented here to incorporate appraisals and the concepts of emotional and behavioral coping.

Advertising

Measuring the construal of advertising messages in terms of appraisals has the potential to illuminate the process of emotional responses to advertising. For example, the knowledge that an advertisement is appraised as incompatible with moral standards is more informative than a simple measurement of negative affect. As another example, an advertisement that is associated with an appraisal of the brand as the agent responsible for a goal-congruent outcome may have more impact on brand evaluations than if the ad emphasizes the consumer as responsible for the outcome. Knowledge of the appraisal of agency has the potential to be more informative and more useful than a simple rating of a positive affective response to the advertisement.

An advertisement that creates a high degree of certainty (or increases in certainty) about the potential of the product to fulfill a goal would likely be effective in stimulating product trial or brand choice. This may be especially true in the case of credence goods, for which quality cannot be judged with certainty even after experience (Steenkamp 1990). Appraisals of the degree of certainty in relation to credence goods should increase repurchase behavior and intentions. Goods that are perceived as easier to evaluate (i.e., associated to a higher degree of certainty) are chosen more often and associated with lower levels of negative affect (Garbarino and Edell 1997). Thus, creating certainty appraisals in consumers may lead to less negative emotional reactions to purchase situations. Consumers may be more likely to experience positive anticipation or hope, rather than anxiety and fear, when they are more certain that their goals will be fulfilled.

Appraisal theories suggest that advertising should seek to create moderate expectations in relation to the goals that the product can fulfill. If expectations are more moderate, product experience is more likely to be goal congruent, and the degree of goal congruence is likely to be higher. In addition, comparative advertising may have unanticipated beneficial effects for the brand that is used as a comparison. Generally, comparative advertising seeks to create a negative expectation of potential goal fulfillment for the comparison brand. However, if the consumer then has a positive experience with the comparison brand, the emotional reaction to that experience is likely to be especially intense due to the degree to which product experience exceeded expectations of goal congruence. These suggestions are consistent with research on the relation of expectations to satisfaction (e.g., Bagozzi and Warshaw 1990; Boulding et al. 1993; Oliver, Rust, and Varki 1997; Rust and Oliver 2000).

A consideration of the influence of advertising on all the appraisal tasks might further inform the study of advertising effects. For example, a comparative advertisement that creates an appraisal of the comparison brand as in opposition to social norms, or as disdained by social groups, may create an expectation or prime an appraisal that is difficult to disconfirm. In addition, such a message may be used to position the advertised brand as fulfilling goals of social acceptance.

Advertising should also account for emotional coping when an advertisement creates negative affect, as in a fear appeal. Instead of taking the preventative measures advocated by the advertiser, the person may revise their goals or reappraise the situation presented such that the negative affect is reduced without the necessity of taking any action. All advertisers hope that consumers will respond to emotions inspired by advertisements by purchasing the advertised good or taking the advocated action in order to fulfill the goals to which the advertisement appeals. Appraisal theory can offer a structure to analyze the appeals made and consumer reactions to them in order to make advertising more effective in inspiring behavioral coping rather than emotional coping.

Finally, many advertisements are designed to evoke an emotion and associate this emotion with the advertised product or service. Such emotional appeals have been difficult to reliably measure when the focus has been on the measurement of the appeal, largely because the effects of particular emotional appeals appear to differ from rater to rater (Stewart and Furse 1986). Appraisal theories have the potential to parse out differences in the way(s) specific consumers interpret specific appeals, and thereby lead to more reliable coding of emotional appeals.

Satisfaction

Satisfaction research is an area that may appreciably benefit from the use of appraisals to differentiate the cognitive bases of emotional reactions to product experience. Satisfaction research has traditionally focused on the determination of satisfaction judgments as separate from emotional reactions. However, because appraisal theories view emotions as determined by a process of cognitive assessments of the situation, the traditional approach to satisfaction is compatible with the use of appraisal concepts. Satisfaction research paradigms commonly measure several constructs that are informative to an interpretation based on appraisal theories.

Research on satisfaction has incorporated the role of expectations in relation to the valence and intensity of satisfaction responses (e.g., Mano and Oliver 1993; Oliver 1993; Westbrook 1987). The process of generating an estimation of satisfaction is conceptualized as dependent on a judgment of the extent of expectancy disconfirmation, in a process of comparison with the expectations that existed before product experience (e.g., Westbrook 1987). This process essentially corresponds to the appraisals of the direction and degree of goal congruence, which have been shown to be consistently related to the valence and intensity of emotion in work on appraisal theory (e.g., Scherer and Ceschi 1997). Thus, satisfaction has been conceptualized as a combination of the valence and intensity of emotional response to product experience.

Given that ratings of satisfaction are likely to be related to goal congruence degree and direction appraisals, it is not surprising that satisfaction is consistently found to be related to ratings of the degree of positive and negative affect in numerous studies (Mano and Oliver 1993; Oliver 1993; Westbrook 1987; Westbrook and Oliver 1991). However, consideration of the effects of additional appraisals can aid in predicting consumers' responses. Folkes (1984) measured the equivalent to appraisals of agency (i.e., locus), and found that complaining behavior was related to appraisals of the product as the agent responsible for a negative product experience. Folkes also found that judgments of the stability and controllability of the cause of the negative experience were related to differentiation of the behaviors that can be interpreted as behavioral coping responses, such as a desire for a refund versus exchange, depending on whether the cause was judged to be stable.

Further, it has been suggested that the appraisal of agency is necessary to determine the impact of consumption experiences on satisfaction. Dube and Menon (2000) propose that satisfaction with a service encounter should not be affected by a negative or positive experience unless the service provider is judged to be responsible for the outcome. There is no reason to expect that the same would not be true of a product experience. Though positive or negative emotions may be experienced in relation to positive and negative product or service outcomes, the emotions would not be focused on the product or service unless they were judged to be the responsible agent in the situation.

In sum, the immediate contribution of appraisal theory to satisfaction research is likely to be a clarification of the concepts involved, as well as increased parsimony in the theory on which satisfaction research is based. In addition, an examination of additional factors that impact emotional responses, such as goal importance and certainty appraisals, may provide increased precision in understanding and predicting reactions to product experience. For example, reactions to consumption involving credence goods are likely to be related to the experience of anticipatory emotions such as hope and fear because certainty about the outcome of consumption is likely to be low (Steenkamp 1990).

In addition, a reconceptualization of product experience as leading to more differentiated emotional reactions can suggest potential behaviors that are associated with the emotions, through specific coping behaviors afforded by the environment. For example, the experience of relief in relation to a product may be more strongly related to word-of-mouth behavior than a measure of general positive affect, because relief specifically references avoiding or escaping a negative outcome or situation, and the consumer may be inclined to share that solution with other consumers who have the same problem.

Satisfaction in Low-Involvement Situations

Work on appraisal theories can also suggest theoretical predictions for the formation of satisfaction judgments in consumption situations that involve little motivation to process information carefully. Appraisals in low-involvement situations are unlikely to be carefully considered judgments of the product or service. Instead, satisfaction judgments and emotional appraisals may be based on the associations that the product brings to mind. This may occur even if the associations lack any logical basis for use as a comparison or analogy. The associations that are activated by the product or service may automatically inspire appraisals that are spontaneously applied to the low-involvement consumption situation on the basis of whatever association exists.

Consumer reactions in low-involvement consumption situations may involve an automatic, heuristic processing route to appraisal. Clore and Ortony (2000) describe a dual process theory of emotion, with two potential routes to emotion. One route involves controlled processing, called the computation of appraisal, and the other route takes place through automatic processing, called the reinstatement of appraisal. Controlled appraisal involves bottom-up processing, where categorization of the situation along the appraisal dimensions is based on decision rules and theories about the underlying properties of the situation. Automatic appraisal leading to emotional experience involves top-down processing, where categorization of the situation along the appraisal dimensions is based on prototypes and associations that are activated automatically upon perception of the situation. The automatic route to emotion, through reinstating an appraisal from a prior similar situation, is akin to the activation of schemas, which can include specified appraisals as well as behavioral tendencies. In fact, recent research indicates that the subtle activation of schemas, which are conceptually similar to reinstated appraisals and relational themes, can result in overt behavior that conforms to the behavioral implications of the schema (Chen and Bargh 1997).

It should be noted that automatic processes such as reinstated appraisals are not necessarily nonconscious (Lazarus 1995). Individuals may be aware that they are reacting to a situation on the basis of its similarity to a previously encountered situation. However, if the individual is not aware of the activation of the prior situation in memory, the emotional reaction may be surprising. This may explain some instances of seemingly irrational emotions, for which the reasons are not accessible to conscious awareness. In addition, it should be noted that these two routes to appraisal can operate in parallel and may give rise to different or conflicting results. For example, one may have an automatic negative emotional reaction in response to interacting with a service person whose appearance is unconsciously perceived to be similar to a former romantic partner who behaved badly, while at the same time having a positive emotional reaction to the conscious appraisal of the service encounter.

This dual process theory of appraisal suggests examining the associations that are spontaneously made with low-involvement goods. Satisfaction with such goods might be predicted by the appraisals linked to those associations. The appraisals that are transferred to the low-involvement good may extend beyond the basic appraisal of goal congruence to appraisals of agency, normative/moral compatibility, certainty, and goal importance. These appraisals may, in turn, predict behavioral outcomes such as purchase intentions and loyalty. For example, if an appraisal of relatively high goal importance is transferred to a low-involvement good, the consumer may become a loyal user of the product as a coping response. This effect is facilitated in low-involvement situations because the consumer is likely to lack the motivation to examine the importance of the goal served by the product.

Product Design

Industrial designers have long recognized that three dimensions of products must be considered when designing a product: (1) functional, (2) cognitive, and (3) emotional (March 1994). Satisfaction with a product is a function of consumers' appraisals of all three dimensions and a product that does not provide satisfaction on all three of these dimensions may produce consumer dissatisfaction. The functional dimension of design focuses on whether the product actually delivers the benefit or outcome sought by the consumer. The functional dimension of product design is directly related to appraisals of the direction and degree of goal congruence. In addition, appraisals of agency, that is, appraisals of whether the product or manufacturer of the product is responsible for the functional failure of a product, will play an important role in consumers' emotional response to the product. The processes by which consumers judge the success of a product on the functional dimension are likely to be quite similar to the process involved in the judgments of satisfaction. However, two other dimensions of the product may also influence consumers' satisfaction and emotional response to a product.

The cognitive dimension of product design refers to whether the product works the way the consumer thinks it should, that is, the extent to which the product is consistent with the consumer's intuition and prior experience. For example, consumers tend to expect control switches to be placed on the front of electronic appliances and were baffled when personal computers appeared on the market because the on/off switch was located in the back, counter to expectations. Similarly, consumers expect a printer to produce page output in the order of the document, from front to back, and were frustrated by early printers that made the default order of printing back to front. While appraisals of the direction and degree of goal congruence play a role in consumers' response to products that work in a counterintuitive fashion, there is also a very strong normative component of the appraisal process at work in such circumstances. There is an expectation about how the product "should" work or how it "should" deliver the benefit, which is independent of whether the product delivers the benefit sought by consumers.

Finally, the emotional dimension of product design is concerned with how the possession or use of the product makes the consumer feel. For example, a product may work quite well but make the consumer feel silly or dumb. For example, an adult consumer may feel foolish and helpless if he or she cannot open a "childproof" cap. Alternatively, a consumer might feel empowered by the simplicity of the user interface of a computer like Apple's MacIntosh. There are, no doubt, elements of appraisal related to the direction and degree of goal congruency, and dimensions of appraisal that may include a normative component in such emotional responses. However, there are also especially strong elements of appraisal of personal agency (as opposed to product agency) in such circumstances.

Thus, appraisal theory provides an especially useful complement to contemporary approaches to product design by identifying the dimensions of consumers' appraisal processes that provide the linkages among goals (functional dimensions of a product), normative expectations (cognitive dimensions of a product), and emotional responses related to as assessment of personal agency when using the product. Appraisal theory suggests that consumer response to a product (or service) is quite complex and involves a constellation of emotions that may arise from quite different dimensions of the product. By examining the likely appraisal processes associated with each of the different dimensions of product design, marketers and industrial engineers may be able to better forecast consumer response to the product, and make improvements that produce more positive responses from consumers.

Retail Distribution

There is no doubt that consumers experience an array of emotional responses in retail shopping and service delivery settings. Retailers often intentionally attempt to create or diminish emotional responses as part of the design of their distribution system (Donovan and Rossiter 1982). Kotler

(2000) defines atmosphere as a "planned atmosphere that suits the target market and draws customers toward a purchase" (p. 527). A key dimension of the atmosphere of any retail outlet is the way it makes consumers feel. A feeling of being uncomfortable and crowded may cause the consumer to quickly transact business and leave. A feeling of warmth, comfort, and relaxation may cause the customer to linger. Appraisal theory would suggest that it is the consumers' appraisal of the retail situation that gives rise to the emotions experienced while in the retail environment. Thus, retailers might use the various dimensions of appraisal as a formal means for assessing the likely emotional responses to the retail setting.

Each of the dimensions of the appraisal process suggests specific design characteristics of the retail setting for a particular type of product and consumer. Especially relevant to consumers' response to the retail setting is the appraisal of the degree and direction of goal congruence. The specific goals of consumers, whether they are shopping for a specific type of product, browsing to gather information or for recreation, or shopping for some other reason, will drive specific outcomes of the appraisal process and potentially lead to quite different emotional responses among consumers. Similarly, there will be strong normative and certainty dimensions of consumers' appraisals of retail settings. There are frequently strong expectations among consumers about how a retailer should be laid out and how a retailer should interact with the consumer; shopping experience leads to certainty related to retailers that are visited regularly.

Consumers' emotional responses to retail settings can be quite complex. It is the constellation of the various emotions experienced by the consumer that ultimately influences the consumer's behavior toward and response to a retailer. Thus, appraisal theories provide an especially useful conceptual framework for identifying and explaining such complex emotional responses.

Conclusion

The application of appraisal theory to consumer behavior has the potential to suggest many novel avenues of research. By emphasizing the role of information processing in emotion, appraisal theories can explicate the links between many common consumer judgments and emotion. Appraisal theories also offer a sound basis for research on consumption emotions and their impact on consumer behavior.

In addition, though appraisal theories are explicitly focused on emotion, they may make contributions to consumer behavior research on affect in general, such as research on mood. Based on the similarity of mood to emotion—specifically, the potential for emotion to generalize from a specific target situation to a broader affective tendency—appraisal theory may point to new directions for research on mood as well. For example, Keltner, Ellsworth, and Edwards (1993) found that emotions influenced subsequent judgments of a target that was unrelated to the emotions' source in a manner consistent with the appraisals related to those emotions. They found that subjects cued with memories of anger were more likely than subjects cued with sad memories to make appraisals of agency to a person in a subsequently presented scenario that was ambiguous as to the responsibility for a negative situation. Because the source is different from the target, these are mood effects. Further, they provide evidence that these effects were due to the appraisals associated with the emotion rather than with any purely cognitive priming effects that may have occurred. These results suggest that moods may be characterized by the tendency to apply the appraisals associated with the emotion that engendered the mood.

Research on emotion and affect is challenging, even when there is a sound theoretical basis for making predictions and designing operationalizations. The biggest methodological challenge involved in investigating emotion and appraisal is the potential for emotional processes to operate automatically and beyond conscious awareness. This is a challenge because studies of appraisal typically rely on self-report. However, this limitation can be addressed by using multiple methods to study the predictions of appraisal theory, including projective and observational techniques (Lazarus 1995). Projective techniques are useful in ruling out social desirability effects, and may also be useful in uncovering appraisals in situations that are likely to involve automatic processing. Observational techniques are also useful in uncovering nonconscious processes, but, as appraisals are internal construals that are not necessarily available to observation, these methods can provide only a suggestion of the possible appraisals and emotions that are being experienced.

In sum, appraisal theories are conceptually sound and empirically well supported. They have been shown to be useful in research in psychology in solving theoretical issues for which other theories could not account, and they have provided a solid foundation for the advancement of empirical research on emotion. Research in consumer behavior can also benefit from adopting this theoretical perspective. Though this review is brief in comparison to the large body of literature available, the conceptual framework and summary of appraisal theories can provide an introduction and a reference for researchers interested in further exploring the application of appraisal theories in consumer behavior and in marketing.

Acknowledgment

The authors wish to thank Deborah MacInnis, Naresh Malhotra, and Dawn Iacobucci for their comments and suggestions for improving this article.

Note

1. Pleasure-Displeasure (P), Arousal-Nonarousal (A) or general level of physical activity and mental alertness, and Dominance-Submissiveness (D) or feelings of control vs. lack of control over one's activities and surroundings.

References

Austin, James T. and Jeffrey B. Vancouver (1996), "Goal Constructs in Psychology: Structure, Process, and Content," *Psychological Bulletin*, 120 (3), 338–75.
Bagozzi, Richard P., Hans Baumgartner, and Rik Pieters (1998), "Goal-Directed Emotions," *Cognition & Emotion*, 12 (1), 1–26.
Bagozzi, Richard P., Mahesh Gopinath, and Prashanth U. Nyer (1999), "The Role of Emotions in Marketing," *Journal of the Academy of Marketing Science*, 27 (2), 184–206.
Bagozzi, Richard P. and Paul R. Warshaw (1990), "Trying to Consume," *Journal of Consumer Research*, 17 (2), 127–40.
Bargh, John A. (1982), "Attention and Automaticity in the Processing of Self-Relevant Information," *Journal of Personality and Social Psychology*, 43 (3), 425–36.
Bargh, John A. and Melissa J. Ferguson (2000), "Beyond Behaviorism: On the Automaticity of Higher Mental Processes," *Psychological Bulletin Special Issue: Psychology in the 21st Century*, 126 (6), 925–45.
Batra, Rajeev and Michael L. Ray (1986), "Affective Responses Mediating Acceptance of Advertising," *Journal of Consumer Research*, 13 (2), 234–48.
Boninger, David S., Faith Gleicher, and Alan Strathman (1994), "Counterfactual Thinking: From What Might Have Been to What May Be," *Journal of Personality & Social Psychology*, 67 (2), 297–307.
Boulding, William, Ajay Kalra, Richard Staelin, and Valarie A. Zeithaml (1993), "A Dynamic Process Model of Service Quality: From Expectations to Behavioral Intentions," *Journal of Marketing Research*, 30 (1), 7–27.
Cacioppo, John T. and Richard E. Petty (1985), "Physiological Responses and Advertising Effects: Is the Cup Half Full or Half Empty?" *Psychology and Marketing*, 2 (2), 115–26.

Chen, Mark and John A. Bargh (1997), "Nonconscious Behavioral Confirmation Processes: The Self-Fulfilling Consequences of Automatic Stereotype Activation," *Journal of Experimental Social Psychology*, 33 (5), 541–60.

Clore, Gerald and Timothy Ketelaar (1997), "Minding Our Emotions: On the Role of Automatic, Unconscious Affect," in *The Automaticity of Everyday Life: Advances in Social Cognition*, Robert S. Wyer, Jr., ed. Vol. 10. Mahwah, NJ: Lawrence Erlbaum Associates.

Clore, Gerald L. and Andrew Ortony (2000), "Cognition in Emotion: Always, Sometimes, or Never?" in *Cognitive Neuroscience of Emotion*, Richard D. Lane and Lynn Nadel, eds. New York: Oxford University Press.

Cohen, Joel B. and Charles S. Areni (1991), "Affect and Consumer Behavior," in *Handbook of Consumer Behavior*, Thomas S. Robertson and Harold H. Kassarjian, eds. Englewood Cliffs, NJ: Prentice Hall.

Creighton, Millie R. (1990), "Revisiting Shame and Guilt Cultures: A Forty-year Pilgrimage," *Ethos*, 18 (3), 279–307.

Donovan, Robert J. and John R. Rossiter (1982), "Store Atmosphere—An Environmental Psychology Approach," *Journal of Retailing*, 58 (1), 34–57.

Donovan, Robert J., John R. Rossiter, Gilian Marcoolyn, and Andrew Nesdale (1994), "Store Atmosphere and Purchasing Behavior," *Journal of Retailing*, 70 (3), 283–94.

Dube, Laurette and Kalyani Menon (2000), "Multiple Roles of Consumption Emotions in Post-Purchase Satisfaction with Extended Service Transactions," *International Journal of Service Industry Management*, 11 (3), 287–304.

Ekman, Paul and Richard J. Davidson, eds. (1994), *The Nature of Emotion: Fundamental Questions*. New York: Oxford University Press.

Ellsworth, Phoebe C. and Craig A. Smith (1988), "From Appraisal to Emotion: Differences Among Unpleasant Feelings," *Motivation & Emotion*, 12 (3), 271–302.

Fleeson, William and Nancy Cantor (1995), "Goal Relevance and the Affective Experience of Daily Life: Ruling Out Situational Explanations," *Motivation & Emotion*, 19 (1), 25–57.

Folkes, Valerie S. (1984), "Consumer Reactions to Product Failure: An Attributional Approach," *Journal of Consumer Research*, 10 (4), 398–409.

Folkman, Susan and Richard S. Lazarus (1988), "Coping as a Mediator of Emotion," *Journal of Personality & Social Psychology*, 54 (3), 466–75.

Fredrickson, Barbara L. (1998), "What Good Are Positive Emotions?" *Review of General Psychology*, 2 (3), 300–19.

——— (2001), "The Role of Positive Emotions in Positive Psychology: The Broaden-and-Build Theory of Positive Emotions," *American Psychologist*, 56 (3), 218–26.

Frijda, Nico H. (1993), "The Place of Appraisal in Emotion," *Cognition & Emotion Special Issue: Appraisal and Beyond: The Issue of Cognitive Determinants of Emotion*, 7 (3–4), 357–87.

Frijda, Nico H., Peter Kuipers, and Elisabeth ter Schure (1989), "Relations Among Emotion, Appraisal, and Emotional Action Readiness," *Journal of Personality & Social Psychology*, 57 (2), 212–28.

Garbarino, Ellen C. and Julie A. Edell (1997), "Cognitive Effort, Affect, and Choice," *Journal of Consumer Research*, 24 (2), 147–58.

Gollwitzer, Peter M. and Gordon B. Moskowitz (1996), "Goal Effects on Action and Cognition," in *Social Psychology: Handbook of Basic Principles*, Arie W. Kruglanski, ed. New York: Guilford.

Groeger, John A. (2000), *Understanding Driving: Applying Cognitive Psychology to a Complex Everyday Task*. Philadelphia: Psychology Press.

Hetts, John J., David S. Boninger, David A. Armor, Faith Gleicher, and Ariel Nathanson (2000), "The Influence of Anticipated Counterfactual Regret on Behavior," *Psychology & Marketing Special Issue: Counterfactual Thinking*, 17 (4), 345–68.

Higgins, E. Tory (1997), "Beyond Pleasure and Pain," *American Psychologist*, 52 (12), 1280–1300.

Hirschman, Elizabeth C. and Morris B. Holbrook (1982), "Hedonic Consumption: Emerging Concepts, Methods and Propositions," *Journal of Marketing*, 46 (3), 92–101.

Holbrook, Morris B. and Rajeev Batra (1987), "Assessing the Role of Emotions as Mediators of Consumer Responses to Advertising," *Journal of Consumer Research*, 14 (3), 404–20.

Holbrook, Morris B. and Elizabeth C. Hirschman (1982), "The Experiential Aspects of Consumption: Consumer Fantasies, Feelings, and Fun," *Journal of Consumer Research*, 9 (2), 132–40.

Hui, Michael K. and John E. Bateson (1991), "Perceived Control and the Effects of Crowding and Consumer Choice on the Service Experience," *Journal of Consumer Research*, 18 (2), 174–84.

Izard, Carroll E. (1971), *The Face of Emotion*. East Norwalk, CT: Appleton-Century-Crofts.
——— (1992), "Basic Emotions, Relations Among Emotions, and Emotion-Cognition Relations," *Psychological Review*, 99 (3), 561–65.
Keltner, Dacher, Phoebe C. Ellsworth, and Kari Edwards (1993), "Beyond Simple Pessimism: Effects of Sadness and Anger on Social Perception," *Journal of Personality & Social Psychology*, 64 (5), 740–52.
Klebba, Joanne M. (1985), "Physiological Measures of Research: A Review of Brain Activity, Electrodermal Response, Pupil Dilation, and Voice Analysis Methods and Studies," *Current Issues and Research in Advertising*, 8 (1), 53–76.
Klein, William M. P. (2001), "Post Hoc Construction of Self-Performance and Other Performance in Self-Serving Social Comparison," *Personality & Social Psychology Bulletin*, 27 (6), 744–54.
Kotler, Philip (2000), *Marketing Management: Millennium Edition* (10th ed.). Upper Saddle River, NJ: Prentice Hall.
Lazarus, Richard S. (1991a), "Cognition and Motivation in Emotion," *American Psychologist*, 46 (4), 352–67.
——— (1991b), *Emotion and Adaptation*. New York: Oxford University Press.
——— (1991c), "Progress on a Cognitive-Motivational-Relational Theory of Emotion," *American Psychologist*, 46 (8), 819–34.
——— (1994), "The Stable and the Unstable in Emotion," in *The Nature of Emotion: Fundamental Questions*, Paul Ekman and Richard J. Davidson, eds. New York: Oxford University Press.
——— (1995), "Vexing Research Problems Inherent in Cognitive-Mediational Theories of Emotion—and Some Solutions," *Psychological Inquiry*, 6 (3), 183–96.
——— (1999), *Stress and Emotion: A New Synthesis*. New York: Springer.
——— (2001), "Relational Meaning and Discrete Emotions," in *Appraisal Processes in Emotion: Theory, Methods, Research*, Klaus R. Scherer and Angela Schorr, eds. New York: Oxford University Press.
Lazarus, Richard S. and Craig A. Smith (1988), "Knowledge and Appraisal in the Cognition-Emotion Relationship," *Cognition & Emotion*, 2 (4), 281–300.
Luce, Mary Frances (1998), "Choosing to Avoid: Coping with Negatively Emotion-Laden Consumer Decisions," *Journal of Consumer Research* 24 (March), 409–33.
Luce, Mary Frances, John W. Payne, and James R. Bettman (1999), "Emotional Trade-Off Difficulty and Choice," *Journal of Marketing Research*, 36 (2), 143–59.
Luce, Mary Frances, James R. Bettman, and John W. Payne (2000), "Attribute Identities Matter: Subjective Perceptions of Attribute Characteristics," *Marketing Letters*, 11, 103–16.
MacInnis, Deborah J. and Gustavo de Mello (2002), "The Role of Hope in Consumer Behavior: The Case of Motivated Reasoning," unpublished working paper, Department of Marketing, University of Southern California.
MacInnis, Deborah J. and Linda L. Price (1987), "The Role of Imagery in Information Processing: Review and Extensions," *Journal of Consumer Research*, 13 (4), 473–91.
Mano, Haim and Richard L. Oliver (1993), "Assessing the Dimensionality and Structure of the Consumption Experience: Evaluation, Feeling, and Satisfaction," *Journal of Consumer Research*, 20 (3), 451–66.
Manstead, A. S. and Philip E. Tetlock (1989), "Cognitive Appraisals and Emotional Experience: Further Evidence," *Cognition & Emotion*, 3 (3), 225–39.
March, A. (1994), "Usability—the New Dimension of Product Design," *Harvard Business Review*, 72 (5), 144–49.
Maxham, James G. and Richard G. Netemeyer (2002), "A Longitudinal Study of Complaining Customers' Evaluations of Multiple Service Failures and Recovery Efforts," *Journal of Marketing*, 66 (October), 57–71.
Merriam-Webster Dictionary (2003), http://www.m-w.com/cgi-bin/dictionary?schadenfreude.
Oatley, Keith and P. N. Johnson-Laird (1987), "Towards a Cognitive Theory of Emotions," *Cognition & Emotion*, 1 (1), 29–50.
Oliver, Richard L. (1993), "Cognitive, Affective, and Attribute Bases of the Satisfaction Response," *Journal of Consumer Research*, 20 (3), 418–30.
Oliver, Richard L., Roland T. Rust, and Sajeev Varki (1997), "Customer Delight: Foundations, Findings and Managerial Insight," *Journal of Retailing Special Issue: Service Marketing*, 73 (3), 311–36.
Olney, Thomas J., Morris B. Holbrook, and Rajeev Batra (1991), "Consumer Responses to Advertising: The Effects of Ad Content, Emotions, and Attitude toward the Ad on Viewing Time," *Journal of Consumer Research*, 17 (4), 440–53.

Ortony, Andrew, Gerald L. Clore, and Allan Collins (1988), *The Cognitive Structure of Emotions*. New York: Cambridge University Press.

Perugini, Marco and Richard P. Bagozzi (2001), "The Rôle of Desires and Anticipated Emotions in Goal-Directed Behaviours: Broadening and Deepening the Theory of Planned Behaviour," *British Journal of Social Psychology*, 40 (1), 79–98.

Plutchik, Robert (1982), "A Psychoevolutionary Theory of Emotions," *Social Science Information*, 21 (4–5), 529–53.

———— (1984), "Emotions and Imagery," *Journal of Mental Imagery*, 8 (4), 105–11.

Reisenzein, Rainer and Christine Spielhofer (1994), "Subjectively Salient Dimensions of Emotional Appraisal," *Motivation & Emotion*, 18 (1), 31–77.

Richins, Marsha L. (1997), "Measuring Emotions in the Consumption Experience," *Journal of Consumer Research*, 24 (2), 127–46.

Roseman, Ira J. (1984), "Cognitive Determinants of Emotion: A Structural Theory," *Review of Personality and Social Psychology*, 5, 11–36.

Roseman, Ira J., Ann Aliki Antoniou, and Paul E. Jose (1996), "Appraisal Determinants of Emotions: Constructing a More Accurate and Comprehensive Theory," *Cognition & Emotion*, 10 (3), 241–77.

Roseman, Ira J. and Craig A. Smith (2001), "Appraisal Theory: Overview, Assumptions, Varieties, Controversies," in *Appraisal Processes in Emotion: Theory, Methods, Research,* Tom Johnstone, ed. New York: Oxford University Press.

Roseman, Ira J., Martin S. Spindel, and Paul E. Jose (1990), "Appraisals of Emotion-Eliciting Events: Testing a Theory of Discrete Emotions," *Journal of Personality and Social Psychology*, 59 (5), 899–915.

Roseman, Ira J., Cynthia Wiest, and Tamara S. Swartz (1994), "Phenomenology, Behaviors, and Goals Differentiate Discrete Emotions," *Journal of Personality and Social Psychology*, 67 (2), 206–21.

Russell, James A. and Lisa Feldman Barrett (1999), "Core Affect, Prototypical Emotional Episodes, and Other Things Called Emotion: Dissecting the Elephant," *Journal of Personality & Social Psychology*, 76 (5), 805–19.

Russell, James A. and Albert Mehrabian (1977), "Evidence for a Three-Factor Theory of Emotions," *Journal of Research in Personality*, 11 (3), 273–94.

Rust, Roland T. and Richard L. Oliver (2000), "Should We Delight the Customer?" *Journal of the Academy of Marketing Science*, 28 (1), 86–94.

Schachter, Stanley and Jerome Singer (1962), "Cognitive, Social, and Physiological Determinants of Emotional State," *Psychological Review*, 69 (5), 379–99.

Scherer, Klaus R. (1982), "Emotion as a Process: Function, Origin and Regulation," *Social Science Information*, 21 (4–5), 555–70.

———— (1988), "On the Symbolic Functions of Vocal Affect Expression," *Journal of Language & Social Psychology*, 7 (2), 79–100.

———— (1997), "Profiles of Emotion-Antecedent Appraisal: Testing Theoretical Predictions across Cultures," *Cognition & Emotion*, 11 (2), 113–50.

———— (1999), "On the Sequential Nature of Appraisal Processes: Indirect Evidence from a Recognition Task," *Cognition & Emotion*, 13 (6), 763–93.

———— (2001), "Appraisal Considered as a Process of Multilevel Sequential Checking," in *Appraisal Processes in Emotion: Theory, Methods, Research*, Klaus R. Scherer and Angela Schorr, eds. New York: Oxford University Press.

Scherer, Klaus R. and Grazia Ceschi (1997), "Lost Luggage: A Field Study of Emotion-Antecedent Appraisal," *Motivation & Emotion*, 21 (3), 211–35.

Scherer, Klaus R., Angela Schorr, and Tom Johnstone (2001), *Appraisal Processes in Emotion: Theory, Methods, Research.* New York: Oxford University Press.

Smith, A. K. and R. N. Bolton (2002), "The Effect of Customers' Emotional Responses to Service Failures on Their Recovery Effort Evaluations and Satisfaction Judgments," *Journal of the Academy of Marketing Science*, 30 (1), 5–23.

Smith, Craig A. and Phoebe C. Ellsworth (1985), "Patterns of Cognitive Appraisal in Emotion," *Journal of Personality & Social Psychology*, 48 (4), 813–38.

———— (1987), "Patterns of Appraisal and Emotion Related to Taking an Exam," *Journal of Personality & Social Psychology*, 52 (3), 475–88.

Smith, Craig A., Kelly N. Haynes, Richard S. Lazarus, and Lois K. Pope (1993), "In Search of the 'Hot' Cognitions: Attributions, Appraisals, and Their Relation to Emotion," *Journal of Personality & Social Psychology*, 65 (5), 916–29.

Sonnemans, Joep and Nico H. Frijda (1995), "The Determinants of Subjective Emotional Intensity," *Cognition & Emotion*, 9 (5), 483–506.

Spielman, Lisa A., Felicia Pratto, and John A. Bargh (1988), "Automatic Affect: Are One's Moods, Attitudes, Evaluations, and Emotions Out of Control?" *American Behavioral Scientist*, 31 (3), 296–311.

Steenkamp, Jan-Benedict E. (1990), "Conceptual Model of the Quality Perception Process," *Journal of Business Research*, 21 (4), 309–33.

Stewart, David W. (1984), "Physiological Measurement of Advertising Effects: An Unfulfilled Promise," *Psychology and Marketing*, 1 (1), 43–48.

——— (1985), "Differences Between Basic Research and The Validation of Specific Measures: A Reply to Weinstein, et al.," *Psychology and Marketing*, 2 (1), 41–50.

Stewart, David W. and David H. Furse (1986), *Effective Television Advertising: A Study of 1000 Commercials*. Lexington, MA: Lexington Books.

Stipek, Deborah (1998), "Differences between Americans and Chinese in the Circumstances Evoking Pride, Shame, and Guilt," *Journal of Cross-Cultural Psychology*, 29 (5), 616–29.

Tangney, June Price, Paula M. Niedenthal, Michelle Vowell Covert, and Deborah Hill Barlow (1998), "Are Shame and Guilt Related to Distinct Self-Discrepancies? A Test of Higgins's (1987) Hypotheses," *Journal of Personality & Social Psychology*, 75 (1), 256–68.

Tesser, Abraham (1990), "Smith and Ellsworth's Appraisal Model of Emotion: A Replication, Extension, and Test," *Personality & Social Psychology Bulletin*, 16 (2), 210–23.

Tesser, Abraham and James E. Collins (1988), "Emotion in Social Reflection and Comparison Situations: Intuitive, Systematic, and Exploratory Approaches," *Journal of Personality & Social Psychology*, 55 (5), 695–709.

Watson, David and Auke Tellegen (1985), "Toward a Consensual Structure of Mood," *Psychological Bulletin*, 98 (2), 219–35.

Weiner, Bernard (1985), "An Attributional Theory of Achievement Motivation and Emotion," *Psychological Review*, 92 (4), 548–73.

Weiner, Bernard, Dan Russell, and David Lerman (1979), "The Cognition-Emotion Process in Achievement-Related Contexts," *Journal of Personality & Social Psychology*, 37 (7), 1211–20.

Weinstein, Sidney, Ronald Drozdenko, and Curt Weinstein (1984), "Advertising Evaluation Using Brain-Wave Measures: A Response to the Question of Validity," *Journal of Advertising Research*, 24 (April/May), 67–70.

Westbrook, Robert A. (1987), "Product/Consumption-Based Affective Responses and Postpurchase Processes," *Journal of Marketing Research*, 24 (3), 258–70.

Westbrook, Robert A. and Richard L. Oliver (1991), "The Dimensions of Consumption Emotion Patterns and Consumer Satisfaction," *Journal of Consumer Research*, 18 (1), 84–91.

Wyer, Robert S. Jr., ed. (1997), *The Automaticity of Everyday Life*. Mahwah, NJ: Lawrence Erlbaum Associates.

Zajonc, Robert B. (1980), "Feeling and Thinking: Preferences Need No Inferences," *American Psychologist*, 35 (2), 151–75.

Zajonc, Robert B. and Hazel Markus (1985), "Must All Affect Be Mediated By Cognition?" *Journal of Consumer Research*, 12 (3), 363–64.

CHAPTER 2

THE EYE OF THE BEHOLDER

Beauty as a Concept in Everyday Discourse and the Collective Photographic Essay

MORRIS B. HOLBROOK

Abstract

This article explores the concept of beauty, as experienced by ordinary consumers in their everyday lives. We begin by considering the definitions of beauty typically supplied by philosophers of art from the perspective of aesthetic experience. Such definitions operate in the realm of langue—*semantics, language use, or linguistic competence—that is, a form of language that exists according to certain semantic and syntactic rules but that does not necessarily reflect how the language is generally spoken in the vernacular. The latter concern belongs to the realm of* parole—*pragmatics, usage, or psycholinguistic performance—in which words are deployed by actual speakers of the language in ways that shape the common culturally shared discourse. Exploring the concept of beauty as it appears in* parole—*as opposed to* langue—*requires some sort of empirical investigation involving actual users of the language as an aid to the emergence of data-grounded theory. Toward this end, the present study applies the method of the* collective photographic essay. *That is, ordinary consumers take photographs intended to elucidate the concept of "What Beauty Means to Me" and explain their photographic intentions by means of short paragraphs or vignettes. The meanings of these vignettes and photos are analyzed semiologically by means of hermeneutic interpretation that moves back and forth between general overviews of the text and careful scrutiny of the detailed textual evidence. The application of this hermeneutic circle produces a typology of beauty in ordinary discourse. This typology conceptualizes everyday usage of the term "beauty" as falling into* eight categories *distinguished on the basis of* three dichotomies: *(1) Extrinsically/Intrinsically Motivated (E/I), (2) Thing(s)-/Person(s)-Based (T/P), and (3) Concrete/Abstract (C/A). These eight types of beauty include (1) Function (ETC), (2) Symbol (ETA), (3) Achievement (EPC), (4) Image (EPA), (5) Nature (ITC), (6) Aesthetics (ITA), (7) Relationships (IPC), and (8) Character (IPA). Detailed examples, drawn from the texts of the informants' vignettes and photographs, illustrate each of the eight types of beauty. The major conclusion is that the philosophically grounded definition of aesthetic beauty* (langue) *fails to capture the diverse ways in which the concept of beauty appears in everyday discourse among ordinary consumers* (parole). *Indeed, common usage reveals at least eight distinguishable types of beauty. Though distinct conceptually, these types tend to commingle in consumption experiences in the sense that any one consumer activity may well encompass multiple or even all aspects of beauty.*

Introduction

Background in the Philosophy of Art

Philosophers have long argued about the meaning of beauty without any noticeable tendency to reach agreement. Indeed, the beauty-related literature in the philosophy of art is characterized more by its diversity and fragmentation than by any common thread that might emerge to guide the eager inquisitor. Some have regarded beauty as an entirely subjective aspect of experience—as summarized by the cliché that "beauty is in the eye of the beholder." At the other extreme, some have viewed beauty as an objective property that inheres within (say) a work of art. Others insist that beauty entails an interaction between a subject (some consumer) and an object (some product) such that it stems from a relationship between the two (for reviews, please see Holbrook 1994, 1999a, 1999b; Holbrook and Zirlin 1985).

Along with countless others, the present author has categorized beauty as an example of *aesthetic value*—that is, as one type of *interactive relativistic preference experience* (Holbrook 1994, 1999b). In this connection, a well-developed literature on *aesthetics* justifies a conception of beauty as (1) *intrinsically motivated,* (2) *self-oriented,* and (3) *reactive* in the type of consumer value it creates.

1. First, in aesthetic appreciation, we prize some experience involving an object such as a work of art or a piece of entertainment *for its own sake;* we care not about any utilitarian function that the object or experience might perform (which confers a different type of extrinsically motivated value), but rather appreciate the experience of beauty as an intrinsically motivated *self-justifying end-in-itself.*
2. Second, the value experienced as aesthetic beauty serves *our own purposes* rather than those of others; it is self-oriented insofar as it depends on *how we respond* or on *how it affects us* rather than on how others respond or on how it affects them.
3. Third, the experience of aesthetic beauty involves a reactive *response to some object* rather than its active manipulation; we admire, apprehend, or appreciate it by virtue of *how it acts on us* rather than how we act on it in doing something to shape, manage, or control the object in question.

Illustrations of Aesthetic Beauty in the Philosophy of Art: The Narrow View

As already mentioned, the view of beauty as an example of aesthetic value has characterized much of the work in the philosophy of art. Though a complete review of this literature lies outside the scope of the present article, one conspicuous example appears in the pair of essays contributed by Jerome Stolnitz (1967) and John Hospers (1967) to *The Encyclopedia of Philosophy.*

Stolnitz on Beauty. Stolnitz (1967) provides a brief history of the concept of "Beauty" in which he shows how the concept of beauty has narrowed over time. Thus, this author views beauty as just part of the field of *aesthetics* and, indeed, as a part that has diminished in centrality from the time of the ancient Greeks to that of the present-day psychological aestheticians and philosophers of art. During the time of Plato and Aristotle, beauty was viewed as a property—an ingredient or structural relation—inherent in something not necessarily or even usually a work of art and knowable in an objective and absolute sense by virtue of its presence (p. 263). Here, the Greeks referred not to painting, tragedy, comedy—much less to the appearance of people or other human significations—but rather to a general mode of *goodness* treated as more or less synonymous with *"excellent, perfect,* and *satisfying"* (p. 264). This objectivist/absolutist spirit descended to the neoclassical period in which sixteenth- and seventeenth-century critics sought legitimacy for their renderings of judgment in an appeal to various rules (e.g., the unities of time and space) certified by the "authority of antiquity" (p. 264).

All this changed radically during the eighteenth century when philosophers of art came to regard the appreciation of beauty as just one aspect of "disinterested" (i.e., intrinsically motivated) *aesthetic experience:*

> The century was a Copernican revolution, for instead of looking outward to the properties of beauty or the art object, it first examined the experience of the percipient, to determine the conditions under which beauty and art are appreciated. (p. 264)

In this, beauty became just one type of relevant aesthetic experience—along with, say, *the sublime* (as characterized by feelings of amazement and awe). The latter emphasis on profundity or emotional intensity—the vast, the infinite, the terrible, even the ugly—opened the door to a preoccupation during the romantic era of the nineteenth century with the role of *expression* and with the capacity of something to evoke a certain experience (e.g., by virtue of its unity-in-variety). Some suggested that such capacities are "devoid of meaning" so that *beautiful* becomes just "a general term of approbation" (p. 265).

Increasingly, throughout the twentieth century, philosophers (even those focusing on the arts) got along without or proceeded in opposition to the concept of beauty. Some have taken "beauty" to refer to the delivery of *aesthetic value* (as this varies from one context to another). Others have regarded the term "beautiful" as a relativistic concept that shifts meaning from one application to the next and that has become so narrow as to be essentially "irrelevant for evaluation" (p. 266).

Hospers on Aesthetics. Along similar lines—stressing a narrow conception of beauty as a facet of aesthetic experience—Hospers (1967) sees questions concerning beauty as one aspect of "the discipline known as aesthetics" (p. 36). Aesthetics—because it includes such issues as the beauty of nature—is broader than the philosophy of art, in his view, but nonetheless he maintains that "most of the interesting and perplexing aesthetic questions through the ages have been concerned specifically with art" (p. 36), including such questions as "What features make objects beautiful?" From this, we see that contemporary philosophers concerned with the nature of beauty tend to turn to aesthetics and the philosophy of art as the omnibus disciplines of primary relevance.

Hospers (1967) nicely summarizes the manner in which aesthetic experience involves intrinsic as opposed to extrinsic value:

> The aesthetic attitude, or the "aesthetic way of looking at the world," is most commonly opposed to the *practical* attitude, which is concerned only with the utility of the object in question. The real estate agent who views a landscape only with an eye to its possible monetary value is not viewing the landscape aesthetically. To view a landscape aesthetically one must "perceive for perceiving's sake," not for the sake of some ulterior purpose. One must savor the experience of perceiving the landscape itself, dwelling on its perceptual details, rather than using the perceptual object as a means to some further end. (p. 36)

As made clear by this passage, the essence of aesthetic value lies not in an artwork as a means to any end—including the end of providing pleasure or enjoyment—but rather in an appreciation of the *consumption experience,* for its own sake, as an end in itself. As clarified elsewhere by Lewis (1946), only an experience—never an artwork, thing, event, good, service, or any other kind of product—can be the object of intrinsically appreciated aesthetic value (see Holbrook 1994, 1999b). Later, Hospers (1967) further clarifies the sense in which an artwork may possess extrinsic value (as a means of evoking an aesthetic experience), whereas the experience itself entails intrinsic value (as an end appreciated for its own sake):

> A good work of art is one that successfully evokes an aesthetic experience in an audience and is therefore a good instrument toward the achievement of aesthetic experience as an end in itself. It should be noted, however, that the work of art itself possesses instrumental value, for it and other members of its function-class fulfill the end of evoking aesthetic experience; but the experience of works of art is an intrinsic value, worth having for its own sake alone and not as a means toward any further end. (p. 55)

A similar view of beauty that acknowledges the importance of the subject-object interaction as a foundation for this type of value identifies "beauty" as a name that we give to some situation that evokes an aesthetic experience. Bourgeois (1998), a sculptress, expresses this thought nicely:

> Beauty? It seems to me that beauty is an example of what the philosophers call reification, to regard an abstraction as a thing. Beauty is a series of experiences. . . . People have experiences. If they feel an intense aesthetic pleasure, they take that experience and project it into the object. (p. 331)

This perspective identifies beauty with the celebration of pleasure and art with the embodiment of a desire to please: "Uncontrollable beauty is in the effort to seduce one through my sculpture. It is *le désir de plaire*" (p. 341). A comparable celebratory view of beauty appears in an essay by another artist when Martin (1998) explicitly connected the experience of beauty with human happiness:

> All artwork is about beauty. . . . Beauty is an awareness in the mind. It is a mental and emotional response we make. . . . The goal of life is happiness. . . . Artwork is responded to with happy emotions. (pp. 399–400)

Hospers (1967) takes pains to point out that the concept of beauty—though a subcategory of aesthetics, in his view—applies beyond the realm of art, as when speaking of a beautiful natural object. Art, in his view, entails being made by a human as a necessary condition. Hence, "If what we thought was a piece of sculpture turns out to be a piece of driftwood, we would continue to regard it as an aesthetic object, and it would still be as beautiful (or ugly) as before, but it would not be a work of art" (p. 39). Of course, not all human-made objects are works of art. Nonetheless, note the point that philosophers of art, aesthetics, and beauty have tended to regard these concepts as comprising something of a self-contained world of inquiry—namely, the world of "fine art, upon which philosophers of art have focused most of their attention" (p. 40).

As a principle of form to which we shall return in what follows, assumed to be a foundation for aesthetic response, Hospers (1967) spells out the role of unity—balanced against chaos, confusion, or disharmony—as achieving *formal complexity,* by which he means "variety in unity" (p. 43): "The unified object should contain within itself a large number of diverse elements, each of which in some way contributes to the total integration of the unified whole, so that there is no confusion despite the disparate elements within the object. In the unified object, everything that is necessary is there, and nothing that is not necessary is there" (p. 43). Notice also that this sort of complexity—encapsulated by the slogan "variety in unity"—captures the dialectical sense of a resolution, reconciliation, or synthesis of order and chaos, structure and departure, pattern and deviation, organization and richness, theme and variation, expectation and surprise by which the aesthetic appreciation of artistic creation occurs. Following Pepper's conceptualization, Hospers (1967) maintains that "the way to avoid monotony is variety, and the way to avoid confusion is unity": "A delicate balance between these two qualities must be maintained" (p. 44; see also Holbrook 1984, 1995, 1997a).

In sum, Hospers (1967) views *beauty* as an aspect of aesthetic value, where the latter is "the more general concept" (p. 53), having a broader reach that extends to aesthetic objects not appealing to the eye or ear (e.g., a novel) and perhaps displeasing or even ugly (e.g., Picasso's *Guernica*). Concerning the nature of aesthetic value, he rejects *subjectivist* positions attempting to reduce statements of the form "X is good" to statements of the form "Y likes X"—whether "Y" refers to oneself (autobiographical preference), to others (popular appeal), or to critics (expert judgment). In short, "There always seems to be a difference in meaning between a statement about the merit of a work of art and a statement about the verdict of those judging it" (p. 54). In lieu of such subjectivist theories, Hospers favors what he calls an *objectivist* account "grounded in the nature of the object itself" or what I would call an *interactionist* perspective in that a "judgment of its merit . . . is based upon the work's properties alone, not on the properties of any observers" (p. 54)—where, in my view, this appraisal hinges on an *interaction* between a subject (the "judgment") and an object (the "properties"). At any rate, Hospers locates *beauty* at the heart of such a "property or set of properties that constitutes aesthetic value":

> One view of this issue is that there is a property of all aesthetic objects which may be present in varying degrees. . . , but which to the degree that it is present confers upon the work its aesthetic value. This property is usually called "beauty." (p. 54)

This discussion leaves little doubt that Hospers (1967)—despite occasional qualifications—regards beauty as an aspect of aesthetic experience and aesthetics as generally dealing with works of art. Though he notes exceptions, this Venn-like overlapping of treatments constitutes the heart of contemporary philosophical approaches to art, aesthetics, and beauty. Such intersections of these three topics appear, for example, in the definition of *aesthetics* offered by Munro (1962): "Traditionally, the branch of philosophy dealing with beauty or the beautiful, especially in art, and with taste and standards of value in judging art" (p. 6).

Explanations for Aesthetic Beauty—the Role of Complexity

When viewed in the "narrow" manner just described, beauty is seen as the outcome of a process leading to an aesthetic experience and thereby raising questions concerning the dynamic explanation of this process. In one way or another, when analyzing aesthetic experience, numerous commentators have pointed to the role of *complexity*. Thus, far from "old fashioned," the views of beauty espoused by Hospers (1967) find their echoes in more contemporary accounts provided by such eclectic aestheticians as Frederick Turner (1991).

Turner on Beauty as Value. Turner (1991) draws on every source of insight he can find, from Greek philosophy to chaos-and-complexity theory (for a recent review of complexity science, please see Holbrook 2003). In essence, Turner views beauty as an objective aspect found in every facet of the universe, from the most atomic to the most cosmic level, and as a universal standard for both truth and goodness. His central concept for expressing this vision involves *complexity* as a combination of order and chaos:

> A beautiful thing, though simple in its immediate presence, always gives us a sense of depth below depth, almost an innocent wild vertigo as one falls through its levels. Complexity is contained within simplicity. . . . You can never get to the bottom of something beautiful, because it always finds space inside itself for a new and surprising recapitulation of its idea that adds fresh feeling to the familiar pattern. (pp. 2–3)

In short, "Beauty is always paradoxical": "It is not mere chaos and non-linearity but the paradoxical coexistence of chaos with order, non-linear discontinuity with linear flow and predictable repetition" (p. 4). Turner finds such paradoxes, for example, in the *golden section,* with the implicit contradiction between "its irrational decimal expression" (1:1.618. . .) and "the logical simplicity of the Fibonacci series that generates it" (1, 2, 3, 5, 8, 13, 21, 34, 55. . .) (p. 5). (See also pages 94–95, where Turner reveals the Fibonacci series as the basis for the spiral shape "found throughout nature" as well as the construction of a five-pointed star and where he describes this series as "only the simplest of a whole class of iterative algorithms or formulae" that include the fractal patterns developed by Mandelbrot and reviewed by Holbrook 2003.)

Thus, for Turner (1991), beauty entails the notion of a higher-level order containing a lower-level disorder: "The indescribably beautiful is always, I believe, partially describable because higher hierarchical levels contain and reference lower ones . . . to unify disparate material, to preserve the surprise of difference precisely by holding it within a frame of unity" (p. 10). Later, sounding a great deal like Meyer (1956, 1967) in his classic treatment of *Emotion and Meaning in Music* (1956), Turner (1991) gives a more detailed example:

> In music the same thing happens: Mozart will often pile two or three twists of melodic or harmonic surprise upon each other, and yet in retrospect the structure of his piece will hold firm, perfectly braced, airy, yet as strong as adamant. (p. 80)

Still later, borrowing from Gerard Manley Hopkins, Turner (1991) views beauty as "a mixture of regularity and irregularity": "Patterns are beautiful that exist at the margin between order and disorder, that exhibit a hierarchical organization which is troubled and opened up by contradictory elements" (p. 93). He sees this vision of beauty as "central to all meaningful human life and . . . to the objective reality of the universe" (p. 15).

In another contemporary view of beauty as embodying a sort of *anima mundi* ("soul of the cosmos"), Hillman (1998) describes beauty as an "inherent radiance" that is "permanently given, inherent to the world in its data, there on display always, a display that evokes an aesthetic response" (p. 267). On this theme, Hillman quotes Whitehead to the effect that, "The teleology of the universe is directed to the production of Beauty" (p. 268). Hillman concludes,

> If life itself is biologically aesthetic and if the cosmos itself is primarily an aesthetic event, then beauty is not merely a cultural accessory, a philosophic category, a province of the arts, or even a prerogative of the human spirit. It has always remained indefinable because it bears sensate witness to what is fundamentally beyond human comprehension. (p. 270)

Psychological Views of Aesthetic Experience. Meanwhile, psychologists and others concerned with tracing the process of aesthetic experience have often developed conceptions analogous to those of Turner (1991) and couched in terms of a dialectic (thesis → antithesis → synthesis) in which structure →   departure → resolution or in which order → disorder → complexity. I have described this process-oriented view of beauty in aesthetic experience at length elsewhere (Holbrook 1984, 1995, 1997a). I first encountered a highly influential exposition of the dialectical view via a clearly expressed and even profound articulation in the work of Meyer (1956, 1967), who analyzes emotional responses to music as the outcome of a process in which musical *structure* builds expectations that are, in turn, violated by *departures* subsequently seen as the basis for a newly emerging structural *resolution.* Moving beyond music, Berlyne (1971) gives a more general account in terms of an arousal jag in which "collative" or uncertainty-producing properties build tension that gets resolved via specific exploration. Arnheim (1971) traces similar thinking all the way back to the ancient principle of "unity in variety" (p. 50), with attention to "Eysenck's attempt to identify the 'good gestalt' with the 'beautiful'" (p. 52; see Eysenck 1942); to Birkhoff's quest for an aesthetic measure (p. 51; see Birkhoff 1933); and even to Freud's emphasis on tension reduction in his *Beyond the Pleasure Principle* (p. 44; see Freud 1990). Essentially, Arnheim (1971) is concerned with the paradox whereby systems tend toward greater entropy (the second law of thermodynamics or SLT) even while the human mind exhibits a "pervasive striving for order": "Order is a prerequisite of survival; therefore the impulse to produce orderly arrangements is inbred by evolution" (p. 3). In this connection, he draws on the gestalt psychologists such as Wolfgang Köhler as well as the work of physicists such as Sir Joseph J. Thomson, tending to show that "orderly form will come about as the visible result of physical forces establishing . . . the most balanced configurations attainable" (p. 6). How can we square such observations with SLT's principle of increasing entropy? Arnheim's answer appears to rest on the concept of equilibrium seen as "the very opposite of disorder" (p. 25):

> A system is in equilibrium when the forces constituting it are arranged in such a way as to compensate for each other. . . . It also represents the simplest structure the system can assume under the given conditions. This amounts to saying that the maximum of entropy attainable through rearrangement is reached when the system is in the best possible order. (p. 25)

Ultimately, Arnheim (1971) seeks to resolve all this by positing two counteracting forces at work—a *catabolic effect,* whereby things tend to fall apart in accord with SLT (p. 27), and an *anabolic tendency,* which tends to create structure, shape, or pattern (p. 31). The result of these counteracting forces is the creation of a new order that is generally "quite complex" (p. 32) and that organizes energy "according to the simplest, most balanced structure available to a system" (p. 35). Thus, Arnheim summarizes his view under the heading "A Need For Complexity":

> Man's striving for order, of which art is but one manifestation, derives from a similar universal tendency throughout the organic world; it is also paralleled by, and perhaps derived from, the striving towards the state of simplest structure in physical systems. This cosmic tendency towards order . . . must be carefully distinguished from catabolic erosion, which afflicts all material things and leads to disorder or more generally to the eventual destruction of all organized shape. A counterprinciple . . . must supply what is to be ordered. I described this counterprinciple as the anabolic creation of a structural theme. . . . Subjected to the tendency toward simplest structure, the object or event or institution assumes orderly, functioning shape. (pp. 48–49)

Hofstadter's Golden Braid. A similarly complexity-based conception of beauty—expressed via lengthy and elaborate meditations on the subjects of beauty, truth, mind, and brain—appears in the multidisciplinary tour de force entitled *Gödel, Escher, Bach: An Eternal Golden Braid* by Douglas Hofstadter (1979). This learned and versatile professor of computer science attempts to tie together—metaphorically if not literally—currents of thought collected from such diverse areas as art, music, literature, mathematics, geometry, philosophy, linguistics, logic, computer science, artificial intelligence, religion, physics, and biology (just to name a few). In other words, his 756 pages of convoluted ruminations aspire to nothing less than a worldview appropriate to an understanding of the human condition.

If challenged to summarize Hofstadter's major theme in two words or less, I would choose the complexity-related terms "reflexivity" and "self-similarity." To paraphrase quite freely, Hofstadter (1979) chooses Bach as a musical prototype for the creation of such works as fugues and canons in which the fugal subject or canonic motif recurs systematically and refers recursively to itself in the form of various augmentations (lengthened in duration), diminutions (shortened in duration), inversions (turned upside down), and "crabs" (played backwards). Weaving such patterns together into a coherent musical form creates works of staggering complexity—thereby suggesting an intellect of awesome power. In one canon from the *Musical Offering,* for example, successive appearances of the theme enter a whole tone higher until the piece has modulated through six keys and returned to its starting tonality.

Visually, such virtuosic principles of construction ("strange loops" or "tangled hierarchies") are echoed in the work of M. C. Escher, as in his repeating patterns wherein (say) a frog is transformed into (say) a bird. Other aspects of Escher's inveterate habit of self-commentary appear, for example, when he sketches a hand drawing a second hand that is, in turn, drawing the first hand. Elsewhere, Escher presents highly paradoxical pictorial puzzles in which going up a staircase leads one to a position lower than that at which one started (and so forth).

Such pictorial displays remind Hofstadter (1979) of Gödel's incompleteness theorem, which bears some resemblance to Epimenides paradox or the liar's paradox: "This statement is false." Colloquially, Gödel's important proposition held that no self-consistent system could be complete. A number theory, for example, must generate statements that are true but that cannot be proved: "All consistent axiomatic formulations of number theory include undecidable propositions" (p. 17) or "This statement of number theory does not have any proof in the system" (p. 18). Here, to repeat, the key is reflexivity:

> The proof of Gödel's Incompleteness Theorem hinges upon the writing of a self-referential mathematical statement, in the same way that the Epimenides paradox is a self-referential statement of language. But whereas it is very simple to talk about language in language, it is not at all easy to see how a statement about numbers can talk about itself. In fact, it took genius merely to connect the idea of self-referential statements with number theory. Once Gödel had the intuition that such a statement could be created, he was over the major hurdle. The actual creation of the statement was the working out of this one beautiful spark of intuition. (p. 17)

All these observations suggest parallels and analogies from which Hofstadter (1979) draws some rather sweeping conclusions about the nature of mind, the potential for artificial intelligence, the limits to truth, and the role of beauty. Consistent with our concerns in the present context and central to Hofstadter's preoccupation with Gödel-Escher-Bach, I shall focus briefly on the latter beauty-related sorts of issues.

Hofstadter (1979) makes it clear from the start that he finds beauty in the *impossibility* of the creations by Gödel-Escher-Bach (p. 29). He takes delight in such philosophical games as Zeno's paradox attempting to show why (the fleet) Achilles can never catch (the slow) Tortoise in a foot race. He finds proofs by the likes of Euclid to be "simple, compelling, and beautiful" (p. 59). He marvels at Bach's use of self-reference—as in his inclusion of a theme based on the musical notes B-A-C-H ("H" = B-flat in German) where a piece from the *Art of Fugue* broke off at the moment when the great composer passed away (p. 80). He reveres Escher's astonishing self-referential exercises in visual paradox—as in a work characterized by "the beauty and ingenuity with which he made one single theme mesh with itself going both backwards and forwards" (p. 199). He compares a mathematical proof to a piece of music and concludes that "The mathematician's sense of tension is intimately related to his sense of beauty, and is what makes mathematics worthwhile doing" (p. 227). One section entitled "Prelude" weaves together a discussion of Fermat's last theorem with comments on the "beauty" of Escher and Bach (p. 281). Here, Hofstadter draws explicitly on the concept of unity-in-variety:

> Fugues have that interesting property, that each of their voices is a piece of music in itself; and thus a fugue might be thought of as a collection of several distinct pieces of music, all based on one single theme, and all played simultaneously. And it is up to the listener . . . to decide whether it should be perceived as a unit, or as a collection of independent parts, all of which harmonize. . . . The art of writing a beautiful fugue lies precisely in this ability, to manufacture several different lines, each one of which gives the illusion of having been written for its own beauty, and yet which when taken together form a whole, which does not feel forced in any way. (p. 283)

Hofstadter (1979) emphasizes that this whole/parts dichotomy "applies to many kinds of structures built up from lower levels" (p. 283)—as in his verbal metaphor for the structure of a fugue as composed of letters ("MU") built from words ("HOLISM" and "REDUCTION-ISM") composed of contrary terms ("R-E-D-U-C-T-I-O-N-I-S-M" and "H-O-L-I-S-M") (p. 310). Rather brilliantly, this scheme gives a visual linguistic parallel to the structure to be found in a Bach fugue. Hofstadter sees such multilayered cases as illustrations of "order emerging from chaos" (p. 317). On first reading this section, I wrote in the margin: "Cool! This is a wonderful metaphor for how Fugues-Bach, Art-Escher, and Math-Gödel play their fascinating mind games." Indeed, speaking through the dialoguing voices of his protagonists (Achilles and Tortoise), Hofstadter (1979) considers the proposition that—as suggested in a picture by Escher—"chaos might be an integral part of beauty" (p. 398) in that "Order and chaos make a pleasing unity" (p. 399).

In all this, Hofstadter (1979) weaves together themes (that need not detain us here) concerning number theory, mental functioning, the nature of consciousness or selfhood, Zen koans, ant colonies, DNA codes, and other aspects of systems involving self-reference, recursiveness, multiple layers, and potential incompleteness in ways that he characterizes as "of a sort more complex and beautiful than any human mind ever imagined" (p. 504). Especially relevant metaphorically, at several junctures, are works by René Magritte showing this artist's penchant for self-referential paradox—as in his reflexively self-contradictory masterpieces incorporating pictures of pipes labeled "Ceci n'est pas une pipe" (p. 494, p. 701). Further relevant are figurative analogies between the truth of mathematics and the beauty of music (p. 555)—making it reasonable to contemplate the possibility of "mathematical esthetics" (p. 565) and to consider the likelihood that "the process by which we decide what is valid or what is true is an art; and that it relies as deeply on a sense of beauty and simplicity as it does on rock-solid principles of logic or reasoning or anything else which can be objectively formalized" (p. 695).

When returning to the themes of Gödel-Escher-Bach, near the book's end, Hofstadter (1979) reminds us about the interwoven aspects of reflexivity wherein "Escher has thus given a pictorial parable for Gödel's Incompleteness Theorem" (p. 717) and wherein Bach's "Endlessly Rising Canon" serves as a prototype for the beauty of multileveled paradoxically self-referential complexity:

> One cannot look deeply enough into the *Musical Offering*. There is always more after one thinks one knows everything. . . . Things are going on on many levels in the *Musical Offering*. There are tricks with notes and letters; there are ingenious variations on the King's Theme; there are original kinds of canons; there are extraordinarily complex fugues; there is beauty and extreme depth of emotion; even an exultation in the many-leveledness of the work comes through. The *Musical Offering* is a fugue of fugues, a Tangled Hierarchy like those of Escher and Gödel, an intellectual construction which reminds me, in ways I cannot express, of the beautiful many-voiced fugue on the human mind. (p. 719)

And which reminds *us* of Hofstadter's own extraordinary achievement in writing or, indeed, composing his beautifully conceived *Gödel, Escher, Bach*.

Rescher on Complexity. Rounding out our consideration of complexity as the essence of beauty in the aesthetic experience typical of artistic appreciation, we find a recent treatise by the philosopher Nicholas Rescher (1998) entitled *Complexity: A Philosophical Overview*. Rescher (1998) devotes his book to exploring "the nature of complexity" (p. xiii) in the world around us—seeing "complexification" in a "common pattern of growing complexity that confronts us all" (p. xvi). Most important for our purposes, he defines *complexity* as the property of "a structured whole consisting of interrelated parts" where the degree of complexity increases with "the number and variety of an item's constituent elements and . . . the elaborateness of their interrelational structure" (p. 1): "the concept fuses and integrates a plurality of distinct elements into an elaborately articulated coordination" (p. 10). With special relevance to our focus on beauty, Rescher suggests that increasing complexity tends to characterize all aspects of human endeavor, including the arts: "complexity growth also characterizes the domain of human creativity—in art and literature, for example, which knows virtually no limits" (p. 3).

Much of Rescher's philosophizing—for example, his speculations on *why* complexity increases in human enterprises and on *how* complexity increasingly typifies the natural sciences—need not detain us here. Rather, we are primarily concerned with his conviction *that* complexity tends to permeate all human artifacts, including all forms of artistic creation. Thematically for Rescher (1998), in all such endeavors,

> An inherent impetus towards greater complexity pervades the entire realm of human creative effort. We find it in art; we find it in technology; and we certainly find it in the cognitive domain as well (p. 58). . . . All of our creative efforts—in material, social, and intellectual contexts alike—manifest a historical tendency of moving from the simpler to the more complex. (p. 174)

Indeed, Rescher views the intellectual effort required to comprehend something as the single best indicant of its degree of complexity:

All in all . . . , the best overall index we have of a system's complexity is the extent to which resources (of time, energy, ingenuity) must be expended on its cognitive domestication (p. 16). . . . A prime index of a system's complexity is the extent to which effort—intellectual and physical—is needed to come to adequate cognitive grips with it (p. 191).

In this connection, Rescher (1998) comes closest to speaking specifically about beauty when he addresses the subject of how the fine arts (as a whole) have evolved over time to their contemporary status as a highly complex body of work, taken as a whole, in which "There is no question that painting, collectively considered, has been ever more diversified, variegated, and complex" (p. 19): "Here, as elsewhere, local simplicity has been riding on the back of globally systemic complexity" (p. 19). Clearly, this view stops short of identifying complexity with beauty. But it does suggest that complexity forms an essential part of the context in which beauty appears. Hence, it would not be amiss to identify complexity as a key aspect of aesthetic experience. In this, Rescher progresses toward an embrace of ideas drawn from complexity science (for a review, see Holbrook 2003) and a view of complexity as a post-postmodern synthesis that inspires an account of "Complexities Bearing on Philosophical Anthropology" (chapter 11), wherein Rescher (1998) applies his own penchant for dialectic synthesis to a consideration of modernism (Mod), postmodernism (PoMo), and what lies beyond (Post-PoMo). In this connection, Rescher envisions a sort of dialectic process in which the Mod Thesis ("orderly, lawful, intelligent, explicable, . . . tidy," p. 205) gives way to the PoMo Antithesis ("randomness, transvalued values, cultural relativism, incoherence, disintegration, anarchy," p. 205) but, in turn, yields to a Post-PoMo Synthesis ("chaos, fuzzy logic, . . . complexity," p. 206) wherein the Post-PoMo episteme recognizes "*the self-generation of order in a universe of chance*" (p. 206). Here, the emergence of complexity clearly represents the outcome of a dialectic tension between order and anarchy. Thus, in concluding, complexity represents the Post-PoMo Synthesis that moves us to the next stage of the dialectic beyond modernism and postmodernism:

> What is perhaps the principal theme of late twentieth century science—and one that distinguishes it from all that has gone before—is nature's tendency to self-organization, the natural dynamic in highly complex systems of an emergence of order from disorder, lawfulness from chance, structure from chaos. . . . This recognition of self-organization and the natural emergence of complex order from chance and chaos has come to pervade the landscape of science. It nowadays occupies the middle ground between modernistic oversimplification of a universe frozen into deterministic order and the postmodern vacuity of a universe viewed as anarchic, irrational, and totally unruly beyond the grasp of rational comprehensibility (p. 206). . . . Where the postmoderns saw incomprehensibility, their post-postmodern successors have come to see a mere complexity that is substantially tractable by new cognitive instrumentalities more powerful than those available heretofore. (p. 207)

Beyond Aesthetic Beauty in the Philosophy of Art: The Broader View

Obviously, not all commentators have confined their attention to the rather narrow conception of aesthetic beauty emphasized thus far. For example—as a kind of counterpoint to the treatments by Stolnitz (1967) and Hospers (1967), reviewed earlier—Beardsley (1967) contributes a piece to the same *Encyclopedia* in which he presses beyond those aspects of beauty that are coextensive with aesthetics or the arts. Thus, Beardsley (1967) suggests that—though Plato in the *Republic* saw the arts as able to "embody in various degrees the quality of beauty" (p. 19)—he described in the *Symposium* the path to beauty as progressing "from bodily beauty to beauty of mind, to beauty of institutions and laws and the sciences themselves, and finally to beauty in itself" (p. 19). Further, in the *Philebus,* Plato adopted a general view of beautiful things as those "made with care in due proportion of part to part, by mathematical measurement" according to "the qualities of measure . . . and proportion" (p. 19). Clearly, to flip to a contemporary analogy, such criteria could apply as well to a fire hydrant, a piece of legislation, or a movie star as to a marble sculpture. As already noted, Plato saw this beauty of measure and proportion as "closely allied to goodness and virtue too" (p. 20). Meanwhile, Aristotle viewed "beauty in general" as applicable to "either a living creature or any structure made of parts" that has "an orderly arrangement of those parts" (p. 20) so that, again, the term serves as an omnibus expression of admiration. Similarly, the Stoics regarded beauty as dependent on "the arrangement of parts" and connected this concept with "the virtue that expresses itself in an ordered life, with decorum" (p. 21). And Plotinus, following Plato, found beauty not only in "things seen and heard" but also in "good character and conduct"—envisioning a ladderlike ascent "from the contemplation of sensuous beauty to delight in beautiful deeds, to moral beauty and the beauty of institutions, and thence to absolute beauty" (p. 22).

During the Middle Ages, St. Augustine still considered beauty to be an "objectively valid" judgment dependent on "the emergent unity of heterogeneous whole" (p. 23). Regarding beauty as "a part of goodness" that "has different senses when applied to different sorts of things," St. Thomas Aquinas proposed three requisite conditions: "integrity or perfection," "due proportion or harmony," and "brightness or clarity" (p. 23).

After the Renaissance—with its emphasis on "faithfulness of representation" (p. 24) via (say) the mathematical laws of linear perspective—the neoclassical period, in the wake of Cartesian rationalism, carried its penchant toward "rules for making and for judging works of art" (p. 25) to sometimes extreme lengths in the pursuit of reason. But with the Enlightenment's enshrinement of empiricism came also a new interest in the nature of "the creative process and the effects of art upon the beholder" (p. 25). In adumbrating questions concerning the problem of *taste,* Shaftesbury deemed beauty to be a form of virtue apprehended by the "moral sense" (p. 26); and, borrowing from Shaftesbury, Hutcheson developed the former's concept of disinterestedness into the concept of a "sense of beauty" that depends on "a compound ratio of uniformity and variety" (p. 26). Hume wanted to map this sense of beauty by means of "inductive inquiry into those features of works of art that enable them to please most a highly qualified perceiver" (p. 26). Burke and others distinguished the beautiful (comparable to physical attraction, minus the lust) from the *sublime* (involving an admixture of horror). In his *Critique of Judgment,* Kant concerned himself with questions about how such assertions of beauty or sublimity could be vindicated in terms of their "implicit claims to general validity" (p. 27)—finding answers in the concepts of "disinterested satisfaction" (p. 27), "purposiveness without purpose" (p. 28), and the sense that others "*ought* to take the same satisfaction we do in it" (p. 29). Pushing German Idealism to its most fully articulated level of aesthetic relevance, Hegel treated beauty as the dialectical embodiment of the "idea" in "sensuous form" (p. 29).

Thence flowered the eighteenth-century Romantic emphasis on emotional expression (e.g., Wordsworth's lyrical poetry), imagination (e.g., Shelley's creative act), and organic wholeness (e.g., Coleridge's unity in multeity). Similar trends appeared in Nietzsche's early view of tragedy as a conjunction of the Dionysian urge (joyful experience) with the Apollonian spirit (orderly proportion)—the first of which gained ascendancy in his later thinking. Such impulses led both toward *aestheticism* (as in the art-for-art's-sake or *l'art-pour-l'art* doctrines) and toward the *functionalism* found in socially concerned attacks on the Industrial Revolution (by Ruskin, Morris, and others).

The twentieth century saw continued attention to expression via intuition (Croce, Collingwood, Bergson); the empirically based view of beauty as objectified pleasure (Santayana); the artistic moment as *"an* experience" (Dewey); the nature of aesthetic appreciation as a form of intrinsic value (Lewis, Pepper); judgments of beauty as purely emotive (Ogden and Richards); the semiotic approach to art as (say) a "presentational symbol" (Langer) or "iconic sign" (Peirce, Morris); the Marxist conception of art as a sociohistorically constructed reflection of reality (Caudwell, Lukács); an emphasis on the autonomy of the artwork as an "object in itself" (Hanslick, Bell, Fry) and the embrace of this conception by the "new criticism" (Richards, Empson, Wimsatt, Beardsley); various phenomenological approaches to aesthetic experience (Ingarden, Dufrenne); empirical investigations of "scientific aesthetics" by means of such approaches as Gestalt psychology (Koffka, Arnheim, Meyer); more interpretivistic psychoanalytic approaches (Freud, Jung); introspectively descriptive psychological accounts of "empathy" (Lipps) or "psychical distance" (Bullough); and applications of analytic philosophy to the meaning of "ordinary language" about art, aesthetics, beauty, and related concepts (Beardsley 1967, pp. 31–33). Indeed, the latter perspective will concern us at some length as the present inquiry develops further.

Langue *or Linguistic Competence versus* Parole *or Psycholinguistic Performance*

The "narrow" conceptualization of beauty described earlier covers the case of how certain philosophers concerned with the phenomenon of artistic appreciation wish to define the nature of aesthetic value. In that sense, as envisioned by Saussure (1915, ed. 1966), it represents a rigorously specified aspect of the *langue*—that is, a formal definition for the correct use of language or the specification of a semantic convention that certain thinkers regard as consistent with a set of distinctions they wish to preserve. However, as anticipated by the "broader" view of Beardsley (1967), a moment's thought will suggest that such aspects of the *langue* may depart dramatically from the *parole*—that is, the actual usage of language in everyday practice. Numerous thinkers have insisted on this contrast between *langue* versus *parole* (Saussure 1915, ed. 1966), semantics versus pragmatics (Morris 1946), use versus usage (Ryle 1964), competence versus performance (Chomsky 1965), or, to combine some key terms, competence in linguistic use versus performance in psycholinguistic usage (Holbrook 1994).

As made clear by McEvilley (1998), the contrast between *parole* and *langue* or between psycholinguistic performance and linguistic competence resembles that in cultural anthropology between "the emic viewpoint—that of the tribal participant" and "the etic one—that of the outside observer" (p. 157). This is to say that—as in the case of *parole/langue*—these contrasting emic/etic perspectives employ, in effect, different languages to describe the phenomena of interest: the first employs the everyday discourse of the relevant culture; the second employs the refined articulation of the detached scientist. Quoting Marvin Harris, McEvilley (1998) summarizes as follows:

> Emic operations have as their hallmark the elevation of the native informant to the status of ultimate judge of the adequacy of the observer's descriptions and analyses. The test of the adequacy of emic analyses is their ability to generate *statements the native accepts as real, meaningful, or appropriate. . . .* Etic operations have as their hallmark the elevation of observers to the status of ultimate judges of the categories and concepts used in description and analyses. . . . Rather than employ concepts that are real, meaningful, and appropriate

from the native point of view, the observer is free to use alien categories and rules derived from *the data language of science.* (Marvin Harris quoted by McEvilley 1998, p. 158, italics added)

For our present purposes, the key point is that, in common discourse, people can and do use the word "beauty" and related concepts in ways very different from those envisioned by philosophically inclined students of aesthetic experience—that is, in colloquial ways that do not refer to intrinsically motivated self-oriented reactive value. It behooves us to pay careful attention to these differences between the idealized and realistic uses of language.

Beauty in the Everyday Usage of Language

Some intimation of how our inquiry into the usage of everyday language and imagery concerning the nature of beauty might progress can be gleaned from an examination of the work by Guy Sircello (1975) entitled *A New Theory of Beauty.* Sircello practices the sort of analytic philosophy that delves deeply into the use of language. This is to say that he frequently asks how a term is ordinarily employed and derives from such questions some sense of its significance. For example, he notices perceptively that—though "'X is beautiful' does not entail 'X is agreeable to me'"—judging something beautiful with respect to F implies finding it agreeable with respect to F: "there is *something wrong* in *my* saying that blue color on the chair is beautiful but I dislike it" (p. 69). Later, his analysis of *sublimity*—which he takes to be "a species of beauty"— hinges on the fact that it makes sense to say that something is "sublimely beautiful" but not that it is "beautifully sublime" (as also in the case of "joyously happy" versus "happily joyous" or "ponderously heavy" versus "heavily ponderous") (p. 99). From such observations, we might anticipate keen insights into the nature of beauty; but, in this, we would perhaps be disappointed— for a couple of reasons.

First, Sircello (1975) deploys his analytic powers with the finesse of a surgeon using a scalpel or—when the need for logic chopping arises—with the bludgeoning forcefulness of a butcher wielding a cleaver. Consider, for example, his articulation of the book's centerpiece—namely, the "New Theory of Beauty" (NTB). Toward this end, he develops a concept known as a "property of qualitative degree" (PQD) and, thereafter, proposes that "*A PQD of an 'object' is beautiful if and only if . . . it is present in that 'object' in a very high degree*" (p. 43). Or ponder what he considers to be "an astounding conclusion":

> All that a perfectly comprehensive theory of beauty need do . . . is to determine what, for all X and F such that X is beautiful with respect to F-ness and such that F-ness is beautiful as instantiated in X, makes X *beautifully* F. (p. 16)

Few readers will easily follow the tortured logic of such arguments. And when Sircello suggests that an "interchangeability between 'is' and 'appear' vocabularies obtains with respect to many, if not most, beautiful properties" (p. 36), who can resist the thought that this analytic maneuver resembles the verbal shenanigans of a disgraced president claiming that the truth "depends on what your definition of 'is' is"? Much of the book has that sort of rigorous but sterile flavor, as if to defy ready access. Sircello seems to apprehend this difficulty when he admits,

> But to say that beauty is the presence in an "object" to an extremely high degree of a property of qualitative degree [exactly what he *did* say when articulating the NTB] is to say

something so dry, colorless, and dispassionate that it must cause us to wonder that anything like *that* could ever be *enjoyed*. (p. 127)

Second, whenever Sircello (1975) verges on making statements about how we use—or at least how he himself uses—language, he often reveals himself to dwell on the senior side of a generation gap that opened up during the latter part of the past century. Thus, for example, he ponders whether "beauty" could refer to moral excellence and allows, "I can *imagine* using the term to apply to a person's moral character; and, when invited, so can other people I know" (p. 82). As Sircello himself admits (footnote 21), this comment locates his observations "on the depressing side of the generation gap"—the side not populated by anyone coming of age after the advent of (say) the Beatles.

Nonetheless, a careful reading of Sircello (1975) does allow us to extract at least one clear premonition concerning the manner in which the concept of beauty is applied in everyday discourse. Specifically, it appears clear that the Sircellean view extends to every sort of object that one might imagine—ranging from the arts to nature to vivid colors to other visual objects to sounds to taste-smell-and-tactile sensations to intellectual accomplishments to the useful or the good or the moral or the emotionally satisfying. As he puts it, understating the sweep of his analysis, "Just consider the range of objects to which beauty can be attributed: people, rocks, snakes, daisies, horses, trees, mountains, rivers, paintings, symphonies, buildings, spoons, books, chairs, hats" (p. 5).

In a similar spirit, Welish (1998) points out helpfully that the term "beauty" has been used casually to express preference in personal taste, culturally to designate what a society values, philosophically as part of a theory of art, psychologically as a root of aesthetic experience, and so forth. In essence, it has lost meaning by virtue of its widespread deployment in a number of different contexts: "*BEAUTY* . . . is a word that has come to mean nothing—or everything" (p. 61).

Further, Sircello (1975) makes room for the sublime, the harmonious, and even the ugly as potential sources of beauty. Hence, like Beardsley (1967), Sircello (1975) encourages us to look broadly rather than narrowly for the types of beauty that characterize everyday consumption experiences. And he ends on an optimistic note whose cheerfulness survives his apology for offering a "mere speculation":

> Yet if this speculation is anywhere near the truth, then we ultimately enjoy beauty because in perceiving beauty we seem to be *better* off than merely well off. For in perceiving beauty we seem to be perceiving with a much greater degree of clarity than our ordinary clear perception has. In perceiving beauty we are filled, if only for a moment and if only in a limited respect, by a feeling of transcendent well-being. (p. 138)

Beauty and the Illuminating Power of Photography

The sense of "transcendent well-being" just adumbrated by Sircello (1975) comes more fully to light—with additional insights into the role of photography, as incorporated into the methodological approach proposed and demonstrated in what follows—in a treatise by Alfred Appel (1993) entitled *The Art of Celebration*. Specifically, while traversing the history of twentieth-century art, Appel intends his book as "urging that we properly appreciate an enriching body of work that can be called 'celebratory modernism'" (p. 5). Toward that end, he proposes the appropriate contents for what he calls a "celebratory bookshelf"—that is, one "devoted to the life-affirming, celebratory works of the twentieth century" (p. 6). The work of Henri Matisse, Pablo

Picasso, Paul Klee, Constantin Brancusi, and Alexander Calder will be there. Also, W. B. Yeats, William Carlos Williams, and James Joyce (especially Molly Bloom's soliloquy from *Ulysses*). Plus recordings of compositions by Darius Milhaud and of performances by Louis Armstrong, Benny Goodman, and Count Basie. And photos by Alfred Stieglitz, Edward Steichen, and Henri Cartier-Bresson.

But perhaps most tellingly, Appel (1993) hits his stride when he begins a remarkable series of chapters devoted to such artists and photographers as Fernand Léger, Stuart Davis, Walker Evans, Russell Lee, Ralph Goings, Georgia O'Keeffe, and Edward Weston. Herein, he dwells on the pre-postmodern discovery of pervasive beauty in the everyday world:

> Modernists in the West such as Fernand Léger (France) and Stuart Davis (the United States) sought to celebrate quotidian life by basing entire works on commercial or vernacular sources, another kind of radical act. "Beauty is everywhere, perhaps more in your kitchen than in your eighteenth-century salon or in official museums," Léger said in 1924. . . . Davis's . . . motto . . . is an early product of his sustained, programmatic ambition to base his art on the American scene: "The brilliant colors on gasoline stations, chainstore fronts, and taxi-cabs . . . fast travel by trains, auto, and aeroplane, which brought new . . . perspectives; electric signs . . . 5 & 10 cent store kitchen utensils; movies and radio; Earl Hines' hot piano and Negro jazz music in general," as Davis explained in 1943. His son, Earl, was named after Hines. (p. 108)

Appel (1993) cites the painter Charles Demuth as a prophet of the premise that "industrial and vernacular objects are an artist's potential treasure trove" in the attempt to capture "quotidian beauty" (p. 112). Thus, the German photographer Albert Renger-Patzsch entitled his 1928 collection *The World Is Beautiful* (p. 114). Thus, also, Appel honors "Walker Evans, whose more formal, strictly frontal black-and-white photographs of industrial paraphernalia and vernacular signs and symbols from the 1930s are still teaching us how to take delight in our unnatural, manmade environment" (p. 115). His primary piece of evidence in this connection is a marvelous Evans photo of the signage at a shoeshine stand in the rural south circa 1936:

> Evans discovered and photographed ample evidence of a bracing populist ethic and aesthetic: hand-painted and sometimes framed commercial signs and messages that express their makers' good humor and self-respect, their natural impulse toward balance, symmetry, and an uncompromising sense of elegance. . . . Saul Steinberg . . . once told an interviewer that Walker Evans had "taught a generation what and how to see." . . . Framed by Evans's camera, the shoeshine site [with its intriguing arrangement of a shoe painted in white, a white-lettered sign saying "SHINE," and eight white shoes lined up under the five letters] . . . is as perfectly arranged as any museum display. (pp. 115–117)

Along similar lines, a magnificently cluttered photo by Russell Lee shows "Signs in Front of a Highway Tavern"—featuring a wild array of brand-advertising reminders to drink Coca-Cola, Dr. Pepper, Budweiser, Grand Prize, 7up, and Delaware Punch at the "HiWay Tavern" (p. 119). Commenting on this sort of work in general and on a photo-realist piece by Ralph Goings entitled "Blue Tile with Ice Water" (p. 123) in particular, Appel comments:

> Goings's picture is a more elaborate version of the still life he's been executing since around 1977 of luminous lunch-counter objects, including ketchup and mustard bottles; napkin

and straw holders; sugar; creamers; and salt and pepper shakers—all arranged very neatly, in various combinations. . . . In the last decade, Goings's principal subject has been the interiors of diners and restaurants . . . a contemporary, vernacular version of the time-honored pastoral mode. . . . If Goings's crystalline interiors, perused in an art gallery or book, can be accepted as idyllic, symbolic structures . . . , then some viewers who enter his pictures in this spirit will emerge renewed, having achieved the promise of traditional pastoral. . . . "SHINE!" exhorts Walker Evans's one-word visual poem, another version of pastoral. (pp. 122–124)

Comparable epiphanies await us in Appel's treatments of the "surprisingly sensuous or sensual" flower portraits by Georgia O'Keeffe (p. 174) or the "erotic and ambiguous" vegetable photographs by Edward Weston (p. 178).

All this leads to a premise comparable to that which motivates my use in the present study of the collective photographic essay (CPE), described later. As Appel (1993) puts it, "Let's look at some more photographs": "They won't lie" (p. 194). Here, Appel features the remarkable photos by László Moholy-Nagy, André Kertész, Lewis Hine, and other like-minded modernists—which lead him to a conclusion remarkably similar to the fundamental assumption behind photographic autoethnography as a route to exploring the experience of beauty: "Photography . . . is . . . an injunction to us to be free-wheeling or floating camera-eyes and continue the photographer's open-minded if dizzying hunt for quotidian beauty" (p. 209). In this light, Appel describes the catalog of a recent photo exhibition as follows:

> *The New Vision* . . . is . . . a sourcebook still capable of providing a few of us with elevating symbols . . . that are best appreciated in the context of history. Add *The New Vision* catalog to your Twentieth-Century Celebratory Shelf. (p. 219)

At the end, as Appel celebrates Piet Mondrian's yellow-saturated painting entitled "Broadway Boogie Woogie" (reputedly created while listening to recordings by some of the great stride pianists, including James P. Johnson), his prose becomes more tangled but also more lyrical. We sense that he is trying to create an effect something like that of Molly Bloom's closing soliloquy, much admired for its riveting power of affirmation. Appel does not come close to matching Joyce in this epigonic endeavor. But who could? The point is that he tried.

Beauty in Ordinary Discourse

One Example of the Broader View: Physical Beauty

As one example of beauty beyond the confines of aesthetic experience in the appreciation of art, in her book entitled *Survival of the Prettiest: The Science of Beauty,* Nancy Etcoff (1999) focuses primarily on physical beauty, viewing its display and appreciation in evolutionary terms as key traits deployed to foster the survival of the fittest. Specifically, in the context of a Darwinian process of natural selection, those members of the species seen by potential mates as most beautiful gain an advantage in maximizing their chance to reproduce and, hence, to foster the perpetuation of their gene pool. In this, Etcoff—a psychological researcher at the Harvard Medical School and the Massachusetts General Hospital—rejects such feminist critiques as those by Naomi Wolf (1992) in *The Beauty Myth: How Images of Beauty Are Used Against Women.* Wolf sees beauty as a patriarchal subterfuge serving to foster male dominance by keeping women in their subservient place at a low level in the power structure. By contrast, Etcoff (1999) entertains the possibility that "women cultivate beauty and use the beauty industry to optimize the power beauty brings" (p. 4). In that spirit, from an evolutionary viewpoint, she pursues "an inquiry into what we find beautiful and why" (p. 7).

Etcoff's book is not the place to look for a scholarly treatment of aesthetic philosophy. She dispenses with the philosophy of beauty in just a few pages (pp. 7–10), tending to regard the experience thereof as always connected with *pleasure*. She does suggest the existence of a *beauty canon*—grounded in such concepts as symmetry, balance, or harmonious proportion—in which "Common to all these theories is the idea that the properties of beauty are the same whether we are seeing a beautiful woman, a flower, a landscape, or a circle" (p. 15). However, she hastens to add that, objective measures based on this canon—wherein physical dimensions of models and other people are statistically related to subjective judgments of beauty—have tended to show poor predictive validity: "Measurement systems have failed to turn up a beauty formula" (p. 17).

Nonetheless, Etcoff (1999) strongly resists the conclusion that beauty is subjective or "in the eye of the beholder." Rather, she maintains that beauty follows "a universal grammar" (p. 22) in which "aspects of judgments of beauty may be influenced by culture and individual history, but the general geometric features of a face that give rise to the perception of beauty may be universal" (p. 23). Such aspects of universality result from the role that beauty plays in signaling the suitability of a potential mate for purposes of successful reproduction and procreation of the species. In simple terms, more beautiful sexual partners make better—that is, healthier—babies:

> The argument is a simple one: that beauty is a universal part of human experience, and that it provokes pleasure, rivets attention, and impels actions that help ensure the survival of our genes. Our extreme sensitivity to beauty is hard-wired, that is, governed by circuits in the brain shaped by natural selection. We love to look at smooth skin, thick shiny hair, curved waists, and symmetrical bodies because in the course of evolution the people who noticed these signals and desired their possessors had more reproductive success. We are their descendants. (p. 26)

Besides offering a powerful excuse for admiring (say) Cheryl Tiegs, Cindy Crawford, Claudia Schiffer, or Naomi Campbell, Etcoff's perspective provides a scientific rationale for the beneficial role of taking pleasure in physical attractiveness. That we possess prewired beauty detectors follows from the tendency of babies to gaze longer at faces judged by adults as more attractive (p. 31): "When babies fix their stare at the same faces adults describe as highly attractive, their actions wordlessly argue against the belief that culture must teach us to recognize human beauty" (p. 34).

Research has shown that experimental subjects are more likely to display altruistic behavior toward better-looking people (p. 44). Further, more attractive people are more successful in winning arguments, persuading others, or evoking conciliatory behavior (p. 46). They elicit more favorable treatment by teachers (p. 48) and—as we might have guessed—are more popular with potential sexual partners (p. 50).

To repeat—as Etcoff (1999) does, rather incessantly—the reason for all this, in terms of evolution, is that beauty is a biological signal of a healthy, fertile body well suited to the purpose of sexual reproduction (p. 69) and therefore to "the survival of the genes" (p. 70). Specifically, men are attracted to the *nulliparous female*—"a woman who is fertile, healthy, and hasn't been pregnant before" (p. 71)—because such a mate stands the best chance of reproductive success: "Males focus . . . on pure physical appearance because appearance gives many clues about whether a woman is healthy and fertile, able to successfully carry off a pregnancy" (p. 76). By contrast, women are most attracted to men showing signs of status, power, income, or other emblems of the ability to provide a safe, secure, and protective environment (p. 79).

From this, it follows that the beauty-products industry—dedicated to facilitating the ability of an individual to project an image of beauty—plays an important role in the lives of both men and women. In America, we spend twice as much on cosmetics as on reading materials—namely $14 billion a year (p. 95). For women, makeup and hair-care products foster the impression of youthfulness, clear skin, shining hair, and other signs of fertility (p. 105). Where cosmetics don't do the trick, plastic surgery waits in the wings (p. 110). (For further discussion of such issues from the perspective of consumer research, see especially Holbrook, Block, and Fitzsimons 1998; Richins 1999; Schouten 1991; Solomon 1999; Thompson and Hirschman 1995; Wagner 1999.)

Recent studies have shown that the aforementioned criteria of beauty are also *universal* in that they command agreement across cultures (p. 139): "People tend to agree about which faces are beautiful, and to find similar features attractive across ethnically diverse faces" (p. 139). One point of agreement is a liking for such signs of *youthfulness* as large eyes and small chins (p. 139). Another is *koinophilia*—a favorable response to the average as a signal of good health (p. 145). However, striking beauty often involves one or another telling departure from the norm. For example, *Vogue* models have "larger eyes, smaller noses, and plumper lips than the average" (p. 151). Indeed, based on their facial proportions, a computer program estimated their age to be between six and seven years old (p. 151). Therein lies still more potential, it would seem, for cosmetic surgery (p. 152).

Etcoff (1999) summarizes all this as follows:

> Babies and adults automatically recognize beautiful faces. People make snap judgments about appearance all the time. They tend to agree with each other about who is beautiful, and they tend to be guided in their judgments by mechanisms that detect symmetry and averageness as well as exaggerated markers of femininity in women's faces. This suggests that the general geometric features of a face that give rise to the perception of beauty may be universal, and the perception of these features may be governed by circuits shaped by natural selection in the human brain. (p. 163)

Meanwhile, females also tend to prefer males who are larger and more symmetrical: "Symmetry is tied to beauty because it acts as a measure of overall fitness. . . . Symmetrical animals have higher growth rates, are more fecund, and survive longer" (p. 185). While males also value symmetry in females, a woman's beauty depends especially on the waist-to-hips (w-to-h) ratio (p. 192). For example, despite all their other obvious differences, Marilyn Monroe and Audrey Hepburn were remarkably similar in this respect—with virtually identical w-to-h ratios of .71 (36–24–34 and 31.5–22–31, respectively). Surprisingly similar w-to-h statistics prevail across a wide variety of other beauty icons (p. 193). Wide hips are, of course, well suited to the purpose of delivering healthy babies: "Thus, although waist-to-hip ratio is an excellent modern indicator of health in general, its primary evolutionary importance for detection of beauty probably had more to do with what it signified about fertility" (p. 194).

To the extent that aspects of what we call "beauty" tend to change over time or vary from place to place, Etcoff (1999) tends to refer to them as *fashion*. This allows her to admit what is obvious—namely, that fashion (unlike beauty) is *not* universal. To some extent, this viewpoint begs the question. If some aspect of taste changes rapidly or varies widely, she labels it "fashion"; if not, "beauty." This permits her to conclude that the former/latter isn't/is universal. Hence, for example, the use of clothing as a status marker belongs to the realm of fashion (p. 211). Ditto the manipulation of body parts as a sign of conspicuous leisure—long fingernails and so forth (p. 215). As an illustration, the current vogue among cashiers at the supermarket on my corner is to grow their fingernails so long that their length makes it impossible for these women to work a cash register— the only problem being that, after all, they *are* cashiers. All this takes Etcoff into the realm of designer labels (p. 222) and supermodels (p. 223)—in other words, into the realm of fashion as opposed to beauty. To repeat, unlike the former, the latter does not change from time to time or place to place—precisely because it is rooted in the evolutionary imperatives of natural selection:

> Our minds evolved by natural selection to solve problems crucial to our survival and repro-
> duction. To find the sight of potentially fertile and healthy mates beautiful and the sight of
> helpless infants irresistibly cute is adaptive. Despite the vagaries of fashion, every culture
> finds the large eyes, small nose, round cheeks, and tiny limbs of the baby beautiful. All men
> and women find lustrous hair, clear taut skin, a woman's cinched waist, and a man's sculpted
> pectorals attractive. Beauty is one of the ways life perpetuates itself, and love of beauty is
> deeply rooted in our biology. (p. 234)

Some Further Intuitive Examples

In sum, vernacular uses of the term *beauty* do not necessarily reflect the rigorous definitions developed by philosophers of art in describing aesthetic experience. For example, as indicated by the work of Etcoff (1999), many ordinary consumers employ the word "beauty" to refer to image-related aspects of personal appearance associated with the impressions we make on others (Holbrook, Block, and Fitzsimons 1998; Richins 1999; Schouten 1991; Solomon 1999; Thompson and Hirschman 1995; Wagner 1999). Here, clothing, cosmetics, and other fashions are regarded as tools of *impression management* whereby we create a beautiful personal appearance as a means of attaining one or another form of status or social success. The related type of value must be classified as diametrically opposed to that discussed previously; that is, status-oriented "beauty" is extrinsically motivated, other oriented, and active in nature (Holbrook 1994, 1999b). Status involves manipulating one's consumption-related image as a means to the end of obtaining a reward from someone else.

Further, others might regard beauty as an aspect of *product quality* (Garvin 1988; Steenkamp 1989) or *service quality* (Rust and Oliver 1994; Zeithaml 1988; Zeithaml, Parasuraman, and Berry 1990). In this sense, the visual design of a product such as a car or computer plays a role in determining the quality of its performance. One cannot separate the aerodynamic styling of a Ferrari from its speed and handling. (For debates concerning the aesthetic- versus quality-related aspects of product design, please see Bloch 1995; Norman 1988.)

Still others would regard beauty as an aspect of a living object that potentially carries quasi-spiritual connotations. When they speak of a person's beauty or of a beautiful relationship with a friend or loved one, they mean to evoke certain *inner characteristics* that make that person or that relationship especially estimable in their eyes. In these senses, another person or even an animal might be homely to look at while possessing certain inward virtues that accompany a *beautiful spirit* or *beautiful character*.

Preview

Obviously, other conceptions of beauty are entirely possible and are even likely to be found in the common parlance. Yet, to the best of my knowledge, no one in general and no consumer researcher in particular has taken the trouble to collect or chronicle these different colloquial meanings of this frequently invoked and marketing-relevant word. The purpose of the present investigation is to begin the task of conceptualizing how the notion of beauty enters into the everyday lives of ordinary consumers. Toward that end—rather than engaging in further refinements of the pure concept of aesthetic beauty (*langue*)—we shall collect samples of how consumers actually employ the term "beauty" in everyday discourse so as to conceptualize the different ways in which this term appears in common usage (*parole*).

Method

The Collective Photographic Essay

The method used to explore the questions just raised draws on an approach called the collective photographic essay (CPE), as already proposed and discussed at length in the context of studies dealing with consumers' responses to the experience of living in New York City (Holbrook and Kuwahara 1998) and with the relationships of pet owners to their animal companions (Holbrook et al. 2001). This method is analogous to those advocated for the discovery of grounded theory in qualitative social science (Strauss and Corbin 1990) and for the use of pictures-based photoelicitation (Harper 1988) in visual sociology; autodriving (Heisley and Levy 1991) in ethnographic studies of consumers; and metaphor elicitation (Zaltman 1997, 2003) in marketing research.

Specifically, the CPE rests on the use of photos and short vignettes collected from a small sample of informants (usually under 100 in number). These informants employ disposable cameras, supplied by the researcher, to shoot pictures of scenes, objects, or situations that they see as embodying the relevant concept (e.g., New York City, animal companionship, or, in the present case, beauty). They then write brief paragraphs to explain their reasons for choosing those particular subjects for their photographs and to elucidate how they intend their photos to capture the essence of the focal concept (NYC, pets, or, here, beauty). The photos and vignettes are then analyzed with an eye toward seeking common themes and/or categorization schemes that capture the main motifs conveyed by the informants in a manner that builds toward better conceptualizing the phenomenon of interest.

Samples

The relevant samples included two major groups of informants: an *analysis sample* and a *validation sample*.

Analysis Sample

The analysis sample was used for purposes of developing a basic classification for major types of beauty experienced by the initial set of informants. Construction of this analysis sample began with thirty-three members of two MBA-level marketing courses at Columbia University's Graduate School of Business. Each of these student informants was asked to supply his or her own photograph and vignette while contacting one or two informants from outside the school community. The latter instruction resulted in the inclusion of an additional forty-four ordinary consumers for an overall analysis sample of seventy-seven informants. Because three of these gave two answers, the analysis sample supplied eighty responses in all.

Validation Sample

The validation sample was used to check the appropriateness of the typology of beauty that emerged from the analysis sample by applying it to a fresh set of data drawn from the same basic pool of informants. Here, thirty-seven members of two different MBA classes at the Columbia Business School supplied photos and vignettes while also collecting responses from one or two additional informants. The latter included twenty-three ordinary consumers for an overall validation sample of sixty informants. Because eight of these gave two or three answers, the validation sample supplied seventy responses in all.

Task

Student and ordinary informants were asked to follow a set of instructions spelled out at some length (for full details, please see Appendix 1). Basically, these instructions asked the informant to take a picture, using a disposable color flash camera, of "What Beauty Means to Me in My Daily Life" or "What I Find Beautiful in the World Around Me" and then to clarify the intentions behind this photo in a short explanatory paragraph. The resulting photographs and vignettes served as the basis for the emerging interpretation.

Guiding Rationale

As proposed and illustrated by the present study, the approach just described resembles not so much methods drawn from qualitative approaches to the social sciences—which typically involve an overriding concern for reliability and validation (often masquerading under different names)—as it does methods associated more with the humanities in general and with semiotics or hermeneutics in particular. Specifically, I shall not speak of intercoder reliability, triangulation, audits, or member checks (the traditional concerns of sociological or ethnographic approaches to consumer research). Rather, I shall pursue a form of validity associated with the *hermeneutic circle* in which successive movements back and forth between general overviews and close readings of the text lead toward the emergence of an interpretation that has, in fact, been developed according to principles analogous to the logic of falsificationism (Gadamer 1975; Ricoeur 1976, 1981).

Here, in the spirit of hermeneutics, I claim *not* to attain the *Truth* or even *truth(s)* in the sense(s) pursued by the typical quantitative or qualitative social sciences, but rather to achieve *understanding* in the sense that we have arrived at an emergent interpretation of a suitable consumption-related text. My reading of this text reflects the self-corrective hermeneutic circle to the extent that it begins with a broad overview, tests that overview against a detailed consideration of the textual evidence, reformulates the general view accordingly, checks this revised scheme against further close readings, and continues to proceed in this manner until a satisfactorily self-consistent interpretation has emerged. Thus, while this approach owes more to the humanities than to the social sciences, the basic logic of falsificationism—as embodied here by the self-corrective hermeneutic circle—applies to both. (For further discussion and justification of this guiding rationale, please see Hirschman and Holbrook 1992; Holbrook and O'Shaughnessy 1988.)

It would be tedious in the extreme to lead the reader through successive stages of the essentially reiterative process just described. For this reason, here as elsewhere, we consider the conclusions from the hermeneutic interpretation without detailing the self-corrective analytic process that led toward these conclusions.

Alternative or Complementary Approaches

Before proceeding, we should pause to remind ourselves that alternative or complementary approaches are, of course, available and widely practiced in various applications to the study of consumer behavior. Specifically, the method employed here—namely, the CPE—builds on qualitative approaches that first surfaced in marketing and consumer research about the time of the Consumer-Behavior (CB) Odyssey (Belk 1991; Belk, Sherry, and Wallendorf 1988; Wallendorf and Belk 1987). These approaches emphasize elements drawn from ethnography—especially the use of depth interviews (cf. McCracken 1986) and the inclusion of corroborative evidence in the form of photographs and other artifacts (cf. Becker 1986, 1995; Collier 1967; Collier and Collier 1986), where photos are also often used as ways of prompting informants via photo elicitation (Harper 1988) or autodriving (Heisley and Levy 1991) to provide more probing, rich, and insightful accounts of the meanings carried by consumption and other events in their lives en route to the creation of thick descriptions of consumer behavior (cf. Geertz 1973).

Since the time of the CB Odyssey, both key aspects of ethnography have been pushed further and developed in more depth by marketing and consumer researchers working in a large number of different content areas. Techniques of depth interviewing and related introspective data-collection methods have shed light on any number of consumption-related phenomena ranging from the behavior of homeless people (Hill 1991; Hill and Stamey 1990) to river rafting (Arnould and Price 1993) to skydiving (Celsi, Rose, and Leigh 1993) to motorcycle clubs (Schouten and McAlexander 1995) to class-based differences in tastes (Holt 1998) to consumption as a form of product-based relationship (Fournier 1998). Meanwhile, the use of photographs and other visual images to prompt deeply rich accounts of the meanings carried by consumption experiences—often included in the studies just mentioned—has reached a sort of apotheosis in the technologically sophisticated image-construction approaches developed as part of the Zaltman Metaphor Elicitation Technique (ZMET) (Zaltman 1997, 2003).

Against this background of variegated qualitative methods, the CPE provides yet another way to elicit introspective accounts by photo elicitation in the service of seeking insights into the meanings of consumer behavior. Here, the CPE deploys a more surface-level and briefer type of introspective account (i.e., a short written vignette) prompted by a report of the informant's intentions in taking a photograph (i.e., the self-interpreted meaning of a picture shot with a disposable camera). The CPE therefore lends itself to the use of samples somewhat larger than those typically found in other ethnographic, autoethnographic, or quasi-ethnographic methods. For interested readers, Holbrook and his colleagues have discussed the development of this CPE approach in considerable detail (Holbrook and Kuwahara 1998; Holbrook et al. 2001)—sometimes, though not in the present case, with an emphasis on the use of stereographic three-dimensional pictures (Holbrook 1997b, 1998a, 1998b).

Overall, my claim is *not* that the CPE is superior to other qualitative, ethnographic, or introspective methods of collecting data on consumption experiences but rather that it offers one more approach in our set of tools for investigating consumer behavior—namely, an approach well suited for gathering picture-based minivignettes from a larger-than-usual number of informants. Far from claiming that the CPE is superior to other techniques—much less that it should replace other methods of data collection—I am devoutly committed to a pluralistic embrace of multiple different approaches to gathering and interpreting data on consumer behavior (Hirschman and Holbrook 1992).

A Typology of Beauty in Ordinary Discourse

The main results of the present study take the form of a typology of beauty in ordinary discourse. I shall first present this typology and shall then provide detailed illustrations of each relevant category, drawn from the data at hand.

Emergent Conceptualization

The typology of beauty in ordinary discourse that emerges from the semiological/hermeneutic interpretation of informants' responses in the analysis sample rests on three key distinctions or dimensions outlined in what follows. Here, because I view the data as providing helpful illustrations of the underlying conceptual scheme that emerges from the analysis, I present major conclusion(s) in the form of a typology before discussing detailed examples from the data on which this typology is based.

Please note that, although they are described as dichotomies for the sake of convenient exposition, the key contrasts underlying the beauty typology would more properly be regarded as continua that range between one extreme and the other with various intermediate, fuzzy, or gray areas in between. In that sense, the typology could be envisioned as a three-dimensional "beauty space" (based on three continuous dimensions) rather than as the $2 \times 2 \times 2$ "beauty typology" (based on three dichotomous distinctions) toward which we are headed.

Extrinsically Versus Intrinsically Motivated Beauty (E/I)

First, the distinction (continuum) between extrinsically motivated beauty and intrinsically motivated beauty resembles the dimension of extrinsic/intrinsic value emphasized by the aforementioned typology of consumer value (Holbrook 1994, 1999b).

Specifically, some beauty is valued extrinsically as a means toward another end, as when a beautifully styled automobile enjoys certain benefits of functional performance or when physical beauty helps a prospective employee negotiate a successful job interview. These extrinsically motivated aspects of beauty are prized for the ulterior purposes they serve; they are utilitarian, instrumental, or banausic in nature.

By contrast, an experience of beauty may be valued intrinsically as an end in itself—for example, when a painting makes a favorable aesthetic impression or when a person's inner character shines forth as an inspiration to others. These intrinsically motivated aspects of beauty are appreciated for their own sake; they are self-justifying or autotelic in nature.

Thing(s)- Versus Person(s)-Based Beauty (T/P)

Second, the distinction (continuum) between thing(s)-based beauty and person(s)-based beauty refers to whether the beauty in question stems from an experience with some inanimate object(s) or from the way one relates to one or more other living person(s). This contrast is partly overlapping or analogous—though certainly not synonymous—with the self-oriented/other-oriented dimension of the aforementioned customer-value typology (Holbrook 1994, 1999b).

Specifically, some beauty arises from our interactions with an inanimate object such as a house, a camera, a piano, a painting, or a piece of sculpture. This type of beauty is thing(s)-based in nature.

Table 2.1

Typology of Beauty in Ordinary Discourse

		Extrinsically Motivated	*Intrinsically Motivated*
Thing(s)-Based	*Concrete*	FUNCTION (ETC)	NATURE (ITC)
	Abstract	SYMBOL (ETA)	AESTHETICS (ITA)
Person(s)-Based	*Concrete*	ACHIEVEMENT (EPC)	RELATIONSHIPS (IPC)
	Abstract	IMAGE (EPA)	CHARACTER (IPA)

By contrast, some beauty stems from aspects of other living people, as when others react favorably to one's appearance or when one prizes a relationship with another or admires the depth of another's inner spirit. This type of beauty is person(s)-based in nature. Here, by the way, I treat animal companions as potentially qualifying to be considered quasi-"persons" in accord with the fact that many consumers regard their pets as full-fledged friends, surrogate children, or beloved members of the family (Holbrook et al. 2001).

Concrete Versus Abstract Beauty (C/A)

Third, the distinction (continuum) between concrete beauty and abstract beauty refers to whether the beauty in question depends on tangible, physical, or objective aspects of the relevant thing(s) or person(s) or on more intangible, symbolic, or subjective aspects.

Specifically, some beauty arises from such physical properties as (say) the aerodynamic shape of an automotive design, the color of a flower, the arc traveled by a home-run baseball, or the physiognomy and physique of a blind date. This type of beauty is concrete in nature.

By contrast, some beauty stems from such intangible properties as (say) the nostalgic implications of a brand logo, the significance of a school uniform, the subtlety of an actor's facial expressions, or the kindness of a generous gesture. This type of beauty is abstract in nature.

Conclusions Concerning the Typology of Beauty in Ordinary Discourse

Combining the three distinctions (dichotomies) or continua (dimensions) just described produces the typology of beauty in ordinary discourse shown in Table 2.1. In this typology, the three key distinctions or dimensions appear in *bold italics,* whereas the types of beauty appear in CAPITAL LETTERS. The resulting eight major types of beauty—suggested by the relevant data and illustrated in the remainder of this essay—are as follows: (1) Function (ETC), (2) Symbol (ETA), (3) Achievement (EPC), (4) Image (EPA), (5) Nature (ITC), (5) Aesthetics (ITA), (6) Relationships (IPC), and Character (IPA).

The following discussion draws on the vignettes and photographs supplied by informants to provide illustrations of the eight major types of beauty that emerge from data in the analysis sample and that are checked against responses from the validation sample. In each case, four illustrative photographs are included to enrich the description of key findings and to add visual substance to the discussion of verbal vignettes.

Illustrations

In the illustrations that follow, each of the informants' responses is categorized according to the type of beauty that it exemplifies most prominently. As noted later, any one example may relate to multiple aspects of beauty. However, each illustration focuses on the one type that appears to predominate.

I shall present illustrations separately for the analysis and validation samples. The former led originally to the formulation of the aforementioned typology of beauty in ordinary discourse. The latter serve to check the helpfulness of this typology in interpreting a fresh set of data drawn from the same pool of informants.

Function (ETC)

Analysis Sample

In the analysis sample, six informants—viewing beauty as an aspect of function—adopt an extrinsically motivated orientation that emphasizes the role of concrete properties of things as means to some worthwhile end(s).

For example, one 25-year-old male management consultant from India stresses the importance of "intricate construction, elegant design, admirable function" and photographs "the insides of a computer." Similarly, a 31-year-old American male student prizes the utilitarian beauty of his seven-foot $180.00 bookshelves as "a step towards more comfortable living." From the more feminine side but also for instrumental reasons, a 28-year-old media researcher and marathon runner values her own right foot as "the beautiful embodiment of the unlimited possibilities that lie ahead": "A foot, or a pair of feet can take you anywhere. . . . Mine have taken me around the world."

A more successful photograph came from a U.S. female writer, age 33, who focuses on the desk where she works to edit her first novel, capturing the various writing tools (loose-leaf binder, laptop, printer, etc.) that contribute to her literary project (Figure 2.1A).

Even more clearly functional in nature is a 28-year-old Hispanic financial analyst's description of his "prized possession"—namely, a "sleek," "smooth," "polished" BMW that he views as, among other benefits, an aid to enhancing his "opportunity to travel" (Figure 2.1B).

Perhaps the quintessential depiction of beauty as an essentially utilitarian concept appears in a vignette and photo presented by a 30-year-old engineer, who singles out the virtues of a bulldozer as "the ultimate tool," which he regards as "an extension of our own bodies that magnifies our muscle and power" and as "a symbol of productivity" where the "beautiful aspects of design are . . . there to see, hear, and feel . . . Raw, efficient, beautiful" (Figure 2.1C).

Validation Sample

In the validation sample, nine responses adopt the functional orientation that views beauty as a means to some worthwhile end(s).

For example, one informant—a 27-year-old male U.S. student—produces three different slants on the functionality theme. First, he admires the double buses that he takes every day to get to school because they are "clean, above ground, and free of subway smells": "The fact that the buses are so large but still very maneuverable is a remarkable feat of engineering and design."

Figure 2.1A **Writing Desk**

Figure 2.1B **Sleek, Smooth, Polished BMW**

Figure 2.1C   **A Bulldozer as the Ultimate Tool**

Second, he values his "clean and sleek and shiny" Wilson F6–51 forged-blade golf clubs—not the woods, just the irons—because "When swinging irons or using them in a round, I have extreme confidence in my ability to hit a good shot." Third, as shown in a rather inscrutable picture of a steel frame against a white wall, he prizes his "steel squat rack" for its usefulness as the chinning bar in his regimen of pull-ups: "In addition to being a superb piece of exercise equipment, it is a very attractive manifestation of industrial design."

One theme that surfaces among three members of the validation sample concerns the functional beauty found in various forms of nourishment. Thus, one 28-year-old U.S. student presents a photo of his water pitcher with a few words about its powers of fulfilling desire by means of quenching his thirst: "One of the roots of beauty can be desire. . . . I had just gone for a long run [and] was especially fatigued when I returned, dying for a drink of water. . . . Pure desire. When I opened the refrigerator, the pitcher of water . . . was beautiful." Another 28-year-old U.S. student snaps a photo of his "quick take-out order of sushi," calling it "the perfect food . . . low in fat, high in protein, and very fresh" as well as "fast." Along similar lines—but with considerably more effusiveness on the merits of his favorite food—a U.S. student, age 30, describes his love of pizza as the comestible that "changed my life" so that "My picture of pizza and seltzer and newspaper is beautiful to me": "To be able to sit down, read the sports section with 3 slices (note Sicilian and regular) and my favorite drink is truly a pleasure. I have loved pizza since the dawn of time. . . . Add to that the quite refreshing, delicately flavored lemon-lime seltzer and a sports page and what more could any person ask for?"

Interestingly, three members of the validation sample focus on themes related to linens and beds. Thus, one 52-year-old Japanese woman finds beauty in "clean towels, just out of the dryer,

Figure 2.1D **Inviting Bed as a Relief After a Fourteen-to-Sixteen-Hour Day**

fluffy and smelling pretty, stacked up in a perfect tower." Comparable functional pleasures are associated by a U.S. student, age 28, with his "large, warm, inviting" bed, which he regards as a "wonderful invention": "It is the only place in New York where I feel relaxed and comfortable." Along similar lines, a 30-year-old banker describes the "simple" beauty of her bed—into which she loves to "crawl" in search of "relief" after a day of "14 to 16 hours"—with an insistent emphasis on her requirement that the bed must be "made" and *not* "unmade" and with an attractive photo to match (Figure 2.1D).

Symbol (ETA)

Analysis Sample

In more abstract ways, one or more thing(s) may also perform as a mode of conveying significance, meaning, or an idea—thereby fulfilling an extrinsically motivated but abstract purpose as a symbol or symbols. Here, the important point concerns not what the thing(s) symbolize(s) but rather that the thing(s) symbolize(s) some concept of importance or interest. Thus, the symbolic items chosen for attention by twelve informants range from the trivial to the exalted.

At the mundane extreme, one 25-year-old male U.S. "professional" sees a "glass of Guinness" as a symbol of the "fleeting beauty . . . that lasts a few moments before being consumed"—as found in a sunrise at the shore, fresh powder snow, a steak dinner, a speeding Ferrari, a sunset, or daffodils blooming in the spring. A 30-year-old U.S. student associates his golf clubs with "a beautiful day, green grass, friendly competition." And a 30-year-old female U.S. student associates a turret-topped brownstone with "a touch of country nostalgia" that suggests "a pastoral peaceful family warm inside."

Moving toward loftier concerns, a 21-year-old female U.S. student responds to a map of the world as a reminder of "the vibrancy and immensity that surrounds us": "If one reflects upon . . . the dominant blue of the oceans and waters, one begins to comprehend one's own miniscularity." A 32-year-old male U.S. student links beauty with "experience and contemplation, living in the present moment," as symbolized by some shots of Central Park—one of people gathered around a fountain, another of an empty field of grass. A 27-year-old male Hispanic student finds that "The American flag represents the great opportunities that Americans experience": "Since my family emigrated from Cuba to the United States, . . . I understand firsthand how being able to grow up in a country that offers its citizens so much is a privilege." And a 31-year-old U.S. artist poses for a picture of herself as an expectant mother to provide a symbolic evocation of "Chaos— Because that is where God's most powerfully revealed . . . When the essence of something is revealed . . . That moment when the form that captures energy recedes and someone/thing's true nature is revealed."

Particularly successful photographs that emphasize the symbolic nature of beauty include a gigantic Toblerone bar, seen by a 28-year-old male U.S. student as a representation of "good food, indulgence, and international travel"; a gray-against-red stairway, seen by a 23-year-old female Nigerian medical student as a representation of the fact that "Beauty is life in itself" where "life is in itself a number of steps/phases"; and a red Volkswagen Beetle, seen by a 30-year-old female U.S. student as a representation of "urban man-made commercial beauty": "There is something so warm about it . . . The color and soft edges, with a flower on the dash" (Figure 2.2A).

As a vivid pictorial signifier, a 26-year-old French policeman shoots a picture of his neighborhood church near the center of Paris to symbolize sturdiness and solidity, commenting that, "This church is beautiful because it is strong": "It is protecting the city of Paris, just like my job is protecting my city. . . . It protects life, which is the most beautiful thing of all" (Figure 2.2B).

A 29-year-old female U.S. student photographs a baseball diamond—Legends Field in Tampa, Florida (preseason home of the New York Yankees)—as an evocation of childhood, rebirth, and eternal hope: "Baseball evokes for me a peace and comfort which harkens back to the safety of my early childhood. . . . The greenness of the grass, starkly contrasted by the dirt infield, symbolizes each year to me a rebirth after winter. It is a reminder that hope springs eternal" (Figure 2.2C).

Validation Sample

In the validation sample, twelve informants focus on objects whose beauty they find in various symbolic meanings, again ranging from the more trivial to the more exalted.

Among the more mundane concerns, we find the story by a 27-year-old U.S. housewife about her dinner plates (broken in an accident involving some collapsed shelving) and the bread plates, soup bowls, cups, and saucers that survive to round out the rest of the twelve complete place settings (shown lovingly in a photo of their positions on the inside of a well-organized cabinet): "the dishes pictured here . . . are simply waiting to serve."

Two members of the same family present photographs taken on a beach near Monterey, California. A 21-year-old U.S. student describes the meanings of his "fantastic memories" associated with "a wave crashing against a rock": "This picture represents beauty . . . of days spent with family and friends lounging on the sand, sailing, and swimming." His sister (I infer)—a 26-year-old student—also presents a snapshot of the beach at Monterey, complete with a "so cute and so

Figure 2.2A **The Volkswagen Beetle as a Representation of Urban Man-Made Commercial Beauty**

Figure 2.2B **A Neighborhood Church That Protects Life**

Figure 2.2C **A Baseball Diamond as an Evocation of Childhood, Rebirth, and Eternal Hope**

beautiful" sea otter, whose significance lies in what the otter and other objects "mean" to her: "The photo . . . recalls youth and sun and close friends."

Six informants from the validation sample present photos of objects whose meaning lies in their associations with the coming of spring and its sense of rebirth. One 29-year-old student from Singapore points his camera at a distant pair of sparrows (barely discernible amidst the clutter of a trellis) and comments that "the return of the sparrows at the start of spring is a beautiful sight." On a grander level, a 23-year-old U.S. student travels to Ethiopia and shoots a picture of "a lush waterfall," "beautiful trees," and "cascading water" that, to him, represent "not only beauty but the hope of rebirth." On the same theme of rebirth, four additional informants focus on various aspects of trees and flowers. One—a U.S. journalist, age 34—places his camera very close to the buds on a tree, whose (blurred) image represents "the dawn of spring, the most beautiful time of year": "Spring is about new beginnings and second chances." Another journalist, age 41, photographs a small garden of daffodils and tulips, which he sees as a "reminder of the seasons and passing of time . . . an encouraging sign of the coming spring": "Just passing the flowers and checking them out each day has become a bit of a ritual for me, a small moment that takes me out of myself to appreciate the beauty, the effort, the rhythms of nature and the seasons, and the larger world around me." Similarly, a 28-year-old U.S. student finds beauty in a small patch of purple crocuses that she values for their "simplicity" and "the promise of spring they hold": "I find beauty in the reminder of the first flowers of spring."

Pushing toward even grander visions, a Brazilian student, age 26, presents a photo of Central Park as a representation of his belief that "beauty means . . . freedom": "Central Park . . . is a beautiful, quiet place where the sense of freedom is really intense." Similarly, a 62-year-old

Figure 2.2D   **Optimistic Effect of Light from the Living-Room Window**

psychologist from the United States takes a shot of the George Washington Bridge on the horizon in the distance, comments on its "majestic and dramatic" setting, and points out that "Bridges symbolize connections of not only land but people": "It also suggests pathways to new adventures on distant shores." In a comparable mood, a 31-year-old Greek student points his camera heavenward and snaps a shot of the blue sky with one floating cloud, commenting that "Beauty is the sky on a crisp, bright sunny day": "It is pure and eternal . . . happy and cheerful . . . reminds me of summer; a holiday on the beach, by the deep blue Mediterranean sea; a past carefree life with no stress, anxiety, or worry."

Further "optimistic" meanings imbue the significance attributed by a U.S. journalist, age 45, to her photo from the living room of her house, as light streams in from the peaceful neighborhood outside to convey "the idea of what I might see" and to evoke "the hint of something . . . beautiful to me because it is filled with light, stillness and tranquility" (Figure 2.2D).

Achievement (EPC)

Analysis Sample

When person(s) replace(s) thing(s) as the focal point of attention, concretely embodied beauty may take the form of an extrinsically motivated means to gaining recognition from others for one's achievement(s). In this sense, some concrete accomplishment may appear beautiful because it serves to win the admiration or respect of other people.

Only three of the analysis-sample informants emphasize achievement-oriented beauty of the type just described. But in each case, their vignettes and photographs reveal an exceptionally strong degree of involvement.

First, a 37-year-old U.S. "stay-at-home mother" describes her homemade curtains as the beautiful embodiment of "three months and at least 45 hours of hard work to make them" to the point that "When I finished, I felt as proud of them as I was when my children were born": "I know that sounds ridiculous, but true. They represent what I can do when I put my mind to it" (Figure 2.3A).

Second, a 32-year-old Japanese businessman—who supplied his own photo of himself holding the trophy for first place in a tennis tournament—describes the degree to which this victory made him "proud and happy": "I participated in a certain tennis tournament in Atlanta and won the 1st prize. . . . On this day I was so proud and happy to pay $20 . . . because I was the happiest person there" (Figure 2.3B).

Third, a 26-year-old African American male student intends his picture to evoke "the beauty of accomplishment that can be achieved through teamwork"—as when his team of "short" players won a local football contest against teams of taller players: "We had the shortest team . . . yet we prevailed because we communicated and worked together as a team. The end result was truly a beautiful thing" (Figure 2.3C).

Validation Sample

A comparably small subset of only three members of the validation sample comment on aspects of achievement-oriented beauty.

First, an Italian doctor, age 33, presents a photograph of some skyscrapers (including the World Trade Center) in downtown New York City as a token of "how much people are capable of doing": "My definition of beauty is very related to the accomplishments of human beings."

Second, accomplishments on a more private level concern a 28-year-old female student who equates "beauty" with "happiness" and "happiness" with "reading a book" from the personal library captured in her photograph: "I'm happiest when I'm reading a book or re-reading an old favorite *and* when I have a couple of unread books on reserve, waiting to be devoured."

Even more oriented toward personal achievement is a third informant, a 31-year-old male student, who comments on his "battle" for "freedom"—as encapsulated by a photograph of the bicycle that enables him to travel through town, that lets him avoid smelly subways and slow buses, that provides exercise, and that exposes him to "the many incredible sights of the city," one of which appears in the form of the New York City skyline in the background of his well-composed photo (Figure 2.3D).

Image (EPA)

Analysis Sample

Closely related to the achievement-oriented type of beauty just described, one's image hinges not so much on concrete accomplishment as on being admired by others for various abstract qualities that work toward making a good impression. Needless to say, beauty of this type serves as the cornerstone of the fashion industry and drives the value that many people find in cosmetics, clothing, coiffures, cosmetic surgery, and other aspects of personal appearance. Though only three of the analysis-sample informants dwell on image-related beauty, all three offer strong evocations and clear visual evidence.

Figure 2.3A **Hand-Made Curtains as a Representation of Accomplishment**

Figure 2.3B **Pride and Happiness in Winning a Tennis Tournament**

Figure 2.3C   **The Beauty of Accomplishment Through Teamwork**

Figure 2.3D   **A Bicycle as the Vehicle for Personal Accomplishment**

First, one 22-year-old U.S. legal assistant talks about her coat in terms of falling in love—"I saw this coat a year ago and fell in love with it. . . . So I bought it and I love it" (Figure 2.4A).

Second, a 22-year-old Nigerian/American student describes her "amazing long blue skirt" as a favorite mode of self-expression (Figure 2.4B):

> Beauty for me is fun, creativity, and expression. The picture that I took is of this amazing long blue skirt that is decorated with beautiful gold trim and pink designs. This skirt is representative of many things. It is regal and opulent while at the same time funky and outrageous. For me fashion is a way for me to express my mood, my ideas, and my creative energies; it has the [power] to elevate my mood and to play out my dreams. This skirt allows me to do all of this. Thus, the skirt's beauty goes beyond the aesthetic level because it is symbolic of not just a clothing choice but the colorful and expressive way in which I try to live my life.

Third, a 26-year-old Polish/Irish finance manager delves deeply into her collection of shoes and therein finds "beauty" in "the most effective way of expressing myself . . . with my shoes" (Figure 2.4C):

> Beauty can be found in many areas in our lives. . . . To me, beauty is the ability to express myself in whichever way I choose. While it may seem superficial, I find that the most effective way of expressing myself is through the way I look. Specifically, I express myself with my shoes. Each pair that I own has a story behind it and a mood associated with it. For instance, I have a pair of sneakers that you'll really only see me wear when I am taking out my dog in the morning. They are quite worn and tired. However, if you saw me in the morning as I'm walking my dog, you'd see that the look on my face goes well with my shoes—I am not a morning person. The shoes I wear to work are quite different. They reflect the serious, professional side of me. Picture the conservative finance manager, conducting meetings, making a presentation . . . what better way to capture the mood than a pair of simple, black pumps? The summer months bring out an even different side of me. Days are fun and carefree. Beauty is a light breeze, a frozen margarita, a flowing sun dress, and a perfect pair of strappy, white, patent leather sandals. The mere thought makes me long for warmer temperatures! Social evenings with friends bring about my favorite moods and bring out my favorite pair of shoes. A fabulous night out requires a fabulous outfit—a flirty blouse, slim black skirt, and black leather knee-high boots with a three-inch heel. These boots are very chic and very sexy. They exude confidence and when I'm wearing them, so do I.

Validation Sample

Again, three members of the validation sample focus on image-related beauty of the type related to abstract qualities that serve as a means to making a good impression on others.

One—a 29-year-old U.S. information-technologies professional—comments on the "skill" needed "to attune oneself to beauty and to make its appreciation a part of one's daily life" before proclaiming his "enjoyment of the feminine form" and illustrating this with "the immediate, visceral, and powerful sense of beauty stirred up by these fascinating subjects" in the form of two alluring models pictured in a Ralph Lauren print ad.

Figure 2.4A   **A Lovable Coat**

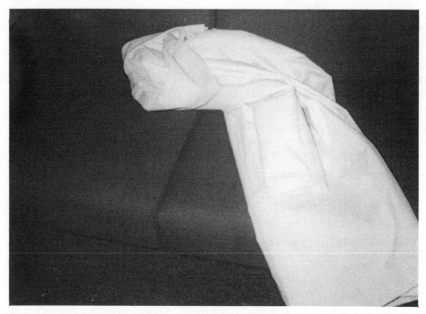

Figure 2.4B   **A Blue Skirt as Self-Expression**

Figure 2.4C **Beauty as Self-Expression Through Shoes**

The second—an Israeli producer/tourist, age 28—expresses her admiration for "Charlie's Angels" as "for years, the symbol of beauty" and captures this reflection via her photo of "a huge wall painting" that towers over Canal Street in New York's Chinatown and shows the angelic Farrah, Kate, and Jaclyn gathered together above the slogan "Times Change. Great TV Doesn't."

The third—a Japanese student, age 28—arranges for someone to photograph her own hands, with the comment that, "To me, hands of others and mine signify beauty in the world": "In Japan where I grew up, it is said that no matter how well a woman puts on makeup, the hands and neck will give away her true age" (Figure 2.4D).

Nature (ITC)

Analysis Sample

Considering beauty in nature returns our focus to concrete things but now regards experiencing these tangible aspects of the environment as worthy of appreciation for its own sake. Thus, twenty of the illustrations from the analysis sample—the most in any single category—identify facets of nature as embodiments of beauty, the variegated experience of which is regarded as an intrinsically motivated end in itself.

Understandably, many of these evocations are somewhat perfunctory and are accompanied by relatively routine photographs. These include—roughly in order of photographic excellence—"a bright sunny day" on which "Sunshine is beautiful to me . . . brings warmth and happiness . . . brightens things up and puts me in a good mood" (26-year-old U.S. female program assistant);

Figure 2.4D **The Hands as a Beauty-Related Sign of True Age**

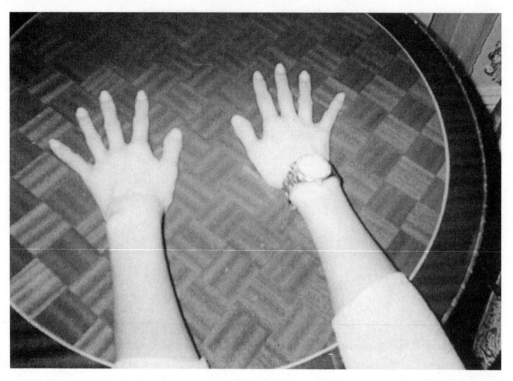

"beauty in tranquil outdoor settings . . . sunny skies, calm waters, and a beautiful landscape" as "what beauty means to me" (30-year-old female TV producer); a tree seen as "my thermometer of the season," viewed as a signal that "it is spring again," and interpreted as "beautiful because it reminds me that no matter where I am, I am at one with the Earth" (21-year-old female U.S. student); a tree viewed as "natural random structures" whose "beauty . . . is unexplainable" (37-year-old male Japanese ad exec); a wet grassy scene at the university on "a warm rainy day" with special enjoyment found in "watching the rain glisten off of grass" (28-year-old U.S. female student); an unexpected "flurry of snow . . . on an April morning," observed through a window from which "the snow seems to dance in the air untouched" (21-year-old U.S. male student); a local park selected "to represent nature" as "pleasing to look at and . . . a wonderful setting to read, exercise, or just relax . . . a backdrop to appreciate a beautiful blue sky" (29-year-old male consultant); and a squirrel in the park to embody the "innocence and serenity of an animal in nature" as "what I find most beautiful in the world around me" or as "the essence of beauty in the most natural sense" (35-year-old U.S. female student).

One ambitious informant—a 29-year-old U.S. computer technician—conveys his appreciation of nature via a three-stage odyssey that takes him and his female companion from one end of New York City to the other and back again, visiting three different parks that "as a whole bring me joy": "These parks . . . bring people together, provide a safe haven from the 'craziness' of Manhattan, and mesh so much natural beauty with concrete."

By far the most common theme among the nature-loving informants focuses on the beauty of plants in general and of flowers in particular. Two present relatively mundane versions of

(1) "springtime flowers" to signify "a new beginning" as "nature's way of telling us that no matter what life may bring us, the flowers will always bloom" (25-year-old Italian/Irish female sales rep) or (2) "brilliant red and green colors" of a houseplant viewed as "my connection to the natural world that NYC has essentially swallowed" (29-year-old male U.S. student). Two pursue the convenient strategy of photographing a local flower stall—featuring (1) "Gerbera flowers sold at a corner grocery" (30-year-old Japanese housewife) or (2) "a burst of multicolored and multi-shaped flowers" as a "small sample of natural beauty" found at a neighborhood market (30-year-old female U.S. student). But one informant—a 24-year-old U.S. financial analyst, drawing on her private photo collection—presents a rather spectacular view of "one of nature's greatest creations," noting that with their "beautiful colors and . . . wonderful scents . . . Flowers always provide me with a sense of joy and happiness."

Finally, several informants produce vignettes and accompanying photographs that offer especially vivid evocations of beauty in nature. Two present descriptions and pictures of bridges in the park: (1) a "flower bridge" that "shows how old and delicate nature is" and "how beautiful the outdoors is when you just take a minute to look at it" (11-year-old U.S. schoolgirl) and (2) a "waterfall, stream, and bridge" in a natural scene that is "beautiful because" it is both "attractive" and "soothing" (29-year-old U.S. male student).

A 27-year-old Argentinean student portrays "trees covered by ice" in a cemetery located near her house: "I have always been fascinated by the beauty of nature, and the effect of light going through the ice on trees' branches is one of the few things that have the power to rescue me from everyday hectic [events] and make me smile" (Figure 2.5A).

A 30-year-old U.S. physician photographs a bowl of fruit on her kitchen table as a form of "natural beauty" evocative of "the interaction between various aspects of the environment which provide for the growth of fruit" and manages to capture a slightly blurred image that strongly resembles a Dutch still-life painting (Figure 2.5B).

A 31-year-old Israeli Ph.D. student presents one nautical vignette and photo wherein "the specific scene of the sea and sailboat expresses a certain calmness that I find beautiful" and another pastoral image that pictures a long path or road winding into the distance between two patches of farmland and vividly conveys "the colors and shapes of the fields and trees and how they are combined . . . the experience of being outdoors, the colors and scents of the general blossom" (Figure 2.5C).

Validation Sample

Again, beauty in nature proves to be the most common theme among members of the validation sample—accounting for twenty responses, the most in any category.

Once more, some of the evocations of natural beauty are somewhat perfunctory and generate fairly routine photographic expressions. These include—again, roughly in order of photographic excellence—"sky . . . deep and rich" between two buildings on the university campus (34-year-old Korean housewife); "the first day of warm weather" at the university, with "People . . . coming out of buildings absorbing the rays and smiling" (33-year-old female Israeli student); "a country scene—in the middle of the big city . . . And right here on campus as well" (35-year-old male U.S. student); "the calm, quiet Lake Michigan in Chicago as seen from my father's apartment . . . calm, peaceful, natural, and blue in color" (25-year-old female student); along the Hudson River, "blue skies, sunshine, birds . . . by the water on a bright and beautiful day" (26-year-old female U.S. publicist); a painting showing "a natural view of an old quiet house" with "trees . . .

Figure 2.5A **Light Through Ice on Trees**

Figure 2.5B **Bowl of Fruit**

Figure 2.5C **A Long and Winding Road**

flowers . . . fruits . . . small rivers with their blue colors and relaxing sound . . . finally the old house that reminds me of my old home town with beautiful old trees that reflect that life is beautiful" (middle-aged male Hispanic physician); the Wollman Skating Rink in NYC's Central Park on "a crisp sunny New York Winter Day" when "The weather was beautiful and the tall New York Skyscrapers provided a great background" (27-year-old female student from Singapore); a fountain in Central Park with "many of the elements that I have noticed are part of the scenes that I find beautiful . . . flowing water . . . ornamentation . . . skies . . . changing clouds and colors . . . vistas . . . the contrast between the solidity of the stone and the fluidity of the water" (24-year-old female U.S. student); and a glacier in Alaska that "represents one of the most beautiful sites I've ever seen . . . because it is natural and not fabricated, because the layers of the sky, clouds, rock, glacier, water are in such contrast to each other and yet there is a fluidity to their form" (27-year-old female student from the United States and the United Kingdom).

Again, by far the most common nature-loving theme concerns the beauty of plants, flowers, and trees; and, again, these evocations range from the trivial to the sublime. At the more mundane end of the spectrum, one informant presents photos of her potted euonymus, which "retains its leaves throughout the winter . . . a stark contrast to its . . . surroundings" (35-year-old female Jamaican student). Two informants find beauty in flowers: (1) where "Flowers are the most beautiful thing in the world [and] cheer me up and create a good mood for me" (28-year-old female Israeli producer/tourist) and (2) where "roses represent nature at its best . . . and . . . reflect the beauty of . . . inner joy triggered by something visual" (57-year-old female U.S. college professor). Four focus on trees: the "green scenes . . . an infusion of green and trees" in Central Park near the Metropolitan Museum of Art (26-year-old female U.S. student); "the first tree that I noticed had bloomed this spring . . . beauty on these often crowded dirty streets of Manhattan" (27-year-old female U.S. media analyst); trees blooming on the university campus where "The beauty of this scene of spring trees blossoming with its calm demeanor while basking in the sunshine is very beautiful and calming" (35-year-old male U.S. student); and, more expansively, "some trees with newly blossomed whitish-pink flowers situated in Riverside Park":

> The light pink blossoms complement the fresh, bright green grass surrounding the trees. . . . Although I have lived in New York for most of my life, I actually love nature and like to take advantage of any opportunity I can to escape the concrete world of NYC or at least to take refuge in the places in the city where there are signs of natural life. Newly blossomed trees are symbolic of the rebirth that occurs in springtime and are a welcomed manifestation that the cold and dreary winter has come to an end. I feel most at ease and calm when I am in nature. . . . Of course in the other direction you can also see the beautiful, majestic Hudson River. Riverside Park is a welcome treasure in Manhattan's Upper West Side and a walk through it is conducive to reflection and reminiscence. (28-year-old female U.S. student)

As before, two informants celebrate the theme of beauty found in trees covered by snow or ice. The first—a female U.S. journalist, age 31—sits in a "favorite spot" at her "parents' kitchen table" and comments that, as shown in her photo, "when I was visiting for spring break, a small snow storm hit and the backyard just looked gorgeous" as "snow covered the ground or hung on the branches of the trees." The second—a female Japanese/German/Dominican student, age 16— suggests that "beauty means nature untouched" and presents a "picture of snow covering the trees" to show "nature in its true essence."

A particularly successful photograph—in sepia tones—comes from the collection of a 65-year-old U.S. physician who supplies his own picture to evoke a scene from nature full of multisensory aspects of beauty: "Fishing boats, all colors, resting in the beautiful Monterey Harbor and gulls in the air and seals honking, the wind blowing, the sun shining and the smell of food rising from the Fish Markets along the piers—that is beauty."

But probably no informant captures a richer sense of the evocative power of natural beauty than does a twenty-something U.S. student who shoots eight photos intended to express the essence of her experience with flowers and blossoms in the spring (Figure 2.5D). The poetic nature of her description deserves to be quoted in full:

> Hyacinths . . . Cherry Blossoms. . . . Spring is in full bloom. Spring flowers represent quintessential beauty. They bloom at Easter—a time when my fellow Episcopalians and other Christians are reflecting on the mystery of life.
>
> Spring flowers have become more and more beautiful to me since my Grandmother's passing in the winter of 1998. The sight and scent of the flowers has both a calming and energizing effect on me. I remember planting hyacinths and daffodils with my Grandmother as a little girl. After her passing, when the ground was soft, I continued this ritual we once shared by planting a small garden of spring flowers at her grave. . . . When the flowers bloom, they bring life to the graveyard.
>
> They bloom as the children come out to play at recess on the other side of the graveyard fence. Spring flowers are beautiful because they help my sorrows fade away. I leave the graveyard with a clearer head, with a skip in my step, with a smile. I leave knowing that I still have life, and I must lead it with the same energy and fearlessness as the children tumbling down the playground slide.

Figure 2.5D **Tree Blossoms in Full Bloom at Easter**

Aesthetics (ITA)

Analysis Sample

The type of beauty that emphasizes aesthetics characterizes the responses of thirteen analysis-sample informants—only the third highest among the categories represented by the beauty typology. This means that the sort of intrinsically motivated thing(s)-based abstract aesthetic beauty most commonly stressed by philosophers of art occupies just a small niche in the more colloquial uses of that term found in ordinary discourse. I consider this an important, if somewhat surprising, finding of the present study.

   Nonetheless, we should not lose sight of the role played by beauty in the form of aesthetic value in the lives of several informants. In this connection, one 32-year-old female French lawyer tries to capture a picture of the "understated elegance, purity, and simplicity" of calla lilies as "a genuine representation of beauty . . . simple . . . yet extremely refined" but produces only a blurred image. Another offers a grainy photo of some costumed drummers to capture "Simplicity, Strength, Innocence" and to indicate that "beauty . . . is fluid, changing, static, permanent,

Figure 2.6A **Beautiful Shiny Apples**

thus unable to define, but able to be appreciated" (33-year-old male American). Another more successfully catches the delicious appearance of "beautiful shiny apples in the middle of a dreary February day" (23-year-old female U.S. graphic designer) (Figure 2.6A).

Curiously, no informant presents a convincing photograph of a visual artwork. One tries but fails to take a photo of "the tranquility and serenity" captured by "the color scheme" in Van Gogh's *Irises in Vase* as "one of the most beautiful things she has ever seen" (28-year-old anonymous female). Another attempts unsuccessfully to photograph a picture of a llama from a Banana Republic advertisement, commenting that, "The texture of the llama's fur against the cashmere scarf, and the contrasting colors, make the aesthetic experience of the photo that much more profound" (23-year-old male U.S. paralegal). Still another cannot deliver a usable snapshot of the architectural beauty found in the "style" and "grandeur" exhibited by the Cathedral of St. John the Divine as "a local commitment to beauty" (27-year-old male U.S. architecture student).

One informant offers a telling description of beauty as "the interaction of elements in a pleasing way" but provides only an out-of-focus photo of the "subtle beige-brown-soft" tones pitted against a "stronger brown color" that decorate his eyeglasses case, finding therein "a beauty that wouldn't exist in each element alone" (31-year-old male Jewish American student). Another presents a clear image of the "tall ceilings" and "ample space" found in his apartment as an example of "beauty to me" but offers no clear aesthetic rationale for this judgment beyond calling these qualities "refreshing" when compared with the hotel rooms where he spends most of his workweeks (34-year-old U.S. engineer). By contrast, another supplies a highly sophisticated aesthetic argument based on "the perception of sensory inputs to any combination of the five senses" but inexplicably follows this with a portrait of his pretty girlfriend, who is presumably flattered to

Figure 2.6B   **Three Guitars**

be regarded as an illustration of beauty but who might not wish to be labeled as a "perception of sensory inputs" (53-year-old U.S. CFO of an online trading company).

Somewhat paradoxically, several informants try to take photos of aesthetic beauty associated with types of artworks high on abstract qualities and therefore especially difficult to capture on film. Thus, one informant focuses on the aesthetic beauty of a literary work, *Mama Day* by Gloria Naylor, to exemplify "beauty as clarity in a pure form of expression" (21-year-old female African American student): "What is beautiful about this book is the honesty and openness of the characters presented by Naylor, as well as the significance given to every detail mentioned however slightly. It highlights the grandness of all things great and small whether we as the reader find any significance in them." Meanwhile, no fewer than four informants tackle the challenging task of representing the beauty of music pictorially—with results that include an unusable photo of the Steely Dan album *Two Against Nature*, regarded as the "perfect antidote for people who think that jazz-pop is a genre meant only for elevators" (26-year-old male Indian student); a pedestrian snapshot of a medium-priced stereo system as the "greatest everyday source of beauty I know" (21-year-old male U.S. model); an impressive shot of a huge country-music collection (roughly 300 CDs) as "a thing of beauty" indicative of "an obsession or an addiction" or even "a way of life" in which "Each CD comes alive once the music begins and I can admire the musical talent of others" (23-year-old male U.S. student); and a successful composition by a 28-year-old Hispanic bank-supervision support analyst portraying his three guitars—"beautiful . . . From their polished bodies to their exquisite craftsmanship" so as to "embody . . . what beauty is all about" (Figure 2.6B).

Validation Sample

In the validation sample, we again find a surprisingly small representation of aesthetic beauty— namely, eight responses, only the fifth highest among the eight categories. In other words, we again see that the sort of intrinsically motivated thing(s)-based abstract experience emphasized by aesthetic philosophers only occasionally finds its way into the manifestations of beauty en- shrined in ordinary discourse. To repeat, this strikes me as a significant and somewhat surprising result of the present research.

Interestingly, those informants who dwell on the aesthetic aspects of beauty again appear to have the most difficulty capturing their observations on film—a curious phenomenon suggest- ing, paradoxically, that aesthetic sensibility does not necessarily lead to good photography. Thus, one informant—a 27-year-old U.S. buyer—rhapsodizes about her vision of the Empire State Building on a night when "it really sparkled" and "stood out amongst the concrete jungle of the city," but produces only a drastically underexposed and grainy picture of . . . the Chrysler Building. Another informant—a male U.S. student, age 35—tries unsuccessfully to capture "The Beauty of the New York Skyline" through a small opening between two walls that reveals only a narrow view of a few tall buildings in the distance. Yet another—a twenty-something female student—offers two responses with convincing aesthetically oriented descriptions ac- companied by badly blurred photos. The first represents a candle—out of focus with its top cut off—appreciated for its "unusual color . . . a blend of orange and brown with a hint of yellow" and for its "lack of symmetry" wherein "the designs on each half are not identical." The second shows some blurred and therefore difficult-to-identify roses—valued according to the pro- vocative premise that, "Wilting roses are beautiful" because "The color of wilting roses is much richer than roses in full bloom": "Wilting roses that were purely red before they started wilting become mixtures of red, burgundy, and a wine color so deep that the color is almost black" (admirable qualities, no doubt, but not evident in the photograph). Finally, a 27-year- old British arts-administration student comments eloquently on her conception of beauty as involving "Grace and patience, uniqueness in color and texture, simplicity and intricacy, an ethereal or other worldly presence, wonder and excitement . . . something that is 'awesome' in the true sense of the word," but demonstrates this almost neo-Kantian view with an unrecog- nizably out-of-focus snapshot of a fish appreciated for its "graceful, fragile, intricate and simple . . . flashes of color."

Happily three somewhat more pictorially successful evocations of aesthetic beauty do appear among the responses in the validation sample. First, a 35-year-old U.S. portfolio manager pre- sents a photo of the staircase in his loft—seen as "an artful combination of form and function steeped in the laws of geometry . . . a structure that will serve as an aesthetically pleasing addition to the loft's overall appeal": "The strength and warmth evoked by the very simple set of lines . . . is a testament to success in this particular design" where "Creative choices of color, stair pitch, and combination of metal and wood materials result in a visually appealing complement to the dwell- ing that I call home."

Second, a 24-year-old U.S. media buyer shares his view that "beauty is found in emotion" and illustrates this claim by photographing a rather attractively designed display of vegetables: "I found the vibrant colors and variety of this busy vegetable stand to be eye-catching, interesting, and well . . . beautiful!" (Figure 2.6C).

Figure 2.6C **An Eye-Catching Vegetable Stand**

Third, a 24-year-old U.S. student shares her photograph (© SR 1999 and used by permission) of some flowers on a city street, which she appreciates for their "juxtaposition of colors and materials": "The riot of color is set against the monochrome palette of typical city materials— stone, concrete and metal" so as to incorporate "elements of both human efforts to create beauty as well as growing life forms" (Figure 2.6D).

Relationships (IPC)

Analysis Sample

The second-most-frequent category of responses in the analysis sample, illustrated by sixteen informants, refers to concrete aspects of persons-based relationships viewed as intrinsically motivated ends in themselves. Here, beauty lies in the way one interacts with others where such interactions are pursued for their own sake rather than as means to any other end(s). Interestingly, by contrast with the aesthetics category just described, the category based on beauty in personal relationships produces some of the stronger visual images found in the present study. Further, virtually all of these examples celebrate the same essential point—namely, the beauty of warm, harmonious, loving connections with family and close friends.

Somewhat indirectly—presumably in the absence of the relevant family or friends involved— some informants take photos of scenes that remind them of the key person(s) of interest. These include an "engagement ring" that "represents . . . the special relationship I share with my significant other and my extended family . . . Partnership, love, companionship, respect, and safety . . . just a few of the many beautiful qualities an engagement ring represents" (32-year-old

Figure 2.6D **A Juxtaposition of Colors and Materials**

female Hispanic assistant VP at a brokerage firm); "two stuffed animals" that "my sister gave me . . . as a peace offering" after a "big argument" and that therefore "represent the beauty of forgiveness and beauty of love and family" (26-year-old U.S. "stay-at-home mom"); "plastic flowers in a Heineken bottle" that "remind me of my grandmother" who "received the flowers from a friend, but . . . thought they were pretty ugly, so . . . was planning to throw them out" (22-year-old female U.S. student); a "sorority photo album" that is "beautiful because it is filled with memories of times that I shared with my sorors" and "Additionally, . . . represents beauty to me because it was presented to me by one of my best friends . . . Made by hand and presented to me in love" (24-year-old female U.S. student); a pair of candles on a tablecloth to "represent relaxation, intimacy, and spirituality . . . with loved ones" (34-year-old female Japanese researcher); a scene in Paris on the Seine of "the bridge where I kissed my girlfriend the very first time" so that "every time I see this bridge I think of that moment, and her beauty" (27-year-old French professional soccer player); along similar lines, the view from a girlfriend's balcony where "the fact that it's [the view's] from her balcony also represents beauty to me, because it's a peaceful place where I can relax and be myself" so that "This view makes me feel safe, because I know when I see it that I am 'home'" (31-year-old male Puerto Rican athlete); a pictorially unsuccessful photo of a family's condo that depicts "our first home together" as "a very important icon of us and the beginning of our life together" (26-year-old female U.S. career counselor); and a "newly purchased house" because, for this 27-year-old female U.S. student, "my home is a place that my husband and I and baby-to-be will share so many memories . . . experiences that a family shares that one reflects upon and in which I find great beauty" (Figure 2.7A).

More directly, several informants take photos of family or friends involved in the personal

Figure 2.7A **House and Family Home**

relationships of interest. Generally, these produce among the most compelling vignettes and pictures collected in the present study. Thus, one 31-year-old Italian American female school psychologist photographs six family members—ranging in age from young children to older grandparents—to portray "ultimate beauty" as "relationships and connections with other people, particularly family" and "the highest form of Beauty" as "the whole concept of reproduction and the creation of new family members, carrying on traits, connections and traditions from one generation to another": "Having had the experience of death of very close family members and the experience of family members not being able to reproduce, I have come to value my connection to family and the miracle of reproducing and the carrying on of family ties."

A 47-year-old U.S. journalist shows his "family lighting Sabbath candles" as "a scene of beauty" involving "customs that have a particular meaning to our family and its heritage" and finds this evocative of "my late mother lighting candles when I was a child, and of her mother lighting candles surrounded by family members on special holiday occasions . . . reflections of loved ones now gone—scenes of beauty that fail to dim with age."

From her own collection, a 36-year-old U.S. student provides a photo of her partner's hands, comments that she "could touch them for long periods of time without saying a word," and considers this an illustration of beauty as an "indescribable thing . . . such that I can't define it but know it when I see it."

A 30-year-old U.S. sound man states that "beauty is family" and presents a cheerful picture of six siblings and cohorts to prove it.

Also in a joyous vein, a 28-year-old female Norwegian student feels that "being out in the sun, playing [music] with my dear friends, is true beauty" and captures photos that express how "the most beautiful moments in my daily life are related to music and the dance experience."

Figure 2.7B   **Clem on the Sofa**

We should also note that—as in previous studies (Holbrook et al. 2001)—some informants include animal companions in the category of beauty that I have labeled as "intrinsically motivated concrete person(s)-based relationships." In this connection, one 30-year-old U.S. equity-research analyst reports that playing with his dog Daisy "is absolutely beautiful to me," as in a ball-throwing scene in which "the majority of the beauty comes from being with my dog and doing something that seems to bring her such pleasure." A 31-year-old male U.S. writer depicts "My dog Clem asleep on our sofa" and comments that "Clem isn't allowed on the sofa but I love her so damn much I can't bring myself to wake her," adding that "if I had a kid sleeping I suppose I'd have taken that picture" and also that "If my wife wasn't at the gym she'd be in the picture too" (Figure 2.7B).

Validation Sample

The theme of interpersonal relationships also appears frequently among the responses of the validation sample—ten times, the third most frequent in number. Again, in contrast to the comparatively unsuccessful photographic evocations of aesthetic beauty, personal relationships inspire some of the stronger visual images—intended to celebrate warm, harmonious, loving connections with family and close friends.

Again, somewhat indirectly, some informants photograph scenes that remind them of key people or loving relationships. For example, a 56-year-old Bolivian housewife presents a photo of a small statuette that represents two children kissing—accompanied by a list of adjectives to describe "my perception of beauty": "Creation of God . . . Happy . . . Innocent . . . Loving . . . Darling. . . ." Along similar lines, a 28-year-old U.S. student takes a picture of "daffodils on a file cabinet in my . . . room" because, by "blooming so bright," they remind him of his girlfriend "on the other side of the continent": "I just picked them up the day before because I was thinking of my long-distance girlfriend (daffodils are her favorite flower)." In a comparable mood, a 47-year-old U.S. journalist photographs his home as "the most beautiful object I see every day" because "It evokes family life for me, time with the people I love."

More directly, several informants again take photos of family or friends with whom they share important relationships. And, again, these often produce among the more compelling vignettes and pictures found in this study. Once more, a ritual feast among intimate acquaintances provides a salient theme—as in the photo by a 33-year-old Israeli student of her close friends gathered for the Seder meal at Passover where "We were all without families in the United States—so we became a new one [a new family]": "I find these interpersonal relationships between people one of the most beautiful things in life." Along similar lines, a 23-year-old U.S. student photographs six friends to illustrate "The sharing of ideas from people of different backgrounds": "Beauty is many things but one of the most beautiful things are people gathering to discuss something" so as "to bring people of common interest and uncommon backgrounds together." Another informant— a U.S. advertising executive, age 30—finds something comparable at a party attended by her closest friend at the restaurant Indochine: "it is her plus the lively environment . . . and the amazing amount of happiness I felt on this night." Yet another student—a 27-year-old American— shoots no fewer than nine photos of classmates who provide comfort during her difficult period of cramming for final exams: "I find beauty in . . . Sunshine, smoke breaks, coffee and friends who understand the stress and misery of cram time" so that "When you know you're not alone, and others are experiencing the same pressure as yourself, the situation takes on a new perspective." Ironically, the most photographically successful picture submitted by this informant shows herself alone, dressed entirely in black, against a white-and-black background of stone and windows, smoking a cigarette and surrounded by cups of take-out latté (Figure 2.7C).

Among informants from the validation sample, relationships with children also figure prominently in the pictorial expression of beauty. Thus, a 29-year-old female U.S. recruiter suggests that "Human kindness represents beauty to me" and points her camera at a woman who "holds a child's hand to cross the street": "people helping people brings out the most beautiful part of themselves." Even smaller children, twin babies, appear in the photograph by a 32-year-old Korean American retail owner and student, who finds "new life beautiful" and who sees babies as "reminders of new beginnings and reflections of our own developments": "They symbolize hope and joy, a gift to parents that enlighten[s] them to . . . deeper appreciations [of] higher existences [in] life." Such higher existences appear in the charming face captured by one proud father—a 38-year-old Korean student—who suggests that "Beauty should be beauty [for] itself" (not as a means to some other end) and who elaborates that, "In this regard, I always feel beauty and recognize beauty whenever I look at the faces of my children" (Figure 2.7D).

Character (IPA)

Analysis Sample

The final type of beauty, emphasized by seven analysis-sample informants, continues the focus on intrinsically valued aspects of person(s)-based relationships but turns attention to the more abstract qualities of inward beauty associated with the more psychological or spiritual aspects of inner character. As in our discussion of personal relationships, we again find that the virtues of a beautiful character are attributed both to animals and to people.

Figure 2.7C **Beauty in Smoke and Coffee Breaks (with friends who understand)**

In the former connection—pets with shining personalities—we find responses ranging from the ridiculous to the sublime. At the former extreme, one informant—a 29-year-old female U.S. foundation employee—claims that her white rats possess "both inner and outer beauty" and, after failing to convince us of the second part of this claim with the observation that "Their soft white fur contrasts well with their red, attentive eyes," contends that "The most adorable thing they do is clean their faces with their tiny front paws." Speaking of face cleaning, a 29-year-old female U.S. engineer proclaims the beauty of her black cat—who "is pure," "gives love unconditionally," and "captures the very essence of what is elegant, graceful, and beauty to me"—but produces no usable photo. Similarly, an 11-year-old U.S. schoolgirl reports that her canine friend Daisy is "beautiful" because she is "a very wonderful animal, with a good personality"—one who is "like a friend . . . playful, fun, . . . always happy, never upset" and who "always loves everybody" (Figure 2.8A).

Turning to descriptions of people, a 34-year-old U.S. editor describes but does not reproduce a picture of her mother that conveys "her inner beauty—her kindness, her gentleness, her deep and abiding love for her family" as "the essence of real beauty . . . what is most beautiful in people and in life." Though he also fails to provide a photograph, a 33-year-old U.S. communication director reports that his 1-year-old son "personifies my definition of beauty" and paints a strong verbal portrait of the boy's "youth" and of "how much potential he has to grow into a marvelous human being—another aspect of beauty." More successful photographically, a 35-year-old U.S. mother sees her son as "the essence of beauty . . . full of love and laughter" when "his eyes and his smile . . . especially beautiful . . . radiate joy" (Figure 2.8B).

Figure 2.7D **Beauty in the Face of a Child**

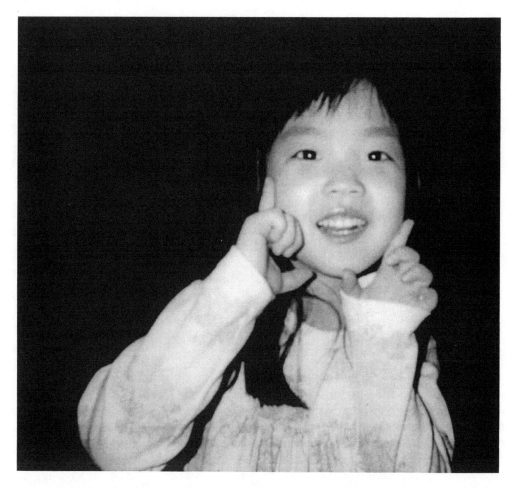

Similarly, a 27-year-old U.S. director of a think tank regards his partner or friend M—— as an embodiment of "the purest form" of "Beauty . . . composed of four elements"—not only physical beauty, but also "Beauty of the heart" ("love and the emotional bond that any two humans might hope to experience"); "Beauty of the mind" ("an intellectual bond between two people"); and "Beauty of the spirit" ("a focused devotion which is able to express . . . faith") (Figure 2.8C).

Validation Sample

Again a small but sincere group of five informants from the validation sample focus on intrinsically valued person(s)-related abstract qualities of inward beauty associated with personality-based aspects of inner character.

Here, more than ever, we find that pets with shining personalities emerge as key embodiments of inner beauty associated with exemplary character traits. Thus, without producing a usable photograph, one twenty-something student provides a touching verbal portrait of his cat "Special Patrol Group" or "SPG" as "the most beautiful animal I've ever known" by virtue of her transfor-

Figure 2.8A **Daisy as Like a Friend with a Good Personality**

mation from a "mean, angry, and frightened" kitten (adopted from a shelter after being mistreated by her former owners) to a lovable pet with whom the informant has "gotten very close": "To see her spirit change so dramatically, albeit slowly, is one of the dearest things I've known. She's family, and she's a beautiful creature." In two cases, similar feelings attach to dogs. First, a 34-year-old U.S. student declares that her dogs are "the two most beautiful things in NY City":

> They have internal beauty that cannot be matched by any human being. They have beautiful souls—love unconditionally and empathize—always know how I feel without my having to express it. They feel whatever they feel without excuses and as intensely as possible and they feel it very quickly and then forgive and forget very quickly. . . . They keep my feet warm every night. They bark no matter what I say when people come by my door because it is more important for them to protect our home than listen to me. They are happy with the smallest things—things which humans take for granted—food, outdoors, other dogs, other people, hugs, etc. . . . They are cute . . . cuddly on the outside . . . and they keep my soul warm. That to me is beautiful.

Second, a 30-year-old U.S. student finds beauty in Roxy, her soft-coated wheaten terrier—a breed, by the way, that has virtually taken over the streets of New York City in the past half decade—who "represents beauty" by virtue of her excellent character: "She is beauty because of her loyalty, vitality, and utter happiness . . . the beauty of youth and innocence" (Figure 2.8D).

Besides these informants who focus on the beauty of character in their animal companions, we do find a couple who attribute similarly admirable attributes to other humans. One informant—a

Figure 2.8B **Son as the Essence of Beauty**

U.S. trial attorney, age 27—finds beauty in people's eyes as "the windows to the soul" and presents a photo of some out-of-focus, blurred, and fuzzy blue eyes taken at very close range—mercifully without flash but also without enough light to capture a decent image. Another informant—a 27-year-old U.S. student—presents a photo of "a school group I often see during the week" to illustrate "beauty in people, especially children who are constantly influenced by the world around them with their young, open minds": "The kids are always holding hands, laughing and eager to learn. . . . Beauty is an open mind, a happy heart, and a love for the world around us."

Statistical Comparison of Analysis and Validation Samples

The comparative frequencies and percentages of responses classified as examples of the eight types of beauty in the analysis and validation samples appear in Table 2.2. As suggested by the columns displaying percentages, the analysis and validation samples show similar profiles among

Figure 2.8C **The Four Components of Beauty: Body, Heart, Mind, and Spirit**

Figure 2.8D **Roxy, the Soft-Coated Wheaten Terrier**

Table 2.2

Distributions of Responses among Types of Beauty in the Analysis and Validation Samples

	Analysis sample		Validation sample	
	No.	%	No.	%
1. Function (ETC)	6	0.075	9	0.129
2. Symbol (ETA)	12	0.15	12	0.171
3. Achievement (EPC)	3	0.0375	3	0.043
4. Image (EPA)	3	0.0375	3	0.043
5. Nature (ITC)	20	0.25	20	0.286
6. Aesthetics (ITA)	13	0.1625	8	0.114
7. Relationships (IPC)	16	0.20	10	0.143
8. Character (IPA)	7	0.0875	5	0.071

Note. These distributions do *not* show a statistically significant difference: $\chi^2 = 5.708$, $df = 7$, $p = .57$ (*NS*).

the various beauty categories. A Chi-square test of the difference between the two distributions indicates that the responses of informants in the validation sample appear to follow the same pattern as those of the informants in the analysis sample: $\chi^2 = 5.708$, $df = 7$, $p = .57$ (*NS*).

We would not want to reach conclusions that overstate the rigor of this validation process. After all, the statistical comparison rests on categorizations made by the same individual who developed the classification scheme in the first place—namely, the author. Hence, the potential for biases toward self-consistency is obvious. Nevertheless, we should note that several months elapsed between the codings of the data from the analysis and validation samples, so that the author did not remember the first distribution of responses when deriving the second. Also, when working with the data, one tends to forget how many responses one has assigned to each category until going back and tabulating the results at a later date. All this suggests that there is, at least, some reason for taking comfort in the absence of a difference in the distributions of responses between the analysis and validation samples.

Discussion

Summary

The lessons learned from the present CPE stem less from the specific types of beauty uncovered in the preceding discussion or from the frequency distribution of the responses than from the style of the approach and the general nature of the findings.

Most basically, the study demonstrates the usefulness of the CPE as a quick and potentially insightful method for gathering data that elucidate a particular phenomenon or concept of relevance to marketing in general or to consumer research in particular. By autodriving informants' photographic intentions (even when the photos themselves do not all necessarily turn out to be high in visual quality), we gain insights into the meanings these informants attach to an idea such as beauty. These insights help to generate "grounded theory" or what I would prefer to call *emergent conceptualizations* likely to encompass key aspects of the relevant phenomenon.

Further, in the present case, the relevant phenomenon in question concerns the meanings of beauty. In this connection, the findings reported here take us a considerable distance from the sorts of definitions offered by philosophers of art when they consider the nature of aesthetic experience. As indicated in our earlier review, such philosophically inclined aestheticians tend to regard beauty as an aspect of intrinsically motivated self-oriented reactive consumption experiences with works of art or pieces of entertainment (Holbrook 1994, 1999b; Holbrook and Zirlin 1985). As a characterization of *langue*—that is, prescriptions for how words should be used in the service of conceptual clarity—such definitions of beauty may recommend themselves to the philosophically rigorous among us. But the present study suggests strongly that as a characterization of *parole*—that is, descriptions of how words actually are used by ordinary speakers of the common discourse—the philosophical definition(s) of beauty may leave a lot to be desired.

Specifically, it appears that ordinary consumers use the term "beauty" in a variety of ways not encompassed by the traditional aesthetic conceptualizations from the philosophy of art. Consideration of these usage patterns via a semiological/hermeneutic approach to interpretive analysis has led in the direction of formulating a tentative typology that—in the tradition of the hermeneutic circle—has survived checking, revising, re-checking, re-revising, re-rechecking . . . and so on . . . against the detailed textual evidence from eighty vignettes and photographs provided by seventy-seven informants in an analysis sample and against further comparisons with seventy responses from another sixty informants in a validation sample.

I do not claim, at this stage, to have arrived at the definitive typology of beauty in ordinary discourse—though I do believe that we have made a worthwhile start in that direction. What I do claim to have shown is that our conceptualization of beauty—as that term appears in everyday usage—must expand considerably to embrace the various types reviewed here. These types include not just aesthetic beauty, as traditionally emphasized, but also beauty of function, symbol, achievement, image, nature, relationships, and character. There may be other varieties of beauty, yet to be discovered, and such potential discoveries should serve as the focus of future research. But on the evidence presented here, at a minimum, the types just mentioned all deserve to be included in any emergent conceptualization.

Directions for Future Research

Simple logic suggests three major possibilities for new directions in future research on methods and topics related to those addressed in the present report—namely, extensions of the CPE toward new applications to the study of beauty, applications of alternative methods to the study of beauty, and extensions of the CPE to new content areas. Let us look briefly at each avenue for new directions in future research.

Extensions of the CPE Toward New Applications to the Study of Beauty

First—as would apply to marketing- or consumer-research efforts of all kinds and descriptions—the findings reported here would benefit from further validation on additional, more representative samples drawn from the general population of American consumers, as well as from cross-cultural studies extending the present approach to the global market of consumers around the world. My premonitions suggest that the types of beauty identified here will adequately characterize the responses of U.S. consumers at large, but that clear differences in underlying dimensions and major types of beauty may well appear when comparing cultures at the global level. For example, more collectivist as opposed to individualistic societies might give greater weight to various social aspects of beauty. Or cultures holding more spiritual as opposed to secular worldviews might tend to emphasize a sacred or idealistic component not found so prominently in Western societies. And so on.

Applications of Alternative Methods to the Study of Beauty

Second, it should be obvious that the CPE is not the only method appropriate to the study of beauty as it affects consumers in America and beyond. Other qualitative techniques drawn from anthropology (e.g., ethnography), sociology (e.g., participant observation), or psychology (e.g., depth interviews) would surely cast illuminating light on the nature and types of beauty experienced in the lives of consumers. Further, quantitative efforts to measure and calibrate the underlying dimensions of beauty—for example, by means of multidimensional scaling or other psychometric approaches—might well lead toward the construction of a multidimensional beauty space that might clarify the structural relationships among various types of beauty-related consumption experiences. Here as elsewhere, convergence or "triangulation" among a pluralistic variety of techniques and procedures appears to offer promising possibilities to pursue (Hirschman and Holbrook 1992).

Extensions of the CPE to New Content Areas

Third, the approach advocated here—that is, the CPE—has already been applied to a number of content areas ranging from the experience of living in New York City (Holbrook and Kuwahara 1998) to the consumption of services provided by pets viewed as animal companions (Holbrook et al. 2001). Further extensions to new content areas might follow any number of disparate paths. One such path that would hold special interest for me might involve the comparison of beauty to *other types* of customer value such as efficiency, excellence, status, esteem, fun, ethics, and spirituality (Holbrook 1999b). As a start, it would be quite interesting to investigate whether the major types of value identified by logical analysis (*langue*) appear as key categories in the everyday discourse of ordinary consumers (*parole*). Extrapolating the findings of the present study would suggest the possibility that our psycholinguistic performance of ordinary discourse (*parole*) might encompass a considerable complexity of richness and gradations in meaning not anticipated by our linguistic competence in logical abstraction (*langue*).

Conclusion

In closing, I must mention a caveat—heavily emphasized in previous work on customer value (Holbrook 1994, 1999b)—that has been implicit but not stressed in everything I have said to this point. Specifically, it should be clear that any consumption experience in general and all those covered in the present study in particular can—indeed, normally will—partake of multiple types of beauty simultaneously. In classifying the vignettes and photographs discussed earlier, I have allocated each example to the one category that it seemed most clearly to illustrate. However, the reader will have noticed that most illustrations have tended to impinge on multiple categories in the typology. Thus, we find automobiles that function flawlessly but that are also aesthetically pleasing to look at while additionally enhancing one's public image. We find natural scenes that serve symbolically to evoke a pleasant association while also conveying a sense of nature's grandeur and the joyous harmony of personal interactions in tranquil locales. We find images of achievement that transpire amidst scenic splendor in the company of people with the highest moral character. In short, everywhere we look, we find examples of how different types of beauty commingle in the enactment of any given consumption experience.

Based on this commingling, philosophers would say that the eight types of beauty we have identified both conceptually and empirically are potentially *compresent* in any given situation—

that is, that they exist together, simultaneously, in the fabric of our lives as consumers. Our everyday language—our common discourse, as explored in the responses of informants—tells us that we intuitively recognize this compresence of multifaceted types of beauty as central to the essence of the human condition. In this, it appears, we are blessed. We find beauty, in multifarious and variegated forms, everywhere in our lives as consumers. Clearly, we would not want it any other way.

Appendix 1
Mini-Project, B8601 and B9601–38, Spring 2000

As anticipated at the end of the introduction to the syllabus, the members of B8601 and B9601–38 are invited to offer their overworked and underpaid instructor some much-needed assistance by providing some data for his ongoing research on the subject of experiential consumption. This brief exercise should be useful to the class members in conveying a sense of interpretivistic methods—both subjective personal introspection and ethnographic approaches—as sources of insights into the consumption experience, in encouraging an enhanced understanding of photographic approaches to collecting data, and in reviewing material potentially relevant to the class projects.

Specifically, each class member is requested to collect a small amount of data (1) from yourself and (2) from a couple of other consumers of your acquaintance. These other consumers can be friends, neighbors, spouses, significant others, siblings, parents, relatives, colleagues at work, et cetera. Where convenient, the latter should differ from yourself in age, gender, occupation, income, education, and/or as many other characteristics as possible. They should *not* be other students. And you should *not* discuss your answers with each other beforehand.

Each informant (yourself plus the other two consumers) is asked to take a couple of *photographs* that represent "What Beauty Means to Me in My Daily Life" or "What I Find Beautiful in the World Around Me" and to explain these photos via *a brief paragraph* that indicates their significance. In other words, working independently, you and the two other informants should reflect deeply on your feelings about what you consider to be beautiful in your daily existence. You should think of some scene that captures the essence of what beauty means to you. You should then take at least *two* photos of the scene in question (preferably from two somewhat different angles and/or set up in two somewhat different ways so that if one view does not work well, the other might be more successful). You and the other two informants should then write a brief paragraph in which you *describe* the relevant scene that captures the essence of your feelings about beauty and in which you convey *why* you have selected this particular scene. You should then return the three paragraphs and the cameras to the instructor so that the next class member can use them as soon as possible. *Please* be absolutely *sure* to return the paragraphs and cameras *within one week* at the most.

When taking the photographs and writing the paragraphs, both you and your other two informants should carefully adhere to the following guidelines:

1. Please be sure to take the photo in a place that is illuminated by a reasonable amount of light. Outdoors in the sun is good. Indoors in a brightly lit room is OK. Down in the subway in the dark is a bad idea.
2. Please be sure always to use the flash—even if you are outdoors in bright light. This will help to eliminate shadows or dark patches on nearby objects. But please also do not turn the flash on when you are not using it because this will wear out the batteries.

3. Please write your descriptive paragraph explaining your view of "What Beauty Means to Me" in the space provided. Please be sure to include the relevant camera and print numbers so that it will be easier to match each paragraph with the relevant pictures. Please do not forget to include your age, your gender, your occupation, your nationality, your name, and your signature (which will be kept entirely confidential in every way).

4. Both you and your two other informants should please be aware that your words may be so profound and/or your picture(s) so striking that the instructor will want to quote or reproduce them in some published form. In the event that this happens, your name will *not* be used. So please do not worry that any of your secrets will be revealed publicly. However, to make things legal (1) please sign the permission statement at the end of the space provided for your paragraph; also, (2) if for any reason you include any other people in the photo(s), please have them also sign the permission statement to the effect that their photo can be used.

Members of B8601 or B9601–38 should please be *sure* to return the written paragraphs from yourself plus two other informants and the cameras *within one week* at the most. This is very important to ensure that everyone gets a chance to use the cameras (in both classes) and so that the instructor will have time to work with these materials in hopes of sharing them with you on the last day of class. The goal is to share the photos and some interpretive comments with the class before the end of the term. So, please, let's *get moving*! This should be *fun*!

MANY THANKS to all class members for their help on this project!!!

Acknowledgments

The author thanks Professors John Schouten and Barbara Stern for their helpful comments on an earlier draft of this article. He also gratefully acknowledges the support of the Columbia Business School's Faculty Research Fund.

References

Appel, Alfred, Jr. (1993), *The Art of Celebration: Twentieth-Century Painting, Literature, Sculpture, Photography, and Jazz.* New York: Knopf.

Arnheim, Rudolf (1971), *Entropy and Art: An Essay on Disorder and Order.* Berkeley: University of California Press.

Arnould, Eric J. and Linda L. Price (1993), "River Magic: Extraordinary Experience and the Extended Service Encounter," *Journal of Consumer Research*, 20 (June), 24–45.

Beardsley, Monroe C. (1967), "Aesthetics, History of," in *The Encyclopedia of Philosophy*, Volume 1, Paul Edwards, ed. New York: Macmillan, 18–35.

Becker, Howard S. (1986), "Photography and Sociology," in *Doing Things Together: Selected Papers*, Howard S. Becker, ed. Evanston, IL: Northwestern University Press, 221–72.

——— (1995), "Visual Sociology, Documentary Photography, and Photojournalism: It's (Almost) All a Matter of Context," *Visual Sociology*, 10, 5–14.

Belk, Russell W., ed. (1991), *Highways and Buyways: Naturalistic Research from the Consumer Behavior Odyssey.* Provo, UT: Association for Consumer Research.

Belk, Russell W., John F. Sherry, Jr., and Melanie Wallendorf (1988), "A Naturalistic Inquiry into Buyer and Seller Behavior at a Swap Meet," *Journal of Consumer Research*, 14 (March), 449–70.

Berlyne, Daniel E. (1971), *Aesthetics and Psychobiology.* New York: Appleton-Century-Crofts.

Birkhoff, George D. (1933), *Aesthetic Measure.* Cambridge, MA: Harvard University Press.

Bloch, Peter H. (1995), "Seeking the Ideal Form: Product Design and Consumer Response," *Journal of Marketing*, 59 (July), 16–29.

Bourgeois, Louise (1998), "Sunday Afternoons: A Conversation and a Remark on Beauty," in *Uncontrollable Beauty: Toward a New Aesthetics*, Bill Beckley with David Shapiro, eds. New York: Allworth Press, 331–41.

Celsi, Richard L., Randall L. Rose, and Thomas W. Leigh (1993), "An Exploration of High-Risk Leisure Consumption through Skydiving," *Journal of Consumer Research*, 20 (June), 1–23.

Chomsky, Noam (1965), *Aspects of the Theory of Syntax*. Cambridge, MA: MIT Press.

Collier, James, Jr. (1967), *Visual Anthropology: Photography as a Research Method*. New York: Holt, Rinehart and Winston.

Collier, James, Jr. and Malcolm Collier (1986), *Visual Anthropology: Photography as a Research Method* (rev. and expanded ed.). Albuquerque: University of New Mexico Press.

Etcoff, Nancy (1999), *Survival of the Prettiest: The Science of Beauty*. New York: Doubleday.

Eysenck, H.J. (1942), "The Experimental Study of the 'Good Gestalt'—A New Approach," *Psychological Review*, 49, 344–64.

Fournier, Susan (1998), "Consumers and Their Brands: Developing Relationship Theory in Consumer Research," *Journal of Consumer Research*, 24 (March), 343–73.

Freud, Sigmund (1990), *Beyond the Pleasure Principle*, James Strachey, ed. New York: W.W. Norton & Company.

Gadamer, Hans-Georg (1975), *Truth and Method*, Garrett Barden and John Cumming, eds. New York: Crossroad.

Garvin, David A. (1988), *Managing Quality: The Strategic and Competitive Edge*. New York: Free Press.

Geertz, Clifford (1973), *The Interpretation of Cultures*. New York: Basic Books.

Harper, Douglas (1988), "Visual Sociology: Expanding Sociological Vision," *The American Sociologist*, 19 (Spring), 54–70.

Heisley, Deborah D. and Sidney J. Levy (1991), "Autodriving: A Photoelicitation Technique," *Journal of Consumer Research*, 18 (December), 257–72.

Hill, Ronald Paul (1991), "Homeless Women, Special Possessions, and the Meaning of 'Home': An Ethnographic Case Study," *Journal of Consumer Research*, 18 (December), 298–310.

Hill, Ronald Paul and Mark Stamey (1990), "The Homeless in America: An Examination of Possessions and Consumption Behaviors," *Journal of Consumer Research*, 17 (December), 303–21.

Hillman, James (1998), "The Practice of Beauty," in *Uncontrollable Beauty: Toward a New Aesthetics*, Bill Beckley with David Shapiro, eds. New York: Allworth Press, 261–74.

Hirschman, Elizabeth C. and Morris B. Holbrook (1992), *Postmodern Consumer Research: The Study of Consumption As Text*. Newbury Park, CA: Sage.

Hofstadter, Douglas R. (1979), *Gödel, Escher, Bach: An Eternal Golden Braid*. New York: Vintage Books.

Holbrook, Morris B. (1984), "Theory Development Is a Jazz Solo: Bird Lives," in *Scientific Method in Marketing: Proceedings of the 1984 AMA Winter Educators' Conference*, Paul F. Anderson and Michael J. Ryan, eds. Chicago: American Marketing Association, 48–52.

——— (1994), "The Nature of Customer Value: An Axiology of Services in the Consumption Experience," in *Service Quality: New Directions in Theory and Practice*, Roland T. Rust and Richard L. Oliver, eds. Thousand Oaks, CA: Sage, 21–71.

——— (1995), *Consumer Research: Introspective Essays on the Study of Consumption*. Thousand Oaks, CA: Sage.

——— (1997a), "Borders, Creativity, and the State of the Art at the Leading Edge," *Journal of Macromarketing*, 17 (Fall), 96–112.

——— (1997b), "Stereographic Visual Displays and the Three-Dimensional Communication of Findings in Marketing Research," *Journal of Marketing Research*, 34 (November), 526–36.

——— (1998a), "Marketing Applications of Three-Dimensional Stereography," *Marketing Letters*, 9 (1), 51–64.

——— (1998b), "Stereo 3D Representations in Postmodern Marketing Research," *Marketing Intelligence & Planning*, 16 (5), 298–310.

————, ed. (1999a), *Consumer Value: A Framework for Analysis and Research*. London: Routledge.

———— (1999b), "Introduction To Consumer Value," in *Consumer Value: A Framework for Analysis and Research*, Morris B. Holbrook, ed. London: Routledge, 1–28.

———— (2003), "Adventures in Complexity: An Essay on Dynamic Open Complex Adaptive Systems, Butterfly Effects, Self-Organizing Order, Coevolution, the Ecological Perspective, Fitness Landscapes, Market Spaces, Emergent Beauty at the Edge of Chaos, and All That Jazz," *Academy of Marketing Science Review*; available at www.amsreview.org.

Holbrook, Morris B., Lauren G. Block, and Gavan J. Fitzsimons (1998), "Personal Appearance and Consumption in Popular Culture: A Framework for Descriptive and Prescriptive Analysis," *Consumption, Markets and Culture*, 2 (1), 1–55.

Holbrook, Morris B. and Takeo Kuwahara (1998), "Collective Stereographic Photo Essays: An Integrated Approach to Probing Consumption Experiences In Depth," *International Journal of Research in Marketing*, 15, 201–21.

Holbrook, Morris B. and John O'Shaughnessy (1988), "On the Scientific Status of Consumer Research and the Need for an Interpretive Approach to Studying Consumption Behavior," *Journal of Consumer Research*, 15 (December), 398–402.

Holbrook, Morris B., Debra Lynn Stephens, Ellen Day, Sarah M. Holbrook, and Gregor Strazar (2001), "A Collective Stereographic Photo Essay on Key Aspects of Animal Companionship: The Truth About Dogs and Cats," *Academy of Marketing Science Review*; available at: www.amsreview.org.

Holbrook, Morris B. and Robert B. Zirlin (1985), "Artistic Creation, Artworks, and Aesthetic Appreciation: Some Philosophical Contributions to Nonprofit Marketing," *Advances in Nonprofit Marketing*, 1, 1–54.

Holt, Douglas (1998), "Does Cultural Capital Structure American Consumption?" *Journal of Consumer Research*, 25 (June), 1–25.

Hospers, John (1967), "Aesthetics, Problems of," in *The Encyclopedia of Philosophy*, Volume 1, Paul Edwards, ed. New York: Macmillan, 35–56.

Lewis, C.I. (1946), *An Analysis of Knowledge and Valuation*. La Salle, IL: Open Court.

Martin, Agnes (1998), "Beauty Is the Mystery of Life," in *Uncontrollable Beauty: Toward a New Aesthetics*, Bill Beckley with David Shapiro, eds. New York: Allworth Press, 399–402.

McCracken, Grant (1986), *The Long Interview*. Thousand Oaks, CA: Sage.

McEvilley, Thomas (1998), "Doctor Lawyer Indian Chief: 'Primitivism' in Twentieth-Century Art at the Museum of Modern Art in 1984," in *Uncontrollable Beauty: Toward a New Aesthetics*, Bill Beckley with David Shapiro, eds. New York: Allworth Press, 149–66.

Meyer, Leonard B. (1956), *Emotion and Meaning in Music*. Chicago: University of Chicago Press.

———— (1967), *Music, the Arts, and Ideas*. Chicago: University of Chicago Press.

Morris, Charles (1946), *Signs, Language, and Behavior*. New York: Braziller.

Munro, Thomas (1962), "Aesthetics," in *Dictionary of Philosophy*, Dagobert D. Runes, ed. Totowa, NJ: Littlefield, Adams & Co., 6.

Norman, Donald A. (1988), *The Design of Everyday Things*. New York: Doubleday (Currency).

Rescher, Nicholas (1998), *Complexity: A Philosophical Overview*. New Brunswick, NJ: Transaction.

Richins, Marsha L. (1999), "Possessions, Materialism, and Other-Directedness in the Expression of Self," in *Consumer Value: A Framework For Analysis and Research*, Morris B. Holbrook, ed. London: Routledge, 85–104.

Ricoeur, Paul (1976), *Interpretation Theory: Discourse and the Surplus of Meaning*. Fort Worth: The Texas Christian University Press.

———— (1981), *Hermeneutics and the Human Sciences: Essays on Language, Action and Interpretation*, John B. Thompson, ed. and trans. Cambridge, England: Cambridge University Press.

Rust, Roland T. and Richard L. Oliver, ed. (1994), *Service Quality: New Directions in Theory and Practice*. Thousand Oaks, CA: Sage.

Ryle, Gilbert (1964), "Ordinary Language," in *Ordinary Language*, V.C. Chappell, ed. New York: Dover, 24–40.

Saussure, Ferdinand de (1915, ed. 1966), *Course in General Linguistics*, Wade Baskin, trans. New York: McGraw-Hill.

Schouten, John W. (1991), "Selves in Transition: Symbolic Consumption in Personal Rites of Passage and Identity Reconstruction," *Journal of Consumer Research*, 17 (March), 412–25.

Schouten, John W. and James H. McAlexander (1995), "Subcultures of Consumption: An Ethnography of the New Bikers," *Journal of Consumer Research*, 22 (June), 43–61.

Sircello, Guy (1975), *A New Theory of Beauty*. Princeton, NJ: Princeton University Press.

Solomon, Michael R. (1999), "The Value of Status and the Status of Value," in *Consumer Value: A Framework for Analysis and Research*, Morris B. Holbrook, ed. London: Routledge, 63–84.

Steenkamp, Jan-Benedict E.M. (1989), *Product Quality: An Investigation into the Concept and How It Is Perceived by Consumers*. Assen/Maastricht, The Netherlands: Van Gorcum.

Stolnitz, Jerome (1967), "Beauty," in *The Encyclopedia of Philosophy*, Volume 1, Paul Edwards, ed. New York: Macmillan, 263–66.

Strauss, Anselm and Juliet Corbin (1990), *Basics of Qualitative Research: Grounded Theory Procedures and Techniques*. Newbury Park, CA: Sage.

Thompson, Craig J. and Elizabeth C. Hirschman (1995), "Understanding the Socialized Body: A Post-structuralist Analysis of Consumers' Self-Conceptions, Body Images, and Self-Care Practices," *Journal of Consumer Research*, 22 (September), 139–53.

Turner, Frederick (1991), *Beauty: The Value of Values*. Charlottesville: University Press of Virginia.

Wagner, Janet (1999), "Aesthetic Value: Beauty in Art and Fashion," in *Consumer Value: A Framework for Analysis and Research*, Morris B. Holbrook, ed. London: Routledge, 126–46.

Wallendorf, Melanie and Russell W. Belk (1987), *Deep Meaning in Possessions*, videotape. Cambridge, MA: Marketing Science Institute.

Welish, Marjorie (1998), "Contratemplates," in *Uncontrollable Beauty: Toward a New Aesthetics*, Bill Beckley with David Shapiro, eds. New York: Allworth Press, 61–73.

Wolf, Naomi (1992), *The Beauty Myth: How Images of Beauty Are Used Against Women*. New York: Anchor.

Zaltman, Gerald (1997), "Rethinking Market Research: Putting People Back In," *Journal of Marketing Research*, 34 (November), 424–37.

——— (2003), *How Customers Think: Essential Insights into the Mind of the Market*. Boston: Harvard Business School Press.

Zeithaml, Valerie A. (1988), "Consumer Perceptions of Price, Quality, and Value: A Means-End Model and Synthesis of Evidence," *Journal of Marketing*, 52, 2–22.

Zeithaml, Valerie A., A. Parasuraman, and Len Berry (1990), *Delivering Quality Service: Balancing Customer Perceptions and Expectations*. New York: Free Press.

CHAPTER 3

CONSUMER INFORMATION ACQUISITION

A Review and an Extension

LAN XIA AND KENT B. MONROE

Abstract

Consumer information search has been an enduring interest of consumer behavior researchers as well as marketers for over three decades. The majority of this research assumes that consumers know what product they want and the purpose of search is to find the appropriate brand. Also, the research also implicitly assumes that there have been no other information acquisition activities prior to the decision to purchase the product. Direct information search is one way that consumers acquire information. However, people also acquire information through more casual information-acquisition activities such as looking at retail display windows or scanning newspaper advertisements and/or through incidental exposure to information such as clicking the wrong link online, passing a roadside sign while driving, or walking through the aisles in a store. Although consumers may not actively seek specific information during such casual activities, their senses are operating, allowing information to be obtained. Moreover, they may use such information without intention and awareness in their subsequent purchase decisions. These more casual information acquisition activities are referred to as browsing.

We first review literature on consumer information search, and then the literature on browsing. Since there is little literature on browsing in marketing, our review on browsing integrates literature from library science and information systems. Third, based on these two reviews, we propose an extended consumer information acquisition framework. Finally, we outline relevant substantive and methodological issues for future research.

Introduction

Consumers draw on available and accessible information when making purchase decisions. How much consumers know about the product or service when they decide to make a purchase and how they obtain this information are important issues. Knowledge of consumer information acquisition is fundamental to understanding buyer behavior, planning marketing communications, and developing strategies and tactics. We begin our review of consumer information acquisition by focusing first on consumer external information search. More importantly, we then extend our understanding of consumer information acquisition activities by including not only those intended, full-attention direct search activities, but also the more casual, less structured, or even nonconscious information-acquisition activities that are conceptualized as consumer browsing behaviors.

Consumer information search has been an enduring interest of consumer behavior researchers as well as marketers for over three decades. Although there is still vagueness concerning what information search behavior really is, implicitly it refers to "direct" search. The majority of research in consumer information search has been conducted at the brand level. Such research assumes that consumers know what product they want and the purpose of search is to find the appropriate brand. Also, the research implicitly assumes that there have been no other information-acquisition activities prior to the decision to purchase the product. A typical early study on information search would ask respondents how many stores they visited, brochures they looked at, and brands they compared when they bought, for example, a stereo several months ago. Or, researchers would ask respondents to choose a stereo among the options provided and see how and how much they searched for relevant information.

Direct information search is one way that consumers acquire information. However, information acquisition is a much broader concept than mere direct search. In this article, *consumer information acquisition* is defined as the set of activities and behaviors through which consumers obtain product or service information, voluntarily and/or involuntarily, and with or without awareness. Our review indicates a lack of research on this broader concept of consumer information acquisition.

The existing literature on direct information search suggests that consumers conduct little information search before making a purchase decision, which has been a puzzle to marketing researchers for years. We suggest that the approach of direct information search misses consumers' everyday information acquisition activities as well as activities they conduct when no specific purchase task is defined. In addition to direct search, people also acquire information through casual, everyday activities such as looking at a retail display window or scanning a newspaper advertisement and/or through incidental exposure to information such as clicking the wrong link online, passing a highway billboard while driving, going through the cereal aisle to get to the frozen food section in the supermarket, and talking with others. Although consumers may not actively seek specific information during such casual and/or involuntary activities, their senses are operating, receiving information. Moreover, they may use such information in subsequent purchase decisions even if they have not intended to do this when acquiring the information. We will refer to these more casual information-acquisition activities as browsing. This aspect of information-acquisition activities has been shown to be an important aspect of consumer behavior, influencing either further specific direct information search or subsequent decisionmaking.

Browsing is a casual, less structured "looking" activity that people conduct for various reasons. Consumers usually do not have specific relevant information in a directly usable format when they begin their decisionmaking processes. They may need first to identify what information would be relevant for their decision. In some other situations, they may not even have a clear idea of what specific information they seek. In such cases, to locate useful information and/or clarify what information they do need, they first need to scan and screen information. Further, consumers may be in the habit of looking around, or automatically attending to information that interests them. Such scanning, screening, and random looking, although not directly related to a specific purchase, may lead to information acquisition that could be stored in consumers' memory and exert an influence on future purchases. It should be noted that although browsing occurs frequently in shopping, it should not be considered to be synonymous with shopping. Browsing is a part of shopping activities but browsing can also occur outside of shopping activities. For example, people may browse when reading a magazine or passing a billboard on the highway.

Although there is a rich literature on how various factors in the shopping environment influence consumers' shopping activities and we can draw inferences on how these factors influence consumer browsing, browsing as an information-acquisition activity has not been examined extensively in a consumer-behavior context. In this article, we focus on the role of browsing as an information-acquisition vehicle. We propose that browsing is an integral part of consumer information-acquisition activities and it should be integrated with research on consumer (direct) information search to further our understanding of general consumer information-acquisition behaviors. In the following sections, we will first review literature on consumer information search, identifying what we know and what is still missing. Second, we review literature on browsing. Since there is little literature on browsing in marketing, we integrate literature from library science and information systems. Third, based on the review of literature in these two areas, we propose an extended consumer information-acquisition framework. Finally, we outline relevant substantive and methodological issues for future research.

Consumer Information Search

The study of information search started as early as the 1920s when Copeland classified products into convenience goods, shopping goods, and specialty goods (Copeland 1923). Different shopping patterns, including extent of information search, was the basis for such a product categorization. Information search is an important step in consumer decisionmaking and is conceptualized as an integral element of major consumer behavior models (Bettman 1979; Engel et al. 1972; Howard and Sheth 1969). Specifically, information search has been conceptualized as a necessary step following the identification of purchasing goals but occurring before consumers make their final choice.

Theoretical Foundations of Research on Information Search

Srinivasan (1990) summarized the theoretical foundations of external information search into three categories: (1) the economics approach using a cost-benefit framework, (2) the psychological approach of motivation and person-/product-/situation-related variables, and (3) the information processing approach stressing the role of memory and human information-processing limitations. However, since the psychological perspective involves both motivation and ability (i.e., information processing), the theoretical foundations of external information search can be summarized into two broad perspectives: economic and psychological.

Economics Perspective

Early economic theories of information search focused primarily on price while ignoring all other potential product differences. Stigler (1961) argued that buyers inform themselves about prices until the marginal return from gathering more information equals or exceeds the marginal costs of doing the search. It was assumed that, at any time, there will be a frequency distribution of prices for a given product and consumers know the distribution of prices. Because different buyers perceive different costs of and benefits from search, some buyers will be better informed than others. The existence of less-informed buyers allows some sellers to charge higher prices, leading to a spread or dispersion of prices for similar products. Information search is beneficial especially when this price dispersion is large. It was also assumed that consumers are perfect information processors and would guide their search by determining the "optimal amount of search." Essentially, buyers need to just keep searching until they find the price that is sufficiently low and any benefit of further search will be offset by the additional search cost. To decide whether or not to search further, consumers would have to know the cost and return of additional search.

Stigler's model may apply when consumers know the exact product they want to buy and merely want to find the lowest price for that item. But even in such situations, they may not be able to execute the proposed price search because the distribution of sellers' prices is usually unknown. Therefore, the model represents an oversimplified situation compared with the general purchasing context where consumers compare several products that differ not only in price but also in quality.

Nelson (1970) extended Stigler's model by acknowledging that consumers may not have full information about prices of products. More importantly, he indicated product quality may vary and product-quality information is even more difficult to obtain compared to price information. Categorizing products into search or experience goods, he suggested that consumer information search strategies vary according to these different types of goods. For search goods, consumers can evaluate their quality prior to purchase or use by searching for information. For experience goods, consumers obtain quality information only after using or consuming them. This experience then provides quality information for their next purchase. However, since quality may not be easily detected on initial trial (e.g., durable products), consumers may also make inferences of quality based on price or other external information (Monroe 2003).

The cost-benefit framework that developed from the economic objective of utility maximization is well accepted and has been used to explain the extent of consumer information search. Cost-related factors such as time and transportation cost (i.e., traveling to the store and time spent to process information) reduce extent of search whereas benefit-related factors such as reduced financial risk (i.e., risk of paying a higher amount of money) enhance extent of search.

Later theories and research accommodated product as well as consumer individual differences (e.g., Klein and Ford 2003; Ratchford 1982). In these developments, consumers' potential gain from information is a function of their preferences and valuations of the product. Also, search activities vary according to dispersion of product class attributes, consumers' prior information, cost of accessing information, consumers' opportunity cost, and education. Consumers form reservation utilities based on these factors and their search activity is guided by these reservation utilities. Any utility equal to or above a predetermined cutoff value would be acceptable. The concept of reservation utility implies that when information is costly, accepting a satisfactory choice actually may represent optimizing behavior. However, the model could only make empirical predictions under strict conditions when consumers have correct prior information about the utility distribution of alternatives (Ratchford 1982).

In summary, the economic approach to consumer information search typically assumes that (a) there is a frequency distribution of product prices that are offered by sellers, (b) consumers know the distribution and search to find the lowest price, and (c) consumers are perfect information processors and will search until the optimal point where the marginal cost of search is equal to the marginal return of search. Although the economic modeling approach has the advantage of parsimony, these assumptions are not realistic and cannot be met in the real marketplace. For example, consumers' individual differences in terms of preferences for search activities, and social as well as psychological factors, would inevitably influence perceptions of benefits and costs. Therefore, incorporating psychological perspectives to understand information-search behavior is desirable.

Psychological Perspective

The psychology literature uses an information-processing approach to investigate consumers' capacity and motivation to search. Research has long recognized that instead of being perfect information processors, human beings have limited cognitive capacity for processing information (Miller 1956). The extent of information search is determined by consumers' motivation to search (i.e., how much they already know and how much they would like to know about the products/services) but constrained by their cognitive capacity to process information. Therefore, consumers are guided by the trade-off between motivation and availability of resources when searching for information.

Motivation is one of the major components of the psychological models. Similarly, consumer-behavior models view motivation as the drive for information-search activities (Engel et al. 1972; Howard and Sheth 1969). These models conceptualize that consumers have various goals to accomplish, and these goals provide consumers with motivation to search both internally and externally (Wright 1975). Factors influencing motivation, such as product involvement, would be potential determinants of extent of information search. Consumer memory connects internal search and external search, and factors such as consumer prior knowledge, familiarity with the product, and experiences are therefore important determinants of search.

On the other hand, the psychological perspective makes it clear that the economic assumption of unlimited information processing resources is unrealistic. Because of this cognitive constraint, consumers may not search up to the optimal point. Since decision tasks are often more complex relative to the cognitive capacity available, consumers tend to use simplifying heuristics such as price or brand name. These heuristics help consumers simplify their purchase problems, and they become satisfied with a reasonable choice. In addition, consumer-behavior researchers also have studied the influence of personal, product, and situational variables on search activities, resulting in a rich body of empirical work.

We recognize these two different theoretical foundations of research on information search but believe that the two approaches are complementary rather than competitive (Moorthy, Ratchford, and Talukdar 1997). Researchers from different backgrounds (whether economics or psychology) have used different methodologies to attack the same research question, thereby enriching our knowledge of the topic.

What Do We Know about Consumer Information Search?

Search Determinants

Empirical research on consumer information search has been wide ranging. One focus of early research was on determinants or correlates of the amount and extent of information search. Since numerous variables have been investigated, it is important to categorize such variables as a basis for organizing previous empirical studies. The early classifications of Newman (1977) and Bettman (1979) included cost-benefit factors as well as personal characteristics. Other classifications include Moore and Lehmann (1980) and Schmidt and Spreng (1996). In this article, we adopt Moore and Lehmann's five basic categories but modify the subcategories to accommodate more recent research. It should be noted that factors within each category are not mutually exclusive. Indeed, the same factor may be in different categories depending on the context of an investigation. Empirical studies investigating the influence of various factors on the extent of external search are summarized in Table 3.1.

Table 3.1

Determinants of Amount/Extent of Consumer External Information Search

Variables	Factors	Relationship with search[a]	Product studied	Study
I. Market environment				
Scope	Number of alternatives	+	Apparel, furniture	Cox and Rich 1964
	Complexity of alternatives, product differences	+	Appliances, cars	Claxton, Fry, and Portis 1974
	City size of residence	+	Cars	Newman and Staelin 1972
	Size of set	+	Cars	Punj and Staelin 1983
		0	Appliances, cars	Newman and Staelin 1972
	Number of information dimensions available	+		Capon and Burke 1977
	Store location (distance)	–	Apparel	Dommermuth and Cundiff 1967
	Store distribution (distance)	–	Apparel, furniture	Cort and Dominguez 1977
	Store distribution (distance)	–	Nonfood items	Bucklin 1969
	Difficulty of store comparison	–	Grocery	Urbany, Dickson, and Kalapurakal 1996
Variation	Perceived price dispersion	+	Nonfood items	Bucklin 1969
	Perceived dispersion of price	+	Grocery	Putrevu and Ratchford 1997
		+	Grocery	Urbany, Dickson, and Kalapurakal 1996
	Variation in offering	+	TV	Duncan and Olshavsky 1982
	Variation in sources of supply	+	TV	Duncan and Olshavsky 1982
	(Product) variation in suitability, quality, price, and style	+	Appliances	Dommermuth 1965
	Perceived variance in retail operations	+	Television	Duncan and Olshavsky 1982
	Interbrand differences	+	Bank service	Maute and Forrester 1991
Other aspects of information	Presentation format: visual cues	0 (More depth of search and less breadth of search)	Pocket camera	Painton and Gentry 1985

Presentation format: memory vs. stimuli	Memory leads to fewer attributes considered; stimuli lead to fewer brands considered	Pocket camera	Painton and Gentry 1985
Information discrepancy	Inverted "U"	Automobiles	Ozanne, Brucks, and Grewal 1992
Bargainable attribute (information uncertainty)	(–) More variability	Microcomputer	Brucks and Schurr 1990
Information uncertainty	(+) Also acquired early	Typewriter/printer	Simonson, Huber, and Payne 1988
Relative uncertainty (prior belief of the structure of the information environment)	Inverted "U"	Automobiles	Moorthy, Ratchford, and Talukdar 1997
Individual brand uncertainty	+	Automobiles	Moorthy, Ratchford, and Talukdar 1997
Negative information	(+) Also acquired early	Typewriter/printer	Simonson, Huber, and Payne 1988
Descriptive brand name (vs. nondescriptive brand name)	–	Bread	Lehmann and Moore 1980
Opportunities available to consumers to exploit the perceived dispersion by locating coupons	+	Grocery	Putrevu and Ratchford 1997
Attractive alternative	(+) Also acquired early	Typewriter/printer	Simonson, Huber, and Payne 1988
Attribute importance	(+) Also acquired early	Typewriter/printer	Simonson, Huber, and Payne 1988
Attribute quality	(Experience +, search and credence –)	Bank service	Maute and Forrester 1991
Macro context			
Grocery shopping environment	+	Grocery	Putrevu and Ratchford 1997
	Inverted "U"	Grocery	Donovan et al. 1994
Mass media	–	Apparel	Dommermuth and Cundiff 1967

(continued)

Table 3.1 (continued)

Variables	Factors	Relationship with search[a]	Product studied	Study
II. Situational variable				
Time	Time pressure	+	Bread	Moore and Lehmann 1980
	Urgency	–	Appliances, furniture	Katona and Mueller 1955
	Immediate need	–	Appliances	Claxton, Fry, and Portis 1974
		–	Cars, appliances	Newman and Staelin 1972
	Urgent need	0	Cars	Kiel and Layton 1981
	Felt time pressure	0	Grocery	Putrevu and Ratchford 1997
	Time constraint	–	Grocery	Urbany, Dickson, and Kalapurakal 1996
	Time pressure	–	Appliances (multiple)	Beatty and Smith 1987
	Opportunity cost of time	–	Grocery	Putrevu and Ratchford 1997
Financial pressure	Financial pressure	0	Bread	Moore and Lehmann 1980
	Financial pressure	+	Appliances, cars	Claxton, Fry, and Portis 1974
		0 (In-store search)	Grocery	Avery 1996
		(–) (Prestore search)	Grocery	Avery 1996
	Tight budget	0	Cars, appliances	Newman and Staelin 1972
	Budget constraint	+	Grocery	Urbany, Dickson, and Kalapurakal 1996
Social factors	Social pressure	0	Appliances	Katona and Mueller 1955
	Perceived obesity	+	Bread	Moore and Lehmann 1980
	Accountability	+	Personal computer, laptop PC	Lee et al. 1999
	Length of commitment necessary	+	Appliances	Katona and Mueller 1955
Physical and mental conditions	Mobility constraint	–	Grocery	Urbany, Dickson, and Kalapurakal 1996
		–	Grocery	Avery 1996

Factor	Sign	Product	Citation
Other			
Quantity of food, bundle of purchase	+	Grocery	Carlson and Gieseke 1983
Store loyalty/preference	–	Nonfood items	Bucklin 1969
Store image, store environment	–	Appliances	Rousseau 1982
Presence of young children	–	Grocery	Urbany, Dickson, and Kalapurakal 1996
Special buying opportunities	"+/–"	Appliances	Katona and Mueller 1955
III. Potential payoff/ product importance			
Price			
Price	+	Nonfood items	Bucklin 1969
	+	Apparel	Dommermuth 1965
	+	Apparel	Dommermuth and Cundiff 1967
	+	Appliances	Katona and Mueller 1955
	+	Cars	Kiel and Layton 1981
	+	Appliances	Newman and Staelin 1972
	0	Cars	Newman and Staelin 1972
		Small appliances	Udell 1966
Price reduction	+	Bread	Lehmann and Moore 1980
Expectation of obtaining a better price	+	Cars	Kiel and Layton 1981
Durable (vs. nondurable) product	+		Capon and Burke 1977
Social visibility			
Style and appearance importance	+	Furniture, appliances	Claxton, Fry, and Portis 1974
	+	Apparel	Cox and Rich 1964
	+	Apparel	Dommermuth and Cundiff 1967
	+	Furniture	LeGrand and Udell 1964
	0	Cars	Newman and Staelin 1972
Perceived risk			
Perceived risk	0	Nondurables	Jacoby, Chestnut, and Fisher 1978
	+		Capon and Burke 1977
	+	n/a	Dowling and Staelin 1994
	+	TV	Duncan and Olshavsky 1982
Perception of product risk	0	Cars	Kiel and Layton 1981
Uncertainty: choice uncertainty	+	Appliances	Wilkie and Dickson 1985

(continued)

Table 3.1 (continued)

Variables	Factors	Relationship with search[a]	Product studied	Study
	Uncertainty: knowledge uncertainty	0	Appliances	Wilkie and Dickson 1985
	Perceived risk for self-use	−	Bread	Moore and Lehmann 1980
	Acceptable risk level	−	n/a	Dowling and Staelin 1994
Product importance	Product importance	+	Furniture, appliances	Claxton, Fry, and Portis 1974
	Attribute importance	+	Phonograph record	Holbrook and Maier 1978
		+	Bread	Lehmann and Moore 1980
	Product class importance	+	Nondurables	Jacoby, Chestnut, and Fisher 1978
	Importance of search	+	Grocery	Urbany, Dickson, and Kalapurakal 1996
IV. Knowledge and experience Subjective knowledge	High perceived knowledge	+	Cars	Kiel and Layton 1981
	Usable prior knowledge	−	Cars	Punj and Staelin 1983
	Subjective knowledge	−	Nutrition information, birth control	Radecki and Jaccard 1995
	Length and breadth	−	Automobile	Hughes, Tinie, and Naert 1969
		−	Bread	Moore and Lehmann 1980
Objective knowledge	Attribute range knowledge	(+) more variability	Microcomputer	Brucks and Schurr 1990
	Product class knowledge: objective knowledge	(+) do not support the "U"- shape relationship	Sewing machine	Brucks 1985
	Product class knowledge	−	Appliances (multiple)	Beatty and Smith 1987
	Knowledge about product	(+) opposite of prediction	Nonfood items	Bucklin 1969

111

Category	Variable	Direction	Product	Reference
	Objective knowledge	0	Nutrition information, birth control	Radecki and Jaccard 1995
Knowledge of how to search	Knowledge of town	+	Homes	Hempel 1969
	Prior memory structure	0	Cars	Punj and Staelin 1983
	Human capital: knowledge capital	+	Grocery	Putrevu and Ratchford 1997
	Human capital: information capital	–	Grocery	Putrevu and Ratchford 1997
	Human capital: knowledge	+	Grocery	Urbany, Dickson, and Kalapurakal 1996
	Human capital: investment search	+	Grocery	Urbany, Dickson, and Kalapurakal 1996
	Human capital: time-management skills	+	Grocery	Urbany, Dickson, and Kalapurakal 1996
Experience	Experience	0	Cars	Bennett and Mandell 1969
	Number of previous usage	–	Bread	Moore and Lehmann 1980
	Times product class purchased	–	Appliances, cars	Newman and Staelin 1972
	Prior usage of product class	–	Furniture, appliances	Claxton, Fry, and Portis 1974
	Past experience	–	Cars	Kiel and Layton 1981
	Past experience	0	Bread	Moore and Lehmann 1980
	Successive purchasing occasion	–	Bread	Lehmann and Moore 1980
		+	Nondurables (cereal)	Jacoby, Chestnut, and Fisher 1978
	Repurchase of same brand	0	Cars	Kiel and Layton 1981
	Repurchase with same dealer	–	Cars	Kiel and Layton 1981
	Positive experience	0	Appliances	Katona and Mueller 1955
		–	Cars, appliances	Bennett and Mandell 1969
	Experience	Inverted "U" shape (decrease no. of alternatives search but increase no. of attributes search)	Automobiles	Moorthy, Ratchford, and Talukdar 1997

(continued)

Table 3.1 (continued)

Variables	Factors	Relationship with search[a]	Product studied	Study
Satisfaction and brand loyalty	Experience	0	Homes	Hempel 1969
	Satisfaction (with past results)	–	Cars	Bennett and Mandell 1969
	Satisfaction	– (With dealer search)	Cars	Kiel and Layton 1981
	Attitudinal brand loyalty	–	Nondurables	Jacoby, Chestnut, and Fisher 1978
	Brand loyal	(–) (Avoid sources that may favor other choices)	Cars	Hughes, Tinie, and Naert 1969
	Switchers	+	Cars	Hughes, Tinie, and Naert 1969
V. Individual differences				
Demographics and psychographics	Education	+	Furniture, appliances	Claxton, Fry, and Portis 1974
		+	Homes	Hempel 1969
		+	Appliances	Katona and Mueller 1955
		–	Sports shirts	Katona and Mueller 1955
		+	Cars, appliances	Newman and Staelin 1972
		+	Ranges of products	Schaninger and Sciglimpaglia 1981
		+	Cars	Kiel and Layton 1981
	Income	–	Small appliances	Udell 1966
		–	Cars	Kiel and Layton 1981
		0	Range of products	Schaninger and Sciglimpaglia 1981
		+	Furniture, appliances	Claxton, Fry, and Portis 1974
	Wealth/income	+	Food	Bucklin 1969

Variable	Relationship	Product category	Study
Hourly wage	—	Grocery	Avery 1996
Age	—	Grocery	Putrevu and Ratchford 1997
	—	Homes	Hempel 1969
	—	Cars	Kiel and Layton 1981
	—	Appliances	Katona and Mueller 1955
	—	Bread	Moore and Lehmann 1980
Marital status: married (vs. single)	0	Care	Kiel and Layton 1981
Gender	+	Food	Bucklin 1969
Household size (large appetite of household)	+	Nonfood items	Bucklin 1969
Perceived role (household role)	—	Range of products	Schaninger and Sciglimpaglia 1981
Household ownership: owner (vs. nonowner)	—	Food	Bucklin 1969
Liberal women	—	Food	Bucklin 1969
Social standing	—	Food	Bucklin 1969
Transient social standing	+	Cars	Kiel and Layton 1981
Personality Self-confidence	+	Range of products	Schaninger and Sciglimpaglia 1981
Self-esteem	0	Nutrition information, birth control	Radecki and Jaccard 1995
Self-esteem	0	Range of products	Schaninger and Sciglimpaglia 1981
Rigidity	—	Range of products	Schaninger and Sciglimpaglia 1981
Cognitive style: simplifier (vs. optimizer)	0 (For purposeful search)		Steenkamp and Baumgartner 1992
Optimal stimulation level	(+) (For exploratory search)		Steenkamp and Baumgartner 1992

(continued)

Table 3.1 (continued)

Variables	Factors	Relationship with search[a]	Product studied	Study
	Dependence on others	0	Cars, appliances	Newman and Staelin 1972
	Tolerance for ambiguity	+	Range of products	Schaninger and Sciglimpaglia 1981
	Self-monitoring	0	Nutrition information, birth control	Radecki and Jaccard 1995
Ability	Ability to judge	+	Television	Duncan and Olshavsky 1982
Approach to search	Shopping enjoyment	+	Grocery	Urbany, Dickson, and Kalapurakal 1996
	Enjoyment	+	Grocery	Putrevu and Ratchford 1997
	Market maven motives	+	Appliances	Katona and Mueller 1955
	Attitude toward shopping	+	Grocery	Urbany, Dickson, and Kalapurakal 1996
	Positive attitude toward search	+	Appliances (multiple)	Beatty and Smith 1987
		+	Cars	Kiel and Layton 1981
		+	Cars	Punj and Staelin 1983
	Perceived search benefits	+	Television	Duncan and Olshavsky 1982
Involvement	Involvement	+	Personal computer, laptop PC	Lee et al. 1999
		-	Grocery	Avery 1996
	Product class involvement	+	Automobiles	Moorthy, Ratchford, and Talukdar 1997
	Ego involvement	0	Appliances (multiple)	Beatty and Smith 1987
	Purchase involvement	+	Appliances (multiple)	Beatty and Smith 1987
	Personal relevance	0	Nutrition information, birth control	Radecki and Jaccard 1995
	Frame of reference	+	Nutrition information, birth control	Radecki and Jaccard 1995
	Absence of spending money as a child	+	Food	Bucklin 1969

[a] + represents positive relationship, − represents negative relationship, and 0 represents nonsignificant relationship.

Market Environment. Factors in this category can be further organized into three subcategories. One is the *scope* of market environment, which includes factors such as number and complexity of alternatives and store distribution. The effects of these factors correspond to a general cost-benefit (both economic and psychological cost and benefit) framework. For example, when information varies and the amount of information is large, the need or benefit of search increases (Claxton, Fry, and Portis 1974; Cox and Rich 1964; Newman and Staelin 1972; Punj and Staelin 1983). However, increased obstacles of search such as store locations (i.e., longer distances between stores) will impede such search tendency because of the increased cost of time and transportation (Bucklin 1969; Cort and Dominguez 1977; Dommermuth and Cundiff 1967; Urbany, Dickson, and Kalapurakal 1996).

Another subcategory is the *variation* within the market environment, which includes factors such as price dispersion, number of varieties and brands offered within the same product category, and differences among models of the same brand. Large variations may lead to greater uncertainty about which alternative is a good choice; therefore, there will be a higher need and benefit of searching (Bucklin 1969; Dommermuth 1965; Duncan and Olshavsky 1982; Maute and Forrester 1991; Mehta, Rajiv, and Srinivasan 2003; Putrevu and Ratchford 1997).

The last subcategory concerns the *different natures of information* available in the market environment. The effects of this category seem more complicated. Information helps consumers make purchase decisions, but during the process of information search, some information may induce ambiguity, thereby stimulating consumers to search more. However, because of cognitive, time, and energy constraints, they are not likely to consider all information before making their choice, and instead may use heuristics to make inferences.

Situational Variables. Two major situational variables are time and financial pressure (i.e., budget constraint). Time pressure has a negative influence on extent of search (Beatty and Smith 1987; Katona and Mueller 1955; Newman and Staelin 1972; Urbany, Dickson, and Kalapurakal 1996). However, Kiel and Layton (1981) and Putrevu and Ratchford (1997) did not find a statistically significant effect. Financial pressure has had a positive influence on search in some studies (Claxton, Fry, and Portis 1974; Urbany, Dickson, and Kalapurakal 1996), but other studies found no statistically significant effects (Avery 1996; Moore and Lehmann 1980; Newman and Staelin 1972). The inconsistency in the statistical results may be due to factors such as different experiment manipulations, or sample size and composition (Malhotra 1983). Therefore, it may be beneficial to conduct a meta-analysis on the existing studies on the influence of time and financial pressure to obtain an empirical estimate of the effect.

Other situational variables include social pressure, physical and mental conditions, purchase quantity, store image, and presence of children. Social pressure such as negative attitude toward obesity may motivate consumers to search for information for relevant products (e.g., bread) (Moore and Lehmann 1980). Physical conditions such as mobility constraints inhibit search activities (Avery 1996; Urbany, Dickson, and Kalapurakal 1996). Carlson and Gieseke (1983) examined the influence of quantity of (the same kind of) food and different product bundles on search and found product bundle and a higher quantity of product purchase enhance information search. Abdul-Muhmin (1999) found that multiple-item purchases led to more alternative search but less attribute search, and a broader but less in-depth information search. Such findings enrich our understanding of consumer information search because most research has focused on choosing one product from alternatives of the same product class while many real-world decision tasks involve multiple purchases and consumers may evaluate the cost and benefit of search at an overall level.

Potential Payoff/Product Importance. Price has been the most studied factor in information search and it has been found that consumers search more when the product price is high (Bucklin 1969; Dommermuth 1965; Dommermuth and Cundiff 1967; Katona and Mueller 1955; Kiel and Layton 1981; Newman and Staelin 1972; Udell 1966). A higher price may signal the importance of the purchase, enhance consumer involvement, and lead to more extensive search. A look at the products studied shows that the effects of price tend to apply more to durables such as cars and major household appliances than nondurables such as consumer packaged goods, which may be due to the relatively higher price of durables.

Perceived risk is another factor that may enhance information search. That is, information search is an effective means of risk reduction; therefore, higher perceived risk would lead to more information search. While most of the studies concerning risk used it in an absolute sense, Dowling and Staelin (1994) considered "acceptable risk level" to examine the relative effect of perceived risk. A higher acceptable risk level lessens the threats of perceived risk and, therefore, may decrease the extent of information search. Overall, there are mixed findings. A meta-analysis of 100 empirical findings found that fifty-one studies failed to show the positive risk-search association (Gemunden 1985).

Other factors in this category include social visibility, product importance, and psychological factors. All five studies reviewed found that social visibility had a positive effect on search (Claxton, Fry, and Portis 1974; Cox and Rich 1964; Dommermuth and Cundiff 1967; LeGrand and Udell 1964; Newman and Staelin 1972). The social visibility effect tends to apply to products that have physical appearance properties such as apparel, furniture, and cars. Product class importance and attribute importance also show a positive influence on search (Holbrook and Maier 1978; Jacoby, Chestnut, and Fisher 1978). Interestingly, the concept of importance seems to be subjective to each individual consumer because the products studied showed a great variety ranging from nondurables (e.g., groceries) to durables (e.g., appliances). Psychological factors such as accountability enhance tendency of search. When decision makers take responsibility for their choices and/or are required to justify their decisions, they tend to search for more information (Lee et al. 1999; Moore and Lehmann 1980).

Knowledge and Experience. Knowledge is one of the most studied factors in research on external information search and explains a large portion of the variances in searching behaviors (Punj and Staelin 1983). One reason for this effect could be that it represents the interface between internal search and external search (Srinivasan 1990). As Newman and Staelin (1972) pointed out, experience leads to knowledge, which leads to future internal search. Consumers tend to search for information both internally and externally (Bettman 1979). Therefore, what they already know or do not know may signal what they will look for. Also, knowledge facilitates interpretation of new external information.

However, at first glance, empirical research on the influence of knowledge and experience on information search appears to be inconsistent and confusing (Raju, Lonial, and Mangold 1995). Positive effects, negative effects, as well as noneffects or inverted "U" shape effects all have been found. One reason for the variation in empirical findings could be due to the differences in definition and measurement of knowledge and experience. For example, Jacoby, Chestnut, and Fisher (1978) measured experience by number of brand names searched, number of different brands purchased, frequency of consumption, and number of purchases whereas Putrevu and Ratchford (1997) included experience with both grocery shopping and the local market conditions. Radecki and Jaccard (1995) asked subjects how much they felt they knew the topic (subjective) while Brucks and Schurr (1990) gave subjects a test on product-attribute range as an indicator of knowledge (objective). The wide variation in how knowledge has been operationalized suggests that it could be a multidimensional construct and its influence on extent of information search is not straightforward.

Early research assumed knowledge is a single dimension construct and defined it vaguely as "prior knowledge" (Punj and Staelin 1983). The subjective and objective nature of knowledge was not distinguished in its early operationalization. Later research recognized the multidimensional characteristics of knowledge and categorized existing research into three groups: perceived knowledge (what consumers think they know, or subjective knowledge), actual knowledge (what they really know, or objective knowledge), and usage experience (Brucks 1985). It was suggested that both perceived knowledge and actual knowledge influence information search, but perhaps in different ways. When Brucks (1985) found a positive effect of objective knowledge on search (but not the inverted "U" shape) and no statistically significant effect of subjective knowledge, it was suggested that subjective knowledge might not be a valid measure of knowledge. However, Radecki and Jaccard (1995) believed that subjective knowledge is central in information-search behavior. As for experience, Brucks (1985) suggested that it is a different construct from knowledge and it is listed as a separate factor in the knowledge category. In measurement, experience is usually measured by previous consumption and repeat purchases. However, there is overlap between the measurement of experience and knowledge, and they have not been clearly distinguished, especially in early studies (Jacoby, Chestnut, and Fisher 1978; Punj and Staelin 1983).

The majority of studies of consumer knowledge and experience implicitly refer to the domain of product class. Two studies went beyond this domain to include other knowledge. Hempel (1969), examining the influence of subjects' knowledge of a town when searching for homes, found that people with a better knowledge searched more. Punj and Staelin (1983) suggested that other than knowledge that is directly related to product class, knowledge of how to obtain and/or process target information may also help. In other words, "metaknowledge" could also help consumers search for information more efficiently (Wright 2002).

More recently, Putrevu and Ratchford (1997) and Urbany, Dickson, and Kalapurakal (1996) incorporated "human capital," which captures consumer knowledge accumulated over time. Human capital is defined as "the stock of information and knowledge obtained in the past that makes the consumer more productive in the current period" (Putrevu and Ratchford 1997, p. 467). It includes information capital (information about attribute and price) and knowledge capital (knowledge about how to search). It suggests that consumers are not that myopic. They may treat current search as an investment for future purchases and/or use their general knowledge from previous search or purchase experiences to guide their current search. Therefore, knowledge can influence search in both directions. It makes consumers more efficient in terms of locating and processing information, thereby facilitating more extensive search (Shim et al. 2001); but it can also reduce search when the future gains of searching are small (Putrevu and Ratchford 1997; Urbany, Dickson, and Kalapurakal 1996).

To summarize, the research literature shows two types of objective knowledge accumulated over time: market knowledge, which is knowledge of specific products (e.g., price range, attributes of a product class), and knowledge on how to search for information, which may or may not be related to the product class at hand. Product knowledge tends to decrease search while knowledge on how to search can either reduce or enhance search.

As Table 3.1 shows, available empirical research suggests that subjective knowledge has a negative effect, objective knowledge has a positive or inverted "U"-shaped effect, knowledge of how to search for information has either a positive or a negative effect, and experience has a negative effect on the extent of search. Satisfaction and brand loyalty are also included in the knowledge/experience category because they are partly the result of previous experiences with the product/service or attitude developed based on previous experiences. Both factors have a negative effect on further information search.

Individual Differences. Demographic variables are usually included in studies of information search. Education consistently has a positive relation to search. This effect is usually explained by relating education to ability and knowledge to search. Age tends to have a negative effect due to deteriorated cognitive resources. Moreover, although empirical evidence is lacking, aging may be correlated with experience/knowledge, further decreasing the need to search.

Information acquisition may occur during shopping activities. Shopping enjoyment and attitude toward search have a consistently positive influence on search (Beatty and Smith 1987; Duncan and Olshavsky 1982; Katona and Mueller 1955; Kiel and Layton 1981; Punj and Staelin 1983; Putrevu and Ratchford 1997; Urbany, Dickson, and Kalapurakal 1996). This positive effect suggests that information search does not serve only a utility function, but also provides hedonic values at least to some consumers. Shopping can be both work and fun (Arnold and Reynolds 2003; Babin, Darden, and Griffin 1994). Finally, consumer involvement with the purchase has a positive effect on search (Beatty and Smith 1987; Bloch, Sherrell, and Ridgway 1986; Bucklin 1969; Lee et al. 1999; Moorthy, Ratchford, and Talukdar 1997; Radecki and Jaccard 1995).

Other Aspects of Information Search

The above review has focused on the correlates of information search, which comprises the bulk of studies in consumer information search. Jacoby, Chestnut, and Fisher (1978) proposed four general classes of variables for studying information search: search correlates (i.e., search determinants), search statistics, search strategies, and search outcomes. Research on search correlates and search statistics dominate existing empirical research. Search strategies such as across-alternative search versus within brand search, and search sequences are embedded in much of the research on search correlates. Consequently, consumer search strategies need more extensive research.

Moreover, few studies have examined the influence of search on decision outcomes. It has been assumed implicitly that the outcome of more extensive search is a better choice (Hughes, Tinie, and Naert 1969). A similar lack of attention exists in the research on the relationship between searching and postchoice affect and behaviors. Cardozo (1965) found a positive relationship and suggested that search may lead to perceived effort in decision process, which enhances consumers' postchoice satisfaction because of the self-justification mechanism. Applying equity theory, Huppertz, Arenson, and Evans (1978) suggested that search effort is part of consumers' input into an exchange. More information search increases consumers' input; therefore, consumers may perceive the exchange as relatively unfair to them and feel less satisfied. Kennedy and Thirkell (1983), Thirkell and Vredenburg (1982), and Hempel (1969) all found a negative influence of information search on choice satisfaction. They reasoned that extensive information search increased consumers' levels of expectation, increasing the likelihood of disconfirmation between expectation and actual results. This issue between information search and consumer satisfaction is still unresolved, and it needs further research.

How Has Information Search Been Studied?

A variety of methodologies have been used in the research on information search. This methodological diversity could be attributed to both the nature of the research and the two theoretical foundations on which the issue is based. Analytical modeling is the major method used in studies originating from the economic foundation. In addition, data gathered through interviews and/or surveys are used to model the influence of various correlates of search behaviors. On the other hand, studies originating from psychology tend to follow the information-processing paradigm and design experiments to examine the influence of one or a few correlating variables while controlling other variables.

Surveys and Interviews

Surveys and interviews have been criticized as not revealing actual search activities. First of all, consumers may not actually behave as they report because it is based on self-report, not on observation (Beatty and Smith 1987; Kiel and Layton 1981; Putrevu and Ratchford 1997). Self-reports are less reliable because individuals have difficulty recalling the cognitive processes they used (Beatty and Smith 1987; Moore and Lehmann 1980; Newman and Staelin 1972). Memory research suggests that memory can be fallible (Schacter 1999). Self-reports based on subjects' recall could be inaccurate due to weak memory because of shallow processing in encoding, decreased information accessibility over time, and/or temporary inaccessibility of information. Besides, self-reports could also be influenced by social desirability (Wilkie and Dickson 1985). At least one study found little or no correlation between observation-based and survey-based scores of in-store search (Newman and Lockeman 1975). Second, causal inferences cannot be made due to the nature of the method, and it is difficult to account for individual differences (Punj and Staelin 1983). Finally, the method is obtrusive, requires more effort to gather data, and only goal-directed acquisition of information is captured (Wilkie and Dickson 1985).

Survey methods have improved over the years. Early studies using one-time surveys requested subjects to recall their search behaviors about a purchase made as long as eighteen or twenty-four months previously (Claxton, Fry, and Portis 1974; Katona and Mueller 1955). Recognizing the disadvantages of such methods, more recent studies have tried to use a longitudinal approach. For example, Moorthy, Ratchford, and Talukdar (1997) surveyed subjects once during their purchasing processes and a second time after they made the purchase. Such studies have provided richer information than previous ones. In such designs, recall may impose a less serious problem for the researcher.

Experiments

Experimental studies have been criticized as not studying information search behaviors at all (Beatty and Smith 1987). People may behave differently in a controlled setting compared with the real world. In addition, experiments typically capture only intentional acquisition and do not allow other casual and unintentional search activities (Lehmann and Moore 1980). However, experiments offer benefits that survey studies cannot achieve. For example, search patterns other than merely the amount of search can be obtained. Experiments offer opportunities to investigate detailed search processes in addition to providing a quantitative measure of search amount. Lehmann and Moore (1980) used a longitudinal study to validate the method and found that experiments using Information Display Boards (IDB) are particularly good at capturing the effect of changes in the marketing environment such as a price reduction and introduction of new alternatives. Surveys and experiments are complementary rather than competing and can be combined to provide insights from different angles on the issue of consumer information search.

Likewise, the equipment used in experiments has progressed over the years. The IDB was the early equipment used in the laboratories to track subjects' search processes as well as measure the amount of search. IDBs make it easy to detect search patterns but their ecological validity is questioned due to the constraint of what can be displayed, and they do not mimic the actual information environment, nor do they allow motivation to actually search at all. This method has been further computerized. A computerized program can keep the original information matrix (e.g., Mouselab; Johnson, Payne, and Bettman 1988) or can resolve some of the constraints by removing the matrix and asking subjects to input their requests (i.e., search monitor; Brucks 1988). Computerized programs provide advantages over the original IDB such that activity can be monitored more precisely; researchers have tighter control over task variables; researchers can build contingencies into the computer program; a number of factors can easily be incorporated, creating a richer and more complex environment; and researchers can run multiple subjects simultaneously (Brucks 1988; Jacoby et al. 1994). With the development of advanced technologies such as hypertext and the Internet, more sophisticated equipment has been developed. Hauser, Urban, and Weinberg (1993) used a multimedia computer lab to examine subjects' use of different information sources. The multimedia environment provides a richer setting for studying information search. It not only records amount and extent of search, but also provides insights on the search processes such as search sequence and time allocation, without all the constraints that early experiments (using IDB) have. Such a multimedia environment is becoming popular in studying consumer decision processes (Tabatabai 1997). It greatly enhances the level of experimental realism (DiFonzo, Hantula, and Bordia 1998).

Other Methods

Besides the methods mentioned above, verbal protocols have been used in research on human problem solving as well as decisionmaking and information search (Payne 1976). Although there have been debates on the validity of verbal protocols as data (Biehal and Chakravarti 1983), research has shown that verbal protocols can provide valid insights into decision processes (Ericsson and Simon 1980). It is still widely used now in collecting data on human cognitive processes. Eye-tracking equipment was used to monitor subjects' eye movements in order to trace their sequence of information acquisition (Russo and Dosher 1983; Russo and Leclerc 1994). However, it has not been used very frequently because of the cost of the equipment and perceived obtrusiveness. Finally, in terms of empirical modeling, the majority of research has applied additive models. Moorthy, Ratchford, and Talukdar (1997) used a multiplicative model and suggested that it may work better than the additive model.

Dependent Measure of Amount of Search

The amount or extent of search has been the most prevalent dependent measure of search activities. Search activity is typically measured by time spent and quantity of information obtained from various sources (Punj and Staelin 1983). However, there is a wide variation in the operationalization of amount or extent of search. Measures of search activity may include only in-store search, or both in-store and out-of-store or prestore search; it may count one trip or multiple trips; it may or may not include mass media; it may assign scores to different sources and make a composite index, or build different dimensions of search. Such measure variation may contribute to at least part of the inconsistency in empirical findings.

Search scores (indices) can provide an overall picture of search, but they also disguise the nature of search. As Hempel (1969) pointed out, search behavior is multidimensional and the dimensions are not necessarily correlated. For example, the same amount of search within a brand has different managerial implications than across brand or across product class search. Moorthy, Ratchford, and Talukdar (1997) found that as knowledge level increased, subjects decreased the number of alternatives searched but increased the number of attributes searched. Jacoby, Chestnut, and Fisher (1978) had similar findings. Further, searching several sources lightly is different from spending effort to search within one information source (Westbrook and Fornell 1979). And, sequence of search may provide more information about search activities (Mehta, Rajiv, and Srinivasan 2003; Simonson, Huber, and Payne 1988). Different segments of consumers have been identified using search patterns (Claxton, Fry, and Portis 1974) and different information sources (Kiel and Layton 1981). Future research should examine not only the amount of search, but also the search processes and patterns, or sequences.

Summary

Overall, What Do We Know?

The review of the literature on information search indicates that research in the area is both encouraging and frustrating. It is encouraging in the sense that numerous variables have been investigated and consensus can be found for some groups of variables. Our review indicates that amount of consumer information search is influenced by a combination of consumer and environmental factors. Consumers identify their purchase problems and evaluate the internal resources that are available to them (i.e., ability and cognitive resources). These resources guide them in searching behaviors. Consumers' individual differences such as shopping enjoyment further moderate the amount of search.

Knowledge has important effects on information search (Malhotra 1983). This claim is supported by the fact that most of the research regarding consumer knowledge has found statistically significant effects on extent of information search. However, specific effects vary according to how knowledge has been conceptualized. Therefore, further conceptualization of different dimensions of knowledge is needed to determine how knowledge affects information search. And, meta-analyses based on studies from the same distribution may be feasible to provide an empirical estimate of the effect of prior knowledge. Comparatively, the influences of consumers' personality traits such as self-esteem do not produce statistically significant results on the amount of information search.

On the other hand, internal factors further combine with external factors to influence search. Market environment variables such as the amount of available information and variations of such information exert an influence on search. Consumers tend to search more when the amount of information available is large. However, this increasing trend will approach a limit because of cognitive capacity constraints.

In addition, the extent of search is also influenced by situational factors such as the product that is to be purchased, price of the product, and the amount of time available for information search. Product importance consistently has a positive influence on search. Consumers are willing to exert more information search effort when the product to be purchased is of personal importance. A higher product price enhances such importance and positively influences the amount of search. Time pressure seemingly has a negative influence on search. However, it is possible that a moderate amount of time pressure could have a positive effect (Suri and Monroe 2003).

Finally, consumers are social beings. Product purchasing is part of their social activities and the amount of information search is also influenced by social pressures. When the purchase is some kind of "public goods" that has style and appearance dimensions that are visible to others, consumers become more aware of the importance of making a good decision; therefore, they increase their search activities.

As our review shows, many factors have been studied in the context of consumer information search. However, previous research primarily has been descriptive and the underlying mechanisms that influence search need further conceptualization. Stimulation level may be a potential mechanism that mediates search tendency. A moderate level of stimulation or time pressure may encourage consumers to search. For example, in examining the influence of discrepant information on search, Ozanne, Brucks, and Grewal (1992) found that a moderate level of information discrepancy increased search the most. Similarly, some empirical studies on consumer knowledge indicate that consumers with a moderate level of knowledge search for more information compared with low and high level of knowledge consumers.

In addition, the shopping environment, a combination of factors such as retail display, color, background music, and smells, has been found to influence consumer in-store information search activities in an inverted "U"-shape manner. Research results are consistent with the prediction of optimal stimulation level theory (Donovan and Rossiter 1982; Donovan et al. 1994).

Some other factors have not been examined under the stimulation-level theory, but may well be explained by the mechanism. For example, time pressure has been found to decrease search activities. However, time pressure may increase consumers' stimulation levels and, therefore, would have an inverted "U"-shape effect on extent of search. Most studies on the effect of time pressure have compared only situations with and without time pressure. Therefore, the influence of a moderate level of time pressure needs to be further investigated.

What Is Missing?

The variables that have been investigated only explain a small amount of variance in consumer search behaviors (Punj and Staelin 1983). For example, Bucklin's study (1969) explained 24 percent of variance whereas Newman and Staelin (1972) explained only 16 percent (appliances) and 22.7 percent (cars) of the variance. Radecki and Jaccard (1995) achieved a similar level of success (16%). Further, the finding that consumers only exhibit limited search despite availability and low cost of information still puzzles researchers (Grewal and Marmorstein 1994; Kiel and Layton 1981; Moorthy, Ratchford, and Talukdar 1997; Newman and Lockeman 1975). So, the question is: *Do consumers make their decisions based on insufficient information or do they also acquire information through ways other than direct search?*

The literature demonstrates that limited information search does not mean consumers are ignorant (Duncan and Olshavsky 1982; Newman and Staelin 1972). They are reasonably rational in their decisionmaking and they seem to have sufficient knowledge or information when making choices. So why is existing research not explaining a larger part of consumer information-acquisition activities? One reason is the majority of research has been operationalized within the context of brand choice. It is assumed that consumers start to search for information when they know what to buy, and the task is to choose one among alternatives of the same product class (Newman and Lockeman 1975; Punj and Staelin 1983). The measurement of search usually only captures the amount of search within this period of time, ignoring that information acquisition is an ongoing process (Avery 1996; Claxton, Fry, and Portis 1974). Indeed, this problem of "little search" may be because past measures of direct search have not reflected the full extent of buyer information-acquisition activity (Rousseau 1982). Bloch, Ridgway, and Sherrell (1989) suggested that focusing only on the purchasing problem at hand is insufficient and unable to account for information acquisition activity that is recreational or that occurs without a recognized consumption need.

Limiting the study of search to prepurchase settings can underestimate the amount of information consumers have at their disposal when making a purchase, and studies relying on prepurchase contexts may only assess a subset of consumers' total information acquisition activity. Consumers may acquire information, even without intention and awareness, in their everyday lives without a specific goal of buying something, or they may obtain information about one product while shopping for another. They are "investing" in the future while searching for information now, and/or may use their "human capital" instead of explicitly searching when facing a purchase task. Consumers accumulate knowledge over time—not only knowledge of a specific product or brand, but also knowledge of how to find useful information. The issue of how to find specific information is becoming more important as specific information itself may become obsolete very quickly.

Second, if information acquisition is ongoing, how do consumers acquire the information that has not been captured by previous studies? It is suggested that the way consumers capture everyday information and/or "not specifically sought information" may be different from information directly searched. The literature has indirectly indicated that people may not acquire all information in the same way. Painton and Gentry (1985) investigated the nature of the format effect on information acquisition and suggested consumers may use some visual cues to reduce the size of the evoked set first and apply more in-depth search to the remaining alternatives. Putrevu and Ratchford (1997) also mentioned that how much search effort consumers will exert might be the result of early browsing behaviors. Steenkamp and Baumgartner (1992) made a distinction between two types of information search: purposeful search (direct search) and exploratory search (browsing). The former is a means to an end (purchase) whereas the latter is an end in itself (browsing). Exploratory search may well be a way consumers accumulate knowledge for future use when there is no specific purchase goal at hand.

Further, the mechanism underlying direct information search and general everyday information acquisition might also be different. Theoretical foundations of research on direct information search were based on economic cost and benefit, or search motivation and cognitive capacity trade-offs. Urbany, Dickson, and Kalapurakal (1996), recognizing the limitation of such a theoretical foundation, suggested that economic costs and returns are insufficient to explain consumers' information-acquisition behaviors in the marketplace. They tried to apply human capital theory to account for the *habitual nature of search* and for noneconomic returns to search (e.g., enjoyment and opinion leader), under conditions when there is no immediate purchase goal. Also, even though consumers may believe that prices do vary, their motivation to search for lower prices may not increase as otherwise expected if they compare the relative amount of potential savings to the expected price of the product (Grewal and Marmorstein 1994).

On the other hand, a psychological theoretical foundation states that cognitive capacity constrains information search because it is assumed consumers pay full attention when searching for information and that information processing is always conscious and effortful. The majority of empirical studies, especially experiments conducted in the laboratory settings, are based on this assumption. However, research has shown that people acquire information both consciously and nonconsciously. Compared with conscious cognition, nonconscious information acquisition is even faster and structurally more sophisticated (Lewicki, Hill, and Czyzewska 1992). Information acquired without full conscious control is not influenced by divided attention and is not constrained by limited cognitive resources (Baars 1997). Such information may not even be accessible to explicit memory, but it allows the development of knowledge that is unknown to conscious awareness and facilitates task performance (Goschke 1997).

Consumers live in an information-saturated environment. They could be more efficient than researchers think and absorb more information than their limited attention and information processing resources can allow. Existing studies asking subjects to recall their information search activities or asking them to search for information under full attention are unable to detect the information consumers have acquired and used in decision making but that is inaccessible to their explicit memory (Krishnan and Chakravarti 1999). Therefore, to further investigate consumer information acquisition, an extended framework that incorporates activities other than directed search is needed. The framework should incorporate not only goal-directed search, but also less structured search behaviors when there is no immediate purchase goal at hand. The framework should incorporate not only conscious but also nonconscious information acquisition.

We suggest that consumers acquire information through browsing as well as direct search. Including browsing as part of consumer information-acquisition activity extends the existing framework and enriches our understanding of consumer behavior. Next, we review literature from marketing, library science, and computer information systems on browsing and integrate it with information-search literature to form a general information-acquisition framework.

Consumer Browsing

Browsing is a common human behavior that occurs in people's everyday lives. For example, we browse newspapers to see what is new, go window-shopping, look for materials in the library, and scan television channels. However, there has been little systematic study of the concept of browsing. The available research literature is scattered across various disciplines. Marketing and consumer researchers have studied browsing within the context of recreational shopping. Library researchers have studied browsing within the context of finding books, and information-system designers have studied browsing within the context of information retrieval and users' navigation within a system. Browsing behaviors are also embedded in the way consumers attend to mass advertising such as zapping television channels and scanning advertisements in magazines, business executives' environmental scanning, and architects' wayfinding in a complex environment, although browsing behaviors may be only implied.

Theoretical Issues: The Concept of Browsing

What Is Browsing?

Browsing in the Marketing Literature. The concept of browsing is not completely new in the marketing literature. Browsing within a shopping context may be considered as the examination of a store's merchandise for recreational or informational purposes without a current intent to buy (Bloch, Ridgway, and Sherrell 1989; Bloch, Sherrell, and Ridgway 1986). Ongoing search (browsing) can be distinguished from prepurchase search (direct information search) by conceptualizing it as search activities that are independent of specific purchase needs or decisions. That is, it does not occur to solve a recognized and immediate purchase problem. On the other hand, direct prepurchase search is information-seeking and -processing activities that consumers engage in to facilitate decisionmaking regarding their purchase goals. In this sense, browsing is shopping behavior that is not directly motivated by purchasing intent. It could be simply recreational window-shopping motivated only slightly by the desire to make a purchase, or a way of gathering information to be used later when making a purchase.

Janiszewski's (1998) concept of exploratory search is very close to the concept of browsing.

He suggested that visual information search is a combination of two distinct types of behavior: goal-directed search and exploratory search. The former occurs when consumers use stored search routines to collect information in a deliberate manner, whereas the latter occurs when consumers are confronted with multiple pieces of information but have little stored knowledge about how to proceed with information gathering. Exploratory search can be used either as a screening process that identifies candidates for goal-directed search or as an information-gathering device when goal-directed search routines are inadequate. The concept of exploratory search is consistent with the role of browsing in the context of information acquisition.

The Concept of Browsing in Other Disciplines. Library science literature provides more vivid behavioral definitions of browsing. Browsing has been referred to as different types of looking activities where initial search criteria are partially defined (Bankapur 1988; Cove and Walsh 1987, 1988). It is a "don't-know-what-I-want" type of behavior that one engages in separately from regular search (Bates 1989). Browsing consists of a wide spectrum of idiosyncratic processes for searching, sampling, and evaluating documents when significant attributes of a target or goal are not fully articulated or evident (O'Connor 1993). It is an important search strategy for novice and casual users (of libraries) (Hyman 1972). These definitions suggest the less structural characteristics of browsing.

The concept of browsing is also used in (computerized) information systems. In this literature, browsing tends to be viewed as an activity to understand the information environment and as an alternative to, or the prelude for, more structured search. Browsing is used to answer the question "what's there?" without involving a higher level of information processing and integration (Spence 1999). It is exploratory information seeking that depends on serendipity and is appropriate for ill-defined problems and for exploring new task domains (Marchionini and Shneiderman 1988). In addition, browsing is an approach to information seeking that is informal and opportunistic and depends heavily on the information environment (Marchionini 1995).

Finally, the idea of browsing is also implicitly embedded in the concept of environmental scanning in organizational behavior where information about events and relationships in a company's outside environment is scanned. Such information assists top management decisionmaking (Aguilar 1967). Next, we synthesize literature from various streams of research to identify the purpose, processes/types, and consequences of browsing.

Why Do People Browse?

Functional Browsing. People engage in browsing behaviors for various purposes. *Acquiring information* is a general purpose for browsing. Consumers browse to build a bank of information for future use (Bloch and Richins 1983; Bloch, Ridgway, and Sherrell 1989; Bloch, Sherrell, and Ridgway 1986). Library patrons browse catalogues or bookshelves to keep themselves updated with the area in which they are interested (Marchionini 1995). Information-system users browse the system to obtain information about the structure of the information organization. Such information provides an overview so users can have a sense of the scope of the system and amount and structure of information available (Marchionini 1995). In environmental scanning, browsing helps to gain knowledge to reduce uncertainty associated with strategic decisionmaking (Auster and Choo 1991).

Further, browsing is complementary to direct information search. People use browsing strategies to *formulate a formal direct search.* This purpose of browsing is very important because browsing starts with less specific goals. In a library or bookstore, patrons may start with a general interest area but do not know which title to look for. Browsing can help them to refine and articulate the problem at hand before they finally locate books of interest (O'Connor 1993). In information systems, browsing helps to develop a formal search strategy when people do not have well-defined search objectives (i.e., information needs) or are not familiar with the information structure (Marchionini 1987).

Compared to direct information search, browsing requires less attention and information-processing resources. Therefore, browsing is a way for people to *shift or share cognitive overload* because recognition is usually easier than formal planning (Marchionini 1995). Baker (1986) pointed out that people use browsing to handle information overload in decisionmaking—they consciously and/or subconsciously adopt strategies to limit their potential options to a more manageable number of choices. In consumer behavior, Painton and Gentry (1985) also found that visual browsing is used first to reduce the size of the evoked set before in-depth information search on the remaining alternatives was conducted.

Recreational Browsing. Besides the functional purposes mentioned above, browsing can also be motivated by hedonic purposes. A recreational purpose is unique in consumer research literature. Besides acquiring information, consumers may browse to experience fun and enjoyment (Bloch and Richins 1983; Bloch, Ridgway, and Sherrell 1989; Bloch, Sherrell, and Ridgway 1986). Consumers tend to engage in browsing behaviors during their shopping trips. Indeed, browsing was the predominant activity among those who visited a shopping mall, and browsing itself was a type of consumption (Bloch, Ridgway, and Dawson 1994).

Passive Browsing. Besides these active uses of browsing, the information systems literature also discusses a passive use of browsing—the influence of the information environment. Because of the constraints of the display mechanism (i.e., computer monitor), the structure of the information in an information system is not transparent. Users have to explore and browse around in order to locate a piece of specific information even if they know what they are seeking. The design of an information system may support and encourage browsing (Marchionini 1995, 1987). This form of browsing may also facilitate information acquisition even when people have no intention to acquire information and no awareness of such information that is acquired. However, this information acquired without awareness will facilitate both the current as well as future search tasks.

Browsing in a Consumer Context. Although not all the purposes of browsing have been examined in the context of consumer behavior, it is not difficult to find potential applications in the area. First of all, browsing complements existing information search literature by adding the concept of information acquisition when no specific purchase goal can be identified as well as serving as a way to formulate more directed search. Most studies in consumer (direct) information search have assumed that consumers know what to buy and what information to look for. However, decisionmaking does not always start with specific goals and consumers do not always make thorough plans before going shopping. Different levels of goals ranging from abstract to concrete can be found in consumer decisionmaking (Huffman and Houston 1993; Lawson 1997; Pieters, Baumgartner, and Allen 1995). Goal specificity influences actions that consumers may take to accomplish goals such as information searching, encoding, and alternative selection. Because browsing is particularly effective for information problems that are ill defined, it may represent the starting point or prelude to direct information search. Through browsing, consumers refine what they want, and as the process continues, search becomes more directed. Essentially, browsing is an important part of standard information acquisition. Adding browsing to consumer information-acquisition behaviors expands the original search concept and provides a more comprehensive framework of consumer information-acquisition behavior.

Second, consumer shopping involves both visual and physical movements in the shopping environment, which are largely browsing activities. Titus and Everett (1995) conceptualized two navigation strategies (i.e., browsing strategies). Epistemic search strategies are used for the purpose of locating products in the retail environment whereas hedonic search strategies are used to satisfy shoppers' desire for pleasure. Therefore, both functional and recreational browsing occurs during consumers' shopping activities.

Third, passive browsing is also an important part of general consumer information-acquisition behavior. Consumer decision processes are constructed by both the external environment and the decision makers themselves (Bettman, Luce, and Payne 1998). On the one hand, consumers actively control their decision tasks and construct information such as its presentation format to facilitate their decision processes (Coupey 1994). On the other hand, task complexity (e.g., number of alternatives) (Johnson and Payne 1985; Payne 1976), information presentation format (Bettman et al. 1993; Bettman and Kakkar 1977), and time pressure (Payne, Bettman, and Johnson 1988; Wright 1974) construct the choice strategies consumers might use to make their decisions. As part of consumer decisionmaking, consumers' information acquisition is also influenced by the information environment itself. Such an environment may induce both hedonic and functional browsing. Creative product displays in retail stores as well as visual and olfactory cues may encourage consumers to browse. Research has shown that retail store displays encourage consumers to browse and lead to increased sales (Underhill 1999). On the other hand, ill-designed floor layouts or product displays may force consumers to browse in order to find a desired product. D'Astous (2000) characterized factors that lead consumers to look around because they are unable to find what they need due to change of store arrangements and inadequate directions within the store as design irritants. Such design irritants may lead to negative affect and negatively influence consumer shopping experiences.

Finally, as e-commerce expands and consumers acquire information and purchase products online, browsing behavior, especially passive browsing, is becoming an important aspect of consumer information acquisition that needs further study. In Internet "stores," because of the constraints of screen display, consumers may have to browse through pages to get a sense of the structure of the store in order to find the information they are looking for.

How Do People Browse?

In the consumer-behavior literature, definitions of browsing focus on "purposes." But no specific "browsing behaviors" are defined, except that Janiszewski (1998) indirectly refers to browsing as "visual exploratory search." It is distinguished from directed search by how people treat focal and nonfocal information. In exploratory search, nonfocal materials compete for attention and subjects keep switching between focal and nonfocal information. However, the difference is very subtle. Bloch, Sherrell, and Ridgway (1986) pointed out that although pre-purchase search and ongoing search are conceptually distinct, they are difficult to separate in practice and the activities exhibited by each are indistinguishable to observers.

From a behavior perspective, browsing involves various types of "looking" activities. And from a motivation perspective, browsing encompasses different levels of goal specificity. Literature in library science and information systems provides categorizations of such "looking" activities under various levels of goals. Herner (1970) and Apted (1971) provided similar types of browsing, although using different terms. Directed (Herner 1970) or specific (Apted 1971) browsing is systematic and focused, and is often driven by a specific object or target. Semidirected (Herner 1970) or predictive browsing (Apted 1971) refers to browsing that has less definite targets and proceeds less systematically. Finally, undirected (Herner 1970) or general-purpose browsing (Apted

1971) refers to those "looking activities" as having no real goal and very little focus, more like recreation than information seeking. Cove and Walsh (1987, 1988) followed a similar route and used the terms "search browsing," "general purpose browsing," and "serendipity browsing."

Canter, Rivers, and Storrs (1985) categorized browsing from a behavioral perspective as scanning (covers a large area but without great depth), browsing (users are happy to go wherever the data take them until their interest is caught), searching (users are motivated to find a particular target), exploring (consists of many different paths, suggesting users are seeking the extent and nature of the field), and wandering (users amble along and inevitably revisit nodes in an unstructured journey). Similarly, O'Connor (1993), taking a process view, conceptualized four phases of browsing: make glimpses (global level, control over depth of penetration), connect attributes (transfer the representation of both documents and user query), evaluate connection, and evaluate search (as a whole). It suggests that different types of browsing are not only different in terms of goal specification, but also in terms of breadth and depth of information acquisition. Carmel, Crawford, and Chen (1992) applied both goal specification and degree of information processing (e.g., processing strategies used) to categorize browsing as scan browse, review browse, and search browse.

The above categorizations suggest that how people browse may depend on how specific their goal is, and therefore the breadth and depth of information covered. Many consumer behaviors are goal directed (Bagozzi 1997, 1998; Bagozzi and Dholakia 1999; Lawson 1997). Although existing information-acquisition research has focused on consumer behaviors with specific defined goals, consumers do enter markets with more abstract or ill-defined goals. Lawson (1997) provided a goal-driven framework, which includes goals with different levels of abstraction. Decision processes and information search can start at different levels of goals: value level, activity level, product-acquisition level, or brand-acquisition level. These four levels of goals range from abstract to concrete. The degree of goal specificity will influence consumer information acquisition activities. At the abstract goal levels (value and activity), consumers need first to determine what activities may be consistent with the value. Therefore, they may cover a larger scope of information while information processing is at the surface level in order to refine their goals. Then, based on the choice of action, they will select product categories and further select the brand. At this stage, information acquisition is more targeted and information processing is more detailed.

Correlates of Browsing

Most empirical studies on browsing have focused on demonstrating the existence of browsing behaviors and investigating factors influencing browsing. Both external factors such as store environment and internal factors such as consumers' individual characteristics influence browsing activities. Bloch, Ridgway, and Sherrell (1989) surveyed shoppers and found that ongoing search (browsing) did exist. Consumers gather information for either recreational or informational purposes even when they do not have a specific purchase intention. Factors that enhance browsing behavior include complexity of product class, the nature of the product, consumers' product involvement, surroundings and pleasant atmosphere of the store, and stores' displays and facilities. Browsing behaviors also vary across different retail outlets. Dawson, Bloch, and Ridgway (1990) suggested that store prestige positively influenced browsing. Consumers were more likely to browse (for recreational purposes) in an upscale department store than in a grocery store. Baker's (1986) experiment in a library setting showed that accessibility (to the books) was an important antecedent of browsing, which further influenced borrowing frequency. Titles displayed in a prominent place caught consumers' attention and encouraged browsing. Browsing in information systems is closely related to the concept of interface (Bankapur 1988). Research in this area has focused on designs and features that enhance and facilitate user browsing and prevent getting lost. Marchionini (1995) suggested that providing users with their history tree and showing them where they came from and where they had been can prevent disorientation. Knowledge of information structure is important for effective browsing. Such knowledge provides people with control over the information environment.

Similarly, in the context of consumer online shopping, providing consumers with tools such as a "store" structure map and easy-to-access links would facilitate (functional) browsing and help consumers locate information conveniently. For example, providing contextual navigation aids significantly improves performance on the task (Park and Kim 2000). Moreover, context information changed the users' navigation patterns and enhanced convenience of navigation. Finally, previous research on the effects of shopping environment, such as store display, color, background music, and consumers' interaction with store employees, offers insights on what influences consumers' browsing in a shopping context. Since our focus is on the information-acquisition aspect of browsing, we do not review that literature here.

Consumer individual characteristics moderate browsing behaviors. Carmel, Crawford, and Chen (1992), testing differences between experts and novices, found that experts browsed fewer topics but more in-depth while novices tended to rely more on referential links. Experts tended to browse topics based on expert knowledge and reasoning while novices tended to browse topics based on special interests and commonsense knowledge. Based on the findings, he suggested that designers should view hypertext indices as semantic networks and design them to inform the user about the organization and structure of information as well as to provide the location of information. Besides, to attract and retain novices, systems should provide topics related to their everyday, commonsense knowledge, and develop links from commonsense and special-interest topics into expert topics. Similarly, Canter, Rivers, and Storrs (1985) used experiments to trace users' navigation processes through information systems and found differences between experts and novices. He suggested that experts and novices may be different in selecting search strategies and design of information systems would be more effective if individual differences were considered. Similar findings regarding the influence of expertise can be found in consumer behavior literature (Maheswaran, Sternthal, and Guerhan 1996).

Jarboe and McDaniel (1987), characterizing browsers and nonbrowsers, found that browsers tended to be employed females, somewhat downscale compared to other mall patrons, and had lower levels of education and income. They were younger than nonbrowsers and had a larger family size. Browsers had high brand awareness, frequently visited the mall, and made a larger number of purchases per trip but a smaller number of purchases per store shopped. They exhibited a greater level of self-confidence, social extroversion, tension, and enthusism. They tended to feel that they made good choices, experienced a higher level of general purchasing satisfaction, and tended to be opinion leaders. Browsing seemed to help them allocate their limited money efficiently. Jarboe and McDaniel concluded that browsers can be both economic-oriented as well as recreationally oriented shoppers. Browsers are not wandering shoppers; they do buy.

Consequences of Browsing

Corresponding to the purpose of acquiring information, gaining knowledge is the most prevalent consequence of browsing. Through browsing, consumers gain not only specific product class and brand knowledge, but also knowledge of market structures and environment such as number of alternatives, competitive situation, and how to find specific information. Such knowledge will accumulate over time and form the "human capital" that will increase future buying efficiencies (Bloch and Richins 1983; Bloch, Ridgway, and Sherrell 1989). Such knowledge can also be disseminated to other consumers through opinion leadership (Bloch, Sherrell, and Ridgway 1986). Similarly, browsing in a library or bookstore may help to keep a patron updated with an area of interest. Browsing through an information system helps users to learn the information structure and become more efficient in direct search. As they browse the structure and the information available, they begin to know better where they want to go, and, as a result, what they know and don't know (Marchionini 1995). The consequences of browsing also include increased sales, increased product knowledge, and opinion leadership (Bloch and Richins 1983; Bloch, Sherrell, and Ridgway 1986; Underhill 1999).

Overall, browsing leads to discovery. It not only helps to refine vague goals, but it can also help to discover unrecognized needs. It leads to incidental learning as well as intentional learning (Liebscher and Marchionini 1988). As a result, browsing may encourage impulse purchases. Impulse purchasing is an important part of consumer purchasing, although it has not been as extensively investigated as planned purchasing has. An impulse purchase is the purchase of a brand in a product category when a need for the product was not recognized before entering the store (Kollat and Willett 1967). Their study showed that 50.5 percent of subjects' grocery purchases were unplanned while only 25.9 percent were categorized as planned. Beatty and Ferrell (1998) studied various precursors of impulse-purchase behavior and found that browsing has a prominent effect. Further, Iyer (1989) demonstrated that less knowledge of the shopping environment forces shoppers to browse, and availability of time provides opportunity for them to browse, which potentially facilitates unplanned purchases.

Clearly, browsing is not as intense as direct search, but information acquired through browsing may have significant influence on consumer decisionmaking. It has been shown that incidental advertising exposure enhanced liking, despite the lack of prior recognition, and it further influenced consideration set formation (Shapiro 1999; Shapiro, MacInnis, and Heckler 1997). Previously exposed products tended to be included in the consideration set. The results were consistent across memory-based and stimulus-based consideration set formation and were robust across different product categories and purchasing situations. Both conceptual and perceptual information processing could occur during incidental exposure to products while browsing. Thus, browsing can facilitate implicit learning, a form of learning that occurs in the absence of an intention to learn and results in a form of knowledge that is expressed in performance but is difficult to verbalize and not accessible to consciousness (Dienes and Perner 1999).

Successful browsing helps people achieve their purposes. However, when browsing is not successful, it may have negative consequences. One negative consequence of browsing, which may be unique to the study of information systems, is the phenomenon of "getting lost" (Marchionini 1995). One reason for getting lost is because of the design of the information system. Users get confused and don't know where to go. It is often referred to as "disorientation" (Conklin 1987; Dias, Gomes, and Correia 1999). Conklin (1987) characterized "disorientation" as the difficulty for information-system users to figure out where they are in the network and how to get to some other places. Such feeling of disorientation is bound to cause frustration.

Another reason for "getting lost" is because people are diverted from the information needs they are instructed or originally interested in (Liebscher and Marchionini 1988). When people begin with an information target, browsing may divert them to other topics that are interesting to them. In other words, as people browse, their cognition of their goal and the information environment interacts; therefore, their prespecified goals and corresponding information needs change. Such change during the course of information acquisition corresponds to Bates's (1989) berry-picking information-acquisition strategy, which describes the behavior that people change their search strategies in response to the new conditions of information environment in order to acquire new bits of information. The changes lead to a discrepancy between the original goal and the one finally achieved. Liebscher and Marchionini (1988) compared analytic search strategy (specific search) and browsing strategy (browsing) while giving subjects search instructions. They found that those who used an analytic search strategy spent less time and made fewer queries whereas those using browsing strategy felt it was easy but resulted in a longer list and more reference time because they were diverted during the task.

Although "getting lost" has not been investigated in the consumer context, it is not irrelevant. First of all, the emerging Internet "stores" themselves constitute information systems. Information about products is usually organized using hypertext. Consumers need at least some degree of browsing to get the information needed. Lacking navigation skills may cause consumers to get lost in the sea of information and exit the "store" in frustration. Or, exposure to information other than planned may change their original goal and lead to final purchases that are different from what they originally expected. Second, even in a retail setting, disorientation may occur when consumers have difficulty locating the target items and get lost in the store (Abdul-Muhmin 1999; Babin, Darden, and Griffin 1994; Dawson 1988; Dogu and Erkip 2000; Park, Iyer, and Smith 1989). For example, Dogu and Erkip (2000) found that factors such as building configuration, visual accessibility, circulation systems, and signage influence wayfinding in the shopping mall, and most customers indicated that the signage system was insufficient to help them find specific destinations. Unfamiliarity with the store environment, such as product displays, may cause consumers to fail to locate a desired product brand, leading to brand switching.

Finally, compared to browsing that achieves functional utilities such as acquiring information and locating products, browsing activities motivated by recreational purposes may lead to an enhanced consumer shopping experience (Bloch, Ridgway, and Dawson 1994). Shopping itself is a form of consumption; therefore, understanding recreational shopping is an important step to better understand consumer consumption experiences. Browsing is an inherent part of shopping, which could be both work and fun (Abdul-Muhmin 1999; Babin, Darden, and Griffin 1994; Dawson 1988; Dogu and Erkip 2000; Park, Iyer, and Smith 1989). Enhanced shopping experiences may contribute to positive affect and attitude and, further, lead to positive word-of-mouth communications and future sales.

Methodologies Used to Study Browsing

Although different types of browsing are conceptualized, how to research these activities imposes important methodology questions. Limited consumer-behavior research has used surveys and/or interviews (Bloch and Richins 1983; Bloch, Ridgway, and Sherrell 1989; Bloch, Sherrell, and Ridgway 1986; Jarboe and McDaniel 1987). Because it was believed that activities of browsing and searching are behaviorally indistinguishable, these empirical tests focused on capturing browsing *without purchase intentions*. Bloch and colleagues (Bloch, Ridgway, and Sherrell 1989) used a single-item measure, asking subjects to recall how often they visited clothing and computer stores to look around or to get information rather than to make a purchase. Jarboe and McDaniel (1987) used a summated rating scale to classify browsers. Several variables, including unplanned shopping, information seeking, impulse purchasing, the propensity to look around in stores and to look at window displays, and length of shopping trips were used to describe browsing.

However, simple recall is not sufficient for fully capturing browsing behaviors and the influence of browsing activities on subsequent behaviors. If consumers have difficulty in remembering their specific search activities, they would have even greater difficulty in remembering nonpurposeful, casual activity such as browsing (Banaji, Blair, and Schwarz 1996). Besides, some information acquisition while browsing may not be registered with explicit memory at all. Janiszewski (1998) measured subjects' eye movement and viewing time of catalogues to study exploratory behaviors. The method captures the process of browsing but the scope of information environment that can be displayed is constrained by the instrument.

In library science studies, Belkin et al. (1990) proposed a field study methodology that combines methods of transaction logs, online questionnaires, nonparticipant observations of users in libraries, and in-depth interviews of users about the observed behavior. The authors concluded that such multimethods are well suited to the context of browsing, a situation where the user's goals and tasks are not well understood, yet are important to the design of library systems.

Most information systems can capture users' information-acquisition processes through computer log files or other similar types of files. Patterns of different types of browsing can be identified by analyzing these files. For example, Canter, Rivers, and Storrs (1985) traced the pattern of subjects' navigation in the information systems, and then categorized browsing paths as a path, a ring, a loop, or a spike based on interrelationships among pieces of information. Types of browsing then can be described as different combinations of these paths. Marchionini and Shneiderman (1988) suggested that examination of paths taken and decisions made in jumping from one information node to another allows researchers to make inferences about users' cognitive activity and provide evaluations of system effectiveness.

Similar process-tracing methods are also used in the studies of consumer information search. The Mouselab (Johnson, Payne, and Bettman 1988), higher-order cognitive tracing (Jacoby et al. 1994), and the most recent multimedia computer lab (Hauser, Urban, and Weinberg 1993) use such computer-recorded files to analyze consumer search behaviors (as reviewed earlier in the information-search section). It is proposed that by examining consumers' information-search scope (e.g., breadth and depth) and connections made among pieces of information (e.g., cross–product category vs. within category), we can evaluate different degrees of searching or browsing. More recently, Hodkinson, Kiel, and McColl-Kennedy (2000) and Berendt and Brenstein (2001) presented different methods to investigate navigation behaviors diagrammatically on the Internet.

Browsing is an integrative part of information-acquisition activities, and its difference with direct search is not a sharp distinction but more a matter of degree along a continuum. Methods used to study consumer information search can be applied to the study of browsing behaviors. However, because of the less structured nature of browsing, qualitative methods or a combination of qualitative and quantitative methods may be more appropriate. Besides, other than measures that directly test subjects' recognition and recall, indirect tests that assess information acquired implicitly are necessary to tap the influence of nonconscious information acquisition on subsequent behaviors (Krishnan and Chakravarti 1999). Shapiro (1999) and Lee (2002) used such an approach in their examinations of incidental information exposure.

Summary

The above review of browsing indicates that although browsing is a common behavior, it is not well understood. But, as our review indicates, although browsing is mentioned explicitly in the research literature, it is considered to be a self-evident behavior. Moreover, there is no agreement on either the definition of browsing or the conditions under which browsing is browsing and not something else (Kwasnik 1992). Browsing is not a single-dimension construct. Each stream of literature reviewed indicated the multidimensional characteristics of browsing. From a consumer behavior perspective, browsing is neither mere information gathering nor a recreational activity that is independent of consumer purchase. As a means of information acquisition, it differs from direct search in terms of behavior (scanning vs. full-attention "looking"), motivation (less defined vs. specific goal), cognition (automatic vs. controlled information processing), and consequences (implicit vs. explicit use of information).

Chang (1995) took a multidimensional approach to investigate the concept of browsing and proposed a general model for understanding browsing, which includes four components: context, influences, browsing process, and consequences. Browsing behaviors are influenced by both external factors such as the structure and display of a resource, and internal factors such as browser's motivation, goal, and individual characteristics. Browsing is an iterative process among its influences, the processes, and its consequences.

From an information-acquisition perspective, browsing can be regarded as complementary to direct search and an important aspect of information acquisition. The literature shows that the behaviors of search and browsing are difficult to distinguish and they tend to exist simultaneously during consumers' search and/or decisionmaking process. Those factors that influence search may also influence browsing. Because browsing strategies tend to be applied to more informal or general goals, the information encountered during browsing keeps refining the goal. Therefore, the influence of the information environment on browsing may be greater than that on direct search. Marchionini (1987) suggested that browsing is a highly interactive process with multiple decision points, which depends on feedback from the environment to help determine what to do. Browsing is more dependent on interactions between the information seeker and the information environment. In the next section, the relationship between browsing and searching is described and they are further positioned within an information-acquisition continuum.

An Extended Consumer Information-Acquisition Framework

As we have suggested, browsing is a multidimensional concept. In a marketing context, browsing occurs during shopping. Although such browsing may or may not lead to an immediate purchase, research has shown that such browsing has a positive influence on consumers' affect, time spent in a store, and likelihood of making more purchases (Underhill 1999). However, browsing goes beyond specific shopping contexts. Consumers may also browse in certain nonshopping contexts such as browsing a magazine and scanning the advertisements. In addition to the recreational purposes, browsing is a means of information acquisition, especially when consumers do not have a specific purchase goal in mind, and sometimes may even occur without an intention to search for information. We focus on this aspect of browsing and further delineate an information-acquisition framework consisting of both direct information search and browsing.

Relationship Between Browsing and Searching

The literature has exhibited different ways of treating the relationship between browsing and searching. One way has been to consider browsing as related but not identical to searching. Studies of Bloch and colleagues (Bloch and Richins 1983; Bloch, Ridgway, and Sherrell 1989; Bloch, Sherrell, and Ridgway 1986) took this approach. They suggested browsing could be an important part of consumer search behaviors, but they explicitly defined browsing as searching without purchase intentions. The cutoff between the two concepts is the presence of a purchase intention. However, they acknowledged that it is difficult to precisely specify when a purchase problem has been recognized and decision process started. The border is further obscured by instances of impulse purchasing. Some library science literature has also taken this approach (e.g., Bates 1989).

A second way of understanding the relationship between browsing and searching is to treat the two concepts as identical. This view exists mainly in the information systems and related research literature (e.g., Bucklin and Sismeiro 2003). The concept of browsing in the area of information systems originated as a task-oriented, problem-solving technique to cope with problems arising from interacting with the computer interface (Chang and Rice 1993). Browsing is treated as an alternative to the complex Boolean search strategy that is used when users do not have a well-defined search criterion (Liebscher and Marchionini 1988).

A third way of conceptualizing browsing and searching is to treat them as the two ends of multiple overlapping and continuous dimensions of human information-acquisition behaviors (Chang 1995; Chang and Rice 1993). We adopt the continuum approach, and the underlying dimensions of the browsing-searching framework will be developed next.

Dimensions of the Browsing-Searching Continuum

Our review suggests that a consumer information-acquisition framework should include both direct search and browsing. The two concepts complement each other and form a range of consumer information-acquisition activities along several underlying dimensions (see Table 3.2).

The Motivation Dimension

Browsing and searching are motivated by different factors. Different levels of consumer goals are an important motivating factor. Various definitions of browsing show that the most prominent characteristic of browsing, compared to direct search, is its less-specific purpose. This characteristic is present in all streams of research regarding browsing. In consumer behavior, it is no immediate purchase intent at hand (Bloch, Sherrell, and Ridgway 1986). In library science, it is browsers come to the library without a specific title in mind (Baker 1986) or without initial criteria completely defined (Cove and Walsh 1987, 1988). In information systems, browsing occurs when no specific target is being sought (Spence 1999). Overall, it seems that people tend to employ browsing activities instead of explicit direct search prior to formulating a specific goal.

Research in consumer information search has assumed that consumers know what they are looking for. The purchase task usually is clearly defined and information search is specifically goal directed. Such research excludes the more general information-acquisition activities when consumers either do not have a goal or have at best an abstract or ill-defined goal. In fact, consumers may enter the market with different levels of goal specificity; therefore, research in information search should be extended to include activities that relate to more general goals. When consumers' purchase goals are at an abstract level and not well defined, they tend to engage in browsing activities before they formulate a direct search. Browsing helps them to refine their goals and provide purchasing ideas based on information encountered and their interpretation of the information. Browsing thus becomes a natural extension of the specific goal-directed information search.

Another motivating factor for consumer information acquisition comes from the information environment. The refinement of an abstract goal depends on the interaction between consumers and the market/information environment; therefore, browsing is more susceptible to external influences compared with direct searching. Baker (1986) argued (in the context of library patrons) that because browsers come to the library without having a specific title in mind, they are open to

Table 3.2

Dimensions of the Browsing-Searching Continuum

	Browsing	Searching
The motivation dimension	Abstract/general goal-motivated; more susceptible to external influence; more recreational	Specific goal–motivated; more susceptible to internal influence; more functional
The behavior dimension	Casual scanning, skimming	Focused examining
The process dimension	Less effortful, automatic process; engage in more perceptual processing	Effortful, conscious information process and integration; engage in more conceptual processing
The consequence dimension	Influence subsequent decision-making through implicit memory; enhance performance on tasks that rely more on perceptual processing/retrieval	Registered with explicit memory and exert influence on decision-making; enhance performance on tasks that rely more on conceptual processing/retrieval

influences from a variety of sources when selecting materials. Further, people usually depend on the feedback from the information environment to decide what to do next (Marchionini 1987), and the formulation of their task changes as browsing progresses. Such interaction between consumers and the information environment is consistent with the view that consumer goals are not fixed and changes in the environment may lead to refinement, abandonment, or modification of original goals (Bettman 1979). Therefore, it is proposed that browsing is more susceptible to external influences as compared to direct search.

Consumers' individual characteristics also influence their behaviors on the browsing-searching continuum. Consumers search for information to facilitate their purchase decisions. Therefore, the purpose of searching is primarily functional. However, a hedonic function of information search is also identified. The review of literature in consumer search also shows that shopping enjoyment and positive attitude toward shopping enhance the extent of direct information search (see Table 3.1). Although it has not been empirically tested, it is speculated that when people enjoy searching for information and shopping, they may be attentive to a variety of information and not constrained to explicit purchase tasks. People may habitually browse and gather information that fits their interests even without an intention to buy. Bloch and colleagues' (Block, Sherrell, and Ridgway 1986) extension from searching to browsing is mainly along this dimension. Besides, a higher degree of interest in the products/services may lead to high involvement and motivate browsing activities. Therefore, compared to direct search, browsing may be more hedonic than functional and could be influenced by factors such as consumer shopping enjoyment and personal interest in specific products.

Knowledge is an important factor influencing direct information search behaviors, as indicated in our review. Both product knowledge and knowledge of how to locate information facilitate direct search, which then reduces the need for functional browsing. When people have higher content knowledge, they know important attributes of the products, different brands in the market, how to compare them, and what to search for in order to execute the decision criteria and make a final decision. In this situation, it is easier to formulate and carry out a specific directed search. Moreover, it may be more likely that information may be acquired without awareness (i.e., nonconsciously) when browsing or searching. When people lack such content knowledge and have to acquire most of it externally, the information acquisition and processing task is more demanding. Browsing could be an effective way for them to get an overview while not experiencing information overload.

Similarly, specific information search is less likely to be successful if consumers lack the skill of locating information. In a physical shopping environment, such knowledge may refer to information such as which store(s) carry the desired product, how to get there, and the display in the store. In the electronic shopping environment, it may refer to knowledge of the organization of the hypertexts and which link(s) lead to the desired information. Browsing could be an effective strategy for people to get familiarized with the information environment and locate specific information. Indeed, browsing may be path specific whereas searching is content specific (Chang 1995; Chang and Rice 1993). This issue is particularly important for electronic shopping because of the constraint of the screen display. Consumers cannot get the sense of the structure at one glance as in retail stores. Knowledge of how to locate information is especially helpful in direct search and reduces the need for functional browsing. However, when consumers are driven by hedonic information needs, such knowledge may facilitate and enhance browsing and searching activities.

The Behavior Dimension

Browsing and searching may exhibit differences at the behavioral level, although the differences could be hard to capture empirically. Browsing and searching can be characterized by different types of "looking" activities. Compared to direct search, which is assumed to be voluntary, utilizes full attention, and covers a small scope of information, browsing is more casual and less structured "looking" such as scanning and skimming. Direct search concerns "focal information" while browsing (exploratory search) includes "non-focal information" (Janiszewski 1998). When browsing, people's attention is more spread and probably divided among several information cues. However, information can be acquired under such conditions (Lewicki, Hill, and Czyzewska 1992; MacLeod 1998). Using a combination of nonparticipant observations, in-depth interviews, and accompanied shopping trips with informants, Xia (2003) found that consumer information acquisition consists of a range of visual and physical activities including glancing and scanning the shelves while walking through the aisles, stopping to skim and read product information, and examining and comparing different products by touching and picking up products from the shelves. These activities differ in terms of attention resources allocated to the information as well as level of information processing.

The Information-Processing Dimension

In terms of information processing, direct search is characterized by information integration and is assumed to be conscious, effortful, and constrained by consumers' cognitive capacity (Beatty and Smith 1987). However, people also process information automatically without full attention or even without awareness (DeSchepper and Treisman 1996; Ganor-Stern, Seamon, and Garrasco 1998; Gardiner and Parkin 1990; Grunert 1996; MacLeod 1998). Theories suggest that attention and controlled processing are important to memory, especially long-term memory (Fisk and Schneider 1984; Schneider and Shiffrin 1977). However, people have limited attentional resources (Kahneman 1973). Because they cannot attend to and process unlimited amounts of information, information search is constrained by cognitive capacity.

Because browsing is more casual and brief "looking," intuitively it may put less demand on attention resources. Theories on attention suggest there is a continuum of attention resource allocation from no attention to full attention. People can allocate attention resources based on the requirements of the task (Umilta and Moscovitch 1994). When browsing, because information acquisition is unintended for a specific purchase occasion, consumers are influenced more by personal interests or store and information environments. Depending on the occasion, they may allocate a minimal amount or a sufficient amount of attention to a product. Compared to direct search, browsing is less cognitive-resource demanding and information is processed using less cognitive effort. Because such information processing could be even without people's awareness, it has important implications in people's everyday lives. A sufficient amount of attention and exposure time provides opportunities for controlled, effortful, higher-level, and meaningful information processing. Such processing may occur when consumers examine a product in detail. In the case of glances or scans, limited attention resources and exposure time devoted to browsing activities may lead to automatic processing and the information acquired may be stored in implicit memory. Therefore, it is an important question as to what information is acquired during brief browsing, compared to more detailed, controlled browsing. Hence, different types of browsing activities could differ in terms of level of processing and type of information acquired.

Thus, what information is acquired through different levels of browsing, how it is stored in memory, and how it may be retrieved later are important research questions. Since less attention will lead to poorer performance on explicit memory tasks such as recall and recognition (Fisk and Schneider 1984), the implicit information acquired through brief browsing may not be revealed in these memory tasks. The information acquired and stored in implicit memory can be demonstrated using indirect memory tasks instead of direct memory tasks.

The Outcome Dimension

Both direct information search and browsing influence consumer decisionmaking. When facing a purchase task, consumers search information externally and internally. Hence, information searched or browsed on one occasion may become internal information and influence future information search and purchase activities. While direct search and browsing are different aspects of external information acquisition activities, both influence consumer memory, contribute to consumers' internal information, and influence future information-acquisition activities. The influences of these two activities on future information acquisition are mixed together. That is, information acquired during direct search may become internal information and guide future browsing. On the other hand, information acquired from browsing may evoke further interests and lead to future, more intensive direct search. However, examining the potential memory and storage of information acquired through searching and browsing, we suggest that there may be qualitative differences due to different encoding purposes and conditions in searching and browsing processes.

Information that people have directly searched, processed, and integrated would enter their explicit memory. Such memory facilitates later recognition and recall and helps consumers in subsequent purchase decisions. Comparatively, information acquired through browsing may not leave obvious retrievable traces in explicit memory. However, such information may be stored in people's implicit memory and exert influence on their subsequent behaviors without conscious awareness (Kirsner et al. 1998; Milech and Finucane 1998; Schacter 1987).

Implicit Versus Explicit Memory

According to Graf and Schacter (1985, p. 501): "Implicit memory is revealed when previous experiences facilitate performance on a task that does not require conscious or intentional recollection of those experiences. [On the other hand,] explicit memory is revealed when performance on a task requires conscious recollection of previous experiences." Empirical studies have shown that implicit and explicit memories are influenced by different factors and are dissociable. Some factors have an impact on explicit memory but not on implicit memory, and some factors even have the opposite effect on implicit and explicit memory. First, research generally agrees that divided attention influences explicit memory but has no effect on implicit memory (Gardiner and Parkin 1990; Jacoby, Toth, and Yonelinas 1993; Mulligan 1997). Second, although people's memory is a function of information elaboration (usually the semantic aspect of the stimuli) during encoding, research shows that levels of processing have no effect on implicit memory (Graf and Schacter 1985; Jacoby and Dallas 1981). Third, research also supports the general conclusion that manipulations of incidental learning versus intentional learning affect explicit memory but have no effect on implicit memory (Bowers and Schacter 1990; Greene 1986; Roediger and Challis 1992; Shapiro 1999; Shapiro, MacInnis, and Heckler 1997). Fourth, exposure time influences subjects' opportunity for processing information, which has a profound effect on recall and recognition. However, a similar effect was not found on implicit memory tests (Hirshman and Mulligan 1991). Similarly, the rate of forgetting is a function of time that has passed by. However, research on explicit and implicit memory has found that compared to explicit memory, implicit memory deteriorates at a much slower speed (Tulving, Schacter, and Stark 1982). Finally, the change of modality between study and test has an effect on implicit tests, but only a small or no effect on explicit tests (Blaxton 1989; Weldon 1991).

Research has offered several theoretical explanations for these observed differences (Cohen and Squire 1980; Graf and Mandler 1984; Roediger and Challis 1992; Squire 1987; Tulving 1972). The processing view has received the most empirical support and it emphasizes that there are different mental procedures underlying performance on different tasks. The Transfer-Appropriate-Processing model proposes that performance on memory tests benefits to the extent that the cognitive operations involved in the test recapitulate or overlap those engaged during initial learning (Roediger and McDermott 1993). Typical explicit memory tests such as recall and recognition rely primarily on conceptual processing; therefore, task performance is influenced by manipulations of level of processing and elaboration. On the other hand, implicit memory tests usually employ different mental processes and performance on these tests depends on the match of types of processing between study and test. Overall, research shows that explicit memory is more conceptual while implicit memory is more perceptual.

An examination of these factors indicates that they are very similar to different conditions or characteristics under which consumers browse versus directly search for information. Hence, not only do consumers acquire information through browsing, such acquired information may have an important effect on consumers' purchase behaviors. Researchers in consumer behavior have recognized that many consumer decisions are made under conditions of low involvement (Foss 1989; Hawkins and Hoch 1992; Hawkins, Hoch, and Meyers-Levy 2001). Although explicit memory measures still dominate consumer research, increasingly attention is being paid to the implicit aspects of consumer memory (Janiszewski 1993; Krishnan and Chakravarti 1999; Lee 2002; Sanyal 1992). For example, Krishnan and Chakravarti (1999) recognized that explicit measures alone may not extract all the information that consumers have acquired after being exposed to an advertisement; therefore, *explicit measures tend to underestimate the influence of marketing communications.* A comprehensive measure of communications effectiveness should be obtained using both direct and indirect tests. Similarly, applying implicit memory to consumers' acquisition of price information, Monroe and Lee (1999) suggested that both implicit and explicit memory measures should be considered when examining consumers' processing of price information. In other words, just because consumers do not explicitly *remember* the specific price of a product does not mean they do not *know* it. Price information that is stored in their implicit memory but not recalled may exert an important influence on their internal reference prices and subsequent behaviors.

Recent research provides evidence that consumers perceive unattended stimuli and learn without intention. Moreover, such learning has an important influence on consumers' decisionmaking, although they are not aware of such learning (Shapiro 1999; Shapiro, MacInnis, and Heckler 1997). Holden and Vanhuele (1999) found that after being exposed to some fake brand names, subjects judged that these brands actually exist a day later although they were not able to recall when they were exposed to these names. Distinguishing the type of information that is stored in implicit memory, Lee (2002) demonstrated that conceptually driven implicit memory affects memory-based choices whereas perceptually driven implicit memory affects stimulus-based choices.

Summary of the Framework

The various dimensions of the information-acquisition framework do not operate in isolation so much as they interact with each other. For example, the goal dimension describes browsing-searching as sequential—when the goal is abstract, consumers may browse first to refine their goals, then conduct direct search. However, browsing-search is also influenced by consumers' personal interests. The moderating role of personal interest may cause browsing and searching to operate simultaneously. While directly searching for information concerning a specific product, consumers may browse other information that is readily accessible at the time and of interest to them. Placing browsing and searching within the broader context of consumer behavior, we find that one activity may blend with the other. Consumers may search for information about one product while browsing another one. Casual browsing may become an intense search at any time. A search for information on one product may lead to browsing of similar products. Browsing on one occasion may reduce the need to search for information later.

By integrating browsing into searching, we continue with the "on-going" and "pre-purchase search" paradigms developed by Bloch, Ridgway, and Sherrell (1989) and broaden the existing research on consumer information search to consumer information acquisition. It is proposed that consumers acquire information through different routes, under different situations, with different purposes, and yet all such information may be at their disposal consciously or nonconsciously. Therefore, although they may not *remember* a lot of information, they may *know* more than researchers' data indicate, and they may even know more than they think they know.

Consumers apply both direct and indirect information acquisition in their daily lives. Direct information acquisition is information-acquisition activities that are intentional and serve a specific purchasing task. Existing research on direct information search primarily has focused on this type of information acquisition. Consumers need to acquire information (when they do not have it internally) if they want to buy a specific product and need to make a choice among alternatives. Direct information search can fulfill this need. However, consumers may need to browse first when they have a desire or goal that is at a more abstract level. For example, consumers who go shopping with a goal of purchasing some winter clothes may look around first to see what fits their desires. New stores, new products, discounted products, or something that catches their eye may help them to decide what information they need to further investigate. Browsing activities can serve as the prelude to direct information search, and therefore are also forms of direct information acquisition.

Indirect information acquisition is information-acquisition activities that are intentional or unintentional but do not directly serve the purpose of a specific purchase. However, such information could be used in future purchases with or without awareness and, therefore, exert informational influences. For example, consumers may intentionally browse some products in a store due to personal interest with no intentions to purchase anything. Later, when they want to make a purchase, they do not need extensive information search. Or, consumers may unintentionally but incidentally look at a highway billboard while driving. When they later develop the desire to buy that product, they may intentionally (i.e., remember that they saw this product on the billboard) or unintentionally (i.e., feel that they are familiar with the product and know some information about the product but do not remember when and where they got this information) use the information to make a purchase decision. It is proposed that such information is usually obtained indirectly through browsing.

Guidelines for Future Research and Implementation

Consumer information acquisition is an important area of research by itself. On the other hand, it is important also because it is closely related to consumer decisionmaking. Therefore, we will discuss the implication of our framework for research on consumer information acquisition and for consumer decisionmaking.

Implications for Consumer Information-Acquisition Research

Be Aware and Clear about the Underlying Assumptions

As we have argued, most existing research on consumer information search assumes that consumers know what they want to buy and what information they need. This implicit assumption may contribute to why we do not observe a close relationship between the amount of information searched and purchases made. Therefore, it is important to make this assumption clear and be aware of it when making inferences. As our framework suggests, consumers acquire information under various conditions. Depending on the specificity of consumer goals, the amount of attention they devote to the information and level of processing may vary. Depending on contextual information such as how information is presented, the length of exposure to a specific piece of information may vary. Depending on both information-exposure conditions and how a question is asked, the memory and retrieval of a piece of information may vary. Hence, corresponding to the caution of information-acquisition motivation and conditions, researchers should also be cautious about how to ask appropriate questions and should be concerned with not only what information consumers acquire but also how and when the information was acquired, before making inferences about consumers' information-acquisition behaviors.

Ask the Right Questions: Need for a Multimethod Approach

Little research has been conducted in marketing to investigate consumer browsing behaviors. Although research from library science and information systems can enrich our understanding of browsing, consumer browsing in a marketing context may be more dynamic when considering an individual's interactions with other consumers, shopping environments, and task characteristics. Research on browsing conducted in a marketing context has used surveys, asking subjects to recall their previous browsing activities (e.g., Beatty and Ferrell 1998; Bloch, Ridgway, and Sherrell 1989; Jarboe and McDaniel 1987). Janiszewski (1998) conducted experiments to demonstrate the existence of exploratory search behavior but did not study browsing per se. Such research does not allow serendipitous information search, nor does it capture information acquisition that is exploratory in nature. In addition, because browsing is casual and less structured, it is difficult to capture using one specific method. Further, browsing activities are also more dynamic, interacting with shopping environments and consumers' own temporal mood states. Because the consumer information-acquisition framework proposed here is multifaceted in nature, it requires multiple methods to capture the dynamic processes of information acquisition through browsing.

Research in library science has applied multiple methods to investigate browsing behaviors. For example, Belkin et al. (1990) combined methods of transaction logs, online questionnaires, nonparticipant observations, and in-depth interviews to gain an understanding of library browsing. They suggested that multiple methods are suitable for less structured phenomena such as browsing, where the user's goals and tasks are not well understood.

Research in social sciences has long advocated using multiple sources of data to achieve convergence. Multiple methods could be used to provide information on various aspects of browsing behaviors. For example, observations may reveal how consumers browse from a researcher's or observer's perspective, while interviews allow informants to articulate their browsing activities and experiences from their own perspective. In addition, shopping with consumers may potentially provide a rich source of data. Although shopping with consumers is not used frequently due to the high cost related to time and money, it provides researchers opportunities to get close to consumers in a natural setting (Otnes, McGrath, and Lowrey 1995). When studying browsing, shopping with consumers gives researchers the opportunity to obtain information that informants may fail to retrieve from memory or not voluntarily tell during interviews. Combining shopping trips with follow-up interviews may provide a vivid presentation of informants' interactions with vendors and their personal feelings and experiences, hence providing insights on consumer browsing processes (Xia 2003). Also, videotaping shoppers in a store or when online would provide more information about their browsing habits and activities. Finally, specific techniques such as eye-tracking technology may be used to measure consumers' attention allocation in a shopping environment. Such technology potentially could be used to study consumer browsing.

Implications for Consumer Decisionmaking Research

Information acquired through either direct search or browsing may ultimately influence consumer decisionmaking. Hence, another implication of the framework is for research on consumer decisionmaking. A typical experiment on consumer decisionmaking provides subjects with product information and then examines how consumers utilize such information when making a choice. In such research, subjects explicitly use such information and are aware of the sources of information. However, research has shown that consumers may not need to explicitly recall a piece of information to use it in their decisionmaking processes (Lee 2002; Shapiro, MacInnis, and Heckler 1997). To make a finer distinction of how consumers use what kind information under what conditions, it is important to consider the different types of choice tasks they face.

Types of Choice Tasks

Consumer choice tasks could be either stimulus based or memory based or a mixture of both (Alba, Hutchinson, and Lynch 1991). For example, when thinking of where to have dinner, consumers need to retrieve information from memory. Such choices are based mainly on their memory, and information accessibility is crucial. Consumers may retrieve information of several restaurants on the type of food, food quality, environment, and restaurant location to help them make a decision. Therefore, memory-based tasks tend to require more conceptual than perceptual information processing. On the other hand, in stimulus-based tasks, consumers are presented information from the environment. A particular name of the restaurant or a picture may prompt consumers to pick one restaurant instead of another. Such tasks tend to require perceptual as well as conceptual processing.

The implication of distinguishing different types of choice tasks is to try to access the influences of information consumers have acquired through different ways. If, as we discussed, information acquired through direct search is more extensively processed and tends to be conceptual in nature and stored as explicit memory, then that information may have a larger influence on memory-based choice tasks, which requires information accessibility. On the other hand, if information acquired through browsing is more perceptual and stored as implicit memory, then that information may have a larger influence on stimulus-based choice tasks. Although not much research has been done, there is some evidence that this might be the case. Lee (2002) conducted experiments to examine the influence of implicit versus explicit memory on different types of tasks. When subjects were exposed only to brand names, this type of information exposure led to better performance later in a stimulus-based choice task. However, when exposed to these brand names in the context of other relevant information that enhanced elaboration, subjects later performed better in a memory-based choice task.

Measuring Nonconscious Information Processing and Implicit Memory

Methodology and measurement issues impose a big hurdle for the study of nonconscious information processing and implicit memory. Several methods developed and used in psychology may be borrowed and adapted for marketing research.

Direct Versus Indirect Memory Tests. In a typical memory test in marketing research, subjects are usually asked to recall a previous episode. In implicit versus explicit memory research, such a test is called a direct test. However, people do not need to be able to make the association between memory and a specific previous exposure to use that information when performing a task. In the context of browsing and search, a consumer may forget where he or she browsed but still can apply information obtained to a choice task. Therefore, it may be appropriate to apply indirect tests in memory and choice research. Direct and indirect tests are distinguished in terms of instructions and measurement criteria (Richardson-Klavehn and Bjork 1988). In a direct test, people are referred to a particular study episode and asked to indicate their knowledge of that episode in some way, as in a recognition or cued recall test. In an indirect test, people are instructed to undertake a task without referring to the previous study episode. Successful performance on the task does not depend on clearly recalling information during the prior study episode, although performance nevertheless may be influenced by that episode.

Based on direct versus indirect tests technique, Schacter, Browers, and Booker (1989) argued that while explicit memory is intentional retrieval of specific information, implicit memory is unintentional retrieval of information from a specific prior episode. They proposed the *retrieval intentionality criterion* as the major principle for testing the influence of implicit memory. The criterion comprises two key elements. First, all external cues other than task instructions provided to subjects on direct and indirect tests should be the same. Second, a variable should be identified such that manipulation of the variable would show an effect on one test but have no or an opposite effect on the other test. For example, in the context of browsing and searching, researchers could identify major characteristics that distinguish one from the other, such as amount of attention paid to the stimuli or level of processing. Then, researchers can manipulate this characteristic and later test memory of this information using direct and indirect tests. The logic of the retrieval-intentionality criterion is that if manipulation of a variable produces differential effects on two tests while the two tests differ only in instruction (direct vs. indirect), then the effects observed can be attributed to differences in intentional versus incidental retrieval processes used in task performance.

Other similar methods are also available. For example, the different influence between implicit and explicit memory can also be demonstrated by the correlation between the performances on different tasks. Tulving, Schacter, and Stark (1982) suggested a stochastic independent criterion, which demonstrated near zero correlation between direct and indirect tasks performed by the same subject. Hayman and Tulving (1989) using a *triangulation* method and a between-subject design demonstrated the same low correlation.

The Process-Dissociation Procedure. The process-dissociation procedure seeks to separate the contribution of conscious and automatic memory processes within one task (Jacoby 1991; Jacoby, Toth, and Yonelinas 1993). In this procedure, subjects first study the stimuli (usually a list of words) under different conditions such as incidental versus intentional learning or full versus divided attention. Then the subjects receive a memory test. One group of subjects will be instructed to first recall the studied items and complete the stems/fragments with the recalled old items (inclusion). The other group of subjects, while receiving the same study and testing cues, would be instructed to respond to the test with items not in the study phase (exclusion). The logic of the process-dissociation procedure is that while both inclusion and exclusion conditions promote intentional retrieval, the exclusion condition may actually reveal the influence of the study phase without subjects' awareness. Since they are instructed to exclude any studied items but unintentional retrieval works against this instruction, any studied items included in their responses will provide evidence of retrieval of studied items without awareness. Jacoby, Toth, and Yonelinas (1993) have used the process-dissociation procedure extensively to demonstrate automatic processing and retrieval. The process-dissociation procedure has been applied to marketing research for studying the effect of incidental and intentional learning and has proven useful (e.g., Shapiro, MacInnis, and Heckler 1997).

Measures of Awareness. We suggest that consumers acquire, process, and retrieve information with or without awareness (see Adaval and Monroe 2002). Therefore, measuring consumers' awareness in a task could be an important issue. Awareness is a crucial but fuzzy issue in implicit memory. Research suggests that there could be different "levels" of awareness. Schacter, Bowers, and Booker (1989) used five scenarios to illustrate awareness. Depending on how a researcher defines implicit memory, different scenarios could qualify.

Different measures have been used to measure awareness. Awareness can be measured by either subjective or objective measures. In studies where awareness is controlled by varying stimulus presentation time or degree of degradation, subjective awareness can be obtained by asking subjects to indicate whether they see the stimulus, see something but are not sure, or do not see anything at all (see Bargh and Chartrand 2000). Objective measures of awareness can be obtained by asking subjects to discriminate between a target and an alternative stimulus. In studies where awareness is controlled by divided attention, awareness status is usually measured by the subjective method. Subjects are asked to report whether they *see* the stimuli located outside of focus of attention. Both subjective and objective measures have been used in studies of implicit memory and have supported perception without awareness. Some have argued that objective measures are stricter and provide a more accurate method to assess awareness. However, awareness by nature is a subjective experience of the subjects, so a subjective measure is valid (Merikle, Smilek, and Eastwood 2001).

Overall, we have outlined a set of methods that are available and could be modified and adapted to research on browsing and searching. Each of these methods has its pros and cons and should be studied carefully when applying them to marketing research. For example, although the process-dissociation procedure has been used widely, it is not without criticism. The assumptions underlying the method, such as independence between intentional and automatic components of a response, are often violated.

Conclusion

Consumer information acquisition is an important issue in consumer-behavior research. The literature we have reviewed shows that existing research in consumer direct information search captures only part of consumer information-acquisition behaviors. The purpose of this article has been to go beyond direct information search and include browsing as an integral part of consumer information-acquisition behavior. We have extended Bloch, Ridgway, and Sherrell's (1989) concept of ongoing information search, delineated different dimensions of the searching-browsing continuum, and suggested some methods to test these issues empirically. Theoretically, this approach broadens the scope of research in consumer information search and provides a new area and methods for research. In addition, most consumer decisionmaking models conceptualize the decisionmaking process as conscious and effortful. However, research in information processing and memory has shown that a large amount of information processing could be nonconscious, and information could be stored in people's memory systems without their awareness. Consumer browsing is an activity that may tap this implicit information processing and storage. Since consumer information acquisition is a crucial element of consumer decisionmaking, understanding consumer browsing behavior and its potential influence on consumer decisionmaking will contribute to our knowledge of consumer information acquisition as well as consumer decisionmaking.

Methodologically, the unique characteristics of browsing impose challenges to study the phenomenon. First, compared to direct search, browsing is more casual and less structured. Such phenomena may be difficult to capture using a single method or a single study. Multiple methods may be necessary to gain insights on the multifacets of consumer browsing. Second, since some browsing activity and its potential influences may be without consumers' awareness, carefully crafted specific tests need to be designed.

Browsing and searching are complements to each other. Although they can be distinguished conceptually, it is hard to separate the two behaviorally because browsing and searching could operate at the same time, and/or consumers can switch smoothly back and forth from browsing to searching to browsing, even without awareness. Although the transitory and less-structured characteristic of browsing imposes difficulty on empirically capturing and analyzing the phenomena, it is worthwhile to look beyond direct search and integrate browsing into the framework of consumer information acquisition. Finally, in the context of consumer behavior, it is interesting to examine in detail how people browse, what factors influence browsing, and how browsing further influences consumer decisionmaking. These are questions to be answered in order to get a fuller picture of consumer information acquisition. Previous research on consumer shopping environments may offer valuable insights on these issues. This review has focused on browsing as an information-acquisition activity, but the broader role of browsing in consumers' experiences in the shopping environment also deserves further exploration. In addition, since the Internet is increasingly becoming an important vehicle for consumers' information acquisition and purchasing, searching and browsing in an online context may exhibit different characteristics than those activities in an offline context. Our review does not address this issue explicitly, and this issue deserves future examination.

Acknowledgment

The authors acknowledge with gratitude the helpful comments by Sharon Beatty, Nancy Ridgway, and Naresh Malhotra on an earlier draft of this manuscript.

References

Abdul-Muhmin, Alhassan G. (1999), "Contingent Decision Behavior: Effect of Number of Alternatives to Be Selected on Consumers' Decision Processes," *Journal of Consumer Psychology*, 8 (1), 91–111.

Adaval, Rashmi and Kent B. Monroe (2002), "Automatic Construction and Use of Contextual Information for Product and Price Evaluations," *Journal of Consumer Research*, 28 (March), 572–88.

Aguilar, Francis Joseph (1967), *Scanning the Business Environment*. New York: Macmillan.

Alba, Joseph W., J. Wesley Hutchinson, and John G. Lynch, Jr. (1991), "Memory and Decision Making," in *Handbook of Consumer Behavior*, Thomas S. Robertson and Harold H. Kassarjian, eds. Englewood Cliffs, NJ: Prentice Hall, 1–49.

Apted, S.M. (1971), "General Purposive Browsing," *Library Association Record*, 73 (12), 228–30.

Arnold, Mark J. and Kristy E. Reynolds (2003), "Hedonic Shopping Motivations," *Journal of Retailing*, 79 (2), 77–95.

Auster, E. and C.W. Choo (1991), "Environmental Scanning: A Conceptual Framework for Studying the Information Seeking Behavior of Executives," *Proceedings of the American Society for Information Science*, 28, 3–8.

Avery, Rosemary J. (1996), "Determinants of Search for Nondurable Goods: An Empirical Assessment of the Economics of Information Theory," *Journal of Consumer Affairs*, 30 (Winter), 390–420.

Baars, Bernard J. (1997), "Some Essential Differences Between Consciousness and Attention, Perception, and Working Memory," *Consciousness and Cognition*, 6, 363–71.

Babin, Barry J., William R. Darden, and Mitch Griffin (1994), "Work and/or Fun: Measuring Hedonic and Utilitarian Shopping Value," *Journal of Consumer Research*, 20 (March), 644–56.

Bagozzi, Richard P. (1997), "Goal-Directed Behaviors in Marketing: Cognitive and Emotional Perspectives," *Psychology & Marketing*, 14 (September), 539–43.

———— (1998), "The Role of Emotion and Volition in the Regulation of Economic Behavior," in *Will and Economic Behavior*, Lennart Sjoberg, Richard P. Bagozzi, and David Ingvar, eds. Stockholm: Stockholm School of Economics, 59–84.

Bagozzi, Richard P. and Utpal Dholakia (1999), "Goal Setting and Goal Striving in Consumer Behavior," *Journal of Marketing*, 63 (Special Issue), 19–32.

Baker, Sharon (1986), "Overload, Browsers, and Selections," *Library and Information Science Research*, 8 (4), 315–29.

Banaji, Mahzarin R., Irene V. Blair, and Norbert Schwarz (1996), "Implicit Memory and Survey Measurement," in *Answering Questions: Methodology for Determining Cognitive and Communicative Processes in Survey Research*, Norbert Schwarz and Seymour Sudman, eds. San Francisco: Jossey-Bass, 347–72.

Bankapur, M.B. (1988), "On Browsing," *Library Science with a Slant to Documentation*, 25 (3), 131–37.

Bargh, John A. and Tanya L. Chartrand (2000), "The Mind in the Middle: A Practical Guide to Priming and Automaticity Research," in *Handbook of Research Methods in Social and Personality Psychology*, Harry T. Reis and Charles M. Judd, eds. Cambridge: Cambridge University Press, 253–85.

Bates, Marcia J. (1989), "The Design of Browsing and Berrypicking Techniques for the Online Search Interface," *Online Review*, 13 (5), 407–24.

Beatty, Sharon E. and M. Elizabeth Ferrell (1998), "Impulse Buying: Modeling Its Precursors," *Journal of Retailing*, 74 (2), 169–91.

Beatty, Sharon E. and Scott M. Smith (1987), "External Search Effort: An Investigation Across Several Product Categories," *Journal of Consumer Research*, 14 (June), 83–95.

Belkin, Nicholas J., Shan-Ju Chang, Trudy Downs, Tefko Saracevic, and Shuyuan Zhao (1990), "Taking Account of User Tasks, Goals and Behavior for the Design of Online Public Access Catalogs," in *Proceedings of the American Society for Information Science (ASIS) 53rd Annual Meeting*, D. Henderson, ed. Volume 27. Toronto, Canada: Learned Information, Inc., for ASIS, 69–79.

Bennett, Peter D. and Robert M. Mandell (1969), "Purchase Information Seeking Behavior of New Car Purchasers—the Learning Hypothesis," *Journal of Marketing Research*, 6, 430–33.

Berendt, Bettina and Elke Brenstein (2001), "Visualizing Individual Differences in Web Navigation: STRATDYN, a Tool for Analyzing Navigation Patterns," *Behavior Research Methods, Instruments & Computers*, 33 (2), 243–57.

Bettman, James R. (1979), *An Information Processing Theory of Consumer Choice*. Reading, MA: Addison-Wesley.

Bettman, James R., Eric J. Johnson, Mary Frances Luce, and John W. Payne (1993), "Correlation, Conflict, and Choice," *Journal of Experimental Psychology: Learning, Memory, and Cognition*, 19 (July), 931–51.

Bettman, James R. and Pradeep Kakkar (1977), "Effects of Information Presentation Format on Consumer Information Acquisition Strategies," *Journal of Consumer Research*, 3 (March), 233–40.

Bettman, James R., Mary Frances Luce, and John W. Payne (1998), "Constructive Consumer Choice Processes," *Journal of Consumer Research*, 25 (December), 187–217.

Biehal, Gabriel and Dipankar Chakravarti (1983), "Information Accessibility as a Moderator of Consumer Choice," *Journal of Consumer Research*, 10 (June), 1–14.

Blaxton, Teresa A. (1989), "Investigating Dissociations Among Memory Measures: Support for a Transfer Appropriate Processing Framework," *Journal of Experimental Psychology: Learning, Memory, and Cognition*, 15 (4), 657–68.

Bloch, Peter H. and Marsha L. Richins (1983), "Shopping without Purchase: An Investigation of Consumer Browsing Behavior," in *Advances in Consumer Research*, volume 10, Richard P. Bagozzi and Alice M. Tybout, eds. Ann Arbor, MI: Association for Consumer Research, 389–93.

Bloch, Peter H., Nancy M. Ridgway, and Scott A. Dawson (1994), "The Shopping Mall as Consumer Habitat," *Journal of Retailing*, 70 (1), 23–42.

Bloch, Peter H., Nancy M. Ridgway, and Daniel L. Sherrell (1989), "Expanding the Concept of Shopping: An Investigation of Browsing Activity," *Journal of the Academy of Marketing Science*, 17 (1), 13–21.

Bloch, Peter H., Daniel L. Sherrell, and Nancy M. Ridgway (1986), "Consumer Search: An Extended Framework," *Journal of Consumer Research*, 13 (June), 119–26.

Bowers, Jeffrey S. and Daniel L. Schacter (1990), "Implicit Memory and Test Awareness," *Journal of Experimental Psychology: Learning, Memory, and Cognition*, 16, 404–16.

Brucks, Merrie (1985), "The Effects of Product Class Knowledge on Information Search Behavior," *Journal of Consumer Research*, 12 (June), 1–16.

——— (1988), "Search Monitor: An Approach for Computer-Controlled Experiments Involving Consumer Information," *Journal of Consumer Research*, 15 (June), 117–21.

Brucks, Merrie and Paul H. Schurr (1990), "The Effects of Bargainable Attributes and Attribute Range Knowledge on Consumer Choice Processes," *Journal of Consumer Research*, 16 (March), 409–19.

Bucklin, Louis P. (1969), "Consumer Search, Role Enactment, and Market Efficiency," *Journal of Business*, 42 (4), 416–38.

Bucklin, Randolph E. and Catarina Sismeiro (2003), "A Model of Web Site Browsing Behavior Estimated on Clickstream Data," *Journal of Marketing Research*, 40 (August), 249–67.

Canter, David, Rod Rivers, and Graham Storrs (1985), "Characterizing User Navigation Through Complex Data Structures," *Behaviour and Information Technology*, 4 (2), 93–102.

Capon, Noel and Marian Burke (1977), "Information Seeking Behavior in Consumer Durable Purchases," in *Contemporary Marketing Thought*, Barnett A. Greenberg and Danny N. Bellinger, eds. Chicago: American Marketing Association, 110–15.

Cardozo, Richard N. (1965), "An Experimental Study of Customer Effort, Expectation, and Satisfaction," *Journal of Marketing Research*, 2 (August), 244–49.

Carlson, John A. and Robert J. Gieseke (1983), "Price Search in a Product Market," *Journal of Consumer Research*, 9 (March), 357–65.

Carmel, Erran, Stephen Crawford, and Hsinchun Chen (1992), "Browsing in Hypertext: A Cognitive Study," *IEEE Transactions on Systems, Man and Cybernetics*, 22 (5), 865–84.

Chang, Shan-Ju L. (1995), "Toward a Multidimensional Framework for Understanding Browsing," unpublished doctoral dissertation, Department of Library and Information Science, Rutgers University.

Chang, Shan-Ju L. and R.E. Rice (1993), "Browsing: A Multidimensional Framework," in *Annual Review of Information Science and Technology*, M. Williams, ed. Volume 28. White Plains, NY: Knowledge Industries, 231–76.

Claxton, John G., Joseph N. Fry, and Bernard Portis (1974), "A Taxonomy of Prepurchase Information Gathering Patterns," *Journal of Consumer Research*, 1 (December), 35–42.

Cohen, Neal J. and Larry R. Squire (1980), "Preserved Learning and Retention of Pattern Analyzing Skill in Amnesia: Dissociation of Knowing How and Knowing That," *Science*, 210 (4466), 207–209.

Conklin, Jeff (1987), "Hypertext: An Introduction and Survey," *Computer*, 20 (9), 17–41.

Copeland, Melvin T. (1923), "Relation of Consumers' Buying Habits to Marketing Methods," *Harvard Business Review*, 1 (April), 282–89.

Cort, Stanton G. and Luis V. Dominguez (1977), "Cross-Shopping and Retail Growth," *Journal of Marketing Research*, 14 (May), 187–92.

Coupey, Eloise (1994), "Restructuring: Constructive Processing of Information Displays in Consumer Choice," *Journal of Consumer Research*, 21 (1), 83–99.

Cove, J.F. and B.C. Walsh (1987), "Browsing as a Means of Online Text Retrieval," *Information Services & Use*, 7 (6), 183–88.

——— and ——— (1988), "Online Text Retrieval Via Browsing," *Information Processing and Management*, 24 (10), 31–37.

Cox, Donald F. and Stuart Rich (1964), "Perceived Risk and Consumer Decision Making—A Case of Telephone Shopping," *Journal of Marketing Research*, 1 (November), 32–39.

d'Astous, Alain (2000), "Irritating Aspects of the Shopping Environment," *Journal of Business Research*, 49 (August), 149–56.

Dawson, Scott (1988), "An Exploration of the Store Prestige Hierarchy: Reification, Power, and Perceptions," *Journal of Retailing*, 64 (2), 133–52.

Dawson, Scott, Peter H. Bloch, and Nancy M. Ridgway (1990), "Shopping Motives, Emotional States, and Retail Outcomes," *Journal of Retailing*, 66, 408–27.

DeSchepper, Brett and Anne Treisman (1996), "Visual Memory for Novel Shapes: Implicit Coding Without Attention," *Journal of Experimental Psychology: Learning, Memory & Cognition*, 22 (1), 27–47.

Dias, Paulo, Maria Joao Gomes, and Ana Paula Correia (1999), "Disorientation in Hypermedia Environments: Mechanisms to Support Navigation," *Journal of Educational Computing Research*, 20 (2), 93–117.

Dienes, Zoltan and Josef Perner (1999), "A Theory of Implicit and Explicit Knowledge," *Behavioral and Brain Sciences*, 22, 735–808.

DiFonzo, Nicholas, Donald A. Hantula, and Prashant Bordia (1998), "Microworlds for Experimental Research: Having Your (Control and Collections) Cake, and Realism Too," *Behavior Research Methods, Instruments & Computers*, 30 (2), 278–86.

Dogu, Ufuk and Feyzan Erkip (2000), "Spatial Factors Affecting Wayfinding and Orientation: A Case Study in a Shopping Mall," *Environment & Behavior*, 32 (6), 731–55.

Dommermuth, William P. (1965), "The Shopping Matrix and Marketing Strategy," *Journal of Marketing Research*, 2 (May), 128–32.

Dommermuth, William P. and Edward Cundiff (1967), "Shopping Goods, Shopping Centers and Selling Strategies," *Journal of Marketing*, 31 (October), 32–36.

Donovan, Robert, and John R. Rossiter (1982), "Store Atmosphere: An Environmental Psychology Approach," *Journal of Retailing*, 58 (Spring), 34–57.

Donovan, Robert, John R. Rossiter, G. Marcoolyn, and A. Nesdale (1994), "Store Atmosphere and Purchasing Behavior," *Journal of Retailing*, 70, 283–94.

Dowling, Grahame R. and Richard Staelin (1994), "A Model of Perceived Risk and Intended Risk-Handling Activity," *Journal of Consumer Research*, 21 (June), 119–34.

Duncan, Calvin P. and Richard W. Olshavsky (1982), "External Search: The Role of Consumer Beliefs," *Journal of Marketing Research*, 19 (February), 32–43.

Engel, James F., T. David, T. Kollat, and Roger D. Blackwell (1972), *Consumer Behavior.* Hinsdale, IL: Dryden.

Ericsson, K. Anders and Herbert A. Simon (1980), "Verbal Reports as Data," *Psychological Review*, 87 (May), 215–51.

Fisk, Arthur D. and Walter Schneider (1984), "Memory as a Function of Attention, Level of Processing, and Automatization," *Journal of Experimental Psychology: Learning, Memory, and Cognition*, 10 (2), 181–97.

Foss, C.L. (1989), "Tools for Reading and Browsing Hypertext," *Information Processing and Management*, 25 (4), 407–18.

Ganor-Stern, Donna, John G. Seamon, and Marisa Garrasco (1998), "The Role of Attention and Study Time in Explicit and Implicit Memory for Unfamiliar Visual Stimuli," *Memory & Cognition*, 26 (6), 1187–95.

Gardiner, John M. and Alan Parkin (1990), "Attention and Recollective Experience in Recognition Memory," *Memory & Cognition*, 18 (6), 579–83.

Gemunden, Hans Georg (1985), "Perceived Risk and Information Search. A Systematic Meta-analysis of the Empirical Evidence," *International Journal of Research in Marketing*, 2 (2), 79–100.

Goschke, Thomas (1997), "Implicit Learning and Unconscious Knowledge: Mental Representation, Computational Mechanisms, and Brain Structures," in *Knowledge, Concepts and Categories*, Koen Lamberts and David Shanks, eds. Cambridge, MA: MIT Press, 247–329.

Graf, Peter and George Mandler (1984), "Activation Makes Words More Accessible, but Not Necessarily More Retrievable," *Journal of Verbal Learning and Verbal Behavior*, 23 (5), 553–68.

Graf, Peter and Daniel L. Schacter (1985), "Implicit and Explicit Memory for New Associations in Normal and Amnesic Subjects," *Journal of Experimental Psychology: Learning, Memory, and Cognition*, 11 (3), 501–18.

Greene, Robert L. (1986), "Word Stems as Cues in Recall and Completion Tasks," *Quarterly Journal of Experimental Psychology*, 38 (4-A), 663–73.

Grewal, Dhruv and Howard Marmorstein (1994), "Market Price Variation, Perceived Price Variation, and Consumers' Price Search Decisions for Durable Goods," *Journal of Consumer Research*, 21 (December), 453–60.

Grunert, Klaus G. (1996), "Automatic and Strategic Processes in Advertising Effects," *Journal of Marketing*, 60 (October), 88–101.

Hauser, John R., Glen L. Urban, and Bruce D. Weinberg (1993), "How Consumers Allocate Their Time When Searching for Information," *Journal of Marketing Research*, 30 (4), 452–66.

Hawkins, Scott A. and Stephen J. Hoch (1992), "Low-Involvement Learning: Memory Without Evaluation," *Journal of Consumer Research*, 19 (September), 212–25.

Hawkins, Scott A., Stephen J. Hoch, and Joan Meyers-Levy (2001), "Low-Involvement Learning: Repetition and Coherence in Familarity and Belief," *Journal of Consumer Psychology*, 11 (1), 1–11.

Hayman, C. Gordon and Endel Tulving (1989), "Contingent Dissociation Between Recognition and Fragment Completion: The Method of Triangulation," *Journal of Experimental Psychology: Learning, Memory, and Cognition*, 15 241–49 (2), 228–40.

Hempel, Donald J. (1969), "Search Behavior and Information Utilization in the Home Buying Process," in *Marketing Involvement in Society and the Economy*, Philip R. McDonald, ed. Chicago: American Marketing Association, 241–49.

Herner, Saul (1970), "Browsing," in *Encyclopedia of Library and Information Science*, A. Kent and H. Lancour, eds. Volume 3. New York: Marcel Dekker, 408–15.

Hirshman, Elliot and Neil W. Mulligan (1991), "Perceptual Interference Improves Explicit Memory But Does Not Enhance Data-Driven Processing," *Journal of Experimental Psychology: Learning, Memory, and Cognition*, 17 (3), 507–13.

Hodkinson, Chris, Geoffrey Kiel, and Janet R. McColl-Kennedy (2000), "Consumer Web Search Behaviour: Diagrammatic Illustration of Wayfinding on the Web," *International Journal of Human-Computer Studies*, 52, 805–30.

Holbrook, Morris B. and Karl A. Maier (1978), "A Study of the Interface Between Attitude Structure and Information Acquisition Using a Questionnaire-Based Information Display Sheet," in *Advances in Consumer Research*, volume 5, H. Keith Hunt, ed. Chicago: Association for Consumer Research, 93–98.

Holden, Stephen J.S. and Marc Vanhuele (1999), "Know the Name, Forget the Exposure: Brand Familiarity Versus Memory of Exposure Context," *Psychology & Marketing*, 16 (6), 479–96.

Howard, John A. and Jagdish N. Sheth (1969), *The Theory of Buyer Behavior*. New York: Wiley.

Huffman, Cynthia and Michael J. Houston (1993), "Goal-oriented Experiences and the Development of Knowledge," *Journal of Consumer Research*, 20 (September), 190–207.

Hughes, G. David, Sena M. Tinie, and Phillippe A. Naert (1969), "Analyzing Consumer Information Processing," in *Marketing Involvement in Society and the Economy*, Philip R. McDonald, ed. Chicago: American Marketing Association, 235–40.

Huppertz, John W., S.J. Arenson, and R.H. Evans (1978), "An Application of Equity Theory to Buyer-Seller Exchange Situations," *Journal of Marketing Research*, 15 (May), 250–60.

Hyman, Richard Joseph (1972), *Access to Library Collections: An Inquiry Into the Validity of the Direct Shelf Approach, with Special Reference to Browsing*. Metuchen, NJ: Scarecrow Press.

Iyer, Easwar S. (1989), "Unplanned Purchasing: Knowledge of Shopping Environment and Time Pressure," *Journal of Retailing*, 65 (1), 40–57.

Jacoby, Jacob, Robert W. Chestnut, and William A. Fisher (1978), "A Behavioral Process Approach to Information Acquisition in Nondurable Purchasing," *Journal of Marketing Research*, 15 (November), 532–44.

Jacoby, Jacob, James J. Jaccard, Imran Currim, Alfred Kuss, Asim Ansari, and Tracy Troutman (1994), "Tracing the Impact of Item-by-Item Information Accessing on Uncertainty Reduction," *Journal of Consumer Research*, 21 (September), 291–303.

Jacoby, Larry L. (1991), "A Process Dissociation Framework: Separating Automatic from Intentional Uses of Memory," *Journal of Memory and Language*, 30, 513–41.

Jacoby, Larry L. and Mark Dallas (1981), "On the Relationship Between Autobiographical Memory and Perceptual Learning," *Journal of Experimental Psychology: General*, 110 (3), 306–40.

Jacoby, Larry L., Jeffrey P. Toth, and Andrew P. Yonelinas (1993), "Separating Conscious and Unconscious Influences of Memory: Measuring Recollection," *Journal of Experimental Psychology: General*, 122 (2), 139–54.

Janiszewski, Chris (1993), "Preattentive Mere Exposure Effect," *Journal of Consumer Research*, 20 (December), 376–92.

——— (1998), "The Influence of Display Characteristics on Visual Exploratory Search Behavior," *Journal of Consumer Research*, 25 (December), 290–301.

Jarboe, Glen R. and Carl D. McDaniel (1987), "A Profile of Browsers in Regional Shopping Mall," *Journal of Academy of Marketing Science*, 15 (Spring), 45–52.

Johnson, Eric J. and John W. Payne (1985), "Effort and Accuracy in Choice," *Management Science*, 31 (4), 359–414.

Johnson, Eric J., John W. Payne, and James Bettman (1988), "Information Displays and Preference Reversals," *Organizational Behavior and Human Decision Processes*, 42, 1–21.

Kahneman, Daniel (1973), *Attention and Effort*. Englewood Cliffs, NJ: Prentice Hall.

Katona, George and Eva Mueller (1955), "A Study of Purchasing Decisions," in *Consumer Behavior: The Dynamics of Consumer Reaction*, Lincoln H. Clark, ed. New York: New York University Press, 30–87.

Kennedy, John R. and Peter C. Thirkell (1983), "Consumer Satisfaction as a Function of Search, Experience, Individual Differences and Circumstances of Use," in *International Fare In Consumer Satisfaction and Complaining Behavior: Papers from the Seventh Annual Conference on Consumer Satisfaction, Dissatisfaction, and Complaining Behavior*, volume 7, Ralph L. Day and H. Keith Hunt, eds. Bloomington: Indiana University Press, 17–25.

Kiel, Geoffrey C. and Roger A. Layton (1981), "Dimensions of Consumer Information Seeking," *Journal of Marketing Research*, 18 (May), 233–39.

Kirsner, Kim, Craig Speelman, Murray Maybery, Angela O'Brien-Malone, Mike Anderson, and Colin Macleod, eds. (1998), *Implicit and Explicit Mental Processes*. Mahwah, NJ: Lawrence Erlbaum Associates.

Klein, Lisa R. and Gary T. Ford (2003), "Consumer Search for Information in the Digital Age: An Empirical Study of Prepurchase Search for Automobiles," *Journal of Interactive Marketing*, 17 (Summer), 29–49.

Kollat, David T. and Ronald P. Willett (1967), "Customer Impulse Purchasing Behavior," *Journal of Marketing Research*, 4 (February), 21–31.

Krishnan, H. Shanker and Dipankar Chakravarti (1999), "Memory Measures for Pretesting Advertisements: An Integrative Conceptual Framework and a Diagnostic Template," *Journal of Consumer Psychology*, 8 (1), 1–37.

Kwasnik, Barbara H. (1992), "A Descriptive Study of the Functional Components of Browsing," in *Engineering for Human-Computer Interaction: Proceedings of the IFIP TC2/WG2.7 Working Conference on Engineering for Human-Computer Interaction*, J. Larson and C. Unger, eds. Ellivuori, Finland: North-Holland, 3–10.

Lawson, Robert (1997), "Consumer Decision Making within a Goal-Driven Framework," *Psychology & Marketing*, 14 (5), 427–49.

Lee, Angela Y. (2002), "Effects of Implicit Memory on Memory-Based Versus Stimulus-Based Brand Choice," *Journal of Marketing Research*, 39 (November), 440–54.

Lee, Hanjoon, Paul M. Herr, Frank R. Kardes, and Chankon Kim (1999), "Motivated Search: Effects of Choice Accountability, Issue Involvement, and Prior Knowledge on Information Acquisition and Use," *Journal of Business Research*, 45 (May), 75–88.

LeGrand, Bruce and Jon G. Udell (1964), "Consumer Behavior in the Market Place—An Empirical Study in the TV and Furniture Fields with Theoretical Implications," *Journal of Retailing*, 40 (Fall), 32–40.

Lehmann, Donald R. and William L. Moore (1980), "Validity of Information Display Boards: An Assessment Using Longitudinal Data," *Journal of Marketing Research*, 17 (November), 450–59.

Lewicki, Pawel, Thomas Hill, and Maria Czyzewska (1992), "Nonconscious Acquisition of Information," *American Psychologist*, 47 (6), 796–801.

Liebscher, Peter and Gary Marchionini (1988), "Browse and Analytical Search Strategies in a Full-Text CD-ROM Encyclopedia," *School Library Media Quarterly*, 16 (Summer), 223–33.

MacLeod, Colin (1998), "Implicit Perception: Perceptual Processing Without Awareness," in *Implicit and Explicit Mental Processes*, Kim Kirsner, Craig Speelman, Murray Maybery, Angela O'Brien-Malone, Mike Anderson, and Colin MacLeod, eds. Mahwah, NJ: Lawrence Erlbaum Associates, 57–78.

Maheswaran, Durairaj, Brian Sternthal, and Zeynep Guerhan (1996), "Acquisition and Impact of Consumer Expertise," *Journal of Consumer Psychology*, 5 (2), 115–33.

Malhotra, Naresh K. (1983), "On 'Individual Differences in Search Behavior for a Nondurable,'" *Journal of Consumer Research*, 10 (June), 125–31.

Marchionini, Gary (1987), "An Invitation to Browse: Designing Full Text Systems for Novice Users," *Canadian Journal of Information Science*, 12 (3), 69–79.

——— (1995), *Information Seeking In Electronic Environment*. New York: Cambridge University Press.

Marchionini, Gary and B. Shneiderman (1988), "Finding Facts vs. Browsing Knowledge in Hypertext Systems," *IEEE Computer*, 21 (1), 70–79.

Maute, Manfred F. and William R. Forrester (1991), "The Effect of Attribute Qualities on Consumer Decision Making: A Causal Model of External Information," *Journal of Economic Psychology*, 12 (4), 643–66.

Mehta, Nitin, Surenda Rajiv, and Kannan Srinivasan (2003), "Price Uncertainty and Consumer Search: A Structural Model of Consideration Set Formation," *Marketing Science*, 22 (Winter), 58–84.

Merikle, Phillip M., Daniel Smilek, and John D. Eastwood (2001), "Perception without Awareness: Perspectives from Cognitive Psychology," *Cognition*, 79 (1–2), 115–34.

Milech, Dan and Melissa Finucane (1998), "Decision Support and Behavioral Decision Theory," in *Implicit and Explicit Mental Processes*, Kim Kirsner, Craig Speelman, Murray Maybery, Angela O'Brien-Malone, Mike Anderson, and Colin MacLeod, eds. Mahwah, NJ: Lawrence Erlbaum Associates, 291–307.

Miller, George A. (1956), "The Magic Number Seven, Plus or Minus Two: Some Limits on Our Capacity for Processing Information," *The Psychological Review*, 63 (March), 81–97.

Monroe, Kent B. (2003), *Pricing: Making Profitable Decisions* (3rd ed.). Burr Ridge, IL: McGraw-Hill/Irwin.

Monroe, Kent B. and Angela Y. Lee (1999), "Remembering Versus Knowing: Issues in Buyers' Processing of Price Information," *Journal of the Academy of Marketing Science*, 27 (2), 207–25.

Moore, William L. and Donald R. Lehmann (1980), "Individual Differences in Search Behavior for Nondurables," *Journal of Consumer Research*, 7 (December), 296–307.

Moorthy, Sridhar, Brian T. Ratchford, and Debabrata Talukdar (1997), "Consumer Information Search Revisited: Theory and Empirical Analysis," *Journal of Consumer Research*, 23 (March), 263–77.

Mulligan, Neil W. (1997), "Attention and Implicit Memory Tests: The Effects of Varying Attentional Load on Conceptual Priming," *Memory & Cognition*, 25 (1), 11–17.

Nelson, Philip (1970), "Information and Consumer Behavior," *Journal of Political Economy*, 78 (March-April), 311–29.

Newman, Joseph W. (1977), "Consumer External Search: Amount and Determinants," in *Consumer and Industrial Buying Behavior*, Arch Woodside, Jagdish Sheth, and Peter Bennett, eds. New York: North-Holland, 79–94.

Newman, Joseph W. and B.D. Lockeman (1975), "Measuring Prepurchase Information Seeking," *Journal of Consumer Research*, 2 (December), 216–22.

Newman, Joseph W. and Richard Staelin (1972), "Prepurchase Information Seeking for New Cars and Major Household Appliances," *Journal of Marketing Research*, 9 (August), 249–57.

O'Connor, Brian (1993), "Browsing: A Framework for Seeking Functional Information," *Knowledge: Creation, Diffusion and Utilization*, 15 (2), 211–32.

Otnes, Cele, Mary Ann McGrath, and Tina M. Lowrey (1995), "Shopping with Consumers," *Journal of Retailing and Consumer Services*, 2 (2), 97–110.

Ozanne, Julie L., Merrie Brucks, and Dhruv Grewal (1992), "A Study of Information Search Behavior During the Categorization of New Products," *Journal of Consumer Research*, 18 (March), 452–63.

Painton, Scott and James W. Gentry (1985), "Another Look at the Impact of Information Presentation Format," *Journal of Consumer Research*, 12 (September), 240–44.

Park, C. Whan, Easwar S. Iyer, and Daniel C. Smith (1989), "The Effects of Situational Factors on In-Store Grocery Shopping Behavior: The Role of Store Environment and Time Available for Shopping," *Journal of Consumer Research*, 15 (March), 422–33.

Park, Joonah and Jinwoo Kim (2000), "Contextual Navigation Aids for Two World Wide Web Systems," *International Journal of Human-Computer Interaction*, 12 (2), 193–217.

Payne, John W. (1976), "Task Complexity and Contingent Processing in Decision Making: An Information Search and Protocol Analysis," *Organizational Behavioral and Human Decision Process*, 16 (2), 366–87.

Payne, John W., James R. Bettman, and Eric J. Johnson (1988), "Adaptive Strategy Selection in Decision Making," *Journal of Experimental Psychology: Learning, Memory and Cognition*, 14 (3), 534–52.

Pieters, Rik, Hans Baumgartner, and Doug Allen (1995), "A Means-End Chain Approach to Consumer Goal Structures," *International Journal of Research in Marketing*, 12 (3), 227–44.

Punj, Girish N. and Richard Staelin (1983), "A Model of Consumer Information Search," *Journal of Consumer Research*, 9 (March), 366–80.

Putrevu, Sanjay and Brian T. Ratchford (1997), "A Model of Search Behavior with an Application to Grocery Shopping," *Journal of Retailing*, 73 (4), 463–86.

Radecki, Carmen M. and James Jaccard (1995), "Perception of Knowledge, Actual Knowledge, and Information Search Behavior," *Journal of Experimental Social Psychology*, 31 (2), 107–38.

Raju, P.S., Subhash C. Lonial, and W. Glynn Mangold (1995), "Differential Effects of Subjective Knowledge, Objective Knowledge, and Usage Experience on Decision Making: An Exploratory Investigation," *Journal of Consumer Psychology*, 4 (2), 153–80.

Ratchford, Brian T. (1982), "Cost-Benefit Models for Explaining Consumer Choice and Information Seeking Behavior," *Management Science*, 28 (February), 197–212.

Richardson-Klavehn, Alan and Robert A. Bjork (1988), "Measures of Memory," *Annual Review of Psychology*, 39, 475–543.

Roediger III, Henry L. and B.H. Challis (1992), "Effects of Identity Repetition and Conceptual Repetition on Free Recall and Word Fragment Completion," *Journal of Experimental Psychology: Learning, Memory, and Cognition*, 18, 3–14.

Roediger III, Henry L. and Kathleen B. McDermott (1993), "Implicit Memory in Normal Human Subjects," in *Handbook of Neuropsychology*, volume 8, F. Boller and J. Grafman, eds. New York: Elsevier Science Publisher, 63–131.

Rousseau, Deon (1982), "A Study on Pre-purchase Information Search," *South African Journal of Psychology*, 12 (1), 19–23.

Russo, J. Edward and Barbara A. Dosher (1983), "Strategies for Multiattribute Binary Choice," *Journal of Experimental Psychology: Learning, Memory, and Cognition*, 9 (October), 676–96.

Russo, J. Edward and France Leclerc (1994), "An Eye-Fixation Analysis of Choice Processes for Consumer Nondurables," *Journal of Consumer Research*, 21 (September), 274–90.

Sanyal, Abhijit (1992), "Priming and Implicit Memory: A Review and a Synthesis Relevant for Consumer Behavior," in *Advances in Consumer Research*, volume 19, John Sherry and Brian Sternthal, eds. Provo, UT: Association for Consumer Research, 795–805.

Schacter, Daniel L. (1987), "Implicit Memory: History and Current Status," *Journal of Experimental Psychology: Learning, Memory, and Cognition*, 13 (3), 501–18.

——— (1999), "The Seven Sins of Memory: Insights from Psychology and Cognitive Neuroscience," *American Psychologist*, 54 (3), 182–203.

Schacter, Daniel L., J. Bowers, and J. Booker (1989), "Intention, Awareness and Implicit Memory: The Retrieval Intentionality Criteria," in *Implicit Memory: Theoretical Issues*, S. Lewandowsky, J.C. Dunn, and K. Kirsner, eds. Hillsdale, NJ: Lawrence Erlbaum Associates, 47–65.

Schaninger, Charles M. and Donald Sciglimpaglia (1981), "The Influence of Cognitive Personality Traits and Demographics on Consumer Information Acquisition," *Journal of Consumer Research*, 8 (September), 208–16.

Schmidt, Jeffrey B. and Richard A. Spreng (1996), "A Proposed Model of External Consumer Information Search," *Journal of the Academy of Marketing Science*, 24 (3), 246–56.

Schneider, Walter and Richard M. Shiffrin (1977), "Controlled and Automatic Human Information Processing: I. Detection, Search, and Attention," *Psychological Review*, 84 (1), 1–66.

Shapiro, Stewart (1999), "When an Ad's Influence Is Beyond Our Conscious Control: Perceptual and Conceptual Fluency Effects Caused by Incidental Ad Exposure," *Journal of Consumer Research*, 26 (June), 16–36.

Shapiro, Stewart, Deborah J. MacInnis, and Susan E. Heckler (1997), "The Effects of Incidental Exposure on the Formation of Consideration Sets," *Journal of Consumer Research*, 24 (June), 94–104.

Shim, Soyeon, Mary Ann Eastlick, Sherry L. Lotz, and Patricia Warrington (2001), "An Online Prepurchase Intentions Model: The Role of Intentions to Search," *Journal of Retailing*, 77 (4), 397–416.

Simonson, Itamar, Joel Huber, and John Payne (1988), "The Relationship Between Prior Brand Knowledge and Information Order," *Journal of Consumer Research*, 14 (March), 566–78.

Spence, Robert (1999), "A Framework for Navigation," *International Journal of Human-Computer Studies*, 51 (5), 919–45.

Squire, Larry R. (1987), *Memory and Brain.* New York: Oxford University Press.

Srinivasan, Narasimhan (1990), "Pre-Purchase External Search for Information," in *Review of Marketing*, Valarie A. Zeithaml, ed. Volume 4. Chicago: American Marketing Association, 153–89.

Steenkamp, Jan-Benedict E. and Hans Baumgartner (1992), "The Role of Optimum Stimulation Level in Exploratory Consumer Behavior," *Journal of Consumer Research*, 19 (December), 434–48.

Stigler, George J. (1961), "The Economics of Information," *Journal of Political Economy*, 69 (June), 213–25.

Suri, Rajneesh and Kent B. Monroe (2003), "The Effects of Time Constraints on Consumers' Judgments of Prices and Products," *Journal of Consumer Research*, 30 (June), 92–104.

Tabatabai, Manouchehr (1997), "Investigation of Decision Making Process: A Hypermedia Approach," *Interacting with Computers*, 9 (4), 385–96.

Thirkell, Peter and Harrie Vredenburg (1982), "Prepurchase Information Search and Post Purchase Satisfaction: An Empirical Examination of Alternative Theories," in *An Assessment of Marketing Thought & Practice—1982 Educators' Conference Proceedings.* Chicago: American Marketing Association, 66–70.

Titus, Philip A. and Peter B. Everett (1995), "The Consumer Retail Search Process: A Conceptual Model and Research Agenda," *Journal of the Academy of Marketing Science*, 23 (2), 106–19.

Tulving, Endel (1972), "Episodic and Semantic Memory," in *Organization and Memory*, E. Tulving and W. Donaldson, eds. New York: Academic, 381–403.

Tulving, Endel, Daniel L. Schacter, and Heather A. Stark (1982), "Priming Effects in Word Fragment Completion are Independent of Recognition Memory," *Journal of Experimental Psychology: Learning, Memory, and Cognition*, 8 (4), 336–42.

Udell, Jon C. (1966), "Prepurchase Behavior of Buyers of Small Electrical Appliances," *Journal of Marketing*, 30 (October), 50–52.

Umilta, Carlo and Morris Moscovitch, eds. (1994), *Attention and Performance 15: Conscious and Nonconscious Information Processing.* Cambridge, MA: MIT Press.

Underhill, Paco (1999), *Why We Buy: The Science of Shopping.* New York: Simon and Schuster.

Urbany, Joel E., Peter R. Dickson, and Rosemary Kalapurakal (1996), "Price Search in the Retail Grocery Market," *Journal of Marketing*, 60 (April), 91–104.

Weldon, Mary Susan (1991), "Mechanisms Underlying Priming on Perceptual Tests," *Journal of Experimental Psychology: Learning, Memory, and Cognition*, 17 (3), 526–41.

Westbrook, Robert A. and Claes Fornell (1979), "Patterns of Information Source Usage Among Durable Goods Buyers," *Journal of Marketing Research*, 16 (August), 303–12.

Wilkie, William L. and Peter R. Dickson (1985), "Shopping for Appliances: Consumers' Strategies and Patterns of Information Search," working paper, Cambridge, MA: Marketing Science Institute.

Wright, Peter L. (1974), "The Harassed Decision Maker: Time Pressures, Distractions, and the Use of Evidence," *Journal of Applied Psychology*, 59, 555–61.

——— (1975), "Consumer Choice Strategies: Simplifying vs. Optimizing," *Journal of Marketing Research*, 12 (February), 60–67.

——— (2002), "Marketplace Metacognition and Social Intelligence," *Journal of Consumer Research*, 28 (March), 677–82.

Xia, Lan (2003), "Consumer Browsing Behaviors and the Retail Environment," working paper, Marketing Department, Bentley College, Waltham, MA 02452.

CHAPTER 4

THE RESOURCE-ADVANTAGE THEORY
OF COMPETITION

A Review

SHELBY D. HUNT AND ROBERT M. MORGAN

Abstract

Since its original conceptualization in Hunt and Morgan (1995), the theory of competition known as resource-advantage (R-A) theory has been developed in numerous articles, books, and book chapters in the marketing, management/general business, and economics literatures. This article reviews the progress and prospects of R-A theory. Specifically, it: (1) provides a brief overview of R-A theory, (2) discusses the progress made to date in developing R-A theory's research program, (3) examines in detail the theory's foundational premises, (4) shows how R-A theory can theoretically ground (and be used to teach) business and marketing strategy, and (5) discusses the theory's future prospects.

In the spring of 1994, we began working on a new theory of competition. The theory came to be known as the resource-advantage (hereafter, "R-A") theory of competition, and the original article developing the foundations, structure, and implications of the theory was published in the *Journal of Marketing* in 1995 (Hunt and Morgan 1995). Since then, over a score of publications, written by over a dozen authors, have contributed to developing the theory and/or used it as a theoretical foundation for explaining, predicting, and understanding phenomena.

The works developing R-A theory make numerous contributions to knowledge in the areas of marketing, management, and economics. (To improve readability, instead of providing multiple cites from individual articles, the following provides page numbers from Hunt [2000b], which, in turn, references other articles.) R-A theory contributes to explaining firm diversity (pp. 152–155); makes the correct prediction concerning financial performance diversity (pp. 153–155); contributes to explaining observed differences in quality, innovativeness, and productivity between market-based and command-based economies (pp. 169–170); shows why competition in market-based economies is dynamic (pp. 132–133); incorporates the resource-based view of the firm (pp. 85–86); incorporates the competence view of the firm (pp. 87–89); has the requisites of a phylogenic, nonconsummatory, and disequilibrium-provoking theory of competition (pp. 23–24); explicates the view that competition is a process of knowledge discovery (pp. 29–30, 145–147); contributes to explaining why social relations constitute a resource only contingently (pp. 100–102); and has the requisites of a moderately socialized theory of competition (pp. 100–102).

In addition, R-A theory shows how path dependence effects occur (pp. 149–152), expands the concept of capital (pp. 186–190), predicts correctly that technological progress dominates the capital/labor (K/L) ratio in economic growth (pp. 193–194), predicts correctly that increases in economic growth cause increases in investment (pp. 194–199), predicts correctly that most of the technological progress that drives economic growth stems from actions of profit-driven firms (pp. 199–200), predicts correctly that R-A competition can prevent the economic stagnation that results from capital deepening (pp. 200–203), contributes to explaining the growth pattern of the (former) Soviet Union (pp. 201–203), provides a theoretical foundation for why formal institutions promoting property rights and economic freedom also promote economic growth (pp. 215–228), provides a theoretical foundation for why informal institutions promoting social trust also promote economic growth (pp. 235–237), and has the requisites for a general theory of competition that incorporates perfect competition as a limiting special case, thereby incorporating the predictive success of neoclassical theory and preserving the cumulativeness of economic science (pp. 240–243). (For a more complete list of issues that have been addressed by R-A theory and their bibliographic sources, please see the Appendix.)

This review will provide a brief overview of R-A theory before discussing how the R-A research program was developed. Because the foundational premises of R-A theory have been so controversial, we then review in detail the arguments for each premise. Because the pedagogical usefulness of R-A theory has been underinvestigated, we show how, as originally proposed in Hunt (2002b) and Hunt and Derozier (2004), R-A theory provides a theoretical grounding for business and marketing strategy. By doing so, we argue, R-A theory provides an integrative theory for teaching business and marketing strategy. Finally, we develop the R-A model of customer value creation and discuss future research directions.

An Overview of R-A Theory

R-A theory is an evolutionary, process theory of competition that is interdisciplinary not only in the sense that it has been developed in the literatures of several different disciplines, but also in that it draws on and has affinities with numerous other theories and research traditions, including evolutionary economics, "Austrian" economics, the historical tradition, industrial-organization economics, the resource-based tradition, the competence-based tradition, institutional economics, transaction cost economics, and economic sociology. R-A theory is a general theory of competition that describes the *process* of competition. Figures 4.1 and 4.2 provide schematic depictions of R-A theory's key constructs, and Table 4.1 provides its foundational premises. Our overview will follow closely the theory's treatment in Hunt (2000b).

The Structure and Foundations of R-A theory

Using Hodgson's (1993) taxonomy, R-A theory is an evolutionary, disequilibrium-provoking, process theory of competition in which innovation and organizational learning are endogenous; firms and consumers have imperfect information; and entrepreneurship, institutions, and public policy affect economic performance. Evolutionary theories of competition require units of selection that are (1) relatively durable, that is, they can exist, at least potentially, through long periods of time, and (2) heritable, that is, they can be transmitted to successors. For R-A theory, both firms and resources are proposed as the heritable, durable units of selection, with competition for comparative advantages in resources constituting the selection process.

At its core, R-A theory combines heterogeneous demand theory with the resource-based theory

Table 4.1

Foundational Premises of Resource-Advantage Theory

P_1: Demand is heterogeneous across industries, heterogeneous within industries, and dynamic.
P_2: Consumer information is imperfect and costly.
P_3: Human motivation is constrained self-interest seeking.
P_4: The firm's objective is superior financial performance.
P_5: The firm's information is imperfect and costly.
P_6: The firm's resources are financial, physical, legal, human, organizational, informational, and relational.
P_7: Resource characteristics are heterogeneous and imperfectly mobile.
P_8: The role of management is to recognize, understand, create, select, implement, and modify strategies.
P_9: Competitive dynamics are disequilibrium provoking, with innovation endogenous.

Source: Adapted from Hunt and Morgan (1997). Reprinted by permission of the American Marketing Association.

of the firm (see premises P1, P6, and P7 in Table 4.1). Contrasted with perfect competition, heterogeneous demand theory views intraindustry demand as significantly heterogeneous with respect to consumers' tastes and preferences. Therefore, viewing products as bundles of attributes, different market offerings or "bundles" are required for different market segments within the same industry. Contrasted with the view that the firm is a production function that combines homogeneous, perfectly mobile "factors" of production, the resource-based view holds that the firm is a combiner of heterogeneous, imperfectly mobile entities that are labeled "resources." These heterogeneous, imperfectly mobile resources, when combined with heterogeneous demand, imply significant diversity as to the sizes, scopes, and levels of profitability of firms within the same industry. The resource-based theory of the firm parallels, if not undergirds, what Foss (1993) calls the "competence perspective" in evolutionary economics and the "capabilities" approaches of Teece and Pisano (1994) and Langlois and Robertson (1995).

As diagrammed in Figures 4.1 and 4.2, R-A theory stresses the importance of (1) market segments, (2) heterogeneous firm resources, (3) comparative advantages/disadvantages in resources, and (4) marketplace positions of competitive advantage/disadvantage. In brief, market segments are defined as intraindustry groups of consumers whose tastes and preferences with regard to an industry's output are *relatively* homogeneous. Resources are defined as the tangible and intangible entities available to the firm that enable it to produce efficiently and/or effectively a market offering that has value for some marketing segment(s). Thus, resources are not just land, labor, and capital, as in neoclassical theory. Rather, resources can be categorized as financial (e.g., cash resources, access to financial markets), physical (e.g., plant, equipment), legal (e.g., trademarks, licenses), human (e.g., the skills and knowledge of individual employees), organizational (e.g., competences, controls, policies, culture), informational (e.g., knowledge from consumer and competitive intelligence), and relational (e.g., relationships with suppliers and customers).

Each firm in the marketplace will have at least some resources that are unique to it (e.g., very knowledgeable employees, efficient production processes, etc.) that could constitute a comparative advantage in resources that could lead to positions of advantage (i.e., cells 2, 3, and 6 in Figure 4.2) in the marketplace. Some of these resources are not easily copied or acquired (i.e., they are relatively immobile). Therefore, such resources (e.g., culture and processes) may be a source of long-term competitive advantage in the marketplace.

Figure 4.1   A Schematic of the R-A Theory of Competition

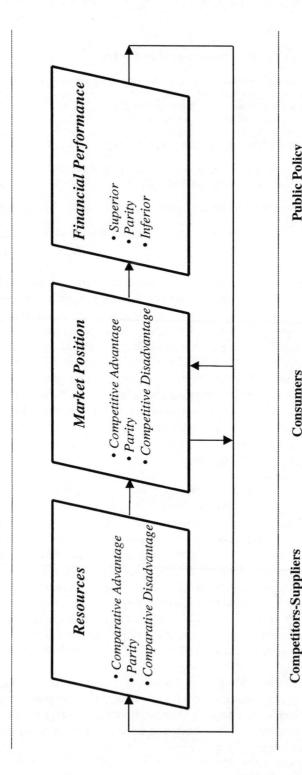

Source: Hunt and Morgan (1997). Reprinted by permission of the American Marketing Association.
Note: Competition is the disequilibrating, ongoing process that consists of the constant struggle among firms for a comparative advantage in resources that will yield a marketplace position of competitive advantage and, thereby, superior financial performance. Firms learn through competition as a result of feedback from relative financial performance "signaling" relative market position, which, in turn signals relative resources.

Figure 4.2   **Competitive Position Matrix**

Relative resource-produced value

	Lower	Parity	Superior
Lower	1 Indeterminate position	2 Competitive position	3 Competitive advantage
Parity	4 Competitive disadvantage	5 Parity position	6 Competitive advantage
Higher	7 Competitive disadvantage	8 Competitive disadvantage	9 Indeterminate position

(Left axis: Relative resource costs)

Source: Adapted from Hunt and Morgan (1995). Reprinted by permission of American Marketing Association.

Note: The marketplace position of competitive advantage identified as Cell 3 results from the firm, relative to its competitors, having a resource assortment that enables it to produce an offering for some market segment(s) that (a) is perceived to be of superior value and (b) is produced at lower costs.

Just as international trade theory recognizes that nations have heterogeneous, immobile resources, and it focuses on the importance of comparative advantages in resources to explain the benefits of trade, R-A theory recognizes that many of the resources of firms within the same industry are significantly heterogeneous and relatively immobile. Therefore, analogous to nations, some firms will have a comparative advantage and others a comparative disadvantage in efficiently and/or effectively producing particular market offerings that have value for particular market segments.

Specifically, as shown in Figure 4.1 and further explicated in Figure 4.2, when firms have a comparative advantage in resources they will occupy marketplace positions of competitive advantage for some market segment(s). Marketplace positions of competitive advantage then result in *superior* financial performance. Similarly, when firms have a comparative disadvantage in resources they will occupy positions of competitive disadvantage, which will then produce *inferior* financial performance. Therefore, firms compete for comparative advantages in resources that will yield marketplace positions of competitive advantage for some market segment(s) and, thereby, superior financial performance. As Figure 4.1 shows, how well competitive processes work is significantly influenced by five environmental factors: the societal resources on which firms draw, the societal institutions that form the "rules of the game" (North 1990), the actions of competitors, the behaviors of consumers and suppliers, and public policy decisions.

Consistent with its Schumpeterian heritage, R-A theory places great emphasis on innovation, both proactive and reactive. The former is innovation by firms that, although motivated by the expectation of superior financial performance, is not prompted by specific competitive pressures—it is genuinely entrepreneurial in the classic sense of *entrepreneur*. In contrast, the latter is innovation that is directly prompted by the learning process of firms' competing for the patronage of market segments. Both proactive and reactive innovation contribute to the dynamism of R-A competition.

Firms (attempt to) learn in many ways—by formal market research, seeking out competitive intelligence, dissecting competitor's products, benchmarking, and test marketing. What R-A theory adds to extant work is how the process of competition itself contributes to organizational learning. As the feedback loops in Figure 4.1 show, firms learn through competition as a result of the feedback from relative financial performance signaling relative market position, which, in turn, signals relative resources. When firms competing for a market segment learn from their inferior financial performance that they occupy positions of competitive disadvantage (see Figure 4.2), they attempt to neutralize and/or leapfrog the advantaged firm(s) by acquisition and/or innovation. That is, they attempt to acquire the same resource as the advantaged firm(s) and/or they attempt to innovate by imitating the resource, finding an equivalent resource, or finding (creating) a superior resource. Here, "superior" implies that the innovating firm's new resource enables it to surpass the previously advantaged competitor in terms of either relative costs (i.e., an *efficiency* advantage), or relative value (i.e., an *effectiveness* advantage), or both.

Firms occupying positions of competitive advantage can continue to do so if (1) they continue to reinvest in the resources that produced the competitive advantage, and (2) rivals' acquisition and innovation efforts fail. Rivals will fail (or take a long time to succeed) when an advantaged firm's resources are either protected by such societal institutions as patents or the advantage-producing resources are causally ambiguous, socially or technologically complex, tacit, or have time compression diseconomies.

Competition, then, is viewed as an evolutionary, disequilibrium-provoking process. It consists of the constant struggle among firms for comparative advantages in resources that will yield marketplace positions of competitive advantage and, thereby, superior financial performance. Once a firm's comparative advantage in resources enables it to achieve superior performance through a position of competitive advantage in some market segment(s), competitors attempt to neutralize and/or leapfrog the advantaged firm through acquisition, imitation, substitution, or major innovation. R-A theory is, therefore, inherently dynamic. Disequilibrium, not equilibrium, is the norm. In the terminology of Hodgson's (1993) taxonomy of evolutionary economic theories, R-A theory is nonconsummatory: it has no end-stage, only a never-ending process of change. The implication is that, though market-based economies are *moving,* they are not moving toward some final state, such as a Pareto-optimal, general equilibrium.

Developing the R-A Theory Research Program

Table 4.2 displays key articles, book chapters, and books in the development of the R-A theory research program. Two comments are worth noting concerning the publications. First, Table 4.2 contains only those publications that focus explicitly on R-A Theory. It does not include the scores of articles, book chapters, and books that use the theory as a theoretical foundation for research. Second, though there are obviously more articles in the marketing literature than in other literatures, note that R-A theory is genuinely interdisciplinary, for there are numerous articles developing the theory in both the economics and management/general business literatures. Although somewhat arbitrary, we can divide the history of the research program into an introductory period, corresponding to 1995–96; a development period, which would be 1997–2000; and a research tradition period, which would be 2001 to the present. Our discussion will focus on significant events in each of the three periods.

Table 4.2

The Resource-Advantage Research Program

Year	Marketing	Management/ general business	Economics
1995–96	JM#1 JM#2	JMI	
1997–98	JM#3 JMM	B&CW EEJ	JEI JSE
1999	JAMS	JBR	
2000	JM-M(4)	IJMR S&H (JAI)	F&R (Routledge)
	A General Theory of Competition: *Resources, Competences, Productivity, Economic Growth* (Sage)		
2001	EJM#1 JPP & M JRM		
2002	JMM(3) EJM#2	JBR	F&K (Elgar)
	Foundations of Marketing Theory: *Toward a General Theory of Marketing* (M.E. Sharpe)		
2003	JMT&P JB&IM		

Source: Hunt (2003). Reprinted by permission of author.

The Introductory Period: 1995–1996

In the spring of 1994, we were reviewing some recent developments in the strategic management literature concerning "resource-based" strategy. In this literature, many writers were suggesting that strategy had been misguided by adopting "industry" as the central focus of strategy development. These new authors were arguing that managers should focus on developing and acquiring rare, valuable, and inimitable resources as a means for achieving "rents," that is, profits in excess of those achieved by a firm under the conditions of perfect competition. The original article that we considered writing was one that developed a new schema for categorizing the various kinds of resources. Indeed, we went so far as to prepare an outline of the structure of the proposed article.

As part of our review, we came across an article by Conner (1991). In this article, Kathleen Conner argued that any theory of the firm should be able to explain the reasons for the existence of firms and what limits their sizes and scopes. Furthermore, she argued that the resource-based theory of strategy, with its focus on heterogeneous, imperfectly mobile resources, constituted the beginnings of a new theory of the firm. We found her arguments to be persuasive. However, because of our background in marketing, we were able to see that the new theory of the firm opened the way for developing a new theory of competition. In particular, we believed, if we joined the resource-based theory of the firm with heterogeneous demand theory and Alderson's (1957, 1965) theory of differential advantage, we might be able to develop a new theory of competition.

After several months of research, we developed a manuscript on the theory and targeted it to the *Journal of Marketing*. The original submission had several key characteristics. First, it defined "resource" as those tangible or intangible entities that were available to firms that enabled them to produce, efficiently and/or effectively, market offerings that had value to any market segment. Second, it provided a set of foundational premises for the theory (see Table 4.1). Third, it provided a key diagnostic tool for understanding competitive advantage, which we labeled the "competitive position matrix" (see Figure 4.2). Fourth, it distinguished between two very different kinds of advantages. Specifically, it distinguished clearly the differences between comparative advantages in resources and marketplace positions of competitive advantage. Furthermore, it theorized that it is comparative advantages in resources that lead to marketplace positions of competitive advantage, which, in turn, lead to superior financial performance. Fifth, it used the emerging theory and its focus on heterogeneous, imperfectly mobile resources to explain firm diversity. Sixth, it used the new theory to contribute to explaining the differences in abundance, innovation, and quality that had been observed between market-based and command economies. Seventh, it explored the issue of whether a market-orientation can be a resource that can lead to sustained, superior, financial performance.

The original submission was reviewed by four scholars. In addition, the editor also provided several pages that had a detailed list of suggestions for revising the manuscript. Many of the reviewers' comments were harbingers of three complaints that have been raised by numerous reviews of works developing R-A theory. First, a common criticism of many reviewers is that perfect competition theory is a "straw man," and we should compare R-A theory to a more robust alternative. (We will return to this complaint in the next section.) Second, reviewers often complain that we do not provide a complete literature review of all the works that have been critical of neoclassical economics over the last hundred years. Indeed, no matter how many works we cite, we always seem to leave out some reviewer's favorite critic of neoclassical economics. Partly as a response to this criticism, fully three chapters of Hunt (2000b) are devoted to other works that are either "antecedents to" or have "affinities with" R-A theory. Third, some reviewers are fundamentally hostile to market-based economies and maintain that R-A theory is too sympathetic to economic freedom. We believe that at least some writers who are harshly critical of competition and its role in market-based economies are so because (1) they presume that neoclassical theories of competition do, indeed, accurately describe the process of competition, and (2) they are reacting with hostility toward certain aspects of neoclassical theory (e.g., the self-interest maximization assumption of utility theory). We maintain that it is at least possible that some critics of market-based economies would not be so *critical* if they started from a base that included R-A theory.

After the acceptance of the Hunt and Morgan (1995) article, we knew that, because of the "silo" nature of academic disciplines, if we wanted R-A theory to be considered seriously in the areas of management and economics, it would be necessary to publish the theory in journals in these areas. As to the management area, the journal that we came upon was the *Journal of Management Inquiry,* which was specifically interested in publishing articles that were radically innovative. Believing—and being informed by reviewers—that R-A theory was, indeed, radical, a manuscript was developed that (1) reviewed the original *JM* article, (2) adopted the "R-A theory" label, (3) modified the process of competition to account for feedback effects of organizational learning (see Figure 4.1), and (4) showed how R-A theory explicates the concept of *productivity.* Specifically, the article showed how R-A theory provides a rigorous distinction between *efficiency* and *effectiveness*. Efficiency is when a firm's market offering moves upward in the marketplace position matrix (Figure 4.2). Effectiveness, in contrast, is when a firm's market offering moves horizontally and to the right in the matrix. Increased productivity, therefore, is both (1) *more* efficiently creating value and (2) efficiently creating *more* value.

The final form of the article prepared for the *Journal of Management Inquiry,* that is, Hunt (1995), had a further, distinguishing characteristic. When we wrote Hunt and Morgan (1995), we were unaware that the standard view of neoclassicists up until the collapse of the Eastern bloc was that the equations of neoclassical theory provided no grounds for preferring market-based over command economies. Indeed, the standard view in the "socialist calculation debate" was that the equations of perfect competition, when combined with general equilibrium theory, implied that planned economies should be at least as productive as market-based ones, if not more so (see, for example, Lavoie 1985). Hunt (1995) was the first article in management or marketing to discuss the socialist calculation debate, and it argued, as did Hunt (2000b, pp. 157–75), that R-A theory can contribute to explaining and, therefore, understanding the factors that depressed the productivity of the command, Eastern bloc economies, when compared with their Western, market-based counterparts. On this issue, neoclassicists had consistently maintained, perfect competition theory and the equations of general equilibrium theory had "proved that a Central Planning Board could impose rules upon socialist managers which allocated resources and set prices as efficiently as a capitalist society of the purest stripe and more efficiently than the capitalist communities of experience" (Lekachman 1959, pp. 396–97).

The final article in the introductory period developing the theory was Hunt and Morgan (1996). This paper resulted from a critique of R-A theory by Dickson (1996), which argued that R-A theory was not sufficiently dynamic and did not give sufficient attention to organizational learning and the phenomenon of path dependencies. Hunt and Morgan (1996) responded by showing that R-A theory is, indeed, a dynamic theory of competition. Specifically, the premise that firms are motivated by the pursuit of *superior* financial performance implies that competition in a market-based economy *must* be dynamic. Because firms always want, for example, more profits than last year, a higher return on investment than competitors', or better profits than some reference point, they will be motivated to develop the proactive and reactive innovations that will make competition dynamic. Furthermore, R-A theory contributes to understanding organizational learning because it shows how the feedback from financial performance causes a firm to learn crucial facts about its marketplace position and resources. Finally, we argued that, because R-A theory is an evolutionary, nonconsummatory theory of competition, it contributes to our understanding of how path dependence effects *can* occur, when such consequences of competition *do,* indeed, occur.

The three articles published in 1995 and 1996 on R-A theory provided a firm foundation for further developing and explicating the theory. We turn now to the period of development, 1997–2000.

The Period of Development: 1997–2000

The years 1997–2000 saw a rapid growth in the number of publications in the marketing, management/general business, and economics literatures that developed the structure and implications of R-A theory. In marketing, Hunt and Morgan (1997) addressed the issue of the relationship between perfect competition and R-A theory. We argued that R-A theory is a general theory of competition that incorporates perfect competition theory as a special, limiting case. Therefore, R-A theory preserves the cumulativity of economic science. Hunt (1999), in contrast, was the first publication that addressed the public policy implications of R-A theory. The article argued that strategy that focused on firm factors (resources) is presumptively procompetitive. After developing three tests for R-A competitiveness, the article argues that R-A competition is prosocial because it fosters productivity and economic growth. In the management/general business area, Hunt (1998) pointed out that neoclassical theory has customarily presumed that it is the efficient allocation of scarce resources that drives productivity and economic growth. In contrast, R-A theory argues that it is resource *creation,* not allocation, that drives productivity and economic growth. Morgan and Hunt (1999) examined the role of relationship marketing in strategy and identified the kinds of resources that might be gained through relationships. Hunt and Lambe (2000) examined marketing's contribution to business strategy and argued that R-A theory integrates the concepts of both marketing and nonmarketing theories of business strategy. Hunt (2000a) and Hunt (2000d) showed how R-A theory can synthesize the competence-based, evolutionary, and neoclassical theories of competition.

As documented by Nelson and Winter (1982), there is an orthodoxy in neoclassical economics that makes it very difficult for heterodox economists to find publication outlets for theories that depart from the position that all economic processes are equilibrating. However, there are some journals that will at least consider publishing articles that advocate dynamic, process-oriented theories, including the *Journal of Economic Issues,* the *Journal of Socio-Economics,* and the *Eastern Economic Journal.* In the first journal, Hunt (1997c) argued that R-A theory is an evolutionary theory of competition. Specifically, both firms and resources are argued to be the heritable, durable units of selection, and competition among firms for comparative advantages in resources is argued to be the selection process that results in the survival of the "locally fitter," not the "universally fittest." In the second journal, Hunt (1997d) explored the nature of sociopolitical institutions that influence favorably the process of R-A competition. The article argues that institutions that promote social trust promote productivity by reducing the transaction and transformational costs in R-A competition. In the third journal, Hunt (1997b) showed how R-A theory can contribute to the area of endogenous growth models in neoclassical economics. Specifically, the article argues that R-A theory, alone among theories of competition, provides a theoretical foundation for endogenous growth models.

By the close of the twentieth century, R-A theory was sufficiently developed in the various journals and academic disciplines to warrant an attempt to pull together the several strands of thought into a research monograph. Hunt (2000b) provided the vehicle for integrating the various articles. Specifically, that monograph argued that R-A theory and its foundations represent the general case of competition, and perfect competition and its foundations are a special case. Therefore, R-A theory incorporates perfect competition, explains the explanatory and predictive successes of perfect competition, and preserves the cumulativity of economic science.

A special symposium was then conducted on R-A theory, as the theory was detailed in the monograph, with commentaries provided by two marketing academics (Falkenburg 2000; Savitt 2000), an industrial-organization economist (Foss 2000), and an institutional economist (Hodgson 2000). The commentators found R-A theory to be highly provocative. Some found the theory to be "too eclectic," while others found it "not eclectic enough." Some found the theory "too incremental," while others found it "not incremental enough." Some found it to be "too neoclassical," while others found it "not neoclassical enough." Hunt (2000c) responded to the commentators and pointed out that it is "heartening to note that none of the three commentators provides convincing argument or evidence that any claim made in the monograph is unwarranted" (p. 80). Specifically, Hunt (2000c) points out that none of the three commentators challenges a single one of the foundational premises of R-A theory.

The Research Tradition Period: 2001–Present

Since 2000, works continue to appear that develop the structure and implications of R-A theory. The issues addressed include antitrust policy (Hunt and Arnett 2001); business alliance success (Hunt, Lambe, and Wittman 2002); efficiency competition versus effectiveness competition (Hunt and

Duhan 2002); R-A theory's philosophical foundations (Hunt 2002b); the relationships among R-A theory, cybernetic systems, and scenario planning (Morgan and Hunt 2002); "Austrian" economics (Hunt 2002c); whether R-A theory is a general theory of marketing (Hunt 2001, 2002b; Schlegelmilch 2002; Wensley 2002); the "embeddedness" of R-A theory (Hunt and Arnett 2004); and the relationships between R-A theory and marketing strategy (Hunt 2002a; Hunt and Derozier 2004).

Even though R-A theory is, as of this writing, scarcely a decade old, we feel justified in characterizing the period starting in 2001 as a *research tradition* phase. Several factors prompt us to do so. First, works developing the theory have appeared in a wide range of journals across several different academic disciplines. Thus, R-A theory appears to have "something to say" to scholars who have very different orientations. Second, the explanatory power and predictive power of the theory are well established. Indeed, the theory has increased our understanding of both micro- and macro-phenomena in marketing, management, and economics. Third, works using R-A theory no longer have to "start from scratch" to explain the characteristic of the theory. Scholars now simply cite the theory and move on to their own contributions. Fourth, there have been no commentaries that have pointed out fundamental flaws in the theory's structure or foundational premises. Fifth, and finally, a host of authors are using the theory as a foundation for further works of both a theoretical and empirical nature in marketing, management, and economics. These, we argue, are characteristics of a theory becoming the foundation for a research tradition.

The rest of this review will focus on (1) the foundations of R-A theory and (2) using the theory to teach business and marketing strategy. We then discuss the future prospects for the theory.

The Foundations of R-A Theory

All theories are derived from their foundational postulates, and Table 4.1 displays the core premises underlying R-A theory. Foundational, as used here, does not imply that the premises are the minimum set of axioms required for deriving theorems, but that these premises are centrally important for understanding the theory. Epistemologically, because R-A adopts scientific realism (Hunt 2002a, 2003), each premise in R-A theory—contrasted with perfect competition—is considered a candidate for empirical testing. Those found false should be replaced with ones more descriptively accurate.

As previously mentioned, a common criticism of R-A theory is that perfect competition theory, its compared alternative, is a "straw man," and we should compare R-A theory with a more robust alternative. However, this section will continue the tradition of contrasting R-A theory with perfect competition for four reasons. First, the foundational premises of perfect competition are well developed and well known. Therefore, contrasting R-A theory with perfect competition communicates efficiently and with great precision the foundations and nature of R-A theory. Second, because neoclassical theory argues that perfect competition is *perfect*, it continues to serve as the ideal form of competition against which all others are compared. Even many of those who have come to question perfect competition's descriptive accuracy still hold it out as an ideal form of competition. Indeed, because perfect competition underlies much public policy, especially antitrust law, perfect competition should serve as the comparison standard (see Hunt and Arnett 2001 for more on R-A theory and antitrust).

Third, even though many scholars question perfect competition theory on numerous grounds, it dominates economics, management, and marketing textbooks. Therefore, it is the only theory of competition that most students ever see that is alleged to be socially beneficial. Discussions of such neoclassical theories as oligopolistic and monopolistic competition in almost all texts are presented (and made meaningful) as departures from the ideal of perfection. Therefore, because

R-A theory argues that perfect competition is not perfect, perfect competition theory should serve as a comparison standard. Fourth, R-A theory is a general theory of competition. Other than neoclassical, perfect competition theory, there may not be a rival, *general* theory to use for comparison purposes (because other theories are too context specific).

Finally, R-A theory is a work in progress. Contrasting R-A theory with perfect competition constitutes an invitation to other scholars to develop rivals to R-A theory. Specifically, we have always invited scholars (in economics, management, and marketing) to identify the foundational premises of rival theories of competition and explicitly contrast them with those of R-A theory. By doing so, we can then evaluate how and why the theories are consistent or inconsistent, saying different things or saying the same things differently, genuinely rival or actually complementary. We again solicit rivals, but we note that, despite numerous past invitations, no rival has been offered. Indeed, no critic has ever shown deficiencies or offered revisions for any of R-A theory's premises.

This section examines the premises in Table 4.1 and follows the discussions in Hunt (2000b) and Hunt and Morgan (1995). We begin with demand.

Demand

For perfect competition theory, demand is (a) heterogeneous across industries, (b) homogeneous within industries, and (c) static. That is, at different configurations of price across generic product categories, for example, footwear, televisions, and automobiles, perfect competition theory allows consumers to prefer different quantities of each generic product. Within each generic product category or "industry," however, consumers' tastes and preferences are assumed to be identical and unchanging through time with respect to desired product features and characteristics. Thus, neoclassical works speak of the "demand for footwear" and the group of firms constituting the footwear "industry" are presumed to face, collectively, a downward-sloping demand curve. Each individual firm in the footwear industry, however, faces a horizontal demand curve because of the homogeneous, intraindustry demand assumption. For perfect competition, the assumptions of homogeneity of demand and supply are necessary for drawing the industry demand and supply curves required for determining the market-clearing, equilibrium price. Absent homogeneous demand, the concept of an industry-demand curve and the market-clearing price make no sense.

Demand and R-A Theory

Consistent with neoclassical theory, R-A theory accepts the premise of heterogeneous interindustry demand. However, drawing on market segmentation theory, intraindustry demand is posited to be both substantially heterogeneous and dynamic: consumers' tastes and preferences differ greatly within a generic product category and are always changing. Heterogeneous intraindustry demand is argued to be the descriptively realistic general case of demand. That is, R-A theory posits that there are far more industries that are radically or significantly heterogeneous, for example, automobile manufacturing (NAICS #336111), women's footwear (#316213), and book publishing (#511130), than there are relatively homogeneous, commodity-type industries, for example, corn (NAICS #111150), gold ores (#212221), and industrial sand (#212322).

The implication of heterogeneous, intraindustry demand is that few industry markets exist. As an example, consider footwear (NAICS #31612). R-A theory views consumers' tastes and preferences for footwear to be substantially heterogeneous and constantly changing. Furthermore, not only do consumers have imperfect information concerning footwear products that might match their tastes and preferences, but obtaining such information is often costly in terms of both time and money. There is no "market for footwear" (NAICS#31612) or even separate, six-digit markets for women's footwear (#3161213) and men's footwear (#3161213). Even though all consumers require footwear and one can readily identify a group of firms that manufacture shoes, there is no shoe-industry market. That is, the group of firms that constitute the footwear industry do not collectively face a single, downward-sloping demand curve—for the existence of such an industry demand curve would imply homogenous tastes and preferences.

R-A theory maintains that, to the extent that demand curves exist at all, they exist at a level of (dis)aggregation that is too fine to be an "industry." For example, even if (for purposes of argument) one considers there to be a homogenous, men's-walking-shoe market, one certainly would not speak of the men's-walking-shoe industry. Nor would one speak of the nineteen-inch-color-television or the minivan industries. Yet, R-A theory maintains that such market segments as these—and those smaller yet—are central for understanding competition.

The heterogeneous, intraindustry demand premise contributes to R-A theory's explanatory and predictive power. First, it implies that identifying those segments most suitable for developing market offerings should be viewed—consistent with Austrian economics—as an entrepreneurial capability that affects firm performance. Second, that intraindustry demand is substantially heterogeneous in most industries contributes to R-A theory's ability (and neoclassical theory's inability) to make the correct prediction as to the diversity in business-unit financial performance.

Consumer Information

Perfect competition theory assumes that consumers have perfect and costless information about the availability, characteristics, benefits, and prices of all products in the marketplace. In contrast, drawing on Austrian economics, Stigler (1961), and Nelson (1970), R-A theory posits that consumers within market segments have imperfect information about goods and services that might match their tastes and preferences. Furthermore, the costs to consumers in terms of effort, time, and money of identifying satisfactory goods and services, that is, search costs, are often considerable. Consequently, one purpose served by the legal protection of trademarks, patents, and licenses is the reduction of consumer search costs. Specifically, trademarks, licenses, and patents are societal institutions that reduce search costs by signaling the attributes of market offerings.

Consider, for example, the issue of trademarks and their relationship to competition. Specifically, are trademarks pro- or anticompetitive? Chamberlin (1933/1962) derives the implications of perfect competition theory for trademarks. He points out that the legal protection of trademarks fosters product differentiation and, therefore, a situation in which prices are higher, quantities produced are lower, excess capacity is permanent, products produced are inferior, and all factors of production are exploited (see Hunt 2002b, section 2.3.1). Therefore, for him (1933/1962, p. 270), "the protection of trademarks from infringement . . . is the protection of monopoly," and he maintains that there are no grounds by which "monopolies protected by the law of unfair competition and of trademarks may be justified" (p. 271). Thus, the standard views in neoclassical theory became that trademarks are anticompetitive.

In contrast, the fact that consumers have imperfect information and often use trademarks as heuristics of quality is not a problem for R-A theory. First, because heterogeneous, intraindustry demand and supply is viewed as natural by R-A theory, it is only natural that, facing imperfect information, consumers will often use trademarks as indicators of quality. Second, because a trademark is viewed as intellectual property and fully worthy of legal protection, R-A theory views firms' protecting the equity—see Aaker (1991) and Keller (1993, 1998)—in their trademarks as providing not only (1) a valuable source of information to consumers, but also (2) a powerful incentive for producers to maintain quality market offerings, and (3) a means by which manufacturers of shoddy or even defective and dangerous products can be held accountable. Third, because R-A theory rejects static-equilibrium efficiency as the appropriate welfare ideal, the heterogeneity of demand and supply does not pose a problem to be solved, but a state of nature—and a desirable one at that. Indeed, R-A theory proposes that the best way to view the role of trademarks in market-based economies is that they are quality-control and quality-enhancing institutions.

The experience of the Soviet Union supports R-A theory's view that consumers' use of trademarks as indicators of quality is not a problem to be solved. Goldman's (1960) work showed that trademarks are institutions that served as important quality-control and quality-enhancing devices in *command* economies. How important? So important that command economies even mandated that firms use trademarks, in those situations where all plants in the Soviet Union were *supposed* to produce homogenous commodities. In short, trademarks and product differentiation are not problems for society to solve; they are institutions that solve societal problems, as R-A theory suggests.

Human Motivation

For neoclassical theory, all human behavior is motivated by self-interest maximization. Thus, in their roles as consumers of products and owners or managers of firms, people maximize their *utility*. Etzioni (1988) shows that neoclassical theory conceptualizes utility and *utility maximization* as being either (a) a pleasure utility (ethical egoism in moral philosophy terms), (b) a tautology, or (c) a mathematical abstraction. He notes that only pleasure utility, or "P-utility," maximization is a substantive thesis that could potentially be empirically tested. Furthermore, in empirical works and public policy recommendations, P-utility is generally assumed.

Human Motivation and R-A Theory

R-A theory posits that human motivation is best viewed as constrained self-interest seeking. That is, the self-interest seeking of individuals is constrained or restrained by personal moral codes, which are, in turn, shaped or influenced by, for example, societal, professional, industry, and organizational moral codes. The concept of personal moral codes in R-A theory draws on the normative theories of ethics in moral philosophy: deontololgy and teleology (Beauchamp and Bowie 1988). Because deontological codes focus on specific actions or behaviors and teleological codes focus on consequences, the former stress the inherent rightness-wrongness of a behavior and the latter emphasize the amount of good or bad embodied in a behavior's consequences.

Deontologists believe that "certain features of the act itself other than the value it brings into existence" make an action or rule right or wrong (Frankena 1963, p. 14). Moral codes based on deontology will emphasize the extent to which a behavior is consistent or inconsistent with such deontological norms as those proscribing lying, cheating, deceiving, or stealing and those prescribing honesty, fairness, justice, or fidelity. Accordingly, deontology emphasizes duties, obligations, and responsibilities to others. Teleologists, on the other hand, "believe that there is one and only one basic or ultimate right-making characteristic, namely, the comparative value (nonmoral) of what is, probably will be, or is intended to be brought into being" (Frankena 1963, p. 14).

Whereas deontological moral codes must address the difficult issue of conflicting norms, those emphasizing teleological factors must grapple with which stakeholders are to be valued. Those moral codes adopting utilitarianism hold that an act is right only if it produces for all people a greater balance of good over bad consequences than other alternatives (i.e., "the greatest good for the greatest number"). Even though it focuses on consequences, because utilitarianism demands that decision makers consider an act's consequences on all stakeholders, it shares at least some common ground with deontology's emphasis on duties and responsibilities to others. In stark contrast, codes adopting ethical egoism—that is, those who adopt the substantive interpretation of utility maximizing—hold that an act is right only if the consequences of the act are most favorable for the individual decision maker. The self-interest, utility-maximizing view of ethical egoism is directly opposed by deontological ethics.

Figure 4.3 shows a model developed by Hunt and Vitell (1986, 1993) that explicates the nature of personal moral codes and shows how such codes are influenced by deontological, teleological, and environmental factors.[1] The Hunt-Vitell (HV) theory of ethics draws on deontological and teleological moral philosophy to explain (1) why people have such radically different views on the ethicality of alternative actions, and (2) why people engage in ethical/unethical behaviors. Briefly, the "triggering mechanism" of the model is the individual's perception that an activity or situation involves an ethical issue, which is followed by the perception of various alternatives or actions one might take to resolve the ethical problem. These alternatives are then evaluated both deontologically and teleologically in the "core" of the model.

For each alternative, the core of the HV model assumes that the decision maker has access to a set of deontological norms that can be applied. The deontological evaluation process, therefore, consists of applying the norms to each alternative, checking for consistency (inconsistency), and resolving the conflicts that result when not all deontological norms can be satisfied simultaneously. Each alternative is also evaluated in the core by a teleological process that combines (1) the forecasting of each behavior's consequences for various stakeholder groups, with (2) estimating the probabilities of the consequences, (3) evaluating the consequences' desirability or undesirability, and (4) assessing the importance of each stakeholder group.

For the HV model, the ethicality of an alternative, that is, *Ethical Judgments,* results from combining the deontological and teleological evaluations. For example, a strict deontologist would ignore totally the results of the teleological evaluation. In contrast, a strict utilitarian would (1) ignore the deontological evaluation, (2) assign equal weights to all individual stakeholders, and (3) maximize the ratio of good consequences over the bad. Like a strict utilitarian, a strict ethical egoist would ignore the deontological evaluation. However, a strict ethical egoist would also assign zero weights to all stakeholders other than the self and maximize the ratio of good consequences over the bad for oneself. Hunt and Vitell do not theorize that individuals are (or ought to be) utilitarians, ethical egoists, or deontologists. Rather, they posit that most people in most situations evaluate the ethicality of an act on the basis of a combination of deontological and teleological considerations.

As to the nature of the personal moral codes that R-A theory posits to constrain or restrain self-interest seeking, the HV model of ethics suggests that they consist of (1) the deontological norms an individual applies to decision situations, (2) the rules for resolving conflicts among norms, (3) the importance weights assigned to different stakeholders, and (4) the combinatory rules for merging the deontological and teleological evaluation processes. R-A theory draws on the HV model and maintains that individuals differ greatly in their personal moral codes. Furthermore, the variance in moral codes is not a "black box" for the purpose of theory development and empirical research. Indeed, personal moral codes are shaped, but not determined, by experience and environment.

168

Figure 4.3   **Hunt-Vitell Theory of Ethics**

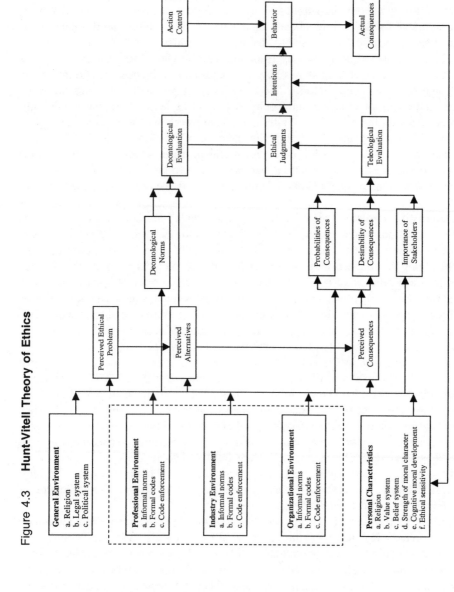

Source: Hunt and Vitell (1986, 1993). Copyright © 1991 Shelby D. Hunt and Scott J. Vitell. Reprinted by permission of the authors.

Note: The portion of the model outside the dashed lines constitutes the general theory. The portion inside the dashed lines individuates the general model for professional and managerial contexts.

As to experience, note that Ethical Judgments in the HV model drives Intentions and Behavior. That is, in most situations, ethical judgments, intentions, and behavior are congruent. (*Guilt* occurs when teleological evaluations drive intentions and behavior in a manner inconsistent with ethical evaluation.) The HV model shows a feedback loop from behavior through actual consequences to personal characteristics. Thus, individuals learn the appropriateness of the moral codes they apply through experiencing positive and negative consequences. This learning-by-experience shapes personal moral codes.

Personal moral codes are also shaped by lifelong, vicarious learning in different environments. First, different societies have different cultures that communicate and "pass on" different moral codes. Second, within societies, different groups, for example, professional associations, industries, and organizations, communicate different moral codes to their members. Third, different families have different moral codes. The HV model views all these environmental factors as shaping—but not determining, for choices are still made as to which code to adopt—an individual's personal moral code.

Returning to the posit that human motivation is best described as self-interest seeking constrained by a personal moral code, R-A theory can account for the economic value to firms and societies of having individuals who are motivated by moral codes that emphasize deontological ethics, rather than ethical egoism.[2] In particular, when people share a moral code based primarily on deontological ethics, trust can exist, and therefore, the costs that firms and societies have that are associated with shirking, cheating, stealing, monitoring, free-riding, "hostage-taking," and opportunism in general are avoided (see Hunt 2000b, section 9.3.3). Thus, R-A theory can provide the kinds of "deeper insights" asked for by Williamson (1994, p. 85) because, not being bound to the neoclassical tradition, it can abandon the assumption of universal opportunism.

Firm's Objective and Information

Consistent with its assumption that humans are self-interest maximizers, perfect competition theory assumes that owner-managed firms profit maximize. (Profits are the self-interest of owners.) Furthermore, maximizing occurs under conditions of perfect and costless information about product markets, production techniques, and resource markets. In order to incorporate time and risk, the neoclassical tradition posits wealth maximization as the firm's long-term objective. That is, owner-managed firms maximize the net present value of future profits using a discount rate that accounts for the time value of money and the risk associated with an expected stream of profits.

Of course, many modern corporations, including most large firms, are not owner managed. The separation of ownership from control and management (Berle and Means 1932) results in situations where the self-interests of owners, that is, the shareholders, in maximizing their wealth may conflict with managers' own personal interests. This "principal-agent" problem is addressed in the neoclassical tradition by agency theory and its "nexus of contracts" view of the firm (Fama 1980; Fama and Jensen 1983; Jensen and Meckling 1976).[3] As with transaction cost economics, agency theory assumes universal opportunism by managers. Thus, measures must be taken to prevent managers from pursuing their self-interests at the expense of shareholders. Measures commonly recommended include developing financial incentives to align managers' interests with shareholder wealth maximization; instituting tight monitoring and control systems; maintaining a high proportion of independent, outside directors on boards of directors; and avoiding "CEO duality," that is, avoiding having the same person as both chief executive officer and chairperson of the board of directors.

Firm's Objective, Information, and R-A Theory

For R-A theory, the firm's primary objective is superior financial performance, which it pursues under conditions of imperfect and often costly to obtain information about extant and potential market segments, competitors, suppliers, shareholders, and production technologies. Consistent with the self-interest seeking aspect of human behavior, superior financial performance is argued to be the firm's primary objective because superior rewards flow to the owners, managers, and employees of firms that produce superior financial results. These rewards include not only such financial rewards as stock dividends, capital appreciation, salaries, wages, and bonuses, but also such nonfinancial rewards as prestige and feelings of accomplishment. Because it enables firms to pursue other objectives, such as contributing to social causes or being a good citizen in the communities in which it operates, financial performance is viewed as *primary*. For-profit organizations differ from their not-for-profit cousins in that the former, but not the latter, are *for profit*. Indeed, prolonged inferior performance threatens the firm's survival and prevents the accomplishment of secondary objectives.

The "superior" in superior financial performance equates with both *more than* and *better than*. It implies that firms seek a level of financial performance exceeding that of some referent. For example, the indicators of financial performance can be such measures as accounting profits, earnings per share, return on assets, and return on equity. The referent against which the firm's performance is compared can be the firm's own performance in a previous time period, the performance of rival firms, an industry average, or a stock-market average, among others. Both the specific measures of financial performance and the specific referents used for comparison purposes will vary somewhat from time to time, firm to firm, industry to industry, and culture to culture. That is, for R-A theory, both measures and referents are independent variables. Therefore, the theory provides a framework for investigating the role of different understandings of financial performance on managers, firms, industries, productivity, economic growth, and social welfare (e.g., Arnett and Hunt 2002).

Superior financial performance does not equate with the neoclassical concepts of "abnormal profits" or "rents" (i.e., profits differing from the average firm in a purely competitive industry in long-run equilibrium) because R-A theory views industry long-run equilibrium as a theoretical abstraction and such a rare phenomenon that the concept of "normal" profits in the neoclassical tradition cannot be an empirical referent for comparison purposes. Furthermore, the actions of firms that collectively constitute competition do not force groups of rivals to "tend toward" equilibrium. Instead, the pursuit of *superior* performance implies that the actions of competing firms are disequilibrating, not equilibrating. Indeed, consistent with Austrian economics, markets seldom if ever are in long-run equilibrium, and activities that produce turmoil in markets are societally beneficial because they are the engine of economic growth.

Positing that the firm's goal is superior financial performance ensures that R-A theory is dynamic, which accords well with the extant dynamism of competition in market-based economies. It is no accident that theories that are static equilibrium in nature assume profit or wealth maximization. But "saving the equations" through profit maximization has a price. If a firm is already making the maximum profit, why should it—absent environmental shocks—ever change its actions? For example, if a firm is maximizing profits producing a product at a certain quality level, why should it ever attempt to improve quality? If, however, firms are posited to (1) always seek *more* profits, *higher* earnings per share, and *greater* return on investment, and (2) they believe that there are always actions that can be taken to accomplish these goals, then (3) competition will be dynamic.

Nelson and Winter (1982, p. 4) maintain that "firms in our evolutionary theory . . . [are] motivated by profit and . . . search for ways to improve profits," which differs from "profit maximizing over well defined and exogenously given choice sets." Likewise, Langlois (1986, p. 252) points out that, though economic "agent[s] prefer more to less all things considered," this "differs from maximizing in any strong sense." Similarly, though R-A theory posits that firms seek superior financial performance, the general case of competition is that they do not "strong sense" maximize because managers lack the capability and information to maximize (Simon 1979).[4] That is, though firms prefer more profits to less profits, a higher return on investment to a lower return, a higher stock price to a lower stock price, more shareholder wealth to less wealth, imperfect information implies that none of these financial indicators equates with profit or wealth *maximization*.

Real firms in real economies are not presented a menu of well-defined sets of alternatives for which the problem is to choose the profit or wealth-maximizing option. Firms do indeed take actions, they do indeed take note of financial indicators, and they do indeed make causal attributions between actions and indicators. But even if—and this is a big if—managers have good reasons to claim to know that actions previously taken have led (or will lead) to increases in financial performance, they cannot know (or warrantedly claim to know) that some alternative action or set of actions (identified or not identified) would not have produced (or will not produce) even higher returns. Therefore *superior* financial performance, not maximum performance, better describes the firm's primary objective.

In addition to informational problems, firms do not "strong sense" maximize because of the personal moral codes of owners, managers, and subordinate employees. Recall that agency theory and transaction cost economics assume self-interest maximization and universal opportunism. In terms of ethical theory, all economic agents are ethical egoists: they ignore deontological considerations, assign zero weights to all stakeholders other than self, and maximize the ratio of good consequences over bad.

In contrast, R-A theory posits that personal moral codes are independent variables that vary across people (and peoples). Moral codes entail (1) the deontological norms an individual applies to decision situations, (2) the rules for resolving conflicts among norms, (3) the importance weights assigned to different stakeholders, and (4) the combinatory rules for merging the deontological and teleological evaluation processes. Thus, R-A theory acknowledges that nonowner managers guided by ethical egoism might not profit maximize when it conflicts with their self-interests. However, by treating personal codes as independent variables, R-A theory expands the kinds of situations beyond those that can be addressed by agency theory.

Consider, for example, the case of distributors of bottled water who could easily charge double the customary price when a natural disaster shuts down a community's water supply. Some firms, guided by ethical egoism, that is, self-interest maximization, might choose to double the price. Other firms, guided by "enlightened" self-interest seeking might choose not to double the price because they believe the long-term, net present value of doubling is less than the "goodwill value" of nondoubling. However, the personal codes of the managers of still other firms might result in their resisting the doubling of prices even though they believe the long-term, net present value of doubling is greater than the goodwill value of nondoubling. In particular, firms guided by deontological ethics might resist doubling because they believe it would constitute exploiting their customers and, hence, would be deontologically wrong. In general (and inconsistent with agency theory and transaction cost economics), some firms do not profit or wealth maximize in particular decision situations because such maximizing behaviors would violate (either owner or nonowner) managers' sense of rightness and wrongness. This sense of rightness and wrongness results from managers' beliefs concerning their duties and responsibilities to nonowner stakeholders; that is, it stems from their personal moral codes based on deontological ethics.

Finally, efforts to profit maximize may also be thwarted by ethical code mismatches between managers and their subordinate employees. Suppose most of a firm's employees have moral codes stressing deontological ethics and, thus, they avoid shirking, cheating, stealing, and other opportunistic behaviors. In such a firm, the costs associated with monitoring and strong controls would be pure economic waste. If, however, the owner-manager is an ethical egoist and assumes that the employees are also ethical egoists (doesn't everyone utility maximize?), then expensive and unnecessary controls will be instituted.[5] Ironically, then, the assumption of utility maximization by managers can thwart efforts at profit maximization. Etzioni (1988, p. 257) puts it this way: "The more people accept the [P-utility maximization part of the] neoclassical paradigm as a guide for their behavior, the more their ability to sustain a market economy is undermined."

In summary, superior financial performance is argued to be the best descriptor of the firm's primary objective because (1) superior rewards flow to owners, managers, and employees of firms that produce superior rewards, and (2) the pursuit of superior financial performance ensures that R-A theory is dynamic, which makes it consistent with the observed dynamism of market-based economies. Although firms do seek superior financial performance, they are argued to not maximize profit or wealth because (1) imperfect information makes maximization impossible; (2) agency problems associated with ethical egoism thwart maximization; (3) firms guided by deontological ethics may, at times, choose not to maximize; and (4) ethical code mismatches between (and among) owners, managers, and subordinate employees may result in nonmaximizing behaviors.

Resources

For perfect competition theory, firm resources are factors of production. Two aspects of "resources are factors" are noteworthy. First, because neoclassical theory is completely mathematized, no entity can be a factor of production unless it can be represented in an equation that can be differentiated. Therefore, the customary factors are land, labor, and capital. Intangible entities, such as entrepreneurship, as Kirzner (1979, p. 187) points out, have no marginal product and cannot be a factor of production. It makes no sense to talk about the extra units of a commodity that can be produced for each additional unit of entrepreneurship.

Second, all resources are perfectly homogeneous and mobile. That is, each unit of labor and capital is identical with other units, and all units—being for sale in the factor markets—can move without restrictions among firms within and across industries. Again, labor and capital must be homogeneous to ensure that equations will be differentiable.

In addition to resources, all firms have access to a *production function,* that is, a technology that enables them to combine the factors of production to produce a product. Because of the assumption of perfect information, the production function for each firm within an industry is identical—no firm has access to a technology, capability, competence, or organizational form that is superior to those available to other firms. Because all innovation is exogenous, new technologies are given to firms by outside sources, for example, by government.

Resources and R-A Theory

Contrasted with "resources are factors," R-A theory adopts a resource-based view of the firm. Specifically, R-A theory defines resources as the tangible and intangible entities available to the firm that enable it to produce efficiently and/or effectively a market offering that has value for some market segment(s). Resources are categorized as financial (e.g., cash reserves and access to financial markets), physical (e.g., plant, raw materials, and equipment), legal (e.g., trademarks and licenses), human (e.g., the skills and knowledge of individual employees, including, importantly, their entrepreneurial skills), organizational (e.g., controls, routines, cultures, and competences—including, importantly, a competence for entrepreneurship), informational (e.g., knowledge about market segments, competitors, and technology), and relational (e.g., relationships with competitors, suppliers, and customers). Each entity is a resource to the firm if, and only if, it contributes to enabling it to produce efficiently and/or effectively a market offering that has value for some market segment(s).

R-A theory posits that resources are both significantly heterogeneous across firms and imperfectly mobile. Resource heterogeneity implies that each and every firm has an assortment of resources that is at least in some ways unique. Imperfectly mobile implies that firm resources, to varying degrees, are not commonly, easily, or readily bought or sold in the marketplace (the neoclassical factor markets). Because of resource immobility, resource heterogeneity can persist through time despite attempts by firms to acquire the same resources of particularly successful competitors.

Note that resources need not be owned by the firm, but just be available to it. For example, the relationships involved in relational resources are never *owned* by firms, but only available to them for the purpose of producing value for some market segment(s). Indeed, just as there is no neoclassical market—no demand or supply curve—for "reputations," there is no market for relationships with suppliers, customers, employees, and competitors. Nonetheless, relational resources have value.

The relationships that a firm has access to become a part of what R-A theory views as organizational capital, Falkenberg (1996) calls "behavioral assets," and Gummesson (1995) refers to as "structural capital." For example, Gummesson (1995, p. 17) defines structural capital as "those resources built into the organization such as systems, procedures, contracts, and brands which are not dependent on single individuals." As he points out, there is a strong shift toward recognizing that the total value of a firm is primarily determined by what he calls "soft" assets, not inventory and equipment. Thus, the value of many organizations "cannot be correctly assessed from traditional information in the balance sheet and the cost and revenue statements of the annual report" (p. 18). Even though accounting procedures for valuing these soft assets are in their infancy, firms are beginning to recognize "the fact that the customer base and customer relationships are . . . assets, even the most important assets" (p. 18).

The work of Falkenberg (1996) provides data on just how important organizational capital or soft assets are in determining the value of a firm. Falkenberg divides a firm's resources into (1) physical assets, (2) valuable paper (e.g., cash), and (3) "behavioral assets," which he defines as the "routines and competencies of the people involved . . . which are located not only inside, but outside the firm" (p. 4). As support for his thesis that it is behavioral assets that are the main source of wealth creation, he calculates the market-price-to-book-value ratio for numerous firms in different industries in different years. Because book value reflects only the (depreciated) value of physical assets and valuable paper, the difference is an (albeit crude) estimate of the value of a firm's behavioral assets.

Falkenberg's (1996) study finds substantial across-industry variation. For example, whereas the behavioral assets of Home Depot, Inc., are valued at 6.6 times its book value, Texaco's behavioral assets are only 2.0 times its book value. Furthermore, he finds substantial within-industry variation. For example, not only did his sample of consumer goods' companies range from 0.8 (RJR Nabisco) to 15.0 (Coca Cola), but even within the petroleum industry the ratios ranged from 2.0 (Texaco) to 3.2 (Phillips Petroleum). Moreover, even across only two years' time (1993–1995), the ratio for individual firms changed dramatically, both up and down. For example, whereas Apple Computer went from 3.1 in 1993 to 2.1 in 1995, IBM went from 1.1 to 2.4 during the same time period.

In short, Falkenberg's (1996) work strongly supports the view that it is organizational capital—including a firm's relational resources—that is viewed by investors as the principal determinant of its wealth-creating capacity. Furthermore, it strongly supports R-A theory's contention that important firm resources are intangible, significantly heterogeneous, and immobile. In contrast, because neoclassical theory customarily admits only capital, labor, and land to qualify as firm resources (where capital is generally construed to be such tangible assets as machinery, inventory, and buildings), such intangibles as relationships are outside the scope of the concept "resources" and are not considered as having value in the production process.

At first glance, one might believe that neoclassical theory could accommodate the concept of organizational capital by the simple expedient of permitting such intangibles as relationships to be resources. But this is problematic in the extreme. The commitment of neoclassical theory to the derivation of demand and supply curves requires that all resources be homogeneous and mobile. That is, it is only by neoclassical theory viewing each unit of each factor of production as being obtainable in the marketplace (and identical with other units) that it can derive demand and supply curves for each factor. Why, then, couldn't neoclassical theory simply discard the necessity of having demand and supply curves for each factor of production? Because demand and supply curves are necessary for determining prices in static equilibrium—which is part of the neoclassical research program's "hard core" (Lakatos 1978). That is, the import of discarding the requirement that all factors of production have demand and supply curves would be that neoclassical theory would no longer be neoclassical.

Role of Management

For perfect competition theory, the role of management is limited, to say the least. Because firms are price takers and quantity makers, the short-term role of management is to determine the quantity of the firm's single product to produce and to implement its standardized production function. Because all firms are profit maximizers, all firms in an industry will inexorably produce at an output rate where marginal cost equals marginal revenue (the product's market price). Therefore, because such resources as plant and equipment are relatively fixed in the short run, each firm will incur profits (or losses) depending on whether price exceeds (or is less than) the average total cost of producing the profit-maximizing quantity.

Management and R-A Theory

R-A theory, in contrast, views the role of management in the firm in a business-strategy manner. Specifically, the role of management (both owner and nonowner managers) is to recognize and understand current strategies, create new strategies, select preferred strategies, implement the strategies selected, and modify strategies through time. "Implementation," of course, encompasses the thousands of day-to-day decisions that must be made and activities that must be undertaken to manage a modern firm (of any significant size). "Recognize and understand" acknowledges that firms sometimes (often?) fail to recognize accurately their respective marketplace positions and/or fail to understand the nature of the resources that led to such positions (McGrath, MacMillan, and Venkataramen 1995; Schoemaker and Amit 1994). Indeed, many strategies emerge through time and, thus, may be implicit (Mintzberg 1987). "Create" and "select" emphasize the cognitive and innovative dimensions of firms. Therefore, the strategic choices that managers make influence performance. "Modify" emphasizes that managers learn through the process of competing and can make adjustments or abandon underperforming strategies.

All strategies (at the business-unit level) involve, at the minimum, the identification of (1) market segments, (2) appropriate market offerings, and (3) the resources required to produce the offerings. Strategies that yield positions of competitive advantage and superior financial performance will do so when they rely on those resources in which the firm has a comparative advantage over its rivals. Sustained superior financial performance occurs only when a firm's comparative advantage in resources continues to yield a position of competitive advantage despite the actions of competitors.

Competitive Dynamics

For neoclassical theory, all resources are variable in the long run and each firm in each industry adjusts its resource mix (e.g., its K/L ratio) to minimize its cost of producing the profit-maximizing quantity. These adjustments inexorably lead to a long-run equilibrium position in which each firm produces the quantity for which market price equals long-run marginal cost, which itself equals the minimum, long-run average cost. The position of long-run equilibrium is thus a "no profit" situation—firms have neither a pure profit (or rent) nor a pure loss, only an accounting profit equal to the rate of return obtainable in other perfectly competitive industries.

Each industry stays in equilibrium until something changes in its environment. Thus, all forms of innovation are exogenous factors and represent "shocks" to which each industry responds. Therefore, rather than "strategic choices matter," the firm's environment strictly determines its performance (i.e., its profits). Pure profits or rents occur only temporarily—just long enough for equilibrium to be restored. Through time, the dynamics of market-based economies are represented as "moving" equilibria.

Because both product and factor markets are interdependent, the possibility of a general equilibrium for an entire economy arises. Walras (1874/1954) was the first to identify the system of equations that an economy would have to "solve" for general equilibrium to exist. Conceptualizing a fictitious, all-knowing "auctioneer" who "cries" prices (i.e., "bids" for all products and resources), Walras theorized that an economy characterized by perfect competition "gropes" toward general equilibrium. Schumpeter (1954, p. 242) calls the work of Walras the "Magna Carta of economic theory." Indeed, precisely specifying and successfully analyzing the "Walrasian equations" is considered to be the crowning achievement of twentieth-century economics—as Nobel prizes to Kenneth Arrow in 1972 and General Debreu in 1983 attest.

The welfare economics literature investigates the conditions prevailing at the position of Walrasian general equilibrium. If—and only if—all industries in an economy are perfectly competitive, then at general equilibrium, every firm in every industry has the optimum-size plant and operates it at the point of minimum cost. Furthermore, every resource or "factor" employed is allocated to its most productive use and receives the value of its marginal product. Moreover, the distribution of products produced is Pareto-optimal at general equilibrium because the price of each product (reflecting what consumers are willing to pay for an additional unit) and its marginal cost (the extra resource costs society must pay for an additional unit) will be exactly equal. Therefore, the adjective "perfect" is taken literally in neoclassical theory: Perfect competition is *perfect,* the ideal form of competition. All other forms of competition are departures from perfection, that is, "imperfect."

Competitive Dynamics and R-A Theory

In contrast, for R-A theory, competition is an evolutionary process in which the actions of firms are disequilibrium-provoking. In this process, innovation is endogenous. Instead of the firm's environment, particularly the structure of its industry, strictly determining its conduct (strategy) and its performance (profits), R-A theory maintains that environmental factors only influence conduct and performance. Relative resource heterogeneity and immobility imply that strategic choices must be made, and these choices influence performance. All firms in an industry will not adopt the same strategy—nor should they. Different resource assortments suggest targeting different market segments and/or competing against different competitors.

R-A competition is not an "imperfect" departure from perfect competition. Rather, the process of R-A competition allocates resources efficiently and, because it creates new resources, the process generates increases in productivity and produces economic growth and wealth. Moreover, rather than R-A competition's being an imperfect departure from perfect competition, perfect competition is a special case of R-A competition.

A Theoretical Grounding for Business and Marketing Strategy

R-A theory can be used in the classroom as an integrative theory to teach such subjects as competitive advantage, by means of the competitive position matrix (Figure 4.2), and *sustainable* competitive advantage, by means of resource immobility, that is, the factors that result in some resources being difficult for competitors to acquire, copy, find substitutes for, or surpass, as discussed in Hunt and Morgan (1995). This section shows how R-A theory can be used to teach business and marketing strategy.

Theories of business and marketing strategy are normative imperatives. That is, they have the following, general form: "In order for a firm to achieve its goals, it *should* . . ." What follows the "should" differs according to the particular theorist's school of thought. For example, one school stresses the importance of industry factors (Montgomery and Porter 1991; Porter 1980, 1985) whereas others stress firm-specific competences (Day and Nedungadi 1994; Hamel and Prahalad 1994a, 1994b; Prahalad and Hamel 1990; Sanchez, Heene, and Thomas 1996) and inimitable resources (Barney 1991; Grant 1991; Wernerfelt 1984). Some schools urge firms to focus on developing their dynamic capabilities (Teece and Pisano 1994) and higher-order learning processes (Dickson 1996; Senge 1990; Sinkula, Baker, and Noordewier 1997) whereas others emphasize the value-creating potential of networks of relationships (Berry and Parasuraman 1991; Grönroos 1996; Gummesson 1994; Morgan and Hunt 1994; Sheth and Parvatiyar 1995a, 1995b; Varadarajan and Cunningham 1995; Weitz and Jap 1995; Wilson 1995). Some schools advocate a market orientation (Jaworski and Kohli 1993; Slater and Narver 1994; Webster 1992, 1994) whereas others focus on "first mover" innovations (Kerin, Varadarajan, and Peterson 1992; Lieberman and Montgomery 1988, 1998) and brand equity (Aaker 1991; Keller 1993).

Choosing wisely from among the various schools of strategic thought requires that managers understand not just the alternative theories, but also the competitive contexts in which each normative imperative would likely work well. A strategy that is highly successful in one competitive context might fail dismally in another. Therefore, using theories of business and marketing *strategy* requires that managers understand the nature of *competition*. Alternatively stated, theories of business and marketing strategy must be *grounded* in a theory of competition.

This section shows that R-A can ground—and, thus, be used to teach—business and marketing strategy. First, we overview the three major schools of business strategy (i.e., industry based, resource based, and competence based) and two prominent schools of marketing strategy (i.e., market orientation and relationship marketing). We then show how business and marketing strategy can be grounded in R-A theory. Our review follows the discussion in Hunt (2000b) and Hunt and Derozier (2004).

Business Strategy: An Overview

Modern business strategy traces to the works on administrative policy of Kenneth Andrews and his colleagues at Harvard (Andrews 1971, 1980, 1987; Christensen et al. 1982; Learned et al. 1965). Viewing business strategy as the match a firm makes between (1) its internal resources and skills and (2) the opportunities and risks created by its external environment, they developed the SWOT framework: Strengths, Weaknesses, Opportunities, Threats. In this framework, the main task of corporate-level strategy is identifying businesses in which the firm will compete. Alternative strategies for the firm are developed through an appraisal of the opportunities and threats it faces in various markets (i.e., *external* factors), and an evaluation of its strengths and weaknesses (i.e., *internal* factors). Good strategies are those that are explicit (for effective implementation) and effect a good match or "fit." Such strategies avoid environmental threats, circumvent internal weaknesses, and exploit opportunities through the strengths or distinctive competences of the firm. Since the work of Andrews and his colleagues, research on strategy has centered on three approaches: industry-based strategy, resource-based strategy, and competence-based strategy.

Industry-Based Strategy

An "external factors" approach, the industry-based theory of strategy, as exemplified by Porter (1980, 1985), turns industrial-organization economics "upside down" (Barney and Ouchi 1986, p. 374). That is, what was considered anticompetitive and socially undesirable under neoclassical, industrial-organization economics, forms the basis for normative competitive strategy. In this view, choosing the industries in which to compete and/or altering the structure of chosen industries to increase monopoly power should be the focus of strategy because:

> Present research [i.e., Schmalensee (1985)] continues to affirm the important role industry conditions play in the performance of individual firms. Seeking to explain performance differences across firms, recent studies have repeatedly shown that average industry profitability is, by far, the most significant predictor of firm performance. . . . In short, it is now uncontestable that industry analysis should play a vital role in strategy formation. (Montgomery and Porter 1991, pp. xiv–xv)

Porter's (1980) "five forces" framework maintains that the profitability of a firm in an industry is determined by (1) the threat of new entrants to the industry, (2) the threat of substitute products or services, (3) the bargaining power of its suppliers, (4) the bargaining power of its customers, and (5) the intensity of rivalry among its existing competitors. Therefore, because "a firm is not a prisoner of its industry's structure" (Porter 1985, p. 7), strategy should aim at choosing the best industries (usually those that are highly concentrated) and/or altering industry structure by raising barriers to entry and increasing one's bargaining power over suppliers and customers.

After choosing industries and/or altering their structure, Porter (1980) advocates choosing one of three "generic" strategies: (1) cost leadership, (2) differentiation, or (3) focus. That is, superior performance can result from a competitive advantage brought about by a firm's, relative to others in its industry, having a lower cost position, having its offering being perceived industrywide as being unique, or having a focus on one particular market segment and developing a market offering specifically tailored to it. Although it is possible to pursue successfully more than one strategy at a time (and the rewards are great for doing so), "usually a firm must make a choice among them, or it will become stuck in the middle" (Porter 1985).

After choosing one of the three generic strategies, internal factors come into play. Specifically, Porter (1985) argues that the firm should implement its strategy by managing well the activities in its "value chain," because "[t]he basic unit of competitive advantage . . . is the discrete activity" (Porter 1991, p. 102). If value is defined as "what buyers are willing to pay," then "superior value stems from offering lower prices than competitors for equivalent benefits or providing unique benefits that more than offset a higher price" (Porter 1985, p. 4).

For Porter (1985), activities in the firm's value chain are categorized as either primary or support. Primary activities include inbound logistics, operations, outbound logistics, marketing and sales, and service. Support activities include procurement, technology development (improvement of product and process), human resource management, and firm infrastructure (e.g., general management, planning, finance). Doing these activities well improves gross margin, promotes competitive advantage, and thereby produces superior financial performance. Therefore, the fundamental strategic imperative of industry-based strategy is that, to achieve competitive advantage and, thereby, superior financial performance, firms should (1) choose industries and/or modify their structure, (2) select one of three generic strategies, and (3) manage well the activities in their value chains.

Resource-Based Strategy

Because (1) empirical studies show that highly concentrated industries are not more profitable than their less concentrated counterparts (Buzzell, Gale, and Sutton 1975; Gale and Branch 1982; Ravenscraft 1983), and (2) similar studies show that the industry market share-profitability relationship is spurious (Jacobson 1988; Jacobson and Aaker 1985), many business strategy theorists have questioned the focus on external factors of industry-based theory. In particular, those labeled "resource-based" theorists argue for the primacy of heterogeneous and imperfectly mobile resources.

Resource-based theory in business strategy, an "internal factors" approach, traces to the long-neglected work of Edith Penrose (1959). Avoiding the term "factor of production" because of its ambiguity, she viewed the firm as a "collection of productive resources" and pointed out, "it is never *resources* themselves that are the 'inputs' to the production process, but only the *services* that the resources can render" (pp. 24–25; italics in original). Viewing resources as bundles of possible services that an entity can provide, "It is the heterogeneity . . . of the productive services available or potentially available from its resources that gives each firm its unique character" (pp. 75, 77). Therefore, contrasted with the neoclassical notion of an *optimum* size of firm, "the expansion of firms is largely based on opportunities to use their existing productive resources more efficiently than they are being used" (p. 88).

Works drawing on Penrose (1959) to explicate resource-based theory in business strategy include the seminal articles of Lippman and Rumelt (1982), Rumelt (1984), and Wernerfelt (1984) in the early 1980s, followed by the efforts of Dierickx and Cool (1989), Barney (1991, 1992), and Conner (1991). The resource-based theory of strategy maintains that resources (to varying degrees) are both significantly heterogeneous across firms and imperfectly mobile. "Resource heterogeneity" means that each and every firm has an assortment of resources that is at least in some ways unique. "Imperfectly mobile" implies that firm resources, to varying degrees, are not commonly, easily, or readily bought and sold in the marketplace (the neoclassical factor markets). Because of resource heterogeneity, some firms are more profitable than others. Because of resource immobility, resource heterogeneity can persist through time despite attempts by firms to acquire the same resources of particularly successful competitors. Therefore, the fundamental strategic imperative of the resource-based view is that, to achieve competitive advantage and, thereby, superior financial performance, firms should seek resources that are valuable, rare, imperfectly mobile, inimitable, and nonsubstitutable.

Competence-Based Strategy

A second "internal factors" theory of business strategy is competence-based theory. The term "distinctive competence" traces to Selznick (1957) and was used by Andrews (1971) and his colleagues in the SWOT model to refer to what an organization could do particularly well, relative to its competitors. Stimulating the development of competence-based theory in the early 1990s were the works of Chandler (1990); Hamel and Prahalad (1989, 1994a, 1994b); Prahalad and Hamel (1990, 1993); Reed and De Filippi (1990); Lado, Boyd, and Wright (1992); and Teece and Pisano (1994). Numerous other theoretical and empirical articles have been developing competence-based theory (Aaker 1995; Bharadwaj, Varadarajan, and Fahy 1993; Day and Nedungadi 1994; Hamel and Heene 1994; Heene and Sanchez 1997; Sanchez and Heene 1997, 2000; and Sanchez, Heene, and Thomas 1996).

Prahalad and Hamel (1990, p. 81) argue that "the firm" should be viewed as both a collection of products or strategic business units (SBUs) and a collection of competences because "in the long run, competitiveness derives from an ability to build, at lower cost and more speedily than competitors, the core competencies that spawn unanticipated products." For Hamel and Prahalad (1994a), business strategy should focus on industry foresight and competence leveraging. *Industry foresight* involves anticipating the future by asking what new types of benefits firms should provide their customers in the next five to fifteen years and what new competences should be acquired or built to offer such benefits. *Resource-leveraging* focuses on the numerator in the productivity equation (i.e., value of output/cost of input). Specifically, they argue that too much attention in analyses of firm productivity has been devoted to resource efficiency—the denominator—and too little on resource effectiveness—the numerator.

For competence-based theorists, productivity gains and competitive advantage come through the resource-leveraging that results from "more effectively concentrating resources on key strategic goals, . . . more efficiently accumulating resources, . . . complementing resources of one type with those of another to create higher-order value, . . . conserving resources whenever possible, and . . . rapidly recovering resources by minimizing the time between expenditure and payback" (Hamel and Prahalad 1994a, p. 160). Therefore, the fundamental strategic imperative of the competence-based view of strategy is that, to achieve competitive advantage and, thereby, superior financial performance, firms should identify, seek, develop, reinforce, maintain, and leverage distinctive competences.

Marketing Strategy

Marketing strategy, of course, overlaps significantly with business strategy. That is, strategic decisions in the functional areas of product, promotion, distribution, pricing, and the sales force, though significantly developed in marketing, are frequent topics in business strategy. Therefore, this section will focus on two distinctive *schools* of marketing strategy: market orientation and relationship marketing.

Market Orientation Strategy

The idea of market orientation traces to the marketing concept, which has been considered a marketing cornerstone since its articulation and development in the 1950s and 1960s. The marketing concept maintains that (a) all areas of the firm should be customer oriented, (b) all marketing activities should be integrated, and (c) profits, not just sales, should be the objective. As conventionally interpreted, the concept's customer-orientation component, that is, knowing one's customers and developing products to satisfy their needs, wants, and desires, has been considered paramount. Historically contrasted with the production and sales orientations, the marketing concept is considered to be a philosophy of doing business that should be a major part of a successful firm's culture (Baker, Black, and Hart 1994; Wong and Saunders 1993). For Houston (1986, p. 82), it is the "optimal marketing management philosophy." For Deshpande and Webster (1989, p. 3), "the marketing concept defines a distinct organizational culture . . . that put[s] the customer in the center of the firm's thinking about strategy and operations."

In the 1990s, the marketing concept morphed into market orientation. In this view, for Webster (1994, pp. 9, 10), "The customer must be put on a pedestal, standing above all others in the organization, including the owners and the managers." Nonetheless, he maintains, "having a customer orientation, although still a primary goal, is not enough. Market-driven companies also are fully aware of competitors' product offerings and capabilities and how those are viewed by customers." At the same time, Narver and Slater (1990) and Slater and Narver (1994) were characterizing a market orientation as having the three components of customer orientation, competitor orientation, and interfunctional coordination. And Kohli and Jaworski (1990, p. 6) defined a market orientation as "the organizationwide *generation* of market intelligence pertaining to current and future customer needs, *dissemination* of the intelligence across departments, and organizationwide *responsiveness* to it" (italics in original). Therefore, the fundamental imperative of market-orientation strategy is that, to achieve competitive advantage and, thereby, superior financial performance, firms should systematically (1) gather information on present and potential customers and competitors and (2) use such information in a coordinated way across departments to guide strategy recognition, understanding, creation, selection, implementation, and modification (Hunt and Morgan 1995).

Relationship Marketing Strategy

The strategic area of relationship marketing was first defined by Berry (1983, p. 25) as "attracting, maintaining, and—in multi-service organizations—enhancing customer relationships." Since then, numerous other definitions have been offered. For example, Berry and Parasuraman (1991) propose that "relationship marketing concerns attracting, developing, and retaining customer relationships." Gummesson (1999, p. 1) proposes that "relationship marketing (RM) is marketing seen as relationships, networks, and interaction." Grönroos (1996, p. 11) states that "relationship marketing is to identify and establish, maintain, and enhance relationships with customers and other stakeholders, at a profit, so that the objectives of all parties involved are met; and that this is done by a mutual exchange and fulfillment of promises." Also for him, relationship marketing is "marketing . . . seen as the management of customer relationships (and of relationships with suppliers, distributors, and other network partners as well as financial institutions and other parties)" (Grönroos, 2000, pp. 40–41). Sheth (1994) defines relationship marketing as "the understanding, explanation, and management of the ongoing collaborative business relationship between suppliers and customers." Sheth and Parvatiyar (1995a) view relationship marketing as "attempts to involve and integrate customers, suppliers, and other infrastructural partners into a firm's developmental and marketing activities," and Morgan and Hunt (1994) propose that "relationship marketing refers to all marketing activities directed towards establishing, developing, and maintaining successful relational exchanges."

Although the various perspectives on relationship marketing differ, one common element is that all view relationship marketing as implying that, increasingly, firms are competing through developing relatively long-term relationships with such stakeholders as customers, suppliers, employees, and competitors. Consistent with the Nordic School (Grönroos 2000; Grönroos and Gummesson 1985) and the Industrial Marketing and Purchasing (IMP) Group (Axelsson and Easton 1992; Ford 1990; Hakansson 1982), the emerging thesis seems to be: to be an effective *competitor* (in the global economy) requires one to be an effective *cooperator* (in some network) (Hunt and Morgan 1994). Indeed, for Sheth and Parvatiyar (1995a), the "purpose of relationship marketing is, therefore, to enhance marketing productivity by achieving efficiency and effectiveness."

It is important to point out that none of the previously cited authors naïvely maintains that a firm's efficiency and effectiveness are always enhanced by establishing relationships with all potential stakeholders. Clearly, advocates of relationship marketing recognize that firms should at times avoid developing certain relationships. As Gummesson (1994, p. 17) observes, "Not all relationships are important to all companies all the time . . . some marketing is best handled as transaction marketing." Indeed, he counsels, "Establish which relationship portfolio is essential to your specific business and make sure it is handled skillfully" (p. 17). Therefore, the fundamental strategic imperative of relationship-marketing strategy is that, to achieve competitive advantage and, thereby, superior financial performance, firms should identify, develop, and nurture a relationship portfolio.

Strategy and R-A Theory

We now argue that R-A theory grounds business and marketing strategies. Each of the five schools of strategy will be discussed. We begin with resource-based strategy.

Resource-Based Strategy and R-A Theory

As discussed, the fundamental imperative of resource-based strategy is that, to achieve competitive advantage and, thereby, superior financial performance, firms should seek resources that are valuable, rare, imperfectly mobile, inimitable, and nonsubstitutable. A positive theory of competition that could ground normative, resource-based strategy (1) must permit such a strategy to be successful, and (2) contribute to explaining why and when (i.e., under what circumstances) such a strategy may be successful.

First, R-A theory permits resource-based strategy to be successful because it specifically adopts a resource-based view of the firm. As premise P7 in Table 4.1 notes, firms are viewed as combiners of heterogeneous and imperfectly mobile resources—which is the fundamental tenet of the "resource-based view" (Conner 1991). Indeed, competition for R-A theory consists of the constant struggle among firms for comparative advantages in such resources.

Note, however, that R-A theory adopts "a" resource-based view of the firm, not "the" view. As discussed by Schulze (1994), many resource-based theorists view competition as an equilibrium-seeking process. Indeed, firms are often described as seeking "abnormal profits" or "economic rents," which in the neoclassical tradition imply "profits different from that of a firm in an industry characterized by perfect competition" and "profits in excess of the minimum necessary to keep a firm in business in long-run competitive equilibrium." Thus, because perfect is posited as ideal, that is, it is *perfect,* viewing competition as equilibrium-seeking and the goal of the firm as *abnormal* profits or *rents* implies that the achievement of sustained, superior financial performance by firms is detrimental to social welfare.

In contrast, R-A theory maintains that competition is dynamic and disequilibrium-provoking (see premise P9 in Table 4.1). In a critique of resource-based strategy, Priem and Butler (2001, p. 35) argue for dynamic theory and suggest that in order for the resource-based view "to fulfill its potential in strategic management, its idea must be integrated with an environmental demand model." They point out that R-A theory's incorporation of heterogeneous demand in a dynamic theory is in the right direction. Barney (2001) agrees that a dynamic analysis using the resource-based view of the firm is important for the further development of strategic research, and he cites R-A theory as an example of an evolutionary approach that incorporates the necessary dynamics.

Also in contrast, R-A theory denies that perfect competition is the ideal competitive form. The achievement of superior financial performance—both temporary and sustained—is procompetitive when it is consistent with and furthers the disequilibrating, ongoing process that consists of the constant struggle among firms for comparative advantages in resources that will yield marketplace positions of competitive advantage and, thereby, superior financial performance. It is anticompetitive when it is inconsistent with and thwarts this process. Therefore, R-A theory maintains that when superior financial performance results from procompetitive ("pro" in the sense of R-A theory) factors, it contributes to social welfare because the dynamic process of R-A competition furthers productivity and economic growth through both the efficient allocation of scarce tangible resources and, more importantly, the creation of new tangible and intangible resources.

Specifically, the ongoing quest for superior financial performance, coupled with the fact that all firms cannot be simultaneously superior, implies that the process of R-A competition will not only allocate resources in an efficient manner, but also that there will be both proactive and reactive innovations developed that will contribute to further increases in efficiency and effectiveness. Indeed, it is the process of R-A competition that provides an important mechanism for firms to learn how efficient-effective, inefficient-ineffective, they are. (See the learning, feedback loops in Figure 4.1.) Similarly, it is the quest for superior performance by firms that results in the proactive and reactive innovations that, in turn, promote the very increases in firm productivity that constitute the technological progress that results in economic growth.

As to why and when a strategy of seeking resources that are "valuable, rare, imperfectly mobile, inimitable, and nonsubstitutable" will be successful, consider the "valuable" criterion. An entity may be valuable in many ways. For example, a firm's assets may include a section of land, or a building, or a painting that has value in the marketplace (and appears in the firm's balance sheet). But what R-A theory highlights is that *marketplace value* is not the key for understanding the nature of competition. Rather, a resource is "valuable" when it contributes to a firm's ability to efficiently and/or effectively produce a marketplace offering that *has value* for some market segment or segments. And, R-A theory maintains, consumer perceptions of value are dispositive. That is, consumer perceptions are the ultimate authority as to the value of a firm's market offering.

Now consider the recommendation that valuable resources should be *rare.* Entities may be "rare" in many ways. What R-A theory highlights and emphasizes is that a valuable, "rare" resource is one that enables a firm, when competing for a market segment's patronage, to move upward and/or to the right in the marketplace position matrix (Figure 4.2). That is, valuable, *rare* resources enable firms to compete by being, relative to competitors, more efficient and/or more effective.

Now, in light of R-A theory's emphasis on proactive and reactive innovation, consider the recommendation that resources should be "inimitable and nonsubstitutable." To the list, R-A theory adds "nonsurpassable" (Hunt 1999). Firms occupying positions of competitive disadvantage (cells 4, 7, and 8 in Figure 4.2) will be motivated to engage in three forms of reactive innovation: (1) imitating the resource of an advantaged competitor, (2) finding (creating) an equivalent resource, or (3) finding (creating) a superior resource. Many authors have tended to focus on the equilibrating behavior of resource imitation and substitution. Although imitation and substitution are important forms of competitive actions, R-A theory highlights the fact that reactive innovation can also prompt disequilibrium-provoking behaviors. That is, reactive innovation in the form of finding (creating) a *superior* resource results in the innovating firm's new resource assortment enabling it to *surpass* the previously advantaged competitor in terms of either relative efficiency, or relative value, or both. By leapfrogging competitors, firms realize their objective of *superior* returns, make competition dynamic, shape their environments, and renew society. In so doing, the process of reactive innovation stimulates the kinds of major innovations described as creative destruction by Schumpeter (1950). Imitation brings parity returns; parity returns are never enough.

Competence-Based Strategy and R-A Theory

The fundamental imperative of competence-based strategy is that, to achieve competitive advantage and, thereby, superior financial performance, firms should identify, seek, develop, reinforce, maintain, and leverage distinctive competences. Organizational competences, all strategy theorists agree, have components that are significantly intangible (e.g., knowledge and skills) and are not *owned* by the firm (i.e., not capable of being *sold* by the firm, except, of course, by selling the division of the firm that houses the competence). Recall that R-A theory acknowledges that both tangible and intangible entities can be resources. Recall also that entities need not be owned by firms to be resources. Rather they need only be *available* to firms.

Premise P6 in Table 4.1 classifies firm resources as financial, physical, legal, human, organizational, informational, and relational. For R-A theory, therefore, a firm competence is a kind of *organizational* resource. Specifically, competences are "higher-order" resources that are defined as socially and/or technologically complex, interconnected combinations of tangible basic resources (e.g., basic machinery) and intangible basic resources (e.g., specific organizational policies and procedures and the skills and knowledge of specific employees) that fit coherently together in a synergistic manner. Competences are distinct resources because they exist as distinct packages of basic resources. Because competences are causally ambiguous, tacit, complex, and highly interconnected, they are likely to be significantly heterogeneous and asymmetrically distributed across firms in the same industry. Therefore, R-A theory permits competence-based strategy to be successful.

Differences in specific competences explain why some firms are simply better than others at *doing* things (Hamel and Heene 1994; Heene and Sanchez 1997; Langlois and Robertson 1995; Sanchez and Heene 1997; Sanchez, Heene, and Thomas 1996). For example, firms can have superior entrepreneurial competences (Foss 1993), research and development competences (Roehl 1996), production competences (Prahalad and Hamel 1990), marketing competences (Conant, Mokwa, and Varadarajan 1990; Day 1992), and competitive agility competences (Nayyan and Bantel 1994).

Highlighted by R-A theory is the role of *renewal* competences, such as those described by Teece and Pisano (1994) and Teece, Pisano, and Shuen (1997) as "dynamic capabilities," by Dickson (1996) as "learning how to learn," and by Hamel and Prahalad (1994a, 1994b) as "industry foresight." Specifically, renewal competences prompt proactive innovation by enabling firms to (1) anticipate potential market segments (unmet, changing, and/or new needs, wants, and desires); (2) envision market offerings that might be attractive to such segments; and (3) foresee the need to acquire, develop, or create the required resources, including competences, to produce the envisioned market offerings. Therefore, because firms are not viewed by R-A theory as just passively responding to changing environment or looking for the best "fit" between existing resources and market "niches," it contributes to explaining why and when a firm developing a renewal competence will be successful. A strategy of developing a renewal competence will be successful (or more successful) when (1) the marketplace is turbulent, (2) competitors are "sleepy," and/or (3) the proactive innovations spawned by a renewal competence promote turbulence.

Industry-Based Strategy and R-A Theory

The fundamental imperative of industry-based strategy is that, to achieve competitive advantage and, therefore, superior financial performance, firms should (1) choose industries and/or modify their structure, (2) select one of three generic strategies, and (3) manage well the activities in its value chain. Of course, as discussed, R-A theory rejects the notion that "choosing industry" is the key factor for strategy success. Indeed, empirical works on financial performance show clearly that "firm effects" dominate "industry effects" and competition is market segment by market segment. However, R-A theory does contribute to understanding when a strategy of expanding the firm's offerings to new segments in (1) the same industry or (2) a new industry will be successful. Such a strategy is more likely to be successful when the resources that the firm has (or can reasonably acquire or develop) are believed to be such that they enable it to produce a market offering that will occupy cells 2, 3, or 6 in Figure 4.2. That is, R-A theory highlights the role of resources in implementing a segment-based variant of industry-based strategy.

R-A theory also addresses the issue of the propriety of the recommendation that firm strategy should be directed at *altering* industry structure. As Fried and Oviatt (1989) point out, the "alter structure" recommendation is often (if not *most* often) interpreted as taking actions that will (1) drive competitors out of the marketplace in order to (2) increase industry concentration and, thereby, (3) achieve superior financial performance. Therefore, the "alter structure" recommendation is customarily interpreted as advocating predatory practices—in potential violation of antitrust law.

As shown in Figure 4.1, R-A theory views competition as "embedded" (Granovetter 1985) within, for example, societal institutions and public policy. It is true that firms are often harmed by the actions of competitors. For example, if a firm introduces a new product at competitive prices that performs better than its rivals, then rival firms' sales and profits will likely be affected. However, R-A theory maintains that the harm to competitors is, or ought to be, a by-product of the process of competition, not the focus of competitors' actions (Arnett and Hunt 2002). The goal of R-A competition is superior financial performance, not harming competitors. Because the goal can be achieved through competing for comparative advantages in resources, success neither implies nor depends on violating norms of public policy.

Finally, consider the recommendation of industry-based strategy that firms should perform well those activities in their value chains. Unfortunately, the value *chain* metaphor has limited applicability beyond manufacturing firms. Service firms and knowledge-based firms are poorly represented by linear, input-output chains of activities. However, though R-A theory minimizes the role of value chains, it highlights the importance of value creation as a key component of strategy. Indeed, value creation is central to Figure 4.2, the marketplace position matrix. Furthermore, R-A theory provides an explanation for the claim that some firms are superior to others in performing value-creation activities: superior-performing firms in terms of value creation have a comparative advantage in resources, for example, specific competences related to specific value-producing activities.

Market-Orientation Strategy and R-A Theory

The fundamental imperative of market orientation (MO) strategy is that, to achieve competitive advantage and superior financial performance, firms should systematically (1) gather information on present and potential customers and competitors and (2) use such information in a coordinated way to guide strategy recognition, understanding, creation, selection, implementation, and modification. R-A theory permits MO strategy to succeed because premise P5 in Table 4.1 assumes that the firm's information is imperfect and premise P6 indicates that information can be a resource. That is, the (1) systematic acquisition of information about present and potential customers and competitors and the (2) coordinated use of such information to guide strategy may contribute to the firm's ability to efficiently and/or effectively produce market offerings that have value for some market segments.

If a firm is market oriented and its competitors are not, then an MO strategy may be a resource that moves the firm's marketplace position upward and to the right in Figure 4.2. Note, however, premise P5 in Table 4.1 also points out that information acquisition is costly. The implication is that if implementing an MO strategy is *too* costly, then the firm's position in Figure 4.2 will shift downward toward positions of competitive disadvantage. Therefore, whether an MO strategy provides a resource that leads to a position of competitive advantage in Figure 4.2 depends on the relative value/relative cost ratio of MO implementation.

Because it consists of a synergistic combination of more basic resources (Hunt and Lambe 2000), the effective implementation of a market orientation may be viewed as an organizational competence. To implement an MO strategy, firms deploy tangible resources such as information systems to store, analyze, and disseminate information about competitors and customers. In addition, firms use intangible resources to implement MO. That is, organizational policies must be in place to encourage MO action, and managers must have the knowledge and experience required to utilize customer and competitor information effectively.

Specifically, a market orientation may be viewed as a kind of renewal competence. That is, a competence in MO will prompt proactive innovation by enabling firms to anticipate potential market segments; envision market offerings that might be attractive to such segments; and prompt the need to acquire, develop, or create the required resources to produce the offerings. Furthermore, a competence in MO will assist efforts at reactive innovation because it provides valuable information about existing competitors and customers.

Relationship Marketing Strategy and R-A Theory

The fundamental imperative of relationship marketing strategy is that, to achieve competitive advantage and, thereby, superior financial performance, firms should identify, develop, and nurture a relationship portfolio. Consider what is required for a theory of competition to permit a relationship marketing strategy to succeed. First, because relationships are intangible, the theory must permit intangibles to be resources. Second, because relationships are not owned (and, therefore firms cannot buy and sell relationships in the "factor" markets), firm ownership must not be a criterion for an entity to be a firm resource. Third, because each relationship has unique characteristics (and, therefore, one cannot take the first derivative of any equation in which a relationship appears), unique entities must be allowed. Fourth, because (at least some) relationships involve cooperation among firms in order for them to compete, the theory must permit some relationships to be procompetitive (and not presumptively assume all instances of cooperation to be anticompetitive *collusion*).

Now consider R-A theory with regard to its view of resources. A firm resource is any tangible or *intangible* entity *available* to the firm that enables it to produce efficiently and/or effectively a market offering that has value for some market segment(s). Therefore R-A theory satisfies criteria one and two. Now recall that R-A theory views firm resources as significantly heterogeneous (premise P7 in Table 4.1). Therefore, it satisfies criterion three. Finally, because R-A theory assumes that (at least some) firm resources are imperfectly mobile (premise P7), yet such resources can nonetheless enable firms to produce offerings efficiently and/or effectively, the theory satisfies criterion four. That is, at least some cooperative relationships are *relational* resources (premise P6), making them procompetitive.

As discussed in Hunt (1997a), R-A theory implies that firms should periodically conduct a strategic resource audit as a standard part of its corporate planning. The strategic resource audit should pay close attention to the competences of the organization and the role that relationships with suppliers, customers, employees, and competitors can play in enhancing the total "mix" of strategic competences. From the perspective of relationship marketing, therefore, firms should develop a relationship portfolio or "mix" that complements existing competences and enables it to occupy positions of competitive advantage, as identified in Figure 4.2. However, it is important to recognize that relationship portfolios are *developed,* not *selected.*

Because it conjures the image of being like a portfolio of stocks, Gummesson's (1999) concept of a relationship portfolio has the same systemic ambiguity as the marketing mix. The standard, textbook versions of the marketing mix concept often imply that some marketing manager sits down at a specific point in time and *selects* both a target market and a particular combination of price, product, place, and promotion that is believed to be optimal. Although this may occur on rare occasions, much more commonly these decisions are made sequentially, that is, through time. For example, it could well be the case that the first decision actually made was the nature of the product. Then a market segment is targeted for the product. Following that, the price, channels of distribution, and promotional programs are developed. The point is that, in contrast with standard textbook treatments, marketing mixes are most often developed through time, not selected at a point in time.

A similar ambiguity emerges in the concept of a relationship portfolio. Even more so than the marketing mix, relationship portfolios are not selected at a point in time, but developed *through* time. Indeed, good relationships take time to develop (Lambe, Spekman, and Hunt 2002). Therefore, though it is important to develop a relationship portfolio that complements existing organizational competences in an optimal manner, and it is important to strategically plan for such relationships, the relationships that comprise the relationship portfolio can only be developed through time. Though both are *portfolios,* the relationship portfolio differs dramatically from a portfolio of stocks, for it is at least possible to select a portfolio of stocks at a single point in time. Consequently, a relationship marketing strategy will be more successful when it is a long-term strategy.

To conclude this section, determining the strategic thrust of the firm may be argued to be the principal task of top management. This task is aided by recent theories of business and marketing strategy, including the normative imperatives based on industry factors, resource factors, competences, market orientation, and relationship marketing. Choosing wisely from among the various theories of strategy requires an accurate understanding of the contexts of competition. R-A theory, an evolutionary, disequilibrium-provoking, process theory of competition, provides that understanding. As such, R-A theory provides an integrative framework for teaching business and marketing strategy. In the next section, we offer our thoughts on how future research in R-A theory might be approached to extend our understanding of strategy and competition. Based on the suggested approach, we also offer further insight into how R-A theory can be used in teaching business and marketing strategy.

Future Research Directions

R-A theory offers tremendous potential for further investigation. Given the foundation that has been developed, we turn now to exploring briefly some of these opportunities.

Relative Value of Resources

As noted earlier, several taxonomies have been proposed to identify and elaborate on the types of resources available to firms. R-A theory proposes that resources can be classified as financial, physical, legal, human, organizational, relational, and informational (Hunt and Morgan 1995). Furthermore, it maintains, some types of resources are more valuable to the firm than others. However, processes by which the various resource types influence the ability of the firm to create unique competences and, eventually, comparative advantages are complex. Individual resources may have direct, indirect, mediating, or moderating effects (or combinations of all four kinds of effects) on firm performance. Furthermore, these effects also may be moderated when some resources are combined with other types of resources. Moreover, it is likely that these effects vary with context.

Many benefits could be derived from understanding how resources differ in their effects on performance in different situations, and articulating their relative value to firms based on these differences in effects. Such research would contribute to competition theory and strategy by providing scholars a more robust foundation for discussing issues such as sustainability of advantage, time delays in building comparative advantages, scope of advantage, impact of strategy on performance, and patterns of value contribution of resources. It would also provide guidance to managers in prioritizing resource creation, acquisition, and bundling efforts.

Perhaps the most extensively studied group of firm resources is human resources (Finkelstein and Hambrick 1996; Hambrick and Mason 1984; Huselid 1995; Pfeffer 1994). In one case, Hitt et al. (2001) investigated the impact of investments in human resources on performance in a professional services firm, as well as the moderating effects of such investments on the strategy-performance relationship. They found that human resources had a curvilinear effect on performance. Specifically, in their early tenure with the firm, the costs of training, acclimating, and managing the professionals outweighed the resulting benefits on firm performance. Over time, however, this relationship was reversed. They also found that human resources moderated the impact of strategy on performance.

Though Hitt et al. (2001) found human resources to have a significant impact on performance in a professional service organization, it is clear that, not all human resources are unique and offer such advantages. In a different context—manufacturing—Schroeder, Bates, and Junttila (2002) found that internal and external learning processes (i.e., organizational resources) had a substantial impact on firm performance. Employees and equipment (i.e., human and physical resources, respectively) were found not to be an effective means of achieving high performance.

We argue that learning and other organizational resources, being "packages" of more basic resources, are more complex and, hence, are less mobile and less vulnerable to substitution and imitation than human resources. Moreover, even within a category, individual resource subtypes can be expected to produce varying degrees of value to the firm. For example, studying four subtypes of organizational resources—that is, firms' market orientation, entrepreneurship, innovativeness, and organizational learning—Hult and Ketchen (2001) found market orientation to have the greatest explanatory power for positional advantage. Indeed, it mediated the effects of the other three organizational resources on firm performance.

It would be useful to study these same issues for other types of resources. Understanding how resources develop over time, as well as identifying their relative performance contribution curves, would both (1) assist scholars in understanding the process of advantage building and (2) inform managers as to processes for creating strategies. Marketing's various activities in the firm touch all seven types of resources; therefore, marketing has plenty of opportunities to participate in these efforts.

Value Creation

One of the major themes of the strategy literature is developing an understanding of the process of customer value creation (Hamel and Prahalad 1994a; Porter 1985; Slater and Narver 1998). The implication is that if managers can understand what their customers value and how that value is created, they can more efficiently and effectively plan and manage the activities of the organization. In turn, superior customer value creation will improve performance.

All issues pertinent to a discussion of competition ultimately come down to customer value creation and the costs associated with such creation (see Figure 4.2). Causal ambiguity is important because the process by which firms *create value* for their customers is not transparent. Thus, the competences that create value are partially shielded from competitors' efforts at imitation. The relative value of a resource to the firm is ultimately determined by the value it creates for the firm's customers—independently or in concert with other resources. Competitively superior firms are those that create unique value for customers, more efficiently and/or effectively than other firms.

Multiple explanations of the customer value creation process exist. Porter (1985) proposed the value chain model as a way of mapping the value creation process. The value chain focuses on firm activities as sources of customer value. The expectation is that if managers explore and evaluate their firms' conduct in the five primary activities (inbound logistics, operations, outbound logistics, marketing and sales, and service) and four support activities (infrastructure, technology, human resources, and procurement), they can identify which value-creating activities are important in their firms and improve their competitiveness. Though valuable in linear manufacturing processes, the "chain" metaphor breaks down in services firms, because services firms are not well represented by a linear process that takes inputs and adds value to make outputs.

In an alternative perspective, Makadok (2001) reviews the strategic management literature and concludes that "two distinct mechanisms—resource-picking and capability-building—have been proposed for understanding how managers create economic rents for their firms." These *rents* (more accurately, superior financial performance; see Hunt and Morgan 1995), he argues, arise from customer value creation. The importance of Makadok's summary is that the activities

Figure 4.4   **The R-A Model of Customer Value Creation**

Identifying, acquiring, and creating resources	→	Bundling resources to create competences	→	Creating the market offering	→	Developing and implementing positioning strategies	→	Protecting, maintaining, and improving resources

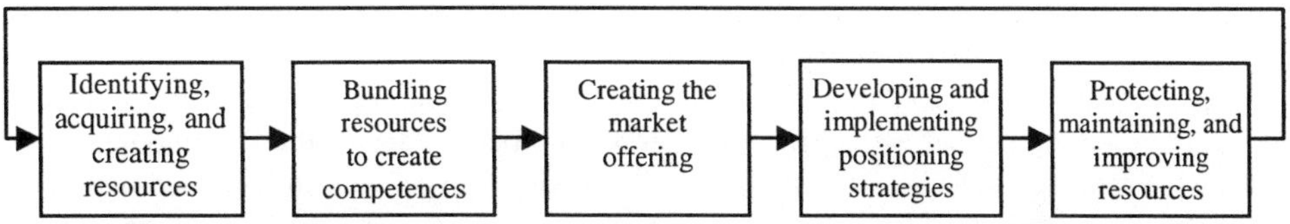

Source: Morgan and Hunt (2003). Reprinted by permission of the authors.

he identifies that managers engage in offer much richer opportunities for understanding how value is created. We agree that identifying resource picking (either through choosing of resources for acquisition or, as R-A theory emphasizes, the *creation* of such resources) and capability building (through resource bundling) constitutes a stronger theoretical foundation for understanding value creation than the "chain" metaphor. However, restricting the process to these two types of activities fails to capture all of the opportunities and responsibilities of managers in the customer value-creation process.

The Resource-Advantage Model of Customer Value Creation (Figure 4.4) separates managers' activities in the process of value creation into five stages. First, needed resources must be identified, created, and/or acquired (Makadok's *resource picking*) to build the firm's inventory of the resources necessary to create unique competences or capabilities. During this stage, managers' efforts are focused on reaching desired inventories of the resources at lower costs than competitors, or finding resources that are highly effective in producing the desired competence(s). At this stage, competitive considerations include the potential for competitors to imitate the resources, the likelihood they may find substitutions for the resources in question, the opportunities for the firm to realize the value of the resources before that value is obvious to others, and the mobility of the resources in the marketplace.

During the second stage of the customer value-creation process, managers bundle resources to create unique competences or capabilities (Makadok's *capability building*). As discussed later, it is at this stage that we begin seeing that both *linkage* and *characteristic* causal ambiguity (because of misunderstanding by competitors) can secure a capability and the basic resources it is based on. Other competitive considerations would include understanding how these capabilities, unique as they may be, will affect how the firm's goods or services will create value for customers. The competences created may result in such outcomes as, for example, efficiencies in transportation of product and a resultant cost savings, new technologies that improve new product-development processes, or improvements in customer service training. In each case, enhancement of customer value drives the return on investing in the capability. Hamel and Prahalad (1994a) also point out the need to understand which competences are *core* competences and which are secondary capabilities. Core competences "are the skills that enable a firm to deliver a fundamental [i.e., core] customer benefit" (p. 224). When considering their own competitiveness, firms must determine the value of these core competences.

Competences or capabilities underlie the eventual, potential embodiment of customer value in the market offering, which is the third stage of the customer value creation process (Hunt 2000a; Sanchez and Heene 1997; Sanchez, Heene, and Thomas 1996). As Hamel and Prahalad (1994a) note, the competences that create value are not generally visible to customers. What is visible is the product—goods or services—that the customer purchases. It is not surprising, therefore, that product innovation has been a frequent topic in the competitive strategy literature

(Campbell-Hunt 2000). For example, looking at one particular competence—that is, that of technical knowledge—McEvily and Chakravarthy (2002) found that the complexity and tacitness of this competence often allow firms to protect major product improvements.

Once a potentially valuable product has been created, positioning strategies must be developed and implemented, such strategies constituting the fourth stage of the R-A model of value creation. Firms integrate their distribution, pricing, service, and promotions decisions to arrive at a positioning strategy that highlights the superior value that the market offering provides for particular market segments. Competitive strategy research typically views these functions as within the domain of marketing (Campbell-Hunt 2000).

The final stage of the R-A model of value creation is the protection, maintenance, and improvement of resources. In this stage, firms engage in activities designed to ensure that the supply of resources is protected, while attempting to identify replacement resources that would offer an improvement in performance. The simple procurement process, involving the replenishment of stocks of resources, though important, may have the least potential for a core competence for the firm and, thus, the least opportunity for value creation. However, through proactive and reactive innovations, firms have opportunities for effecting quantum leaps toward the objective of improved replacement resources. The fifth stage of the value creation process requires *renewal* competences (Hunt 2000b, p. 87).

Resources and Causal Ambiguity

As discussed earlier, the ongoing competitiveness of the firm is dependent in part on the ability of managers to protect advantage-producing resources from imitation by competitors (Barney 1991; Hunt and Morgan 1995). A major protection against imitation is the causal ambiguity that is often inherent in complex resources (Dierickx and Cool 1989; Reed and DeFillippi 1990). When competitors are unable to observe and understand the linkages between resources and competences, it is very difficult to imitate them.

King and Zeithaml (2001) investigate the extent to which two types of ambiguity surrounding basic resources and higher-order resources (i.e., competences) protected those resources from imitation. Using firm performance as an indicator that important resource-competence relationships were protected from competitive imitation, King and Zeithaml examined (1) the ambiguity around managers' shared understanding of the linkages between basic resources and competences (i.e., linkage ambiguity), and (2) the ambiguity that is inherent in the resource or competence due to characteristics of the resource or competence (i.e., resource characteristic ambiguity). Regarding linkage ambiguity, it has often been speculated that when there is disagreement among observers (including managers within the firm) as to how resources relate to competences, such ambiguity would protect the erosion of such competences (Barney 1991; Lippman and Rumelt 1982). After all, if experienced managers of the resources within the focal firm do not agree on the connections between the basic resources they manage and the competences they produce, how could managers of competing firms be expected to understand the relationships, let alone imitate the resources that the competences are attributed to? This becomes problematic, however, for if the managers of the firm that possesses the competence in question fail to understand how it is created and sustained, it is only through chance that the basic resources necessary to sustain it will continue to be provided and combined in the complex manner required.

Because of the inconsistencies surrounding linkage ambiguity, the alternative benefit of causal ambiguity of resources may lie in characteristic ambiguity. King and Zeithaml (2001, p. 77) hold that resource characteristic ambiguity may arise from many sources, but typically results when:

(a) knowledge about the resources and the competence produced is tacit, or (b) the competences "reside in organizational culture and values." Tacit knowledge of the relationships between resources and competences is knowledge that is not formally recorded or "codified." Nonetheless, they maintain, such unarticulated knowledge is often *shared*.

King and Zeithaml (2001) found that linkage ambiguity *among the firm's managers* is detrimental to firm performance, while resource characteristic ambiguity strengthens firm performance. They suggest that managers need to share understandings of how complex resource combinations result in competences, but the firm should also embed knowledge of competences in its culture to protect itself from imitation by competitors.

King and Zeithaml's conceptualization of causal ambiguity—developed in the context of a theory of the firm, that is, the resource-based view—provides a good start. However, the concept of causal ambiguity and its role in strategy can be expanded beyond the bounds of the firm by using the broader scope of a theory of competition, that is, R-A theory. As argued for in Hunt and Morgan (1995), R-A theory expands the scope of potential sources of linkage and characteristic ambiguity to include those that reside in the external environment of the market, allowing us to account for the, arguably greater, ambiguity that arises from the complexities of customers and competitive circumstances. For example, causal ambiguity may exist concerning which product attributes customers value, or how a competitor applies resources and competences to create a superior market offering (Hunt and Morgan 1995). How do certain competitors routinely establish a superior market offering? In Table 4.3 we provide examples of strategic issues, linkage, and characteristic ambiguity that arise from the five stages of value creation under the R-A model from Figure 4.4.

We agree with King and Zeithaml that many instances of causal ambiguity reside within the firm. However, under the richer explanation of R-A theory, the full range of sources of ambiguity, including those that arise from competitive and market situations, can be explored and understood. Many marketing-based competences are based in these types of complex, ambiguous linkages and characteristics, which cut across the boundaries of the firm. High-quality customer service, strong brands, market orientation, successful new product-development processes (Verona 1999), and customer relationships are a few examples. Marketing, under the broader understanding of ambiguity offered by R-A theory, offers valuable opportunities for studying issues surrounding ambiguity.

R-A Theory as a Foundation for Teaching Strategy

Because all business disciplines are ultimately concerned with achieving competitive advantages and superior performance for the firm, it is possible for them to share a common, foundational theory. We believe that R-A theory is the strongest candidate, as it argues that all managers—whether their function is marketing, human resources, production, or otherwise—are ultimately managers of resources, using the resources at their disposal to create customer value.

In discussing *research* directions, we have also further laid the foundations for how R-A theory can be used to *teach* strategy. Students must understand that as managers, they will manage resources, in a competitive environment, with a goal of producing superior customer value. We hold that an excellent framework for understanding this process is the Resource-Advantage Model of Customer Value Creation, shown in Figure 4.4. Here, the student is taught that advantages can be gained in how they create and acquire resources. Further, based on the earlier discussion of relative resource value, students can learn to evaluate which resources offer the best potential return. Next, students are introduced to the complexities of bundling resources—creating more

Table 4.3

Causal Ambiguity and Resource-Advantage Theory

Stage of value creation	Strategic issues	Linkage ambiguity	Characteristic ambiguity
Resource identification, acquisition/creation	How to create or acquire financial, physical, legal, human, organizational, relationship, or information resources that can be used to create value efficiently and/or effectively for market segments?	What activities does the firm engage in that lead to strong customer relationships?	How does the firm partner with its suppliers to co-develop resources? How does the firm build a customer-focused culture?
Bundling resources to create competences	How to choose combinations of resources and find ways to integrate them to create competences, understand which competences are core and which are secondary, and how they may be protected from competitors?	What resources has the firm drawn on to create its core competences? How are particular resources linked to the creation of these competences?	How does the firm bundle its various resources to create such competences as superior processes for new product design, ability to build strong brands, and understand customer needs? What routines has it created to accomplish these abilities that are embedded in the organization?
Creating the market offering	How to use competences and other resources to achieve defensible, superior market offerings?	What competences are used to create market offerings whose attributes are highly valued by customers?	What attributes of the market offering are highly valued by customers?
Developing and implementing positioning strategies	How to develop and implement positioning strategies to achieve defensible, superior market offerings?	What resources and competences does the firm combine to create strategies for positioning its market offering against competitors? What resource/competence strengths are the basis for successful implementation of these strategies?	How do customers use attribute cues to formulate evaluations of market offerings?
Protecting, maintaining, and improving resources	How to continually tend to stocks and flows of resources, developing procurement strategies that enable the firm to meet cost and quality goals, and develop systems for scanning the environment to find improved replacements?	What resources and competences are enabling the firm to preempt competitors from accessing valuable new resources? What competences provide advantage in procurement?	How does the firm consistently gain access to new or improved stocks of resources before competitors can gain such access?

Source: Morgan and Hunt (2003). Reprinted by permission of the authors.

complex resources such as organizational learning, organizational culture, strong brands, and other higher-order resources. In the third phase of the model, students learn how market understanding gained through market research, and concepts such as innovation, creativity, and design, are integrated to create valued products. In the fourth phase, much of this same understanding, as well as competencies in design of promotions, selling, distribution, and pricing strategies, are combined to achieve a desired new or modified position for products—another firm resource. Finally, students learn to maintain and protect resources, including discussions of relationship management, procurement strategies, legal responsibilities, and, of course, managing causal ambiguity.

We have found R-A theory to be a superior theory for teaching strategy, as well as for setting the foundation for any marketing course. It not only provides a well-organized, continually expanded framework for discussing business, but focuses on superior customer value creation as the ultimate goal.

Conclusion

Since its introduction in the marketing literature as a specific theory of competition (Hunt and Morgan 1995) and its subsequent development as a *general* theory of competition (Hunt 2000b; Hunt and Morgan 1997), R-A theory has been critically examined in multiple disciplines on numerous occasions. Our initial hope was that R-A theory would both integrate and expand on concepts developed earlier in a wide range of business and economics literatures and theories—including resource-based theory, competence-based strategy, relationship marketing, and evolutionary economics, to name a few. Our goal was to provide a superior explanation of the process of how firms compete and how such competition produces desired outcomes. To date, R-A theory has withstood critical examination. A review of the contributions to knowledge of R-A theory, a history of the process of developing the theory, an examination of the theory's foundations, and an analysis of how R-A theory provides a theoretical grounding for business and marketing strategy research and practice have been provided here.

Ultimately, the goal of business and marketing strategy for the firm is to achieve superior financial performance by cost-effectively creating market offerings that provide exceptional value for customers, thus leading to superior financial rewards for owners, managers, and employees of those firms. While further critical examination of R-A theory would strengthen the theory, raise awareness, and further refine it, we encourage researchers to focus their attention also on how R-A theory, its structure, and its foundational premises can be *applied* to the practice of business and marketing strategy. We have initiated this process here, discussing how R-A theory compares, contrasts, and extends customary approaches to creating, evaluating, and executing strategy. R-A theory explains at the most fundamental level how relationship marketing and market orientation strategies can provide the firm with a superior approach to competition. R-A theory also overcomes the shortcomings of "outward-looking," industry-based strategy, while enhancing and extending the usefulness of narrowly focused, "inward looking" theories of strategy, such as the resource-based view and competence-based strategy. These types of efforts offer the potential of providing the business and marketing strategy disciplines with a theoretical foundation that can advance these relatively young fields.

Toward the goal of exploring how R-A theory can be applied to business and marketing strategy and research, this article also offers the R-A model of customer value creation. This R-A model organizes the value-creating activities of the firm into a sequence of processes that are informed by the rich, practical, evolutionary, disequilibrating resource focus of R-A theory. We have initiated the process of exploring the model by discussing the differential importance of various categories of resources and how one particular protective mechanism for competitive advantage—causal ambiguity—may be applied to the value-creation model to better understand strategy and its implications. We encourage others to critique, explore, and offer extensions to the model.

Marketing continues to offer a substantial contribution to the competition and strategy theory discussion, and it has the potential to offer much more (Hunt and Lambe 2000). Marketing brings its unique perspective of being outwardly focused on the market. It also understands that firm resources, competences, and capabilities—expressed in, for example, innovative products and superior distribution and promotional strategies—are needed to compete effectively. The importance of firms', and theories about firms, being outward looking and inward looking *simultaneously* has been an underlying and enduring tenet throughout the history of R-A theory's development. It will continue to be a truth that guides the research tradition's continuing evolution.

Acknowledgment

The authors thank Dennis B. Arnett and Sundar Bharadwaj for helpful comments on a draft of this article.

Notes

1. The original model is in Hunt and Vitell (1986). The version reproduced here is a revision from Hunt and Vitell (1993). Discussions and tests of the model may be found in Hunt (1990), Hunt and Vasquez-Parraga (1993), Mayo and Marks (1990), Menguc (1997), Singhapakdi and Vitell (1990, 1991), Sparks and Hunt (1998), and Vitell and Hunt (1990).

2. Etzioni (1988) refers to this view as "moderate deontology." Specifically, he argues that, rather than abandon P-utility, socioeconomics should (1) draw on deontological ethics and (2) theorize that moral commitment is a separate source of valuation. Thus, he hypothesizes that behavior is codetermined by P-utility and a moral commitment based on deontological ethics. By moderating the P-utility thesis with deontological ethics, argues Etzioni (1988, pp. 7, 8), socioeconomics can account for trust, which "is pivotal to the economy . . . as, without it, currency will not be used, saving makes no sense, and transaction costs rise precipitously."

3. See Bergen, Dutta, and Walker (1992); Davis, Schoorman, and Donaldson (1997); Eisenhardt (1989); and Perrow (1986) for reviews of agency theory.

4. However, Simon's (1979) "satisficing" differs from R-A theory's concept of superior financial performance. As Dickson (1992, p. 72) notes:

> Note that this view [Dickson's view]of relentless cost management cannot be accommodated in the satisficing model by simply assuming that the firm keeps raising its efficiency aspiration levels. A firm is likely to change its aspiration levels, but they are still only minimum performance standards, often linked to management and worker reward systems. Once its aspirations levels (performance standard goals) are met, the firm that prefers more profits over less will not stop seeking ways of reducing costs. Such motivation and behavior are antithetic to satisficing because the reality is that the firm is never satisfied with its current performance.

5. Davis, Schoorman, and Donaldson (1997) discuss the differences between agency theory and stewardship theory prescriptions as to corporate governance. They develop a "prisoner's dilemma" scenario concerning the "principal's choice" of either (1) acting opportunistically or (2) acting as a steward. Similar choices are then developed for managers (see their Figure 4.1, p. 39). Among other things, they discuss the costs of what are here called ethical code mismatches.

References

Aaker, David A. (1991), *Managing Brand Equity.* New York: Free Press.
——— (1995), *Strategic Market Management* (4th ed.). New York: Wiley.
Alderson, Wroe (1957), *Marketing Behavior and Executive Action.* Homewood, IL: Irwin.
——— (1965), *Dynamic Marketing Behavior.* Homewood, IL: Irwin.
Andrews, Kenneth R. (1971, 1980, 1987), *The Concept of Corporate Strategy.* Homewood, IL: Irwin.
Arnett, Dennis B. and Shelby D. Hunt (2002), "Competitive Irrationality: The Influence of Moral Philosophy," *Business Ethics Quarterly*, 12 (3), 279–303.
Axelsson, B. and G. Easton (1992), *Industrial Networks: A New View of Reality.* London: Gower.
Baker, Michael J., C.D. Black, and S.J. Hart (1994), "Competitive Success in Sunrise and Sunset Industries," in *The Marketing Initiative*, J. Saunders, ed. London: Prentice Hall.
Barney, Jay (1991), "Firm Resources and Sustained Competitive Advantage," *Journal of Management*, 17 (1), 99–120.
——— (1992), "Integrating Organizational Behavior and Strategy Formulation Research: A Resource-based Analysis," in *Advances in Strategic Management*, P. Whrivastava, A.S. Hugg, and J.E. Dutton, eds. Greenwich, CT: JAI, 39–61.
——— (2001), "Is the Resource-Based 'View' a Useful Perspective for Strategic Management Research? Yes," *The Academy of Management Review*, 26 (1), 41–56.
Barney, Jay and William G. Ouchi (1986), *Organizational Economics.* San Francisco: Jossey-Bass.
Beauchamp, T.L. and N.E. Bowie (1988), *Ethical Theory and Business* (3d ed.). Englewood Cliffs, NJ: Prentice Hall.
Bergen, Mark, Shantanu Dutta, and Orville Walker (1992), "Agency Relationships in Marketing: A Review," *Journal of Marketing*, 56 (3), 1–24.
Berle, Adolph A. and G.C. Means (1932), *The Modern Corporation and Private Property.* New York: Macmillan.
Berry, L.L. (1983), "Relationship Marketing," in *Emerging Perspectives on Services Marketing*, L. Berry, G.L. Shostack, and G.D. Upah, eds. Chicago: American Marketing Association, 25–28.
Berry, L.L. and A. Parasuraman (1991), *Marketing Services.* New York: Free Press.
Bharadwaj, Sundar, P. Rajan Varadarajan, and John Fahy (1993), "Sustainable Competitive Advantage in Service Industries: A Conceptual Model and Research Propositions," *Journal of Marketing*, 57 (4), 83–99.
Buzzell, Robert D., Bradley T. Gale, and Ralph G.M. Sutton (1975), "Market Share: A Key to Profitability," *Harvard Business Review*, 53 (January-February), 97–106.
Bynum, W.F., E.D. Browne, and Roy Porter (1981), *Dictionary of the History of Science.* Princeton, NJ: Princeton University Press.
Campbell-Hunt, Colin (2000), "What Have We Learned About Generic Competitive Strategy? A Meta-Analysis," *Strategic Management Journal*, 21, 127–54.
Chamberlin, Edward (1933/1962), *The Theory of Monopolistic Competition.* Cambridge, MA: Harvard University Press.
Chandler, Alfred D. (1990), *Scale and Scope: The Dynamics of Industrial Capitalism.* Cambridge, MA: Harvard University Press.
Christensen, C.R., K.R. Andrews, J.L. Bower, G. Hamermesh, and M.E. Porter (1982), *Business Policy: Text and Cases.* Homewood, IL: Irwin.
Conant, Jeffrey S., Michael P. Mokwa, and P. Rajan Varadarajan (1990), "Strategic Types, Distinctive Marketing Competencies, and Organizational Performance," *Strategic Management Journal*, 11 (September), 365–83.
Conner, Kathleen (1991), "A Historical Comparison of Resource-Based Theory and Five Schools of Thought Within Industrial-Organization Economics: Do We Have a New Theory of the Firm?" *Journal of Management*, 17 (March), 121–54.
Davis, James H., F. David Schoorman, and Lex Donaldson (1997), "Toward a Stewardship Theory of Management," *Academy of Management Review*, 22 (1), 20–47.
Day, George S. (1992), "Marketing's Contribution to the Strategy Dialogue," *Journal of the Academy of Marketing Science*, 20 (Fall), 323–30.
Day, George S. and Prakesh Nedungadi (1994), "Managerial Representations of Competitive Advantage," *Journal of Marketing*, 58 (April), 31–44.

Deshpande, Rohit and Frederick E. Webster, Jr. (1989), "Organizational Culture and Marketing: Defining the Research Agenda," *Journal of Marketing*, 53 (January), 3–15.

Dickson, Peter Reid (1992), "Toward a General Theory of Competitive Rationality," *Journal of Marketing*, 56 (January), 69–83.

——— (1996), "The Static and Dynamic Mechanics of Competitive Theory," *Journal of Marketing*, 60 (October), 102–106.

Dierickx, Ingemar and Karel Cool (1989), "Asset Stock Accumulation and Sustainability of Competitive Advantage," *Management Science*, 35 (December), 1504–1511.

Eisenhardt, Kathleen M. (1989), "Agency Theory: An Assessment and Review," *Academy of Management Review*, 14 (January), 57–74.

Etzioni, Amitai (1988), *The Moral Dimension: Toward a New Economics*. New York: Free Press.

Falkenberg, Andreas W. (1996), "Marketing and the Wealth of Firms," *Journal of Macromarketing*, 16 (Spring), 4–24.

——— (2000), "Competition and Markets," *Journal of Macromarketing*, 20 (June), 7.

Fama, Eugene F. (1980), "Agency Problems and the Theory of the Firm," *Journal of Political Economy*, 88 (April), 288–307.

Fama, Eugene F. and Michael C. Jensen (1983), "Separation of Ownership and Control," *Journal of Law and Economics*, 26 (June), 301–25.

Finkelstein, S. and Donald Hambrick (1996), *Strategic Leadership*. St. Paul: West.

Ford, D. (1990), *Understanding Business Markets: Interaction, Relationships, and Networks*. London: Academic Press.

Foss, Nicolai (1993), "Theories of the Firm: Contractual and Competence Perspectives," *Journal of Evolutionary Economics*, 3, 127–44.

——— (2000), "The Dangers and Attractions of Theoretical Eclecticism," *Journal of Macromarketing*, 20 (June), 65–67.

Frankena, W. (1963), *Ethics*. Englewood Cliffs, NJ: Prentice Hall.

Fried, Vance and Benjamin Oviatt (1989), "Michael Porter's Missing Chapter: The Risk of Antitrust Allegations," *Academy of Management Executive*, 3 (1), 49–56.

Gale, Bradley T. and Ben S. Branch (1982), "Concentration versus Market Share: Which Determines Performance and Why Does It Matter?" *The Antitrust Bulletin*, 27 (Spring), 83–103.

Goldman, Marshall I. (1960), "Product Differentiation and Advertising: Some Lessons from Soviet Experience," *Journal of Political Economy*, 68, 346–57.

Granovetter, Mark (1985), "Economic Action and Social Structure: The Problem of Embeddedness," *American Journal of Sociology*, 91 (3), 481–510.

Grant, Robert M. (1991), "The Resource-Based Theory of Competitive Advantage: Implications for Strategy Formulation," *California Management Review*, 33, 114–33.

Grönroos, Christran (1996), "Relationship Marketing: Strategic and Tactical Implications," *Management Decision*, 34 (3), 5–14.

——— (2000), *Service Management and Marketing: A Customer Relationship Management Approach*. New York: Wiley.

Grönroos, Christran and E. Gummesson, eds. (1985), *Service Marketing—Nordic School Perspectives*. Stockholm: University of Stockholm, Department of Business Administration, Research Report R.: 2.

Gummesson, Evert (1994), "Making Relationship Marketing Operational," *International Journal of Service Industry Management*, 5 (5), 5–20.

——— (1995), "Focus Shifts in Marketing: A New Agenda for the Third Millennium,"

Presentation at the 20th Anniversary Program of the Marketing Technology Center MTC. Stockholm, Sweden.

——— (1999), *Total Relationship Marketing; Rethinking Marketing Management: From 4Ps to 30Rs*. Woburn, MA: Butterworth-Heinemann.

Hakansson, H., ed. (1982), *International Marketing and Purchasing of Industrial Goods: An Interaction Approach*. Chichester, England: Wiley.

Hambrick, Donald C. and P. Mason (1984), "Upper Echelons: The Organization as a Reflection of Its Top Managers," *Academy of Management Journal*, 14, 401–18.

Hamel, Gary and A. Heene (1994), *Competence-Based Competition*. New York: Wiley.

Hamel, Gary and C.K. Prahalad (1989), "Strategic Intent," *Harvard Business Review*, (May-June), 63–76.

——— and ——— (1994a), *Competing for the Future*. Cambridge, MA: Harvard Business School Press.

THE RESOURCE-ADVANTAGE THEORY OF COMPETITION   197

——— and ——— (1994b), "Competing for the Future," *Harvard Business Review*, (July-August), 122–28.

Heene, Aimé and Ron Sanchez (1997), *Competence-Based Strategic Management*. New York: Wiley.

Hitt, Michael A., Leonard Bierman, Katsuhiko Shimizu, and Rahul Kochhar (2001), "Direct and Moderating Effects of Human Capital on Strategy and Performance in Professional Service Firms: A Resource-Based Perspective," *Academy of Management Journal*, 44 (1), 13–28.

Hodgson, Geoffrey M. (1993), *Economics and Evolution*. Ann Arbor: University of Michigan Press.

——— (2000), "The Marketing of Wisdom: Resource-Advantage Theory," *Journal of Macromarketing*, 20 (June), 68–72.

Houston, Franklin (1986), "The Marketing Concept: What It Is and What It Is Not," *Journal of Marketing*, 50 (April), 81–87.

Hult, G. Tomas M. and David J. Ketchen, Jr. (2001), "Does Market Orientation Matter?: A Test of the Relationship Between Positional Advantage and Performance," *Strategic Management Journal*, 22, 899–906.

Hunt, Shelby D. (1990), "Commentary on an Empirical Investigation of a General Theory of Marketing Ethics," *Journal of the Academy of Marketing Science*, 18 (2), 173–77.

——— (1995), "The Resource-Advantage Theory of Competition: Toward Explaining Productivity and Economic Growth," *Journal of Management Inquiry*, 4 (December), 317–32.

——— (1997a), "Competing Through Relationships: Grounding Relationship Marketing in Resource Advantage Theory," *Journal of Marketing Management*, 13, 431–45.

——— (1997b), "Evolutionary Economics, Endogenous Growth Models, and Resource-Advantage Theory," *Eastern Economic Journal*, 23 (4), 425–39.

——— (1997c), "Resource-Advantage Theory: An Evolutionary Theory of Competitive Firm Behavior?" *Journal of Economic Issues*, 31 (March), 59–77.

——— (1997d), "Resource-Advantage Theory and the Wealth of Nations," *Journal of Socio-Economics*, 26 (4), 335–57.

——— (1998), "Productivity, Economic Growth, and Competition: Resource Allocation or Resource Creation?" *Business and the Contemporary World*, 10 (3), 367–94.

——— (1999), "The Strategic Imperative and Sustainable Competitive Advantage: Public Policy and Resource Advantage Theory," *Journal of the Academy of Marketing Science*, 27 (2), 144–59.

——— (2000a), "The Competence-Based, Resource-Advantage, and Neoclassical Theories of Competition: Toward a Synthesis," in *Theory Development for Competence-Based Management*, R. Sanchez and A. Heene, eds. Volume 6(A) in Advances in Applied Business Strategy Series. Greenwich, CT: JAI, 177–209.

——— (2000b), *A General Theory of Competition: Resources, Competences, Productivity, Economic Growth*. Thousand Oaks, CA: Sage.

——— (2000c), "A General Theory of Competition: Too Eclectic or Not Eclectic Enough? Too Incremental or Not Incremental Enough? Too Neoclassical or Not Neoclassical Enough?" *Journal of Macromarketing*, 20 (1), 77–81.

——— (2000d), "Synthesizing Resource-Based, Evolutionary and Neoclassical Thought: Resource-Advantage Theory as a General Theory of Competition," in *Resources, Technology, and Strategy*, N.J. Foss and P. Robertson, eds. London: Routledge, 53–79.

——— (2001), "A General Theory of Competition: Issues, Answers, and an Invitation," *European Journal of Marketing*, 35 (5/6), 524–48.

——— (2002a), *Foundations of Marketing Theory: Toward a General Theory of Marketing*. Armonk, NY: M.E. Sharpe.

——— (2002b), "Marketing and a General Theory of Competition," *Journal of Marketing Management*, 18, 239–47.

——— (2002c), "Resource-Advantage Theory and Austrian Economics," in *Entrepreneurship and the Firm: Austrian Perspectives on Economic Organization*, N.J. Foss and P. Klein, eds. Cheltenham, UK: Elgar.

——— (2003), "The Resource-Advantage Research Program," working paper, Marketing Department, Texas Tech University, Lubbock.

Hunt, Shelby D. and Dennis Arnett (2001), "Competition as an Evolutionary Process and Antitrust Policy," *Journal of Public Policy and Marketing*, 20 (1), 15–26.

——— and ——— (2003), "Resource-Advantage Theory and Embeddedness: Explaining R-A Theory's Explanatory Success," *Journal of Marketing Theory and Practice*, 11 (1), 1–17.

Hunt, Shelby D. and Caroline Derozier (2004), "The Normative Imperatives of Business and Marketing Strategy: Grounding Strategy in Resource-Advantage Theory," *Journal of Business and Industrial Marketing*, 19 (1), 5–22.

Hunt, Shelby D. and Dale F. Duhan (2002), "Competition in the Third Millennium: Efficiency or Effectiveness?" *Journal of Business Research*, 55 (2), 97–102.

Hunt, Shelby D. and C. Jay Lambe (2000), "Marketing's Contribution to Business Strategy: Market Orientation, Relationship Marketing, and Resource-Advantage Theory," *International Journal of Management Reviews*, 2 (1), 17–44.

Hunt, Shelby D., C. Jay Lambe, and C.M. Wittman (2002), "A Theory and Model of Business Alliance Success," *Journal of Relationship Marketing*, 1 (1), 17–35.

Hunt, Shelby D. and Robert M. Morgan (1994), "Relationship Marketing in an Era of Network Competition," *Marketing Management*, 3 (1), 20–38.

——— and ——— (1995), "The Comparative Advantage Theory of Competition," *Journal of Marketing*, 59 (April), 1–15.

——— and ——— (1996), "The Resource-Advantage Theory of Competition: Dynamics, Path Dependencies, and Evolutionary Dimensions," *Journal of Marketing*, 60 (October), 107–14.

——— and ——— (1997), "Resource-Advantage Theory: A Snake Swallowing Its Tail or a General Theory of Competition?" *Journal of Marketing*, 61 (October), 74–82.

Hunt, Shelby D. and Arturo Vasquez-Parraga (1993), "Organizational Consequences, Marketing Ethics, and Salesforce Supervision," *Journal of Marketing Research*, 30 (February), 78–90.

Hunt, Shelby D. and Scott M. Vitell (1986), "A General Theory of Marketing Ethics," *Journal of Macromarketing*, 6 (Spring), 5–15.

——— and ——— (1993), "The General Theory of Marketing Ethics: A Retrospective and Revision," in *Ethics in Marketing*, N.C. Smith and J.A. Quelch, eds. Homewood, IL: Irwin, 775–84.

Huselid, M.A. (1995), "The Impact of Human Resource Management Practices on Turnover, Productivity and Corporate Financial Performance," *Academy of Management Journal*, 38 (3), 635–72.

Jacobson, Robert (1988), "Distinguishing Among Competing Theories of the Market Share Effect," *Journal of Marketing*, 52 (October), 68–80.

Jacobson, Robert and David A. Aaker (1985), "Is Market Share All That It's Cracked Up to Be?" *Journal of Marketing*, 49 (Fall), 11–22.

Jaworski, Bernard J., and Ajay K. Kohli (1993), "Market Orientation: Antecedents and Consequences," *Journal of Marketing*, 57 (July), 53–70.

Jensen, M.C. and W.H Meckling (1976), "Theory of the Firm: Managerial Behavior, Agency Costs, and Ownership Structure," *Journal of Financial Economics*, 3, 305-60; reprinted in *Organizational Economics*, J.B. Barney and W.G. Ouchi, eds. (1986). San Francisco: Jossey-Bass.

Keller, Kevin L. (1993). "Conceptualizing, Measuring, and Managing Customer-Based Brand Equity," *Journal of Marketing*, 57 (1), 1–22.

——— (1998), *Strategic Brand Management: Building, Measuring, and Managing Brand Equity.* Upper Saddle River, NJ: Prentice Hall.

Kerin, Roger A., P. Rajan Varadarajan, and Robert A. Peterson (1992), "First-Mover Advantage: A Synthesis, Conceptual Framework, and Research Propositions," *Journal of Marketing*, 56 (4), 33–52.

King, Adelaide Wilcox and Carl P. Zeithaml (2001), "Competencies and Firm Performance: Examining the Causal Ambiguity Paradox," *Strategic Management Journal*, 22 (1), 75–99.

Kirzner, Israel M. (1979), *Perception, Opportunity and Profit: Studies in the Theory of Entrepreneurship.* Chicago: University of Chicago Press.

Kohli, Ajay K. and Bernard J. Jaworski (1990), "Market Orientation: The Construct, Research Propositions, and Managerial Implications," *Journal of Marketing*, 54 (April), 1–18.

Lado, Augustine A., Nancy Boyd, and P. Wright (1992), "A Competency-Based Model of Sustainable Competitive Advantage," *Journal of Management*, 18, 77–91.

Lakatos, Imre (1978), *The Methodology of Scientific Research Programmes.* Cambridge, England: Cambridge University Press.

Lambe, C.J., Robert N. Spekman, and Shelby D. Hunt (2002), "Alliance Competence, Resources, and Alliance Success: Conceptualization, Measurement, and Initial Test," *Journal of the Academy of Marketing Science*, 30 (2), 141–58.

Langlois, Richard N., ed. (1986), *Economics as a Process: Essays in the New Institutional Economics.* Cambridge, England: Cambridge University Press.

Langlois, Richard N. and P.L. Robertson (1995), *Firms, Markets and Economic Change: A Dynamic Theory of Business Institutions.* London: Routledge.

Laverty, Kevin J. (1996), "Economic 'Short-Termism': The Debate, the Unresolved Issues, and the Implications for Management Practice and Research," *Academy of Management Review,* 21 (3), 825–60.

Lavoie, Don (1985), *Rivalry and Central Planning, The Socialist Calculation Debate Reconsidered.* Cambridge, England: Cambridge University Press.

Learned, E.P., C.R. Christensen, K.R. Andrews, and W.D. Guth (1965), *Business Policy: Text and Cases.* Homewood, IL: Irwin.

Lekachman, Robert (1959), *A History of Economic Ideas.* New York: Harper.

Lieberman, Marvin B. and David B. Montgomery (1988), "First-Mover Advantages," *Strategic Management Journal,* 9 (Summer), 41–58.

———— and ———— (1998), "First-Mover (Dis)Advantages: Retrospective and Link with the Resource-Based View," *Strategic Management Journal,* 19 (12), 1111–26.

Lippman, S.A. and R.P. Rumelt (1982), "Uncertain Imitability: An Analysis of Interfirm Differences in Efficiency Under Competition," *Bell Journal of Economics,* 13, 418–38.

Makadok, Richard (2001), "Toward a Synthesis of the Resource-Based and Dynamic-Capability Views of Rent Creation," *Strategic Management Journal,* 22 (5), 387–401.

Mayo, Michael A. and Lawrence J. Marks (1990), "An Empirical Investigation of a General Theory of Marketing Ethics," *Journal of the Academy of Marketing Science,* 18 (Spring), 163–72.

McEvily, Susan K. and Bala Chakravarthy (2002), "The Persistence of Knowledge-Based Advantage: An Empirical Test for Product Performance and Technological Knowledge," *Strategic Management Journal,* 23 (4), 285–305.

McGrath, R.C., I.C. MacMillan, and S. Venkataramen (1995), "Defining and Developing Competence," *Strategic Management Journal,* 16, 251–76.

Menguc, Bulent (1997), "Organizational Consequences, Marketing Ethics, and Salesforce Supervision: Further Empirical Evidence," *Journal of Business Ethics,* 16, 1–20.

Mintzberg, Henry (1987), "Crafting Strategy," *Harvard Business Review,* (July-August), 66–75.

Montgomery, Cynthia A. and Michael E. Porter (1991), *Strategy: Seeking and Securing Competitive Advantage.* Boston: Harvard Business School Publishing.

Morgan, Robert E. and Shelby D. Hunt (2002), "Determining Marketing Strategy: A Cybernetic Systems Approach to Scenario Planning," *European Journal of Marketing,* 36, 450–78.

Morgan, Robert M. and Shelby D. Hunt (1994), "The Commitment-Trust Theory of Relationship Marketing," *Journal of Marketing,* 58 (July), 20–38.

———— and ———— (1999), "Relationship-Based Competitive Advantage: The Role of Relationship Marketing in Marketing Strategy," *Journal of Business Research,* 46 (3), 281–90.

———— and ———— (2003), "Customer Value Creation, Causal Ambiguity, and Resource-Advantage Theory," working paper, Marketing Department, University of Alabama, Tuscaloosa.

Narver, John C. and Stanley F. Slater (1990), "The Effect of Market Orientation on Business Profitability," *Journal of Marketing,* 54 (October), 20–35.

Nayyan, Praveen and Karen Bantel (1994), "Competitive Agility = A Source of Competitive Advantage Based on Speed and Variety," *Advances in Strategic Management,* 10A, 193–222.

Nelson, Phillip (1970), "Information and Consumer Behavior," *Journal of Political Economy,* 78, 311–29.

Nelson, Richard R. and Sidney G. Winter (1982), *An Evolutionary Theory of Economic Change.* Cambridge, MA: Belknap Press.

North, Douglass C. (1990), *Institutions, Institutional Change, and Economic Performance.* Cambridge, England: University of Cambridge.

O'Keefe, Michael, Felix Mavondo, and William Schroder (1996). *The Resource-Advantage Theory of Competition: Implications for Australian Competition.* Melbourne, Australia: Monash University Agriculture Research Unit.

Penrose, Edith T. (1959), *The Theory of the Growth of the Firm.* London: Basil Blackwell and Mott.

Perrow, Charles (1986), *Complex Organizations.* New York: Random House.

Pfeffer, Jeffrey (1994), *Competitive Advantage Through People.* Boston: Harvard Business School Press.

Porter, Michael E. (1980), *Competitive Strategy: Techniques for Analyzing Industries and Competitors.* New York: Free Press.

———— (1985), *Competitive Advantage: Creating and Sustaining Superior Performance.* New York: Free Press.

——— (1991), "Towards a Dynamic Theory of Strategy," *Strategic Management Journal*, 12, 95–117.

Prahalad, C.K. and Gary Hamel (1990), "The Core Competence of the Corporation," *Harvard Business Review* (May-June), 79–91.

——— and ——— (1993), "Strategy as Stretch and Leverage," *Harvard Business Review*, (March/April), 75–84.

Priem, Richard L. and John E. Butler (2001), "Is the Resource-Based 'View' a Useful Perspective for Strategic Management Research?" *The Academy of Management Review*, 26 (1), 22–40.

Ravenscraft, David J. (1983), "Structure-Profit Relationships at the Line of Business and Industry Level," *Review of Economics and Statistics*, 65 (February), 22–31.

Reed, Richard and Robert J. DeFillippi (1990), "Causal Ambiguity, Barriers to Imitation, and Sustainable Competitive Advantage," *Academy of Management Review*, 15 (January), 88–117.

Roehl, Tom (1996), "The Role of International R&D in the Competence-Building Strategies of Japanese Pharmaceutical Firms," in *Dynamics of Competence-Based Competition: Theory and the New Strategic Management*, R. Sanchez, A. Heene, and H. Thomas, eds. Elsevier: Oxford, 377–96.

Rumelt, Richard P. (1984), "Toward a Strategic Theory of the Firm," in *Competitive Strategic Management*, R. Lamb, ed. Englewood Cliffs, NJ: Prentice Hall, 556–70.

Sanchez, Ron and A. Heene (1997), *Strategic Learning and Knowledge Management*. New York: Wiley.

——— and ———, eds. (2000), *Theory Development for Competence-Based Management*. Volume 6(A) in Advances in Applied Business Strategy Series. Greenwich, CT: JAI, 177–209.

Sanchez, Ron, A. Heene, and Howard Thomas (1996), *Dynamics of Competence-Based Competition*. New York: Elsevier Science.

Savitt, Ronald (2000), "A Philosophical Essay about *A General Theory of Competition*," *Journal of Macromarketing*, 20 (June), 73–76.

Schlegelmilch, Bodo B. (2002), "Comments on *A General Theory of Competition*," *Journal of Marketing Management*, 18, 221–27.

Schmalensee, Robert (1985), "Do Markets Differ Much?" *American Economic Review*, 75 (3), 341–50.

Schoemaker, P.J.H. and R. Amit (1994), "Investment in Strategic Assets: Industry and Firm-Level Perspectives," in *Advances in Strategic Management*, P. Shrivastava, A.S. Huff, and J.E. Dutton, eds. Volume 10A. Greenwich, CT: JAI, 3–33.

Schroeder, Roger G., Kimberly A. Bates, and Mikko A. Junttila (2002), "A Resource-Based View of Manufacturing Strategy and the Relationship to Manufacturing Performance," *Strategic Management Journal*, 23 (2), 105–17.

Schulze, William S. (1994), "The Two Schools of Thought in Resource-Based Theory," in *Advances in Strategic Management*, volume 10A, P. Shrivastava, A.S. Huff, and J.E. Dutton, eds. Greenwich, CT: JAI, 127–51.

Schumpeter, Joseph A. (1950), *Capitalism, Socialism, and Democracy*. New York: Harper and Row.

——— (1954), *History of Economic Analysis*. New York: Oxford University Press.

Selznick, P. (1957), *Leadership in Administration*. New York: Harper and Row.

Senge, Peter M. (1990), *The Fifth Discipline: The Art and Practice of the Learning Organization*. New York: Doubleday.

Sheth, Jagdish N. (1994), "The Domain of Relationship Marketing," handout at the *Second Research Conference on Relationship Marketing*, Center for Relationship Marketing, Emory University, Atlanta, GA. June 9–11.

Sheth, Jagdish N. and Atal Parvatiyar (1995a), "The Evolution of Relationship Marketing," *International Business Review*, 4, 397–418.

——— and ——— (1995b), "Relationship Marketing in Consumer Markets: Antecedents and Consequences," *Journal of the Academy of Marketing Science*, 23 (4), 255–71.

Simon, Herbert A. (1979), "Rational Decision Making in Business Organizations," *American Economic Review*, 69 (September), 493–512.

Singhapakdi, Anusorn and Scott J. Vitell, Jr. (1990), "Marketing Ethics: Factors Influencing Perceptions of Ethical Problems and Alternatives," *Journal of Macromarketing*, 10 (Spring), 4–18.

——— and ——— (1991), "Research Note: Selected Factors Influencing Marketers' Deontological Norms," *Journal of the Academy of Marketing Science*, 19 (Winter), 37–42.

Sinkula, James M., William E. Baker, and Thomas Noordewier (1997), "A Framework for Market-Based Organizational Learning: Linking Values, Knowledge, and Behavior," *Journal of the Academy of Marketing Science*, 25 (Fall), 305–18.

Slater, Stanley F. and John C. Narver (1994), "Does Competitive Environment Moderate the Market Orientation-Performance Relationship?" *Journal of Marketing*, 58 (January), 46–55.

——— and ——— (1998), "Customer-led and Market-oriented: Let's Not Confuse the Two," *Strategic Management Journal*, 19 (10), 1001–1006.

Sparks, John R. and Shelby D. Hunt (1998), "Marketing Researcher Ethical Sensitivity," *Journal of Marketing*, 62 (2), 92–109.

Stigler, George J. (1961), "The Economics of Information," *Journal of Political Economy*, 71 (June), 213–25.

Teece, David and Gary Pisano (1994), "The Dynamic Capabilities of Firms: An Introduction," *Industrial and Corporate Change*, 3 (E), 537–56.

Teece, David, Gary Pisano, and Amy Shuen (1997), "Dynamic Capabilities and Strategic Management," *Strategic Management Journal*, 18 (7), 509–33.

Varadarajan, P. Rajan and Margaret H. Cunningham (1995), "Strategic Alliances: A Synthesis of Conceptual Foundations," *Journal of the Academy of Marketing Science*, 23 (4), 282–96.

Verona, Gianmario (1999), "A Resource-Based View of Product Development," *Academy of Management Review*, 24 (1), 132–42.

Vitell, Scott J. and Shelby D. Hunt (1990), "The General Theory of Marketing Ethics: A Partial Test of the Model," in *Research in Marketing*, volume 10, Jagdish N. Sheth, ed. Greenwich, CT: JAI, 237–65.

Walras, Leon (1874/1954), *Elements of Pure Economics*. Trans. 1954 by William Jaffe. Homewood, IL: Irwin.

Webster, Frederick E. Jr. (1992), "The Changing Role of Marketing in the Corporation," *Journal of Marketing*, 56 (4), 1–17.

——— (1994), "Executing the Marketing Concept," *Marketing Management*, 3 (1), 9–16.

Weitz, Barton A. and Sandy D. Jap (1995), "Relationship Marketing and Distribution Channels," *Journal of the Academy of Marketing Science*, 23 (4), 305–20.

Wensley, Robin (2002), "Marketing for a New Century: Comments on *A General Theory of Competition*," *Journal of Marketing Management*, 18, 229–37.

Wernerfelt, Birger (1984), "A Resource-based View of the Firm," *Strategic Management Journal*, (5), 171–80.

Williamson, Oliver E. (1994), "Transaction Cost Economics and Organization Theory," in *The Handbook of Economic Sociology*, N.J. Smelser and R. Swedberg, eds. Princeton, NJ: Princeton University Press, 77–107.

Wilson, David T. (1995), "An Integrated Model of Buyer-Seller Relationships," *Journal of the Academy of Marketing Science*, 23 (4), 305–20.

Wong, V. and J. Saunders (1993), "Business Organization and Corporation Success," *Journal of Strategic Marketing*, 1 (March), 20–40.

Appendix 4.1

Issues Addressed by R-A Theory

	H&M 1995	Hunt 1995	H&M 1996	O-M-S 1996	H&M 1997	Hunt 1997a	Hunt 1997b	Hunt 1997c	Hunt 1997d	Hunt 1998	Hunt 1999	M&H 1999	Falk. 2000	Foss 2000	Hodg. 2000	Hunt 2000a
Antitrust											X					
Austrian economics																
Capital						X										
Comparative adv. (res.)	X	X														
Competences				X												X
Competitive advantages	X	X	X													
Dynamic theory		X	X		X								X			X
Economic growth							X		X	X	X					
Economic sociology																
Effectiveness										X			X			
Efficiency										X			X			
Embeddedness																
Endogenous growth models																X
Entrepreneur			X				X			X						
Ethics																
Evolutionary economics			X		X		X	X	X							
Firm diversity	X							X	X		X					X
Firm's objective								X								
Foundations	X	X			X									X		
General theory of competition			X												X	X
General theory of marketing																

Innovation
Institutional economics
Institutions
Learning
Market orientation
Market segments
Monopolistic competition
Opportunism
Path dependencies
Pedigree
Productivity
Property rights
Public policy
Relational resources
Relationship marketing
Resource-based theory
Socialism
Socioeconomics
Soviet economic growth
Strategy
Sustainable advantage
Trust

(continued)

Appendix 4.1 (continued)

	Hunt 2000b	Hunt 2000c	Hunt 2000d	H&L 2000	Sav. 2000	Hunt 2001	H&A 2001	H&Du 2001	Sch. 2002	Hunt 2002a	Hunt 2002b	Hunt 2002c	H,L,&W 2002	Wen. 2002	M&H 2002	H&A 2003	H&De 2004
Antitrust	X	X						X									
Austrian economics	X																
Capital	X																
Comparative adv. (res.)	X									X							
Competences	X		X	X						X	X						
Competitive advantages	X									X							X
Dynamic theory	X	X			X		X				X		X				
Economic growth	X						X										
Economic sociology	X																
Effectiveness	X															X	
Efficiency	X						X	X									
Embeddedness	X							X								X	
Endogenous growth models	X																
Entrepreneur	X		X														
Ethics	X																
Evolutionary economics	X		X				X										
Firm diversity	X		X														
Firm's objective	X					X											
Foundations	X																
General theory of competition	X	X	X		X	X			X	X							
General theory of marketing											X			X			
Innovation	X																
Institutional economics	X	X					X										
Institutions	X	X														X	
Learning	X																

Columns are labeled 1..13 from left to right (Falk., Hodg., H&A, H&De, H&Du, H&L, H,L,&W, H&M, M&H, Sav., O-M-S, Sch., Wen.).

	1	2	3	4	5	6	7	8	9	10	11	12	13
Market orientation			X										X
Market segments	X												
Monopolistic competition	X					X							
Opportunism	X												
Path dependencies	X												
Pedigree	X	X			X								
Productivity	X						X		X				
Property rights	X						X						
Public policy	X						X						
Relational resources	X		X								X		
Relationship marketing			X								X		X
Resource-based theory	X		X								X		X
Socialism	X								X				
Socioeconomics	X												
Soviet economic growth	X												
Strategy	X		X				X	X	X		X	X	X
Sustainable advantage	X						X	X	X		X		
Trust	X												
		X											

Note: Falk. = Falkenberg; Hodg. = Hodgson; H&A = Hunt and Arnett; H&De = Hunt and Derozier; H&Du = Hunt and Duhan; H&L = Hunt and Lambe; H,L,&W = Hunt, Lambe, and Wittman; H&M = Hunt and Morgan; M&H = Morgan and Hunt; Sav. = Savitt; O-M-S = OKeefe et al.; Sch. = Schlegelmilch; Wen. = Wensley.

CHAPTER 5

TOWARD AN INTEGRATED MODEL
OF BUSINESS PERFORMANCE

SUNDAR G. BHARADWAJ AND RAJAN VARADARAJAN

Abstract

Understanding, explaining, and predicting the determinants of performance over different time horizons and organizational levels is an ongoing and important concern to decision makers in organizations. During the past decade, strategy research in marketing focusing on performance-related issues at the business, product-market, and brand levels has been considerably influenced by the resource-based view of the firm. While the intellectual underpinnings of the resource-based view of the firm can be traced to recent works in strategic management and earlier works in economics, at the more aggregate level, published research focusing on the myriad nuances of organizational performance dates back at least to the 1930s. Against this backdrop, this article attempts to provide an interdisciplinary perspective of the evolution of scholarly thought on determinants of organizational performance and advances an integrative model of business performance. In the proposed integrative model, firm-specific intangible resources, and capabilities, industry structure, and competitive strategy variables are modeled as the major determinants of business performance.

Introduction

The evolution of marketing strategy literature over the past quarter century can be viewed as a confluence of perspectives, paradigms, theories, concepts, frameworks, principles, methods, models, and metrics from a number of fields of study, chief among them being industrial organization (IO) economics, strategic management, and marketing. An examination of extant literature in marketing with a strategic focus is indicative of two broad research streams.

- *Marketing Strategy Research:* Research in marketing focusing on marketing-strategy-related issues (e.g., research focusing on marketin-strategy content, formulation process, and implementation-related issues)
- *Strategy Research in Marketing:* Research in marketing with a strategic focus (e.g., research focusing on the role of marketing in the formulation of corporate- and business-level strategy; knowledge management)

Because strategy research in marketing encompasses marketing-strategy research at a more fine-grained level, it is possible to distinguish between the following research streams in marketing characterized by a strategic focus.

- Research focusing on organizational issues germane to marketing strategy (e.g., branding, positioning, and segmentation).
- Research focusing on organizational issues central to marketing strategy but whose scope spans multiple organizational functions (e.g., innovation and quality).
- Research focusing on the outcomes of marketing and business strategy (e.g., competitive positional advantages, market share, customer satisfaction, return on investment (ROI), and market-based assets).
- Research focusing on organizational-level phenomena that influence marketing strategy and management in important ways (e.g., corporate culture, market orientation, organizational learning, and knowledge management).
- Research focusing on issues at the interface of corporate and marketing strategy (e.g., synergy and horizontal acquisitions); business and marketing strategy (e.g., generic strategy of differentiation, market pioneering, and strategic alliances); and corporate, business, and marketing strategy (e.g., global competitive strategy and multimarket competition).
- Research focusing on strategy at the corporate level (e.g., diversification and divestitures) from the perspective of how corporate strategy impacts on and is impacted by marketing strategy. The strategic role of the marketing function in organizations at the corporate level.
- Research focusing on strategy at the business-unit level (e.g., generic competitive strategies and sustainable competitive advantage) from the perspective of how business-level strategy influences and is influenced by marketing strategy. The strategic role of the marketing function in organizations at the business-unit level.

As is evidenced by the above, the scope of strategy research in marketing is vast and expansive. This article provides an interdisciplinary perspective of the conceptual and empirical underpinnings of scholarly research on organizational performance, an issue of enduring interest to decision makers in organizations and to researchers in marketing. Understanding, explaining, and predicting the determinants of performance over different time horizons (long-term, intermediate-term, and/or short-term) and organizational levels (e.g., corporate, divisional, business unit, product-market, product line, product item, brand, and salesperson) are ongoing and important concerns to decision makers in organizations. The assessment of organizational performance is generally based on multiple criteria deemed pertinent to evaluating performance at specific organizational levels and time horizons. Representative of criteria employed to assess organizational performance are effect on shareholder wealth, ROI, earnings growth rate, sales, sales growth rate, market share, market-share growth rate, customer satisfaction, customer retention rate, and the environmental friendliness of the firm's product offerings. A number of competing and complementing perspectives in IO economics, business policy and strategy, and marketing provide valuable insights into the determinants of performance at various organizational levels. For instance, numerous studies in IO economics, strategic management, and marketing that have focused on questions such as those enumerated below have contributed to enhancing our understanding of the determinants of organizational performance:

- Why are some *industries,* on average, more profitable than others?
- Why are some *firms* in an industry, on average, more profitable than others?
- Why are some *businesses* in the portfolio of a multibusiness firm, on average, more profitable than other businesses?
- Given the structural characteristics of an industry and the resource base of a business, what competitive strategy alternatives are available to a *business* to achieve above-average performance?

- How do the structural characteristics of the market in which a *business* competes, the competitive strategy pursued by the business, and its relative competitive position impact on its performance?

An examination of strategy research in marketing focusing on performance-related issues at the business, product-market, and brand levels is indicative of the considerable influence of the resource-based view of the firm during the recent past. However, scholarly research focusing on understanding, explaining, and predicting performance at different levels such as industry, firm, and business dates back to the 1930s, if not earlier. Furthermore, realistically, the resource-based view is a complement to, rather than an alternative to, some of the other perspectives. Against this backdrop, the objectives of this article are to:

- Provide a historical perspective of the evolution of scholarly thought on determinants of organizational performance by reviewing major streams of research that provide insights into the determinants of performance at the industry, firm, and/or business-unit level.
- Propose an integrative model of business performance that builds on this body of research.

The remainder of the article is organized as follows. First, we review the following seven streams of research focusing on issues pertaining to determinants of organizational performance.

- The classical IO school (The Structure-Conduct-Performance Paradigm)
- The efficiency/revisionist school
- The strategic groups school
- The business policy school and the Profit Impact of Market Strategy (PIMS) paradigm
- The Austrian school
- The new empirical IO school
- The resource-based view of the firm

Admittedly, the body of extant literature relating to each of the above research streams is vast and expansive, often spanning literature in the fields of economics, law, sociology, strategy, and marketing. Consequently, the sections devoted to discussion of each of these research streams in this article more realistically constitute an *overview,* rather than an extensive review, of their conceptual underpinnings, representative empirical research, and limitations. Following our review of the seven literature streams, in the discussion section, we draw attention to some of the overlapping and unique aspects of these perspectives. Next, we propose an integrated model of business performance. The proposed model, consistent with the resource-based view, recognizes the importance of firm-specific intangibles (resources and capabilities) as an important determinant of business performance. In the proposed model, firm-specific resources and capabilities are modeled as complementing industry structure and competitive strategy variables as determinants of business performance. In other words, examination of firm-specific intangibles and industry structure and competitive strategy variables are viewed as complementing and not as competing perspectives of determinants of business performance. The article concludes with a brief summary.

The Classical Industrial Organization School

The classical IO school largely draws on the work of Mason (1939) and Bain (1951, 1956). The Bain-Mason paradigm views *industry structure* as influencing *firm conduct* (or strategy), and conduct as, in turn, influencing *performance.* Commonly referred to as the *structure-conduct-performance* (SCP) paradigm, this stream of research was motivated by public policy considerations. Here, performance is construed broadly and from a microeconomics perspective focusing on social efficiency of factors of production. In this conceptualization, performance embodies (among other factors) the goal that the distribution of income should be equitable. This implies that producers do not secure rewards far in excess of what is needed to call forth the amount of services supplied. Conduct or strategy refers to the firm's choice of decision variables such as the advertising and promotional strategy to be employed. Industry structure refers to the relatively stable economic and technical dimensions of an industry that provide the context in which businesses compete with each other (Bain 1972). The primary elements of industry structure identified as important in this stream of research are barriers to entry, industry concentration, product differentiation, and overall elasticity of demand (Bain 1968).

Conceptual Underpinnings

In classical IO research, industry concentration increasing beyond a point is viewed as likely to lead to collusive increases in price by firms in that industry, which, in turn, is reflected in the profit rates[1] of the firms.[2] Oligopoly theory (Cournot 1838), which predicts an increase in price with industry concentration, provides the theoretical rationale for the IO perspective. Although a number of oligopoly theories have been advanced, the differences among them on this issue are a matter of functional form and not direction (Weiss 1989). The Cournot model yields a profit prediction as well. With a straight-line demand, total industry profit declines as the number of firms increases. Confidence in the prediction that profitability will be positively correlated to industry concentration is further buttressed by the assumption that collusive behavior is more likely in concentrated markets than in fragmented markets. Another set of theories identifies the conditions for the presence of successful collusion, tacit or explicit. According to Chamberlin (1933, 1949), although firms act independently, as their market shares increase beyond a critical point,[3] they recognize their interdependence and begin to act collusively. In other words, beyond a critical concentration ratio, collusion will occur. A similar conclusion was arrived at in the modified version of Chamberlin's model (Boulding 1955).

In Stigler's (1964) conceptualization of collusive oligopoly, firms with large market shares can detect secret price-cutting by rivals more readily than small firms can, and the ability of leaders to identify secret price concessions increases at an increasing rate with concentration. Therefore, in a situation of few firms with large market shares in the marketplace, collusion and collusive price increases are predicted.

In the classical IO school, structure is the construct of primary importance. Although initially conceptualized to be of secondary importance, conduct was consistently ignored in empirical studies.[4] The justification for this practice lies in observations such as Bain's (1968, pp. 344–45), below, based on an empirical study of four industries:

> Available evidence from conduct patterns per se, even in intensively studied cases, do not ordinarily reveal enough to support meaningfully precise inferences about the aims of price-calculation pursued, or predictions of the associated market performance. . . . Knowing only what is evident about conduct, there is no clear basis for differentiating the four in terms either of predicted performance. . . . Actual patterns of market conduct cannot be fully enough measured to permit us to establish empirically a meaningful association either between market conduct and performance, or between structure and market conduct. It thus becomes

expedient to test directly for net associations of market structure to market performance, leaving the detailed character of the implied linkage of conduct substantially unascertained.

Teece (1984) provides additional reasons as to why conduct (strategy) has been ignored in the IO school: (a) a stronger concern for consumer welfare and public policy than individual firm performance, and (b) an emphasis on formal quantitative modeling of firm conduct that requires simplification of managerial attributes and behaviors.

Representative Empirical Research

A large number of empirical studies have focused on the SCP paradigm. An early review by Weiss (1974) reported forty-six cross-sectional studies. Gilbert (1984) uncovered forty-five studies in the U.S. banking industry alone. A meta-analysis lists over 100 studies examining the relationship between industry concentration and profitability (Capon, Farley, and Hoenig 1990). A brief overview of relevant empirical research follows.

Bain (1951) was the first test of the SCP paradigm. He used data on forty-two industries, eight-firm concentration ratios and profit, measured as return on equity. Although a strong linear relationship between concentration and profit rates was not found, he found a rather distinct break in average profit rate showing up at the 70 percent concentration line and a significant difference in the average profit rates above and below this line. On the other hand, when Stigler (1963) attempted to test the industry concentration-profitability hypothesis by subdividing the sample into a high concentration group (four-firm concentration over 60%) and a low concentration group (four-firm concentration below 50%), he found no support for the hypothesis.

Brozen (1971) analyzed Federal Trade Commission (FTC) data for practically the same period (i.e., 1939 and 1940) as Bain (1951) and found the earnings of the concentrated and unconcentrated groups of industries to be virtually identical. Industries with concentration ratios greater than 70 percent earned only a statistically insignificant 0.07 percentage point more than the unconcentrated group. Brozen attributed the difference between his and Bain's study findings to the biased sampling adopted by Bain, in that Bain used only industries for which the Securities Exchange Commission (SEC) reported profits for more than two firms. Brozen, on the other hand, used all firms for which SEC reported profits. Analyzing the data further, Brozen (1971) found that while larger firms earned more than smaller ones in seven out of the nine concentrated industries group, larger firms earned more than smaller ones in only two of the seven unconcentrated industries group. Based on the above finding, Brozen surmised that concentrated industries got concentrated because they generated efficiencies that favored larger firms. The smaller firms had not yet adjusted by either dropping out or growing up, and in the interim were earning less. In the unconcentrated industries group, the contrary was observed. In this group, while smaller firms had been able to better adjust to whatever had occurred, the larger firms had neither yet shrunk nor dropped out. Smaller firms earned more because they had made better adjustments. Based on these findings, Brozen concluded that the data on profitability and industry concentration support the theory that market forces concentrate industries where efficiency calls for greater concentration, and deconcentrates industries where efficiency calls for less concentration. Other early empirical studies (primarily, bivariate correlational studies) between industry concentration and profitability found a significant and positive relationship in most cases. The notable exceptions were the works of Stigler (1963) and Brozen (1971). For instance, a survey of fifty-four empirical studies utilizing both domestic and international samples found a robust tendency for a positive association between industry concentration and profitability (Weiss 1974). However, in many cases the correlation was weak. Our summary of sixty-three (illustrative) studies suggests the following:

- Thirteen of the twenty-four bivariate correlation studies (54%) found the relationship between industry concentration and profitability to be positive and significant, and a further seven studies (29%) found the relationship to be positive but not significant.
- Of the bivariate correlation studies, only 17% found the relationship to be negative, and of that, only half found the relationship to be significant.
- Of the multivariate studies, fifteen out of the forty studies (37.5%) found the relationship to be positive and significant, and five studies (12.5%) found the relationship to be positive but nonsignificant.
- Of the multivariate studies, fifteen out of the forty studies (37.5%) found the relationship to be negative and significant, and five studies (12.5%) found the relationship to be negative but nonsignificant.

In summary, multivariate studies, unlike bivariate correlational studies, were less likely to find a positive relationship between industry concentration and profitability. In other words, studies that controlled for other factors were likely to find results contrary to the predictions of the SCP paradigm. However, two meta-analysis studies found the net effect of industry concentration on profitability to be positive (Capon, Farley, and Hoenig 1990; Dutta and Narayan 1989).

Limitations and Critique

Four broad sets of criticisms have been leveled against this stream of research.

Lack of Theory and Model Underspecification

This criticism is mentioned in passing here, since it largely forms the logical basis for the *revisionist/efficiency school* discussed next. Studies examining simple bivariate correlation are open to the criticism of likely "omitted variable bias." By not modeling plausible other variables (e.g., conduct/strategy variables), the variance likely to be explained by the nonspecified/omitted variables is manifested in concentration. As an illustration, Comanor and Wilson (1967) found that after taking advertising expenditure and capital requirements into account, there no longer existed any correlation between industry concentration and profitability (i.e., *there was no unique variation between industry concentration and profitability*).

The revisionist/efficiency school argues that it is efficiency and not concentration that drives profits. Demsetz (1973) contends that efficient firms drive out inefficient firms, and as a consequence, industries become more concentrated. Furthermore, he argues that by not specifying efficiency in the model, a spurious correlation is induced between concentration and profits.

Possibility of Collusion

According to the SCP paradigm, the presence of collusion among firms in an industry is a necessary condition for the achievement of a significant positive relationship between industry concentration and profitability. Stigler (1964), in studying the possibility of collusion, examined the conditions contributing to the enforcement of effective cartels. A necessary condition for a cartel to be effective is the ability of the participants to detect secret price-cutting. Stigler's theoretical analysis indicated that it takes relatively few firms to reduce significantly the gains as well as possibility of collusion.

A similar picture regarding the likelihood of collusive behavior is found in the experimental literature. Experimental economics studies indicate that when two or three sellers exist in a market, collusive outcomes are difficult to establish, much less sustain, and Nash equilibrium abounds (Geroski, Philips, and Ulph 1985; Plott 1989).

Role of Entry Barriers

According to the SCP paradigm, the persistence of the industry concentration-profitability relationship in a market is made possible by the presence of entry barriers. "Entry barriers" refers to "the advantage of established sellers in an industry over potential entrant sellers, these advantages being reflected in the extent to which established sellers can persistently raise their prices above a competitive level without attracting new firms to enter the industry" (Bain 1956, p. 3).

Two criticisms have been voiced in literature concerning entry barriers. Demsetz (1974) argues from a conceptual viewpoint that expenditures on both advertising and capital outlays are needed to produce and sell products. These expenditures are no more barriers than are expenditures on labor and material. Alternatively, if one views entry barriers as the ability of existing firms to be more efficient in the employment of advertising and capital inputs compared to firms that are not in the industry, then it is an indicator of efficiency, and not presence of a barrier. In effect, Demsetz's contention is that theoretical support of the market concentration doctrine is weak at best and nonexistent at worst.

More recent research argues that viewing entry barriers as a determinant of performance could lead to costly errors (McWilliams and Smart 1993). Investments in entry barriers are unlikely to lead to superior performance because firms constructing barriers to entry are subject to a "free-rider problem" (Oster 1990). Since barriers to entry are an industry-level phenomena, while a single firm that invests resources in building barriers bears the cost, the benefits are reaped by other incumbents in the industry as well (Barney, McWilliams, and Turk 1989; McWilliams and Smart 1993). Hence, it seems implausible that organizations will invest in building barriers to entry as suggested by this literature stream.

Assumption of Homogeneity of All Firms within an Industry

The SCP paradigm was developed to explain and predict industry-level phenomena and makes the assumption that all firms within an industry are homogenous (Rumelt 1991). The new IO school (discussed later) modifies this assumption by examining homogenous clusters of firms within an industry, referred to as *strategic groups*. More recently, as elaborated in the section devoted to the resource-based view of the firm, it has been argued that firms are bundles of resources and capabilities, and that in many cases, these resources and capabilities are idiosyncratic to a firm. Therefore, the assumption of homogeneity in IO research, made in the interest of analytical convenience, is questionable.

Summary

The SCP paradigm argues that the key determinant of profits is the structure of the industry in which the firm operates. Using concentration as a proxy for industry structure, the IO school views the positive correlation between industry concentration and profitability as supportive evidence. Empirical results however, have been mixed.[5] Empirical studies appearing prior to the early 1970s, which were predominantly univariate studies, generally found a positive correlation between industry concentration and profitability. However, some of the subsequent studies (most of them incorporating more than one independent variable) found no positive correlation, and in some cases, found a negative correlation, between industry concentration and profitability.

The Efficiency/Revisionist School

The revisionist or efficiency school posits efficiency as the key driver of performance of a firm. Proponents of this school of thought do not view the relationship between industry concentration and profitability as plausible (cf. Bork 1978; Demsetz 1973; McGee 1988). Instead, they view more efficient firms as possessing superior characteristics—methods of organizing production, providing service, nurturing buyer confidence, lowering costs, and satisfying consumer demand better—that positively impact on their market share (Demsetz 1974). This, in turn, forces most marginal firms out of the market. As efficient firms grow larger, their number gets to be fewer. With inefficient firms exiting the market, the industry becomes more concentrated. Since efficiency is not modeled in the SCP paradigm, industry concentration is correlated with profitability.

According to the efficiency school, entry barriers are not necessary in order for firms to achieve superior profits. Above-average profits are a temporary phase in industry evolution. As other firms take note of the above-average profits reaped by a few efficient incumbents, resource reallocation will take place leading to either entry of new competitors or incumbents increasing capacity (Jacobson 1988). According to the efficiency paradigm, there occurs continual reallocation of resources to the highest valued opportunity (Fisher, McGowan, and Greenwood 1983). Industry equilibrium may or may not occur, depending on the ability of the new entrants to replicate the cost structure of incumbents. Thus, unlike the SCP paradigm, which views that incumbents through collusive power and use of market power raise prices, the efficiency paradigm posits that through superior innovativeness or managerial skills, efficient firms can lower their costs, increase their size, and achieve above-normal profits (Demsetz 1973, 1974). Furthermore, since raising prices would encourage firms with less efficient cost structures to persist in the industry, the route to superior performance is through lowering costs.

Representative Empirical Research

Demsetz's (1973) effort was the first empirical test of the efficiency hypothesis. Prior to that, Brozen (1971) and McGee (1971) published efforts that were termed "antecedents" to Demsetz's pathbreaking effort (Scherer 1980). For example, based on an examination of several industries, McGee argues that larger firms in concentrated industries earned higher average profits than smaller firms, and because, by definition, the profits of larger firms are weighted more heavily in calculating average profits, monopoly is not the reason for the high profits. The costs of these firms are lower or consumers prefer their products, or both. In other words, superior efficiency produces higher-than-average profits (McGee 1971).

Demsetz (1973) conducted the first test of the efficiency hypothesis. Using ninety-five three-digit industries as the sample and 1963 as the time period, he sorted firms in each industry into four different asset size classes. The rate of return for the smallest firm was not found to increase with industry concentration, and similar results were found across the classes of smaller firms. He also found that with increases in industry concentration, the differences in earnings between small and large firms increased. Demsetz argued that this provided empirical support for the efficiency hypothesis.

Peltzman (1977) provided a more direct test of the efficiency hypothesis. Based on a study of 165 four-digit manufacturing industries for the period 1947–1967, he concluded that ". . . more concentration raises profitability not because of price increases, but because they fall less than costs. . . . Most practitioners have chosen to interpret the profitability-concentration relationship as evidence for collusion. A minority has emphasized the concentration-efficiency nexus. The emphasis here is consistent with an eclectic view, but one in which efficiency effects predominate" (Peltzman 1977, pp. 257, 262–63).

Our review of studies examining the efficiency hypothesis suggests mixed findings, similar to empirical research examining the SCP paradigm. For example, Clarke, Davies, and Waterson (1984), examining data for U.K.-based firms, found both efficiency and market power effects at work. Porter (1979), in developing the case for *strategic groups,* suggests that it is *mobility barriers,* rather than efficiency, that protect relatively successful firms (research on strategic groups and mobility barriers is discussed in greater detail in the next section). Weiss (1974), a proponent of the SCP paradigm, argued that a proper test of the efficiency hypothesis would be a study that takes market share and industry concentration into account at the same time. In this test, market share could be a proxy for superior products, superior management, as well as scale economies. Following this recommendation, a study by Gale (1972) found a strong positive relationship between the weighted average market share and profitability of large U.S. firms. Ravenscraft (1983), in his multivariate, regression-analysis-based study, found that profits were related to market share but not industry concentration. Later work using line-of-business data by Scherer et al. (1987) also suggested that market share effects were more powerful explanators of performance, and industry concentration effect was, in effect, negative.

Limitations and Critique

Two broad sets of criticisms can be voiced against this school of thought.

Conceptual/Definitional Limitations

Although the efficiency hypothesis is logically compelling, no clear conceptual definition of efficiency effects has been advanced. In empirical studies, researchers have utilized varying operational definitions of efficiency. In a majority of studies testing the efficiency hypothesis, market share has been used as a proxy for efficiency. Business policy researchers, on the other hand, have used market share as a proxy for competitive position. Hence, the absence of a precise conceptual definition poses challenges in assessing the value of the empirical research reported.

Empirical Research

The cumulative empirical evidence is mixed. For instance, Clarke, Davies, and Waterson (1984) did not find unequivocal support for either of the two explanations. Rather, they found both efficiency and market power explanations to be plausible. Scherer (1980) has questioned the validity of some of the studies that found support for Demsetz's (1973) hypothesis. Porter (1979) views his results as indicative of the presence of mobility barriers and strategic groups rather than support for the efficiency hypothesis. Finally, work by Martin (1983), Kwoka and Ravenscraft (1986), Mueller (1986), Cotterill (1986), and Scott and Pascoe (1986) suggests the presence of a variety of complex firm-specific, intraindustry effects not easily explained by Demsetz's hypothesis.

Summary

Compelling logic notwithstanding, empirical support for the efficiency perspective has not been overwhelming. Besides the results being mixed, it also appears that the efficiency explanation constitutes a complementary explanation for explaining performance. In other words, both industry structure and efficiency effects explain variance in performance. The efficiency paradigm however has changed the unit of analysis from the industry to the firm level. From a managerial point of view, this perspective has a great deal more relevance. It provides managers with a more actionable approach. In regard to public policy implications, it supports an antiregulation point of view by suggesting that it is not collusive behavior and monopolistic conditions that cause above-normal profits, but the superior efficiency of some firms in an industry. In effect, this paradigm foreshadows developments in the resource-based view of the firm, discussed later.

The Strategic Groups School

Developing from two separate viewpoints, one emanating from IO economics and the other from the business policy discipline, the strategic groups school introduced the concept of *strategic groups*. Acknowledging that the homogeneity assumption of traditional IO research is questionable, more recent efforts have attempted to identify much finer (homogenous) groupings of firms within the industry. The term "strategic groups," originally coined by Hunt (1972), refers to a set of firms that compete within an industry on the basis of similar combinations of business scope (target market segments, types of goods/services offered, and geographic reach) and resource commitments (Cool and Schendel 1987). Research on strategic groups suggests that, based on a particular set of dimensions, the number of strategic groups in an industry can range from one (all firms competing similarly along the set of dimensions) to the total number of firms in the industry (each firm competing uniquely along the set of dimensions). In effect, firms within a strategic group are assumed to be relatively homogenous, while those across strategic groups are assumed to be relatively heterogeneous. Akin to the SCP school that posits a relationship between industry membership and performance, the strategic school posits a relationship between strategic group membership and performance.

Mobility barriers are factors that inhibit easy/costless entry into a strategic group. These are akin to entry barriers—factors that inhibit easy/costless entry of new firms into an industry. Porter (1979) advanced the presence of mobility barriers as a counterargument to Demsetz's (1973) efficiency hypothesis. Porter argued that, if some firms are more efficient than others, then there must be "some factor" preventing the inefficient firms from copying and achieving similar levels of efficiency as the efficient firms. He points out that the revisionist school provides no clear rationale for the nonimitability of the superior efficiencies of the "efficient" firms. Porter contends that the efficient firms belong to a strategic group, while the inefficient firms belong to another, and it is the presence of mobility barriers that prevents firms from migrating from one strategic group to another. In other words, strategic group research is based on assumptions similar to those of the traditional IO school, albeit at a lower level of aggregation.

Representative Empirical Research

A number of research studies have attempted to examine the presence of strategic groups on the basis of a variety of dimensions. A key objective of research focused on strategic groups is explaining variance in performance based on the membership of firms in strategic groups. A review of relevant empirical research suggests that evidence supportive of strategic group membership-performance relationship is mixed at best. The level of support varies across studies, with many not finding significant support at all. Other reviews of the literature on strategic groups (Cool and Schendel 1988; Thomas and Venkatraman 1988) also draw similar conclusions. For instance, Porter (1979), Frazier and Howell (1983), and Cool and Schendel (1987) found no performance differences between strategic groups. Other studies (e.g., Dess and Davis 1984) found differences on some measures of performance but not others. Still others (e.g., Oster 1982) found significant differences in performance between high and low advertising strategic groups.

More recent efforts have attempted to examine the reasons for the mixed results. Lawless and Tegarden (1991) tested the hypothesis that an incomplete treatment/control of industry forces is the reason for the mixed support. By subdividing their sample into a group in which conditions favor conformity (high concentration, high entry barriers, and low differentiation) and a group in which conditions favor nonconformity (low concentration, low entry barriers, and high differentiation), they found that the strategic group concept is more useful for explaining performance differences in the former group. In brief, they find support for their hypothesis that the mixed results in prior research are due to an incomplete control of important industry forces.

In contrast to early research on strategic groups in IO literature, later research in strategic management literature (1) recognized the presence of heterogeneity within strategic groups, (2) limited focus to specific industries, and (3) employed the firm, rather than the industry, as the unit of analysis. For example, Cool and Schendel (1987), examining the temporal/longitudinal stability and performance differences among strategic groups, concentrated on the pharmaceutical industry. Thomas and Venkatraman (1988) point out that: ". . . rejection of performance differences (across groups) implies that attention should be focussed on 'within-group' differences in performance and on differentiated sets of skills and assets of different players" (p. 548). Lawless, Bergh, and Wilsted (1989) propose that, since capability differences confound the membership-performance relationship, adding firm capabilities to the model may explain persistent intragroup performance variation observed in empirical studies on strategic group. They model the relationship as follows:

$$\text{Performance} = f(\text{industry structure, group membership, firm capabilities})$$

Their results suggest that the strategic group membership-performance relationship may be moderated by firm characteristics associated with the ability to implement strategies. They also found that measures of strategic capability and performance were significantly different and correlated among firms in two strategic groups defined on strategy dimensions. They conclude that:

> Revisions to the conceptual model to include specifications of individual firm characteristics therefore appear to be on the right track. . . . We conclude that even where firms conform on some aspects of conduct, their capabilities constrain pursuit of their strategies, and influence the success of their strategic choices. (p. 658)

Limitations and Critique

Inconclusive Empirical Evidence

The key objective of research on strategic groups is explaining variance in performance. The premise here is that since there are certain shared characteristics among group members, they must achieve similar levels of performance, and across groups they would be dissimilar on both strategy characteristics and performance. In brief, strategic group membership is used to explain variance in performance. However, empirical evidence does not support these views.

Another possible limitation of research focusing on strategic groups and a cause underlying the mixed results is inappropriate control for critical variables. Lawless and Tegarden (1991) point out the absence of control for important industry factors that could explain variance in performance. Lawless, Bergh, and Wilsted (1989) identify the need to control for capability differences among firms. In brief, multiple and conflicting objectives and improper control for critical variables are presented as the major reasons for the mixed results.

Number of Strategic Groups

A major criticism of this research stream has been the lack of strong theory explaining the presence of strategic groups (Barney and Hoskisson 1991). For a given set of firms, the choice of dimensions determines the number of strategic groups as well as the number of firms in a strategic group. For example, in Hunt's (1972) study of the white goods industry, three sources of asymmetry (dimensions) between the firms—extent of vertical integration, degree of product diversification, and differences in product differentiation—produced four strategic groups. Nayyar (1989) points out that if these three sources of asymmetry were dichotomized as "High and Low," there should be potential for $2^3 = 8$ strategic groups rather than four. The question of why there are only four strategic groups rather than eight remains unanswered.

Tautological

As pointed out by Nayyar (1989), studies by Porter (1979) and Caves and Pugel (1980) use measures of performance or firm output (firm size) as dimensions to identify strategic groups. However, given that the objective of strategic group research is to explain differences in performance, using a measure of performance as a group defining/determining variable is tautological.

Haphazard Choice of Dimensions

Empirical studies of strategic groups use a variety of multivariate techniques such as factor analysis, cluster analysis, and regression to identify the strategic groups and their members. However, the choice of dimensions lacks such sophistication. Few, if any, studies emphasize detailed industry knowledge in choosing the dimensions for strategic groups (McGee and Thomas 1986). Since, with a change in dimensions, a different number of strategic groups with different group members emerges, it is empirically derived (Barney and Hoskisson 1991).

Summary

Research focusing on strategic groups evolved as an attempt and response to ameliorate some of the limitations and questionable assumptions of the traditional IO school. Accepting the presence of heterogeneity within industry, this school attempts to identify finer homogenous groups, within which the SCP paradigm would hold (i.e., identify a strategic group membership-performance relationship). However, empirical support is mixed. More recently, there has been a growing recognition that the assumption of homogeneity within groups is questionable. As discussed in the section on the resource-based view of the firm, the presence of capability differences (heterogeneity) among firms within a strategic group cannot be ruled out.

The Business Policy School and the PIMS Paradigm

The Five-Forces Model

Departing from the original objectives of IO school (maintenance of intraindustry competition and monitoring of antitrust behavior), IO inspired research in the field of strategic management focused on models that could aid firms in achieving above-normal profits by circumventing competition (Barney 1986b; Reed and DeFillippi 1990). An influential and representative work in this genre that transcends IO and strategic management literature is Porter's (1980) *five forces model.* As summarized in Figure 5.1, the five-forces model highlights the role of five competitive forces (bargaining power of suppliers and buyers, threat of new entrants, and competition from entrenched rivals and substitutes) as explanators of *differences between industries in their average profitability.* According to this framework, ceteris paribus, the profitability of industries in which suppliers and buyers wield a *high* level of bargaining power, the threat of new entrants is *high,* the level of competition from potential substitutes is *high,* and the intensity of competition between entrenched rivals is *high* will be lower than that of industries in which the above competitive forces are either moderate or low. Table 5.1 provides further elaboration of the potential impact of specific factors underlying the five major competitive forces on industry profitability.

Within any industry, competing businesses differ in their profitability, with some evidencing performance above the industry average and others below the industry average. Key to a business's achieving sustained superior performance is identifying and achieving an advantageous competitive position in the context of the five competitive forces. Labeled in a variety of ways, such as the *market-deterrent approach* (Teece, Pisano, and Shuen 1997) or, more commonly, as the *product-market approach,* the basic premise underlying this approach is that the market and/or industry conditions impose certain pressures to which an organization must effectively respond. This contention is also supported by the literatures in resource dependency theory and evolutionary economics. Firms that successfully adapt to these industry conditions would survive and grow. Firms that do not adapt to these environmental conditions would fail. In other words, superior performance (and survival) is ascribed to a business's responsiveness to external characteristics delineated in this framework.

New Empirical Industrial Organization School

Building on analytical game-theoretic approaches aligned with rigorous econometric foundations, this school developed the perspective that firm profitability was a function not only of the broad structural characteristics of industries, but also of the demand and cost characteristics of specific industries. Cross-industry analysis that was the norm in research based on the SCP paradigm is unlikely to model such industry specific characteristics, leading to the emergence of the New Empirical Industrial Organization (NEIO) school (see Bresnahan 1989 for a detailed review). The NEIO school focuses on the development of structural econometric models with the explicit goal of profit maximization of individual firms, while accommodating the interdependent nature of a single firm's strategic choice with those of its industry competitors. In other words, researchers belonging to this school model a firm's choice as a function of its rival's choices and consequently treat each firm's strategic decisions toward profit maximization as endogenous.

The NEIO school focuses on market power as a proxy for profitability, with market power being measured by the Lerner Index ([price-marginal cost]/price). The school views profitability to be a function of the inherent demand structure (a proxy for consumer preferences), the cost

220

Figure 5.1   **Competitive Forces and Industry Profitability**

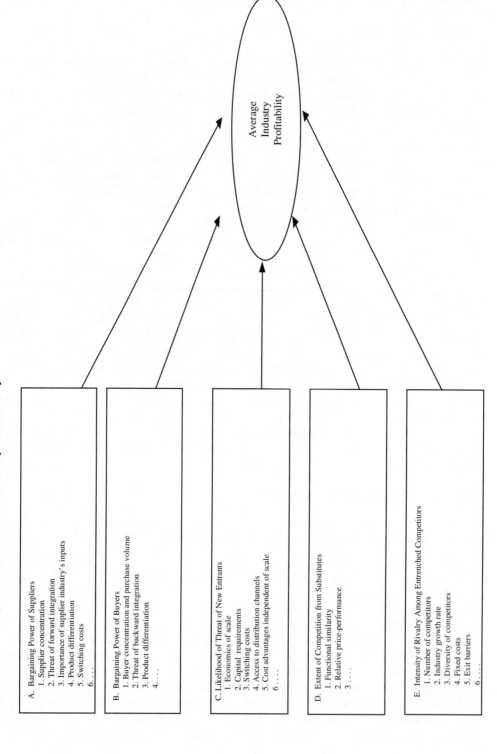

Table 5.1

Impact of Competitive Forces on Industry Profitability

A. Potential Impact of Supplier Forces on Industry Profitability
 A1. A supplier group that is more concentrated than the focal industry it sells to will have a *negative* effect on industry profitability.
 A2. A supplier group that poses a credible threat of forward integration into the focal industry will have a *negative* effect on industry profitability.
 A3. A supplier group that sells a relatively important input to the focal industry will have a *negative* effect on industry profitability.
 A4. A supplier group whose product offerings to the focal industry are differentiated will have a *negative* effect on industry profitability.
 A5. An input from a supplier group that would entail switching costs for the buyer, if the source of supply were to be switched, will have a *negative* effect on industry profitability.
B. Potential Impact of Buyer Forces on Industry Profitability
 B1. A buyer group that is concentrated and purchases a large volume of the focal industry's total output will have a *negative* effect on industry profitability.
 B2. A buyer group that poses a credible threat of backward integration into the focal industry will have a *negative* effect on industry profitability.
 B3. A buyer group to which the focal industry offers an undifferentiated product will have a *negative* effect on industry profitability.
C. Potential Impact of Threat of New Entrants on Industry Profitability
 C1. Cost advantage of incumbents due to scale economies, by deterring potential new entrants, will have a *positive* effect on industry profitability.
 C2. Large capital requirements, by deterring potential new entrants, will have a *positive* effect on industry profitability.
 C3. High switching costs that buyers may have to incur, by deterring potential new entrants, will have a *positive* effect on industry profitability.
 C4. Lack of access to distribution channels, by deterring potential new entrants, will have a *positive* effect on industry profitability.
 C5. Cost advantages independent of scale, by deterring potential new entrants, will have a *positive* effect on industry profitability.
D. Potential Impact of Competition from Substitutes on Industry Profitability
 D1. High functional similarity between the substitute industry's and the focal industry's product offerings will have a *negative* effect on industry profitability due to higher buyer propensity to switch to substitutes.
 D2. Substitute products that provide better price-performance than the focal industry's products will have a *negative* effect on industry profitability.
E. Potential Impact of Rivalry among Entrenched Competitors on Industry Profitability
 E1. Low concentration will have a *negative* effect on industry profitability.
 E2. Low industry growth rate, by increasing market share expansion rivalry among present competitors, will have a *negative* effect on industry profitability.
 E3. Diversity among competitors (in terms of factors such as size, ownership, strategies, and origin) will have a *negative* effect on industry profitability because of their different objectives and goals.
 E4. High fixed costs, by forcing competitors to frequently resort to price cutting to increase utilization, will have a *negative* effect on industry profitability.
 E5. Fewer possibilities available to firms in an industry to differentiate their product offerings from competitors' product offerings will have a *negative* effect on industry profitability.
 E6. High exit barriers, by deterring the exit of marginal firms, will have a *negative* effect on industry profitability.

Source: Adapted from Table 1 in P. Rajan Varadarajan (1999), "Strategy Content and Process Perspectives Revisited," *Journal of the Academy of Marketing Science*, 27 (Winter), 88–100.

structure (a proxy for firm efficiency), and the nature of competitive interaction (a proxy for anticompetitive or tacitly cooperative behavior) of firms within an industry (Kadiyali, Sudhir, and Rao 2001). The analytical model underlying the competitive interactions in this framework relies on game theoretic frameworks such as Bertrand, Leader–Follower, Competitive, and so forth. Managers within firms can then choose to manipulate any of these three sets of variables to enhance their firm's performance.

Although nascent insofar as marketing strategy is concerned, the NEIO school has several interesting aspects that are of great relevance to modeling firm performance and to serve as an alternative to the classical IO school. The modeling of competitive behavior is an important addition, whereas classical IO, to a large extent, treats firms as homogenous. Second, heterogeneity in other aspects such as consumer preferences (influencing demand functions) and firm efficiency (influencing cost functions) is also recognized. Third, the ability to use alternative game theoretic models (each of which has its own assumptions) enables the researcher to test competing models, evaluate stability of results across models, and thereby test and enhance theory development (Kadiyali, Sudhir, and Rao 2001).

Representative Empirical Research

While the research in most cases does not explicitly model firm profitability, it identifies actions relating to competitive behavior, firm efficiency, and demand characteristics that lead to superior profits. For example, Sudhir (2001a) finds that aggressive behavior in entry-level markets, followed with cooperative behavior in luxury markets, leads to superior performance in the auto industry. Kadiyali (1996) examines the role of interactions among manufacturers in influencing wholesale prices, and Sudhir (2001b) relaxes certain assumptions made by these earlier studies and finds that retailers maximize category profits and manufacturers tacitly collude especially when involved in long-term competition in concentrated markets. In a key finding of this research stream, Bresnahan (1989), in his reporting of Lerner indices across industries, finds that concentration is correlated with market power (a proxy for profitability). However, in a specific case study of the cereal industry, Nevo (2001) finds that market power is a function of a firm's ability to deliver differentiated products (a demand advantage) rather than any anticompetitive behavior. In summary, while there is no clear-cut conclusion that can be drawn as yet, the growing number of studies from this school have the potential to provide new insights into the drivers of firm profitability in specific industries.

Summary

The NEIO school is a valuable addition to the field of marketing strategy. Recognizing the concern that heterogeneity in cost, demand, and competitive interactions needs to be modeled to get unbiased estimates of firm profit drivers, this school relies on strong theoretical models and rigorous econometric approaches to model profitability. The need to conduct empirical efforts within a specific industry setting, thereby limiting generalizability of results, is a key criticism of this school. Recent efforts by Putsis and Dhar (2004) to integrate NEIO with SCP is a step in the right direction.

The Profit Impact of Market Strategy (PIMS) Model

The PIMS paradigm is an offshoot of the cross-fertilization of management practice and research in IO economics, strategic management, and marketing. The PIMS database contains historical information on the market structure conditions, competitive strategy actions, competitive position, and financial performance of nearly 3,000 strategic business units (SBUs). The sample, drawn from more than 450 corporations representing a broad spectrum of industry environments, contains data on SBUs for periods ranging from two to twelve years (see Buzzell and Gale 1987). The PIMS paradigm views SBU performance as a function of three sets of variables:

- The structure of the market in which an SBU operates,
- The competitive position of the SBU in that market, and
- The competitive strategy pursued by the SBU.

Figure 5.2 depicts the PIMS competitive strategy paradigm and includes representative variables that belong to each set. The PIMS paradigm posits that market structure, competitive position, and strategy will have main as well as interactive effects on SBU performance.

Representative Empirical Research

Market Share

Overall, the empirical results based on this database have been mixed. Early empirical findings based on PIMS data-based research suggest a positive and significant impact of market share on performance. For instance, a regression analysis of the entire PIMS database with twenty-one other independent variables suggests that a 1 percent increase in market share is associated with a 0.34 percent increase in ROI (see Buzzell and Gale 1987). Three broad theoretical arguments have been advanced to explain this phenomenon:

1. *Efficiency theory:* Businesses with large market shares are cost efficient because of experience and scale effects that ultimately lead to greater profitability (Buzzell and Gale 1987; Day and Montgomery 1983).
2. *Market power theory:* The superior financial performance of businesses with large market shares is attributable to their ability to obtain inputs at lower costs, extract concessions from channel members, and set prices rather than be price takers (Martin 1988; Schroeter 1988).
3. *Product quality assessment theory:* A product's widespread acceptance is likely to be viewed by customers as an indicator of quality (Smallwood and Conlisk 1979). Risk-averse customers would be more inclined to patronize the offerings of a market leader rather than take risks associated with purchasing from a less established competitor.

Product Quality

PIMS data–based studies indicate that the relative product quality is the single most important factor positively impacting on SBU performance over the long run (Buzzell and Gale 1987). It has been suggested that quality leads to (a) stronger customer loyalty, (b) more repeat purchases, (c) less vulnerability from price wars, (d) ability to command premium prices without losing market share, and (e) lower marketing costs.

Other Variables

In addition to market share and product quality, newness of plant and equipment, labor productivity, and vertical integration are among the competitive position and business strategy factors that

Figure 5.2 Profit Impact of Market Strategy (PIMS) Model

Major Influences on Business Performance

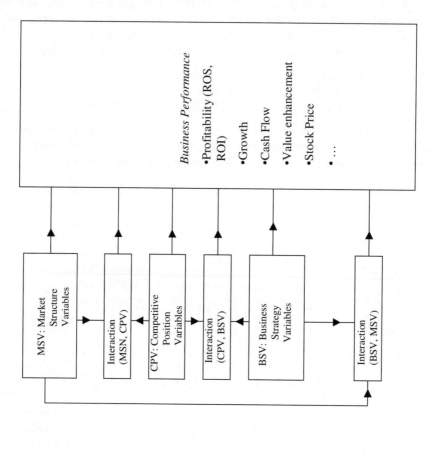

MSV: Market Structure Variables
- Market differentiation
- Market growth rate
- Entry conditions
- Unionization
- Capital intensity
- Purchase amount
- ...

CPV: Competitive Position Variables
- Relative perceived quality
- Relative market share
- Relative capital intensity
- Relative cost...

BSV: Business Competitive Strategy Variables
- Pricing
- R&D spending
- New product introduction
- Change in relative quality and variety of products/services
- Marketing channels
- Relative vertical integration
- ...

MSV: Market Structure Variables

Interaction (MSN, CPV)

CPV: Competitive Position Variables

Interaction (CPV, BSV)

BSV: Business Strategy Variables

Interaction (BSV, MSV)

Business Performance
- Profitability (ROS, ROI)
- Growth
- Cash Flow
- Value enhancement
- Stock Price
- ...

Source: Adapted from Buzzell, R.D., and B.T. Gale (1987), *The PIMS Principles: Linking Strategy to Performance*, New York: Free Press, p. 28.

impact on financial performance (ROI). Fixed capital intensity, inventory investment, rate of new product introduction, and current levels of spending on marketing and R&D are among the factors negatively related to performance. Among the market structure variables, while market growth rate, concentration, and rate of inflation in selling prices were found to be positively related to performance, employee unionization was found to be negatively related to performance.

Limitations and Critique

A number of methodological and theoretical questions have been raised concerning research based on PIMS data.

Small-Share Businesses Achieve Levels of Performance Similar to Large-Share Businesses

A number of PIMS data–based studies have identified the presence of relatively more profitable businesses with low market shares (Woo 1984; Woo and Cooper 1981, 1982). Building on an early study of firms in the *Forbes* annual survey, which identified numerous successful low-market-share businesses (Hamermesh, Anderson, and Harris 1978), Woo and Cooper (1982), using the PIMS database, identified low-market-share businesses that enjoyed pretax rates of ROI of 20 percent or more. These businesses were found to offer high product quality and have low total costs. Woo (1984) also identified market leaders that had poor rates of return. In light of such results, it was argued that the market share–profitability link is overstated.

Spuriousness of the Market Share–Profitability Relationship

Prescott, Kohli, and Venkatraman (1986) tested a PIMS data–based path-analytic model relating performance (measured as ROI) to relative market share (RMS) and sixteen other strategic variables. Based on the study findings, the authors argued that, to the extent that RMS can be explained as a function of these sixteen variables, the relationship between RMS and ROI was spurious, and that their results implied that 55 percent of the RMS-ROI correlation was spurious. However, Buzzell and Gale (1987) criticize this study on methodological grounds, namely the use of a flawed research design and use of accounting ratios that cause identities with the independent variables.

Third-Factor Explanations of the Market Share–Profitability Relationship

Based on earlier work by Rumelt and Wensley (1981), Jacobson and Aaker (1985), Jacobson (1988, 1990), and Boulding and Staelin (1990) have argued that market share reflects the variance due to "third factors." In PIMS data–based studies, since these third factors are not modeled, an omitted variable bias occurs and the variance due to these factors biases the market share–profitability coefficient. Rumelt and Wensley (1981) tested a model wherein ROI in the fifth year is explained by ROI in the first year, growth in market share, and several other factors. Based on their results that showed concurrent increases in rate of return and market share, Rumelt and Wensley argue that market share has no intrinsic value. They contend that "if share had a systematic value, we would expect to see businesses paying for gains in share" (p. 4).

In a model that included market share, Jacobson and Aaker (1985, p. 14) use ROI of the preceding time period as a proxy for firm-specific factors such as customer loyalty, distribution systems, and advertising effectiveness. With the inclusion of lagged ROI, the effect of market share on profitability was found to drop dramatically (five times lower). Hence, they argued that, "market share is not what it is cracked up to be." Jacobson and Aaker justify their use of the lagged ROI by citing similar treatment of dependent variables in Box-Jenkins forecasting models.

Jacobson (1988) addresses the same issue (i.e., controlling for firm-specific unobservable factors such as management quality) by utilizing a panel data set up to estimate the effect of market share on profitability. As in the earlier work with Aaker (Jacobson and Aaker 1985), Jacobson found the effect of market share to be minimal. The central argument in all these works is that unobservable "third factors" drive both market share and profitability. Not controlling for these factors biases the market share–profitability coefficient. Analysis of strictly cross-sectional data seems incapable of controlling for important firm-specific effects. The bias caused by not controlling for unobservables suggests that, "it is imperative to control for unobservable effects in order to assess the influence of strategic factors on business performance" (Jacobson 1988, p. 78). Jacobson (1990) and Boulding and Staelin (1990) draw similar conclusions in other studies. A meta-analysis of fifty-five studies indicates that whereas the effect size of market share on profits is 0.26, when the analysis was limited to PIMS data, the effect size of market share–profit relationship was inflated to 0.28. However, when unobservables are controlled for, the effect size becomes zero (Szymanski, Bharadwaj, and Varadarajan 1993).

Summary

Developing from the efforts of IO researchers and aided by the availability of a large-scale database (i.e., the PIMS database), strategy researchers focused on an alternative model but within the ambit of the product-market approach. With the availability of data on market share, product quality, pricing, profitability, and so forth, researchers have examined the relationship between competitive strategy, industry structure, competitive position variables, and performance. Employing various multivariate techniques, researchers have advanced a wide array of descriptions of the strategic behaviors of businesses such as (a) typologies (e.g., Buzzell, Gale, and Sultan 1975), (b) taxonomies (e.g., Hambrick 1983), (c) gestalts (e.g., Miller and Friesen 1984), (d) generic strategies (e.g., Porter 1980), and (e) strategic groups (e.g., Cool and Schendel 1987). However, a limitation of these efforts is that a business's profitability cannot be explained by product-market factors alone, and, in fact, a significant portion of the variance in performance remains unexplained (Cool and Schendel 1988; Dierickx and Cool 1990; White 1980).

Within marketing, research from an external analysis viewpoint, principally utilizing the PIMS database, focused on explaining differences in profitability among business units with competitive strategy variables as the determinants. Market share was found to be the most important determinant of profitability (cf. Buzzell and Gale 1987). However, questions have been raised about the appropriateness of the specification of these performance models. For instance, it has been pointed out that not controlling for third factors (largely firm-specific intangibles), *omitted variable error* yields biased estimates of factors incorporated in performance models (Jacobson 1988, 1990; Jacobson and Aaker 1985). In other words, strategy research in both management and marketing evidences a convergence of viewpoint, namely that extant literature provides an incomplete and possibly biased explanation for the variance in business performance.

Nevertheless, PIMS data–based research has made important contributions to enhancing our understanding of the determinants of business performance, such as the role of competitive strategy and competitive position variables. For instance, the finding that market share is a key determinant of profitability has a great deal of acceptance in business practice (Buzzell 1990). However, critiques have questioned market share's preeminent role as a determinant of business performance.

Studies controlling (methodologically) for unobservables have found the effect of market share on performance to be insignificant.

The Austrian School

The Austrian school of economics shares a great deal in common with the efficiency and the resource-based schools of thought. The origins of the Austrian school can be traced to the writings of Carl Menger, Frederich Von Weiser, and Eugen Von Bohm-Bawerk, all late-nineteenth-century economists. Subsequent thought leaders of this school include Joseph Schumpeter (a student of Von Weiser and Bohm-Bawerk), Eudwig Von Miser, and Friedrick Hayek. More recently, Israel Kirzner and Dominick Armentano have made contributions to the growing Austrian school of thought. In marketing, the works of Alderson, Jacobson, and Dickson, among others, have been influenced by the Austrian school.

Although a nascent field insofar as marketing strategy is concerned, the Austrian school has certain interesting aspects that are of great relevance to modeling performance. The Austrian school presents an alternative to the traditional IO school of thought. In contrast to the traditional IO view of the strategic objective of a firm as restricting competition, the Austrian school views competition as a dynamic discovery process in which entrepreneurs compete to identify profit opportunities. In an attempt to exploit these profit opportunities, entrepreneurs utilize a variety of strategies such as product differentiation, advertising, price reductions, scale economies, and R&D that are perceived by traditional IO economists as anticompetitive (Kirzner 1973). In brief, in the Austrian school, profits are not viewed as a consequence of monopoly power, but as a consequence of discovery and innovation by entrepreneurs.

While the Austrian school views the market condition to be dynamic and in a state of disequilibrium, strategy researchers inspired by the IO school tend to view the market in static terms. According to the Austrian viewpoint, since the market is in a constant state of flux, some firms are better able to exploit market imperfections to realize above-normal returns for their resources than other firms are. However, unless these firms are able to keep information about market imperfections private, these will be copied by competition and the above-normal returns will dissipate. Alternatively, if a phenomenon is sufficiently understood to be modeled, the business cannot profit from it because it is no longer private information. Hence, a search for empirical regularities through econometric modeling (as is done in traditional strategic management) is viewed as futile.

The key focus of the Austrian school is the emphasis on unobservable/intangible factors as determinants of business performance. The lack of emphasis on intangible/unobservable factors is viewed as neglecting available information that could impact performance. A variety of factors noted by Itami (1987) in the category of intangible factors, such as accumulated consumer information, brand name, reputation, and management skills, are examples of factors that could influence business performance. Furthermore, these could influence strategies adopted by firms (Jacobson 1990).

Representative Empirical Research

Jacobson (1988, 1990), in a variety of empirical efforts, inspired by the Austrian school, emphasized the importance of controlling for unobservables in profitability models. Illustrative of his work in this genre is a study (Jacobson 1990) that controls for unobservable factors in a serial correlation model with ROI as the dependent variable. In this study, he finds that not controlling for unobservables has severe consequences. Since unobservables are correlated to both the dependent and the independent variables, the coefficient estimates for the independent variables are biased. In some cases, they even reverse the sign of the estimated coefficients. For example, when unobservables are not controlled for, the coefficient for marketing expenditures implies an adverse impact on ROI. However, when unobservables are controlled for, the sign for the marketing expenditure coefficient is reversed. Even though tangible strategic factors may influence business performance, it is unobservables that, for the most part, determine business performance. Unobservables not only influence performance directly, but also influence strategic choices and thereby indirectly influence performance.

Summary

The Austrian school serves as an interesting and useful theoretical addition to strategy literature. Its focus on unobservables is particularly important to the modeling of performance. In the Austrian school, the direction of causality implied in the SCP paradigm is viewed as erroneous. Like the efficiency school, the Austrian school contends that more efficient firms win approval from customers and achieve market share gains. The emphasis on unobservable factors in the Austrian school foreshadows the emphasis on resources and capabilities in the resource-based view of the firm, discussed next.

The Resource-Based View of the Firm

The intellectual beginnings of the resource-based view of the firm can be traced to the early writings in strategy literature on distinctive competencies and Penrose's (1959) theory of the firm. Early references to distinctive competencies in the strategic management literature can be traced to a business policy framework often known by its acronym, SWOT (Strengths, Weaknesses, Opportunities, and Threats) analysis. This framework proposed by Learned et al. (1969) emphasizes the importance of assessing an organization's internal capabilities and capability gaps (strengths and weaknesses) and matching these to the external environmental conditions (opportunities and threats) in which it operates. Initial conceptual research in strategy, which focused on internal capabilities, stressed the importance of "distinctive competencies," a term coined by Selznick (1957) to describe the leadership capabilities that were responsible for transforming an unsuccessful public corporation into a successful organization. Hofer and Schendel (1978) defined *distinctive competencies* as the unique competitive position that a firm achieves through resource deployment. Ansoff (1965) viewed the concept of distinctive competency as an integral component of corporate strategy and subsequently argued that it was essential to identify and respond to environmental signals. Snow and Hrebiniak (1980) identified functional areas of a firm that were also areas of competencies. Hitt and Ireland (1985) listed fifty-five distinctive competence activities within functional areas. Empirical research on distinctive competencies, although limited, shares some common themes: (a) the source of competency is always internal to a firm, and (b) competency is produced by the way a firm makes use of its internal skills and resources relative to competition (Reed and DeFillippi 1990).

Penrose (1959) suggested that, "It is the heterogeneity . . . of productive services available or potentially available from its resources that gives each firm its unique character" (p. 75). She suggested that firms achieve superior performance not only because they have better resources, but also due to a distinctive competence to make better use of these resources. More importantly, she viewed the resources of a firm (labor, capital, and managerial capacity) as constraining the choice of markets that it could enter and the levels of profits it could expect (Wernerfelt 1989). Terming it the Penrose effect, she suggested that the growth of a firm was (in the long run) limited/constrained by internal management resources. Firms were viewed largely as administrative organizations and collections of human, physical, and intangible assets. Unused productive resources or excess capacity drove the extent and direction of diversification. This, in turn, spawned a number of research efforts such as on firm diversification and, more recently, on the resource-based view (cf. Chatterjee and Wernerfelt 1991; Harrison et al. 1991; Montgomery and Hariharan 1991).

The growing recognition that a mere external analysis provides an incomplete answer to understanding and explaining variance in firm performance renewed focus on internal firm-specific intangible factors that drive performance. The resource-based view assumes that (1) the resources needed to conceive, choose, and implement strategies are heterogeneously distributed across a set of competing firms, and (2) these firm differences are stable over time (Barney 1991; Peteraf and Barney 2003). Barney views the research objectives of the resource-based model of competitive advantage as being able to tie "a model that facilitates the rigorous analysis of internal organizational strengths and weaknesses with an external analysis."

The resource-based view perceives firm resources to include all assets, capabilities, organizational processes, firm attributes, information, knowledge, et cetera, controlled by a firm that enable it to conceive of and implement strategies that improve its efficiency and effectiveness (Barney 1991). Other resource-based theorists distinguish between resources and capabilities (Grant 1991), types of capabilities (Lado, Boyd, and Wright 1992), and between resource base and dynamic capabilities (Teece, Pisano, and Shuen 1997).

The focus of the resource-based perspective is on the costly to copy attributes of a firm as sources of economic rents and, therefore, as the fundamental drivers of performance and competitive advantage (Rumelt 1984; Barney 1986a, 1986b; Peteraf and Barney 2003). According to this perspective, a firm's ability to attain and hold on to profitable market positions depends on its ability to gain and defend advantageous positions in underlying resources important to production and distribution (Conner 1991). Barney (1991) lays out four essential requirements for a resource to be a source of sustainable competitive advantage. It must be *valuable, rare* among a firm's current and potential competitors, *imperfectly imitable,* and characterized by the *absence of strategically equivalent substitutes.* Firm resources are considered valuable when they enable a firm to conceive of or implement strategies that improve its efficiency and/or effectiveness. However, if valuable resources are possessed by a large number of present and/or potential competitors, it cannot be a source of sustained competitive advantage. In other words, unless the resource is rare, it is unlikely to be a source of competitive advantage. For example, a market pioneer may preempt scarce resources. The concentration of high-grade nickel deposits in a single geographic area in Canada enabled Inco, the first company in the area, to secure rights to virtually the entire supply and thus dominate world production for decades. However, valuable and rare organizational resources can only be sources of sustained competitive advantage if firms that do not possess these resources cannot obtain them—they should be imperfectly imitable (Barney 1986a, 1986b; Lippman and Rumelt 1982). The final requirement for a firm resource to be a source of sustainable competitive advantage is for the resource to be nonsubstitutable. In the presence of substitutable resources, however, a single firm (e.g., a market pioneer) cannot implement a strategy that rival firms (e.g., late entrants) cannot replicate. Substitutability can take two forms:

- A competitor, although unable to exactly duplicate the focal firm's resources, is able to substitute a *similar* resource that enables it to conceive of and implement the same strategies.

- A competitor is able to use very *different* resources as strategic substitutes (Barney 1991). Canon's strategy of making Xerox's strength—after-sales service—irrelevant by making its product highly reliable, is an illustration of a firm using a different set of resources as a strategic substitute.

Peteraf (1993) argues that the above four requirements are necessary but not sufficient conditions for achieving sustainable competitive advantage. The price paid for the resource fills in one sufficient condition. If the market is competitive for the resource, its price will be bid up until it is equal to the present value of the future rent stream (Barney 1986a, 1986b). The point is that benefiting from sustainable competitive advantage and thus economic rents depends crucially on the presence or absence of competition in factor markets. When factor markets are perfect, the prices of resources are bid up and rents are competed away. Beyond the role of private information, the complementary nature of existing resources serves as another reason for a resource to exceed its apparent "market" value. Firms that have an existing portfolio of assets can combine those assets with the new resource to get the benefits of synergy that firms that do not have such a portfolio may not be able to capture.

A growing subfield within the broader umbrella of the resource-based view that stems from the logic of combining capabilities is the emergence of dynamic capability (Teece, Pisano, and Shuen 1997) that argues that a firm can stay ahead of competition by utilizing capabilities built on path-dependent learning. In contrast, Eisenhardt and Martin (2000) characterize dynamic capabilities as best practices. More recently, Miller (2003) contends that firms build capabilities not by copying other firms, but by examining internally to identify those capabilities that they uniquely possess and that they can effectively configure, develop, and exploit for superior performance.

Two streams of work can be characterized as representing the efforts of the resource-based view in marketing. Early efforts were devoted to developing conceptual models of the marketing-oriented resources and skills and their impact on marketing performance (Bharadwaj 1994; Bharadwaj, Varadarajan, and Fahy 1993; Hunt 1997; Hunt and Morgan 1995). Subsequent efforts focused on specific applications of the resource-based view in marketing contexts such as market-based assets (Capron and Hulland 1999; Srivastava, Shervani, and Fahy 1998, 1999), relationship marketing (Day and Van den Bulte 2003; Jap 1999), and complementary capabilities (Slotegraf and Moorman 1999; Slotegraf, Moorman, and Inman 2003). While there has been a growing body of work in strategy on dynamic capabilities, marketing researchers have just begun to work in this domain. Research focused on market learning, marketing strategy-making, creativity, and relational learning are examples of marketing-related issues that fit under this umbrella.

Discussion

The preceding sections provide an overview of alternative perspectives/schools of thought that attempt to explain variance in performance at the industry, firm, or business-unit level. These perspectives overlap in some respects but are unique in other respects. Table 5.2 provides a summary of the perspectives reviewed on some key issues. Table 5.3 provides a summary of the representative research focusing on some of these perspectives. As is evident from Tables 5.2 and 5.3, none of these approaches individually provides a complete explanation of variance in performance. Even the most comprehensive of these perspectives, the PIMS paradigm, suffers from a specification bias (underspecification) as evidenced by the criticism of researchers, some of whose works are in the Austrian tradition (Jacobson 1988, 1990; Jacobson and Aaker 1985).

At one level, the foregoing review of alternative perspectives on determinants of organizational performance provides insights into internal versus external perspectives of determinants of performance, their merits and limitations, and alternative mechanisms available to a business to enhance its performance. At another level, the review also serves to highlight the need to employ an integrative approach in order to gain a better understanding of factors underlying differences in performance. In fact, a number of researchers have argued that rather than focusing exclusively on product-market positions, it is also necessary to examine the resources deployed in the first place to achieve these product-market positions (e.g., Barney 1986b, 1991; Dierickx and Cool 1989; Rumelt 1984; Teece 1984; Wernerfelt 1984). Some have argued that extant literature with an external analysis focus is modeled in a unidimensional manner (Peteraf 1993), while others have viewed the focus on external analysis nearly as a dual of the focus on internal analysis (Ghemawat 1991; Porter 1991; Wernerfelt 1984).

Toward an Integrated Model of Business Performance

As detailed in the foregoing sections, the SCP paradigm views the structural characteristics of the industry as the primary determinant of performance. The PIMS model (Buzzell and Gale 1987, p. 28) views a business's performance as a function of the characteristics of the industry in which it competes, its competitive position within the industry, and the competitive strategy pursued. The resource-based view holds that the type, magnitude, and nature of a firm's resources and capabilities are important determinants of its performance. In research efforts that attempt to explain variance in firm performance by decomposing the effects into industry, corporate, and business-unit level effects, the most important finding is that all three components play complementary roles in explaining variance in firm performance (see, e.g., Rumelt 1991). Here, industry-level effects are representative of the research in the SCP and the new IO tradition, corporate-level effects in the tradition of PIMS data–based research, and business-unit effects are in the tradition of Austrian and the resource-based view.

An *integrated model of business performance* grounded in these complementing theoretical and philosophical underpinnings is reviewed and empirical research is presented in Figure 5.3. The model incorporates industry structure, competitive strategy, and firm-specific intangibles as the three major determinants of business performance. In the proposed model, industry structure variables, competitive strategy variables, and firm-specific intangible resources and capabilities are modeled as impacting on a business's competitive position. A business's competitive position is modeled as impacting on its marketplace performance and financial performance. Firm-specific intangibles (resource and capabilities) are modeled as an antecedent of competitive strategy and impacting on the relative competitive position and performance of a business, both directly and indirectly. For instance, a business's brand equity, customer equity, and channel equity can be expected to positively impact on the market valuation of the firm. Hence, the direct link to financial performance.

The rationale for linkages in both directions between competitive strategy and firm-specific intangibles, and competitive strategy and industry structure is as follows. On one hand, firm-specific intangibles (resources and skills) can be expected to impact on a business's competitive strategy. Also, over time, investments in advertising and achievement of superior quality as a competitive strategy can be expected to positively impact on the strength of the brand equity developed as well as a firm's reputation for quality. Likewise, a business's competitive strategy is likely to be influenced by industry structure factors. Also, industry structure factors are likely to be impacted by a business's competitive strategy (e.g., marginal competitors exiting an industry).

Table 5.2

Explaining Variance in Firm Performance: An Overview of Selected Research Paradigms

Research paradigm	Unit of analysis	Primary objective	Key assumptions	Primary construct of interest	Possibility of attaining abnormal profits in performance	Means to maintain/prevent erosion of abnormal profits
The classical IO school	Industry	Maximizing social welfare	Firms within an industry are homogenous and price takers. Industry concentration facilitates collusion.	Industry structure	Yes	Entry barriers
Revisionist/ efficiency school	Firm	Maximizing social welfare	Firms within an industry are heterogeneous. Market structures resulting from unrestrained competition are efficient market structures.	Firm conduct	Yes	Governmental regulation
The strategic groups school	Strategic groups	Maximizing strategic group performance	Firms within strategic groups are homogenous, and across strategic groups are heterogeneous.	Dimensions that define strategic groups and strategic group membership	Yes	Mobility barriers
The new empirical industrial organization school	Firm, category, and brand	Maximizing profits	The demand and cost structures of firms are heterogeneous. A firm's strategic actions are impacted by a rival's actions.	Demand function; Cost function; Nature of competitive interaction	Yes	Tacit collusion

The business policy school/ the PIMS paradigm	Strategic business unit	Maximizing business-unit performance	The structure of the market, the competitive position, and competitive strategies determine a business unit's performance.	Competitive strategies and competitive position	Yes	With higher market shares
The Austrian school	Firm/ business unit	Maximizing firm/business-unit performance	Firms are heterogeneous in terms of resources and skills.	Intangible assets, resources, and skills owned by a firm	No	
The resource-based view of the firm	Firm/ business unit	Maximizing firm/business-unit performance	Firms are heterogeneous in terms of resources, skills, assets, and capabilities.	Intangible assets, capabilities, resources, and skills owned by a firm	Yes	Presence of valuable, rare, and inimitable resources, skills, capabilities, and assets

234

Table 5.3

Decomposing Variance in Firm Performance: An Overview of Representative Empirical Research

Study	Source of data	Theoretical paradigm	Relative % of variance in firm performance[a]
Schmalensee (1985)	FTC manufacturing firms in 1975	Classical IO school	Industry factors explain 19.6%.
Hansen and Wernerfelt (1989)	Compustat, Trinet, FTC, and survey data	Business policy school	Organizational factors explain twice as much variance as industry factors.
Rumelt (1991)	FTC manufacturing firms 1974–1977	Revisionist school	Industry factors explain 8.32%, business-unit factors explain 46.4%, and corporate factors explain less than 1%.
Roquebert, Phillips, and Westfall (1996)	Compustat manufacturing firms 1985–1991	Business policy school	Industry factors explain 10.2%, corporate factors 17.9%, and business-unit factors explain 37.1%.
McGahan and Porter (1997)	Compustat 1981–1994	Classical IO school	Industry factors explain 18.7%, corporate factors 4.33%, and business-unit factors explain 31.7%.
Brush, Bromiley, and Hendrickx (1999)	Compustat 1986–1995	Business policy school	Industry factors explain 12.5%, corporate factors explain 10%, and business-unit factors explain 36.5%.
McGahan and Porter (2002)	Compustat manufacturing firms 1981–1994	Classical IO school	Industry factors explain 10.3%, corporate factors 11.6%, and business-unit factors explain 36.1%.
Hawawini, Subramanian, and Verdin (2003)	Stern Stewart 1987–1996	Business policy school	Industry factors explain 8.5%, corporate factors explain 30.1%, and, with outliers removed, industry factors explain 21% and corporate factors explain 17.1%.
Ruefli and Wiggins (2003)	Compustat 1980–1996	Business policy school	Corporate factors predict business-unit performance better than industry factors, but business-unit level factors do the best job.

Note: [a]Relative % of variance in firm performance explained.

Also, firm-specific intangibles, in addition to impacting on the competitive strategy of a business in a firm's portfolio, can be expected to influence the choice of industries in which a firm chooses to operate (i.e., a firm's choice of businesses to be in). However, such linkages are outside the scope of a model, given the unit of analysis–business unit.

While the product-market approach views performance as a function of the characteristic of the industry and the business's position within the industry, some proponents of the resource-based view contend that the type, magnitude, and nature of a firm's resources and capabilities are the primary determinants of its performance. In contrast, rather than viewing examination of intangibles and industry structure and competitive strategy variables as competing perspectives of determinants of business performance, the proposed model views the examination of intangibles as complementing examination of the role of industry structure and competitive strategy variables as determinants of business performance.

While the proposed model approaches an integrative model, it is not intended to be construed as a comprehensive model. For instance, in Figure 5.3, organization structure, a construct viewed by organization theorists as a critical determinant of performance (cf. Hrebiniak, Joyce, and Snow [1988] for a detailed review), is not explicitly modeled. Nevertheless, by implicitly viewing implementation ability as a firm-specific intangible, the model attempts to capture a key dimension of organization structure. It should, however, be noted that many other dimensions of organization structure are not captured in this model. Such limitations not withstanding, the proposed model is in accord with:

- Jacobson's (1988, 1990) position that in order to achieve more accurate estimates of the determinants of business performance, a model that incorporates industry structure, competitive strategy, and "third factors or unobservables" is necessary; otherwise, an omitted variable bias would result.
- The resource-based view emphasizes the importance of idiosyncratic firm-specific competencies elicited from managerial volition, organizational assets, reputation, and culture as potential sources of competitive advantage (Barney 1991; Itami 1987). The proposed model is also in accord with the notions of core competencies espoused by Hamel and Prahalad (1991).
- Porter's (1991), Collis's (1991), and Amit and Schoemaker's (1993) position that the resource-based view is complementary to, rather than an alternative to, the role of industry structure and competitive strategy as determinants of firm performance.
- The position of Conner (1991) and Mahoney and Pandian (1992) that the resource-based stream of research has the ability to coalesce extant literature on industry structure and competitive strategy with literature that emphasizes idiosyncratic firm-specific assets and skills.
- The resource-based view and the views espoused in the works of Jacobson (1988, 1990); the proposed model recognizes the importance of firm-specific intangibles (resources and skills) as determinants of performance.

Conclusion

Explaining variance in performance at the industry, firm, and/or business levels has been a central theme in the fields of marketing strategy, business policy and strategic management, and IO economics. Two general explanations dominate this body of literature. IO researchers, drawing largely on the SCP paradigm, have argued that industry structure (e.g., industry concentration, exit barriers, bargaining power of customers and suppliers) influences business conduct (strategy)

236

Figure 5.3   **Toward an Integrated Model of Business Performance**

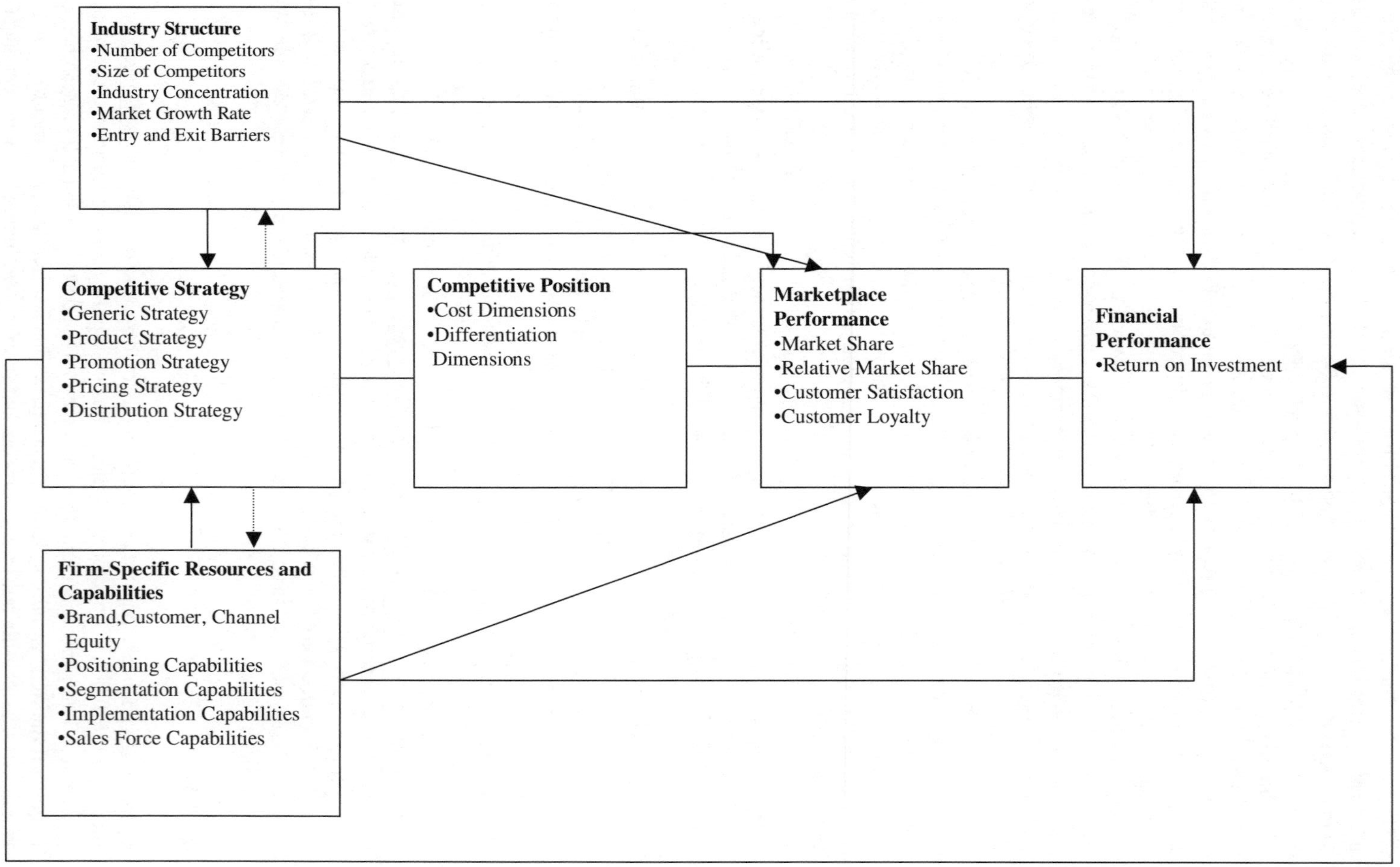

and performance, with industry structure being the primary explanator of variance in performance. Researchers in the marketing strategy and strategic management fields have primarily focused on explaining differences in profitability in terms of competitive strategy variables (e.g., product quality and product line breadth) as the primary determinants. Although both explanations have served to enhance our understanding of determinants of business performance, the explanations have been criticized for (a) being based on questionable assumptions, (b) explaining relatively little variance, and/or (c) being based on underspecified models that focus predominantly on either industry structure or competitive strategy variables.

Motivated by the view that firms within an industry are heterogeneous, and firm-specific resources are an important determinant of performance, the resource-based view argues that businesses that possess better resources and make better use of these resources than their competitors earn higher profits and achieve higher market shares. "Better" resources are those that (a) bestow the business with a competitive advantage and (b) are impossible for competitors to replicate at equal cost. Similarly, research in marketing during the past decade is indicative of a growing recognition that unobservable factors are important drivers of business performance.

A systematic and extensive review of the extant literature reveals not only a dearth of *empirical* research that incorporates firm-specific variables in performance models, but also a lack of *theoretical* models that integrate the SCP, competitive strategy, and resource-based perspectives. In other words, although each of these three research streams are complementary and provide a partial explanation of the variance in business performance, the lack of an integrated view only serves to highlight model underspecification and attendant omitted variable bias. Thus, a more accurate picture can be expected to emerge when these seemingly complementary explanations of business performance are integrated into a more comprehensive and integrated model of business performance. Against this backdrop, this article proposes a conceptual model of business performance that draws on and integrates research from IO, business strategy, and marketing, incorporating industry structure, competitive strategy, and firm-specific factors in the model. In models of business performance that place greater emphasis on external analysis, the structure of the industry or the environment in which a firm operates is viewed as a major determinant of business performance. At the other end of the continuum, the resource-based view of the firm is reflective of near total emphasis on the internal skills and resources of a firm that provide it with the efficiency and effectiveness that are required to achieve superior performance. Against this backdrop, the proposed integrated model of business performance incorporates both factors external to the firm as well as those internal to the firm.

Acknowledgment

The authors thank Sathish Jayachandran (University of South Carolina) and J. Chris White (Michigan State University) for their comments and suggestions provided on an earlier version of this article.

Notes

1. Profits being a more easily available and interpretable variable were used instead of price in empirical studies.

2. This line of research does not recognize the possibility that high profit margins could be due to efficient firms in concentrated markets achieving lower costs. A stream of research stressing this issue is discussed under the revisionist school later in this chapter.

3. Some empirical studies have attempted to examine the presence of this critical concentration ratio. Bain (1951) suggests that his data seemed to show the existence of a critical concentration ratio above which

profit increased dramatically. Others, unlike Bain (1951), found that changes in concentration above or below this critical concentration level had no effect (Dalton and Penn 1976; Kwoka 1979; White 1976). In a study using switching regimes, Bradburn and Over (1982) found evidence for two critical levels. In cases where concentration was low, they found that profits do not increase with increases in concentration until the leading four firms account for 68 percent of industry sales. In cases where concentration was previously high, profits did not drop until the four-firm ratio fell below 46 percent.

4. Although criticized by many, including some proponents of the classical IO school (cf. Scherer 1980; Vernon 1972), empirical researchers have consistently ignored conduct. As discussed later, the business policy school led by PIMS researchers focused on conduct and its implications for performance.

5. The SCP paradigm uses other variables (e.g., size of firms, barriers to entry and exit, and product differentiation) to define industry structure. However, industry concentration is the most common proxy measure of industry structure used in empirical research.

References

Amit, Raphael and Paul J.H. Schoemaker (1993), "Strategic Assets and Organizational Rent," *Strategic Management Journal*, 14 (January), 33–46.

Ansoff, Igor H. (1965), *Corporate Strategy*. New York: McGraw-Hill.

Bain, Joseph (1951), "Relation of Profit Rate to Industry Concentration: American Manufacturing 1936–1940," *Quarterly Journal of Economics*, 65 (August), 293–324.

———— (1956), *Barriers to New Competition*. Cambridge, MA: Harvard University Press.

———— (1968), *Industrial Organization*. New York: Wiley.

———— (1972), *Essays in Price Theory and Industrial Organization*. Boston: Little, Brown.

Barney, Jay B. (1986a), "Organizational Culture: Can It Be a Source of Sustained Competitive Advantage?" *Academy of Management Review*, 11 (July), 656–65.

———— (1986b), "Strategic Factor Markets: Expectations, Luck and Business Strategy," *Management Science*, 32 (October), 1231–41.

———— (1991), "Firm Resources and Sustained Competitive Advantage," *Journal of Management*, 17 (March), 99–120.

Barney, Jay B. and Robert E. Hoskisson (1991), "Strategic Groups: Untested Assertions and Research Proposals," *Managerial and Decision Economics*, 11 (February), 187–98.

Barney, Jay B., Abigail McWilliams, and Thomas Turk (1989), "On the Relevance of the Concept of Entry Barriers in the Theory of Competitive Strategy," paper presented at the *Annual Meeting of the Strategic Management Society*, San Francisco.

Bharadwaj, Sundar G. (1994), "Industry Structure, Competitive Strategy and Firm-Specific Intangibles as Determinants of Business Unit Performance," doctoral dissertation, Texas A&M University.

Bharadwaj, Sundar G., P. Rajan Varadarajan, and John Fahy (1993), "Sustainable Competitive Advantage in Service Industries: A Conceptual Model and Research Propositions," *Journal of Marketing*, 57 (October), 83–99.

Bork, Robert H. (1978), *The Antitrust Paradox*. New York: Basic Books.

Boulding, Kenneth (1955), *Economic Analysis*. New York: Harper and Brothers.

Boulding, William and Richard Staelin (1990), "Environment, Market Share, and Market Power," *Management Science*, 36 (October), 1160–77.

Bradford, Ralph M. and Mead Over (1982), "Organizational costs, Sticky Equilibria and Critical Levels of Concentration," *Review of Economics and Statistics*, 64 (February), 50–58.

Bresnahan, Timothy (1989), "Industries and Market Power," in *Handbook of Industrial Organization*, R. Schmalensee and R. Willig, eds. North Holland: Amsterdam.

Brozen, Yale (1971), "Bain's Concentration and Rates of Return Revisited," *Journal of Law and Economics*, 14 (July), 351–69.

Brush, T.H., P. Bromiley, and P. Hendrickx (1999), "The Relative Influence of Industry and Corporation on Business Segment Performance: An Alternative Estimate," *Strategic Management Journal*, 20 (6), 519–47.

Buzzell, Robert D. (1990), "Commentary on 'Unobservable Effects and Business Performance,'" *Marketing Science*, 9 (Winter), 86–87.

Buzzell, Robert D. and Bradley T. Gale (1987), *The PIMS Principles: Linking Strategy to Performance*. New York: Free Press.

Buzzell, Robert D., Bradley T. Gale, and Ralph G.M. Sultan (1975), "Market Share—A Key to Profitability," *Harvard Business Review*, 53 (January-February), 97–106.

Capon, Noel, John U. Farley, and Scott Hoenig (1990), "Determinants of Financial Performance: A Meta-Analysis," *Management Science*, 36 (October), 1143–59.

Capron, L. and John Holland (1999), "Redeployment of Brands, Sales Forces, and General Marketing Management Expertise Following Horizontal Acquisitions: A Resource-Based View," *Journal of Marketing*, 63 (April), 41–54.

Caves, Richard E. and Thomas Pugel (1980), *Intra-Industry Differences in Conduct and Performance: Viable Strategies in U.S. Manufacturing Industries*. New York University Monograph.

Chamberlin, Edward H. (1933), *The Theory of Monopolistic Competition*. Cambridge, MA: The Harvard University Press.

———— (1949), *The Theory of Monopolistic Competition* (6th ed.). Cambridge, MA: The Harvard University Press.

Chatterjee, Sayan and Birger Wernerfelt (1991), "The Link Between Resources and Type of Diversification: Theory and Evidence," *Strategic Management Journal*, 12 (January), 33–48.

Clarke, Roger, Stephen Davies, and Michael Waterson (1984), "The Profitability-Concentration Relation: Market Power or Efficiency?" *Journal of Industrial Economics*, 32 (June), 435–50.

Collis, David J. (1991), "A Resource-Based Analysis of Global Competition: The Case of the Bearings Industry," *Strategic Management Journal*, 12 (Summer), 49–68.

Comanor, William S. and Thomas A. Wilson (1967), "Advertising, Market Structure and Performance," *Review of Economics and Statistics*, 49 (November), 423–40.

Conner, Kathleen R. (1991), "A Historical Comparison of Resource-Based Theory and Five Schools of Thought Within Industrial Organization Economics: Do We Have a New Theory of the Firm," *Journal of Management*, 17 (March), 121–54.

Cool, Karel O. and Dan E. Schendel (1987), "Strategic Group Formation and Performance: The Case of the U.S. Pharmaceutical Industry, 1963–1982," *Management Science*, 33 (September), 1102–24.

———— and ———— (1988), "Performance Differences Among Strategic Group Members," *Strategic Management Journal*, 9 (June), 207–24.

Cotterill, R.S. (1986), "Market Power in the Retail Food Industry: Evidence from Vermont," *Review of Economics and Statistics*, 68 (August), 379–86.

Cournot, Augustin (1838), *Researches into the Mathematical Principles of the Theory of Wealth*. Reprinted 1963. Homewood, IL: Irwin.

Dalton, James A. and David W. Penn (1976), "The Concentration-Profitability Relationship: Is There a Critical Concentration Ratio?" *Journal of Industrial Economics*, 25 (December), 133–42.

Dutta, Deepak K. and V.K. Narayanan (1989), "A Meta-Analytic Review of the Concentration-Performance Relationship: Aggregating Findings in Strategic Management," *Journal of Management*, 15 (September), 469–83.

Day, George and Christophe Van den Bulte (2003), "Capabilities for Forging Customer Relationships," working paper, The Wharton School, University of Pennsylvania.

———— and David B. Montgomery (1983), "Diagnosing the Experience Curve, " *Journal of Marketing*, 47 (Spring), 44-58.

Demsetz, Harold (1973), "Industry Structure, Market Rivalry, and Public Policy," *Journal of Law and Economics*, 16 (April), 1–19.

———— (1974), "Two Systems of Belief About Monopoly," in *Industrial Concentration: The New Learning*, Harvey Goldschmidt et al., eds. Boston: Little, Brown, 164–84.

Dess, Gregory G. and Peter S. Davis (1984), "Porter's (1980) Generic Strategies as Determinants of Strategic Group Membership and Organizational Performance," *Academy of Management Journal*, 27 (September), 467–88.

Dierickx, I. and K. Cool (1990), "Asset Stock Accumulation and Sustainability of Competitive Advantage," *Management Science*, 35 (November), 1504–11.

Eisenhardt, Kathleen and Jeffrey Martin (2000), "Dynamic Capability: What Are They?," *Strategic Management Journal*, 21 (October–November), 1105–21.

Fisher, Franklin M., John J. McGowan and Joen E. Greenwood (1983), *Folded, Spindled and Mutilated: Economic Analysis and U.S. Vs. IBM*. Cambridge, MA: MIT Press.

Frazier, Gary L. and Roy D. Howell (1983), "Business Definition and Performance," *Journal of Marketing*, 47 (Spring), 59–67.

Gale, Bradley T. (1972), "Market Share and Rate of Return," *Review of Economics and Statistics*, 54 (November), 412–23.

Geroski, Paul A., L. Philips, and A. Ulph (1985), "Oligopoly, Competition and Welfare: Some Recent Developments," *Journal of Industrial Economics*, 33 (July), 369–86.

Ghemawat, Pankaj (1991), "Resources and Strategy: An IO Perspective," mimeo. Cambridge, MA: Harvard Business School.

Gilbert, Richard A. (1984), "Bank Market Structure and Competition: A Survey," *Journal of Money, Credit, and Banking*, 16 (November), 617–45.

Grant, Robert M. (1991), "The Resource-Based Theory of Competitive Advantage: Implications for Strategy Formulation," *California Management Review*, 33 (Spring), 114–35.

Hambrick, D. (1983), "An Empirical Typology of Mature Industrial-Product Environments," *Academy of Management Journal*, 26 (February), 213–20.

Hamel, Gary and C.K. Prahalad (1991), "Corporate Imagination and Expeditionary Marketing," *Harvard Business Review*, 69 (July–August), 81–93.

Hamermesh, R.G., M.J. Anderson, and J.E. Harris (1978), "Strategies for Low Market Share Businesses," *Harvard Business Review*, 56 (May-June), 95–102.

Hansen, George S. and Birger Wernerfelt (1989), "Determinants of Firm Performance: The Relative Importance of Organizational and Economic Factors," *Strategic Management Journal*, 10 (5), 399–412.

Harrison, Jeffrey S., Michael A. Hitt, Robert E. Hoskisson, and R. Duane Ireland (1991), "Synergies and Post-acquisition Performance: Differences Versus Similarities in Resource Allocations," *Journal of Management*, 17 (March), 173–90.

Hawawini, G., V. Subramanian, and P. Verdin (2003), "Is Performance Driven by Industry-or-firm-specific Factors? A New Look at the Evidence?" *Strategic Management Journal*, 24 (January), 1–16.

Hitt, Michael A. and Duane R. Ireland (1985), "Corporate Distinctive Competence, Strategy, Industry and Performance," *Strategic Management Journal*, 6 (July-September), 273–93.

Hofer, C. and David Schendel (1978), *Strategy Formulation: Analytical Concepts*. St. Paul, MN: West.

Hrebiniak, Lawerence G., William F. Joyce, and Charles C. Snow (1988), "Strategy, Structure and Performance: Past and Future Research," in *Strategy, Organization Design, and Human Resource Management*, Charles C. Snow, ed. Greenwich, CT: JAI, 3–54.

Hunt, M.S. (1972), "Competition in the Major Home Appliance Industry 1960–1970," unpublished doctoral dissertation, Cambridge, Massachusetts, Harvard University.

Hunt, Shelby D. (1997), "Resource-Advantage Theory: An Evolutionary Theory of Competitive Firm Behavior," *Journal of Economic Issues*, 31, 59–77.

Hunt, Shelby D. and Robert M. Morgan (1995), "The Comparative Advantage Theory of Competition," *Journal of Marketing*, 59 (April), 1–15.

Itami, H. (1987), *Mobilizing Invisible Assets*. Cambridge, MA: Harvard University Press.

Jacobson, Robert (1988), "Distinguishing Among Competing Theories of the Market Share Effect," *Journal of Marketing*, 52 (October), 68–80.

——— (1990), "Unobservable Effects and Business Performance," *Marketing Science*, 9 (Winter), 74–85.

Jacobson, Robert and David A. Aaker (1985), "Is Market Share All That It's Cracked Up To Be?" *Journal of Marketing*, 49 (Fall), 11–22.

Jap, Sandy D. (1999), "'Pie-Expansion' Efforts: Collaboration Processes in Buyer-Supplier Relationships," *Journal of Marketing Research*, 36 (November), 461–75.

Kadiyali, Vrinda (1996), "Entry, the Deterrence and Its Accommodation: A Study of the US Photographic Film Industry," *Rand Journal of Economics*, 27(3), 452–78.

———, K.Sudhir, and Vithala R. Rao (2001), "Structural Analysis of Competitive Behavior: New Empirical Industrial Organization Methods in Marketing," *International Journal of Research in Marketing*, 18 (1), 161–86.

Kirzner, Israel M. (1973), *Competition and Entrepreneurship*. Chicago: University of Chicago Press.

Kwoka, John E. (1979), "The Effect of Market Share Distribution on Industry Performance," *Review of Economics and Statistics*, 61 (February), 101–109.

Kwoka, John E. and David J. Ravenscraft (1986), "Cooperations Vs. Rivalry: Price-cost Margins by Line-of-Business," *Economica*, 53 (August), 351–63.

Lado, Augustine A., Nancy G. Boyd, and Peter Wright (1992), "A Competency-Based Model of Sustainable Competitive Advantage: Toward a Conceptual Integration," *Journal of Management*, 18 (March), 77–91.

Lawless, Michael W., Donald D. Bergh, and William D. Wilsted (1989), "Performance Variations among Strategic Group Members: An Examination of Individual Firm Capability," *Journal of Management*, 15 (December), 649–61.

Lawless, Michael W. and Linda Finch Tegarden (1991), "A Test of Performance Similarity Among Strategic Group Members in Conforming and Non-Conforming Industry Structures," *Journal of Management Studies*, 28 (November), 645–64.

Learned, Edmund P., C. Roland Christensen, Kenneth R. Andrews, and William D. Guth (1969), *Business Policy*. Homewood, IL: Irwin.

Lippman, S.A. and Richard P. Rumelt (1982), "Uncertain Imitability: An Analysis of Interfirm Differences in Efficiency Under Competition," *The Bell Journal of Economics*, 13 (Autumn), 418–38.

Mahoney, Joseph T. and Rajendran Pandian (1992), "The Resource-Based View Within the Conversation of Strategic Management," *Strategic Management Journal*, 13 (June), 363–80.

Martin, Stephen (1983), *Market, Firm and Economic Performance*. Monograph Series in Finance and Economics, Salomon Brothers Center for the Study of Financial Institutions, Graduate School of Business Administration, New York University.

——— (1988), "Market Power and/or Efficiency," *Review of Economics and Statistics*, 70 (August), 331–35.

Marvel, Howard P. (1980), "Collusion and the Pattern of Rates of Return," *Southern Economic Journal*, 47 (April), 375–87.

Mason, Edward, S. (1939), "Price and Production Policies of Large-Scale Enterprise," *American Economic Review*, 29 (March), 61–74.

McGahan, Anita and Michael Porter (1997), "How Much Does Industry Matter Really?" *Strategic Management Journal*, 18 (Summer Special Issue), 15–30.

——— and ——— (2002), "What Do We Know About Variance in Accounting Profitability?" *Management Science*, 48 (July), 834–51.

McGee, John S. (1971), *In Defense of Industrial Concentration*. New York: Praeger.

——— (1988), *Industrial Organization*. Englewood Cliffs, NJ: Prentice Hall.

McGee, John S. and Howard Thomas (1986), "Strategic Groups: Theory, Research and Taxonomy," *Strategic Management Journal*, 7 (March-April), 141–60.

McWilliams, Abagail and Dennis L. Smart (1993), "Efficiency v. Structure-Conduct-Performance: Implications for Strategy Research and Practice," *Journal of Management*, 19 (March), 63–78.

Miller, Danny (2003), "An Asymmetry-Based View of Advantage: Towards An Attainable Sustainability," *Strategic Management Journal*, 24, 961–76.

——— and Peter H. Friesen (1984), *Organizations: A Quantum View*. Englewood Cliffs, NJ: Prentice Hall.

Montgomery, Cynthia A. and S.A. Hariharan (1991), "Diversified Entry by Established Firms," *Journal of Economic Behavior and Organization*, 15 (March), 71–89.

Mueller, Dennis C. (1986), *Profits in the Long Run*. Cambridge, England: Cambridge University Press.

Nayyar, Praveen (1989), "Strategic Groups: A Comment," *Strategic Management Journal*, 10 (January), 101–107.

Nevo, Aviv, (2001), "Measuring Market Power in the Ready-to-Eat Cereal Industry," *Econometrica*, 69 (March), 307–42.

Oster, Sharon M (1982). "Intraindustry Structure and the Ease of Strategic Change," *Review of Economics and Statistics*, 74 (August), 376–84.

——— (1990), *Modern Competitive Analysis*. New York: Oxford University Press.

Peltzman, Sam (1977), "The Gains and Losses from Industrial Concentration," *Journal of Law and Economics*, 20 (October), 229–63.

Penrose, Edith (1959), *The Theory of the Growth of the Firm*. New York: Wiley.

Peteraf, Margaret (1993), "The Cornerstone of Competitive Advantage: A Resource-Based View, " *Strategic Management Journal*, 14 (March), 179–91.

_____ and Jay B. Barney (2003), "Unraveling the Resource-based Tangle," *Managerial and Decision Economics*, 24 (June/July), 309–23.

Plott, Charles R. (1989), "An Updated Review of Industrial Organization: Applications and Experimental Methods," in *Handbook of Industrial Organization Research*, Richard Schmalensee and Richard D. Willig, eds. Amsterdam: North-Holland, 1109–76.

Porter, Michael E. (1979), "The Structure Within Industries and Companies' Performance," *Review of Economics and Statistics*, 61 (May), 214–27.

——— (1980), *Competitive Strategy*. New York: Free Press.

——— (1991), "Towards a Dynamic Theory of Strategy," *Strategic Management Journal*, 12 (Winter), 95–118.

Prescott, John E., Ajay K. Kohli, and N. Venkatraman (1986), "The Market Share-Profitability Relationship: An Empirical Assessment of Major Assertions and Contractions," *Strategic Management Journal*, 7 (July-August), 377–94.

Putsis, W.P. and Ravi Dhar (2004), "Category Expenditures, Promotion and Competitive Market Interactions: Can Private Labels Expand the Pie?" working paper, Yale University, New Haven, CT.

Ravenscraft, David J. (1983), "Structure-Profit Relationships at the Line-of-Business and Industry Level," *Review of Economics and Statistics*, 65 (February), 22–31.

Reed, Richard and Robert J. DeFillippi (1990), "Causal Ambiguity, Barriers to Imitation and Sustainable Competitive Advantage," *Academy of Management Review*, 15 (January), 88–102.

Roquebert, J.A., R.L. Phillips, and P.A. Westfall (1996), "Markets vs. Management: What 'Drives' Profitability?" *Strategic Management Journal*, 17 (August), 653–64.

Ruefli, Timothy and Robert R. Wiggins (2003), "Industry, Corporate, and Segment Effects and Business Performance: A Non-Parametric Approach," *Strategic Management Journal*, 24 (September), 861–79.

Rumelt, Richard P. (1984), "Towards a Strategic Theory of the Firm," in *Competitive Strategic Management*, R. Lamb, ed. Englewood Cliffs, NJ: Prentice Hall, 556–70.

——— (1991), "How Much Does Industry Matter?" *Strategic Management Journal*, 12 (March), 167–85.

Rumelt, Richard P. and Robin Wensley (1981), "In Search of the Market Share Effect," *Proceedings of the Annual Meeting of the Academy of Management*, Detroit.

Scherer, F.M. (1980), *Industrial Market Structure and Economic Performance*. Boston: Houghton Mifflin.

Scherer, F.M., William F. Long, Stephen Martin, Dennis C. Mueller, George Pascoe, David J. Ravenscraft, John T. Scott, and Leonard W. Weiss (1987), "The Validity of Studies with Line-of-Business Data: A Comment," *American Economic Review*, 77 (March), 205–17.

Schmalensee, Richard (1985), "Do Markets Differ Much?" *American Economic Review*, 75 (3), 341–51.

Schroeter, John R. (1988), "Estimating the Degree of Market Power in the Beef Packing Industry, " *Review of Economics and Statistics*, 70 (February), 158–62.

Scott, John T. and George Pascoe (1986), "Beyond Firm and Industry Effects on Profitability in Imperfect Markets," *Review of Economics and Statistics*, 68 (May), 284–92.

Selznick, P. (1957), *Leadership in Administration: A Sociological Interpretation*. Evanston, IL: Pew, Peterson, and Co.

Slotegraaf, Rebecca J. and Christine Moorman (1999), "The Contingency Value of Complementary Capabilities in Product Development," *Journal of Marketing Research*, 36 (May), 239–57.

Slotegraaf, Rebecca J., Christine Moorman, and J. Jeffrey Inman (2003), "The Role of Firm Resources in Returns to Market Deployment," *Journal of Marketing Research*, forthcoming.

Smallwood, Denise and John Conlisk (1979), "Product Quality in Markets Where Consumers Are Imperfectly Informed, " *Quarterly Journal of Economics*, 93 (February), 1–23.

Snow, Charles C. and Lawerence G. Hrebiniak (1980), "Strategy, Distinctive Competence, and Organizational Performance," *Administrative Science Quarterly*, 25 (April), 317–36.

Srivastava, Rajendra, Tassu Shervani, and Liam Fahey (1998), "Market-based Assets and Shareholder Value: A Framework for Analysis," *Journal of Marketing*, 62 (January), 2–18.

———, ———, and ——— (1999), "Marketing, Business Process, and Shareholder Value: An Organizationally Embedded View of Marketing Activities and the Discipline of Marketing," *Journal of Marketing*, 63 (Special Issue), 168–79.

Stigler, G.J. (1963), *Capital and Rates of Return in Manufacturing Industries*. Princeton, NJ: Princeton University Press.

——— (1964), "A Theory of Oligopoly," *Journal of Political Economy*, 72 (February), 44–61.

Sudhir, K. (2001a), "Competitive Pricing Behavior in the Auto Market: A Structural Analysis," *Marketing Science* 20 (Winter), 42–60.

———. (2001b), "Structural Analysis of Manufacturer Pricing in the Presence of a Strategic Retailer," *Marketing Science* 20 (Summer), 244–64,

Szymanski, David M., Sundar G. Bharadwaj, and P. Rajan Varadarajan (1993), "An Analysis of the Market Share-Profitability Relationship," *Journal of Marketing*, 57 (July), 1–18.

Teece, David J. (1984), "Economic Analysis and Strategic Management," *California Management Review*, 26 (Spring), 87–110.

Teece, David J., Gary Pisano, and Amy Shuen (1997), "Dynamic Capabilities and Strategic Management," *Strategic Management Journal*, 18 (August), 509–33..

Thomas, Howard and N. Venkatraman (1988), "Research on Strategic Groups: Progress and Prognosis," *Journal of Management Studies*, 25 (November), 537–56.

Varadarajan, P. Rajan (1999), "Strategy Content and Process Perspectives Revisited," *Journal of the Academy of Marketing Science* 27 (Winter), 88–100.

Vernon, John Mitchum (1972), *Market Structure and Industrial Performance: A Review of Statistical Findings*. Boston: Allyn and Bacon.

Weiss, Leonard W. (1974), "The Concentration-Profits Relationship and Antitrust," in *Industrial Concentration: The New Learning*, Harvey Goldschmidt et al., eds. Boston: Little, Brown, 185–223.

––––––– (1989), *Concentration and Price*. Cambridge, MA: MIT Press.

Wernerfelt, Birger (1984), "A Resource-Based View of the Firm," *Strategic Management Journal*, 5 (April–June), 171–80.

––––––– (1989), "From Critical Resources to Corporate Strategy," *Journal of General Management*, 14 (March), 4–12.

White, Lawerence J. (1976), "Searching for the Critical Industrial Concentration Ratio: An Application of the 'Switching of Regimes' Technique," in *Studies in Non-linear Estimation*, Stephen Goldfeld and Richard Quandt, eds. Cambridge, MA: Ballinger, 61–75.

White, Roderick E. (1980), "Generic Business Strategies, Organizational Context, and Performance: An Empirical Investigation," *Strategic Management Journal*, 7 (May–June), 217–31.

Woo, Carolyn Y. (1984), "Market-share Leadership—Not Always So Good," *Harvard Business Review*, 62 (January–February), 50–54.

Woo, Carolyn Y. and Arnold C. Cooper (1981), "Strategies of Effective Low Share Businesses," *Strategic Management Journal*, 2 (July–September), 301–18.

––––––– and ––––––– (1982), "The Surprising Case for Low Market Share," *Harvard Business Review*, 60 (November–December), 106–31.

CONSUMERS' EVALUATIVE REFERENCE SCALES AND SOCIAL JUDGMENT THEORY

A Review and Exploratory Study

STEPHEN L. VARGO AND ROBERT F. LUSCH

Abstract

In both consumer satisfaction/dissatisfaction (CS/D) and service quality (SQ) research, the disconfirmation of expectations paradigm has served as the dominant model for understanding consumer reference scales—the psychological scales used to make evaluations of marketing-related stimuli. While dominant, the model has been increasingly questioned in relation to (1) whether standards other than or in addition to expectations influence evaluations, and (2) whether the standards are associated with vector attributes, as implied by the disconfirmation model, or serve as ideal points. Additionally, alternative models have been offered that suggest consumer reference scales comprise zones, latitudes, or ranges—for example, of acceptability, tolerance, and so forth—that have primary roles in evaluative judgments. We first review the disconfirmation model, its related issues, and the latitude models found in the CS/D and SQ literatures. We then investigate social judgment-involvement (SJI) theory, a latitude-based theory from social psychology, both (1) as a potential theoretical framework to augment, replace, and/or elaborate the disconfirmation model and latitude models associated with CS/D and SQ research, and (2) for potential adaptation of its research methods for further inquiry into the nature of consumer reference scales. A preliminary exploratory study using a modified research method from SJI is then reported, and a research agenda is offered.

Traditionally, the disconfirmation of expectations paradigm has served as the dominant model for understanding how consumers make evaluations (e.g., assessments of satisfaction or service quality [SQ]) of marketing-related stimuli. It assumes that consumers compare their perceptions of an offering with their expectations and that positive and negative evaluations are directly proportional to the degree to which perceptions of the offering exceed or fall below these expectations. While dominant, the disconfirmation of expectations paradigm has been increasingly questioned.

This questioning of the model has focused on issues of (1) whether there are other standards, instead of or in addition to expectations, that influence evaluations, and (2) whether the standards are associated with vector attributes, as implied by the disconfirmation model, or they serve as ideal points. Some of the alternative conceptualizations of models of evaluation imply that the standards of comparison may not be single points but rather zones, latitudes, or ranges—for example, acceptability, tolerance, and so forth. More generally, these questions and alternative conceptualizations point to the need for further investigation of the nature of the underlying psychological reference scales used by consumers in making evaluative judgments.

To date, however, most of the empirical research concerning these issues has been limited to testing the relationship between various standards, or disconfirmation of these standards, either singly or in combination, or on dependent variables such as satisfaction or SQ. What is missing is a method for uncovering (1) the underlying reference scales used in the evaluation process and (2) the apparent relative relationship among the various standards, (3) their possible role in the formation of evaluative categories or zones, (4) the relationship between these evaluative categories and behavioral outcomes, and (5) impact on reference scales of various situational variables—for example, involvement, situational criticality, prior knowledge, and so forth.

We propose and argue that social judgment-involvement (SJI) theory and its associated research methods, developed in social psychology by Sherif (e.g., Sherif, Sherif, and Nebergall 1965) and associates, can be used to shed light on the five prior issues. SJI theorists wrestled with very similar issues to the ones faced by marketers in understanding evaluative processes. Their domain was attitude development and change, essentially the same domain as consumer evaluation, and like marketing academics today, they were concerned with multiple standards and evaluative categories, or latitudes, as alternatives to the single-point attitude conceptualizations that had previously been dominant. They identified three latitudes or ranges in the typical evaluative reference scale—acceptability (latitude of acceptance), objectionability (latitude of rejection, or objectionability), and neutrality (latitude of noncommitment).

We combine a review of the literature on the evaluation of service encounters with an exploratory investigation of the use of an SJI research technique to address issues raised in that review. First we review models and issues of evaluation in the context of consumer satisfaction/dissatisfaction (CS/D) and SQ, with particular emphasis on the disconfirmation of expectations model, which is dominant in both contexts. We then review latitude or zone models, with particular attention to social judgment theory and the methods of inquiry developed by SJI theorists to investigate underlying reference scales. Third, we detail the adaptation of one of those methods of inquiry (own categories technique) for use in the investigation of marketing-related stimuli (restaurant service encounters), and in order to better illustrate the method and its potential, we report the findings of an exploratory empirical study. Finally, we briefly discuss the implications of latitude models and the results of the exploratory study for future research.

The Service Encounter and Its Evaluation

The focal domain of the present research is the service encounter, a discrete interaction, usually at the time of delivery, between an enterprise and a consumer. This definition is in general agreement with service-encounter definitions provided by Shostack (1985), Bitner and Hubbert (1994), and Chase and Bowen (1991). However, we argue this research is generalizable to situations in which the "core" offering is commonly considered to be either a "service" or a "good."

The evaluation of service encounters is usually viewed in terms of perceptions and/or feelings of CS/D or in terms of perceptions of SQ. However, we take a broader, and potentially more generalizable, perspective, the investigation of the reference scales that underlie evaluation. This breadth is both desirable and necessary for several reasons; each concerns unresolved issues of definition and domain. First, while both SQ and CS/D research share the disconfirmation paradigm, the specific definition of and relationship between their central constructs (i.e., SQ and satisfaction) continues to be debated (e.g., Bolton and Drew 1991; Dabholkar, Shepard, and Thorpe

2000; Liljander 1995; Strandvik 1994). Second, while CS/D research has been focused on the evaluation of both tangible goods and services, SQ research, by definition, has been limited to services. However, no clear, universal scheme of categorization for differentiating between services and goods as alternative types of market offerings exists (Vargo and Lusch 2004). Consequently, *what* is being evaluated (i.e., an offering, its episodic delivery, or a buyer/seller relationship) under the rubrics of CS/D and SQ is often unclear (Liljander 1995; Strandvik 1994).

Partially ignoring the goods/services and satisfaction/SQ debate and focusing on the general issue of evaluation has the advantage of allowing the inclusion of the previous CS/D and SQ research, as well as the conceptual and empirical work of a number of similar research streams both within and outside of marketing. Our conceptual approach is to look for areas of overlap and similarities among these research streams that may point toward the key components and processes of the reference scales that underlie evaluative processes. Given its prominence in both research streams, the disconfirmation of expectations paradigm is reviewed first.

The Disconfirmation of Expectations Paradigm

The disconfirmation of expectations paradigm has its roots in psychology (e.g., Carlsmith and Aronson 1963), where its investigation was often grounded in cognitive dissonance theory (Festinger 1957). Cognitive dissonance theory posits that in an effort to maintain cognitive consistency, particularly as it relates to self-concept, individuals reduce the negative affect associated with a discrepancy between an internal standard and a perception of reality by the process of assimilation, or perceptual bias in the direction of the standard.

The disconfirmation of expectations paradigm was introduced into marketing by Cardoza (1965), who noted that the assimilation-based dissonance theory (e.g., Festinger 1957) and "contrast" theory (e.g., Spector 1956) make opposing predictions concerning the direction of the perceptual bias. That is, while assimilation theory predicts that perceptions will be biased toward an expectation, contrast theory predicts perceptions will be biased away from the expectation. Cardoza suggested that the level of customer effort, which presumably reflects the importance of an acquisition, moderates the direction of the perceptual bias—that is, assimilation is likely under conditions of considerable effort in obtaining a product, and contrast is likely when little effort is expended. Several of the early studies in the marketing literature continued to focus on this process of comparative judgment and the question of the appropriate model to explain this process (e.g., Anderson 1973; Olshavsky and Miller 1972).

Over time, the disconfirmation of expectations paradigm generally evolved into a relatively static model, emphasizing the distance between the expected and the perceived performance and the relationships among antecedents and consequences, rather than the underlying process. The fundamental proposition is that perception of the actual performance of a focal referent (e.g., a good or service-encounter experience) is compared to the expectation of that performance. If the perception of the actual performance matches the expectation, the result is *simple confirmation*. If the perception is below the expectation, *negative disconfirmation* results; if perceptions exceed expectations, *positive disconfirmation* results. Simple confirmation causes a neutral or mildly positive reaction or attribution of SQ. Positive disconfirmation, in turn, causes satisfaction or positive attributions of SQ, while negative disconfirmation causes dissatisfaction or negative attributions of SQ. The degree of satisfaction or dissatisfaction is usually seen as being a linear function of the degree of disconfirmation.

In the SQ literature, this comparison between perceptions and expectations is often called "Gap 5," from Parasuraman, Zeithaml, and Berry's (1985) identification of various gaps between management, employee, and customer perceptions and standards. Regardless of the terms used, disconfirmation is seen as resulting in the structure of an evaluative domain—that is, the full range of stimuli to be evaluated—depicted in Figure 6.1.

Disconfirmation and Consumer Satisfaction/Dissatisfaction

Most early studies of judgmental and evaluation phenomena within marketing were only nominally concerned with (or later identified with) consumer satisfaction (e.g., Anderson 1973; Cardoza 1965; Olshavsky and Miller 1992). None of these early studies explicitly defined the construct of satisfaction (although Anderson did provide a "dictionary" definition), and only one of them (Swan and Combs 1976) purported to measure it. Rather, most of these studies were concerned with the relationship between expectations and product performance, which, in turn, was typically *assumed* to be a surrogate of satisfaction (Liljander 1995).

One (or more) of three overlapping theoretical frameworks was (were) normally employed in or tested by these studies: (1) contrast, (2) assimilation, and (3) assimilation-contrast (Anderson 1973; Day 1976). A fourth explanation, adopted from Carlsmith and Aronson (1963) and tested by Anderson (1973), was "general negativity," an explanation that suggests that perceptions both above and below a standard will be evaluated negatively (essentially an "ideal point" explanation—e.g., Teas 1993). In each case, the research emphasis was on an overall *emotional (or affective) response,* resulting from a discrepancy between a postpurchase evaluation and a prepurchase expectation.

During the mid-1970s, while the underlying satisfaction process continued to be debated, the focus partially shifted to the measurement of satisfaction as an outcome of (dis)confirmation. For example, Swan and Combs (1976), in what was probably the first attempt to use a direct measurement of satisfaction (Liljander 1995), used the critical incident technique to identify the relationship between "instrumental" (i.e., functional) and "expressive" (i.e., emotional) outcomes and satisfaction. Oliver (1977), using a six-item affective Likert scale measure, was probably first to quantify satisfaction as an outcome.

Beginning about the same time, some of the attention was shifted toward the refinement of antecedent components of satisfaction, especially preformed expectations. Olson and Dover (1976), in line with the multiattribute models popular at the time (e.g., Fishbein and Ajzen 1975), conceptualized expectations as specific belief elements within a cognitive structure. Miller (1977) distinguished between four kinds of standards for comparison: expected, deserved, ideal, and minimum tolerable. Similarly, Swan and Trawick (1980) distinguished between predicted (expected) and desired (ideal) expectations. Spreng and Mackoy (1996) found desired and expected standards to be distinct and to play different roles in evaluation. Oliver (1980) suggested that expectations were equivalent to Helson's (1964) "adaptation level"—a neutral level to which the individual has adjusted. Woodruff, Cadotte, and Jenkins (1983) suggested that expectations be replaced with "experience based norms"—that is, brand-based and product-based experience-grounded standards of comparison around which there exists a "zone of indifference."

Other aspects of the disconfirmation process also became the objects of both refinement and scrutiny. LaTour and Peat (1979) reviewed assimilation, contrast, and combined assimilation/contrast explanations and proposed "comparison level" theory as an alternative explanation. Oliver (1980) reviewed the issues in the CS/D process and came down on the side of adaptation level (AL) theory, but suggested that expectations had both a direct and an indirect effect, through disconfirmation, on satisfaction. Prakash (1984) questioned the disconfirmation of expectations

Figure 6.1 **Alternative Models of Evaluation**

a. Disconfirmation model (single standard)

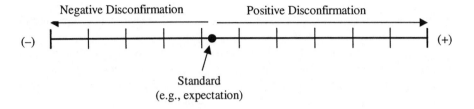

b. Zone of tolerance model (multiple standard, bounded range)

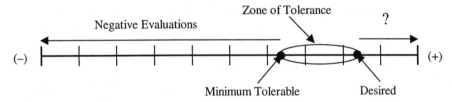

c. Latitude model of social judgment theory (multiple standard, anchor-based)

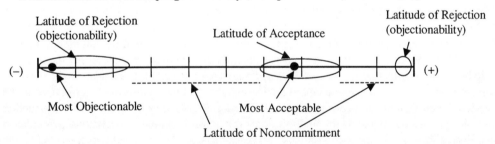

paradigm on the basis of measurement issues related to problems with difference scores (see also Peter, Churchill, and Brown 1993), rather than on conceptual grounds.

This increased questioning of the disconfirmation of expectations paradigm and the search for adjustments to the model, or for more isomorphic models, has become a salient focus in (dis)satisfaction research. Pieters, Koelemeijer, and Roest (1996, p. 30) objected to the disconfirmation of expectations model on the basis of its assumption that experience and expectations are independent. They noted that while it provides an "elegant framework, it may assume that a customer is both motivated and able to form prior expectations, and who is motivated and able to compare these with subsequent experiences." They suggested and found support for the view that experiences, rather than expectations, dominate satisfaction formation. Oliver found support for his contention (Oliver 1980) that satisfaction is a joint function of expectation and disconfirmation and for his adaptation-level-based contention that this satisfaction is compared to (and is used to update) anticipated satisfaction (attitude), which serves as an antecedent to behavioral intentions. He reiterated that expectation measurement should be based on a multiattribute affect-belief (ab) scale (e.g., Fishbein and Ajzen 1975) and found support for his contention that direct ("greater than or less than expected") measures of confirmation have a more meaningful relationship to satisfaction than do indirect measures (e.g., difference scores).

Oliver (1981, p. 27) defined satisfaction as "an evaluation of the surprise inherent in a product acquisition and/or consumption experience." But he distinguished further between attitude and satisfaction by noting that satisfaction is a more complex emotional response whereas attitude is an affective orientation. He proposed an integration of adaptation-level theory and "dynamic opponent-process theory," which predicts that individuals seek homeostasis through opposing forces in the face of disconfirmation. In a later study, Oliver (1988) suggested three major categories of (dis)confirmation (cf. Woodruff, Cadotte, and Jenkins 1983):

1. A region where performance in deviations are considered acceptable;
2. A range of disconfirming performance that is "plausible" and considered "gratifying" or "disappointing"; and
3. Levels that are unexpected or "surprising."

The movement in satisfaction research has increasingly been away from simple linear-function disconfirmation models, in which satisfaction is directly proportional to the distance between expectations and perceptions, and toward more complex models. These models often imply multiple standards, which may play different roles in evaluation. Increasingly, they suggest at least the possibility of nonlinear relationships between perceptions and satisfaction, resulting in zones or latitudes in which evaluations are relatively constant. These latitude models are discussed in more depth below.

Disconfirmation and Service Quality

Service quality as a construct of academic focus has followed a pattern of development similar to that of CS/D. While the notion of quality, as a quantifiable, comparative measure of the relationship between manufacturing specifications and manufactured output, has a well-established history in the study and practice of tangible production, the term was not formally introduced in the services literature until Gronroos (1982, p. 54) first defined SQ as an outcome of the "production of a service." Based largely on the findings of the relationships among expectations, perceptions, and evaluations in consumer (dis)satisfaction research, Gronroos defined perceived SQ as the outcome of the comparison of expected service to perceived service. Thus, from this formal introduction of the perceived SQ construct into the marketing literature, it has been defined in terms of the same disconfirmation of expectations paradigm as has (dis)satisfaction.

Parasuraman, Zeithaml, and Berry (1985) further associated the SQ concept with the disconfirmation of expectations paradigm by defining SQ in terms of "the magnitude and direction of the gap between expected service and perceived service." Based on their exploratory focus group analysis, they identified this "gap" as "Gap 5" and postulated that it was, in turn, a function of other gaps among consumer expectations, management's perceptions of consumer expectations, SQ specifications, actual service delivery, and external communication about services. Additionally, based on their focus-group data, they postulated an initial set of dimensions of SQ. They distinguished between satisfaction and SQ by construing the latter to be "a global judgment, or attitude, relating to the superiority of service, whereas satisfaction is related to a specific transaction" (p. 16).

In an empirical investigation of their gap model, Parasuraman, Zeithaml, and Berry (1988) developed a multiple-item scale for measuring perceived SQ, which they called SERVQUAL. Using exploratory factor analysis, they reduced their original ten dimensions to five:

1. Tangibles: physical evidence of the service
2. Reliability: consistency of performance and dependability
3. Responsiveness: willingness or readiness of employees to provide service and timeliness of service provision
4. Assurance: Knowledge and courtesy of employees
5. Empathy: Caring, individualized attention

The SERVQUAL score was a linear combination of the five difference scores (i.e., perceived performance less should-expectations) derived for each of these five dimensions.

In a follow-up study, Parasuraman, Berry, and Zeithaml (1991) offered a number of refinements to the SERVQUAL instrument. For example, noting that asking respondents to indicate how dimensions of a service *should be* to establish a standard of comparison produced unrealistically high standards, they changed the standard to one of actual expectations by asking how the respondents thought the actual service dimension *would be* performed.

With some modifications, this disconfirmation of expectations–based gap model and the SERVQUAL instrument developed from it have dominated the SQ literature. Despite this dominance, neither has had universal acceptance. The primary criticisms are usually grounded in issues concerning (1) the appropriateness of the overall model itself, (2) the dimensionality proposed, and (3) the appropriate definition and nature of the standards that should be used if the gap model is employed.

As with the employment of the disconfirmation paradigm in (dis)satisfaction research, the primary criticism of its use in SQ research has been based on the lack of independence between expectations and perceptions. Carman (1990) noted that expectations vary between service-encounter situations and, in turn, differentially influence perceptions. Bolton and Drew (1991) found perceived SQ to be a function not only of disconfirmation, but also perceptions of actual performance. That is, perceptions of performance had both a direct effect on SQ and an indirect effect through disconfirmation. They noted the similarity between this finding and the CS/D literature.

Perhaps the most ardent protagonists of the disconfirmation of expectations model for the understanding of SQ have been Cronin and Taylor (1992, p 56). They suggested that, despite its popularity in the SQ literature, the gap model has "little if any theoretical or empirical support." They further suggested that the fundamental flaw in SERVQUAL is the fact that it is based on this gap model, which is a *satisfaction* model, rather than an attitude model as they feel it should be. They posited that a performance-only assessment of SQ, which they operationalized as the performance-perception half of SERVQUAL, is more isomorphic with this attitude conceptualization than the perception-minus-expectations $(P - E)$ score used in SERVQUAL. In support of this contention, they found that this performance-only measure, which they call SERVPERF, accounts for more variance in a direct assessment of SQ than does the full SERVQUAL difference score. Parasuraman, Berry, and Zeithaml (1991) and Parasuraman, Zeithaml, and Berry (1994) acknowledged the potential superiority of perceptions versus the difference score operationalization for predictive purposes but maintained that the difference score approach has greater diagnostic value.

Much as Prakash (1984) criticized the use of difference score operationalization of the disconfirmation of expectations model in satisfaction research, and Cronin and Taylor had pointed out the superiority of performance-only measures, Peter, Churchill, and Brown (1993) again issued a caution concerning the use of difference scores on methodological grounds. Specifically, they argued that difference scores were often characterized by (1) low reliability, (2) false indications of discriminant validity, (3) spurious correlations, and (4) restricted variance resulting from one measure's (e.g., expectations) being almost always higher than the other measure (e.g., perceptions) (see also Page and Spreng 2002).

Considerable debate can also be found in the operationalization of the standard of comparison. This debate involves two issues. The first is a definitional issue similar to Miller's (1977) distinction among ideal, expected, deserved, and minimum tolerable standards of comparison in (dis)satisfaction research. The other issue involves the nature of the standard; that is, whether it has vector attributes or an ideal point (Teas 1993).

As noted, in the original SERVQUAL study (Parasuraman, Zeithaml, and Berry 1988), expectations were defined in terms of how the service "should" be performed. However, in their reassessment, Parasuraman, Berry, and Zeithaml (1991) changed the wording so that expectations reflected what the respondent *would* experience at a similar company that provided excellent service. Boulding et al. (1993) found evidence that *should* expectations negatively affect perceptions of quality whereas *will* expectations positively affect perceptions of quality. Cronin and Taylor (1992), drawing on Woodruff, Cadotte, and Jenkins's (1983) work in the satisfaction literature, suggest that a better standard would be a normative expectation based on previous experience with similar service providers. In a further revision of their SQ conceptualization, Zeithaml, Berry, and Parasuraman (1993) suggested the simultaneous use of two comparison standards: desired service and adequate service (see below).

Drawing on all of these conceptualizations of comparison standards, as well as Miller's (1977) delineation in the satisfaction literature, Liljander (1995) investigated eight standards in both inferred and direct comparison models: excellent service, adequate service, predictive episodic expectations, brand norm, product type norm, best brand norm, deserved service, and equity. She found that while all expectation measures correlated with performance measures, there was little support for the disconfirmation of expectations model, and that different comparison standards may be used by individuals when making evaluations of SQ or satisfaction and when evaluating intentions to behave (e.g., repeat patronage).

The other issue is whether the comparison standard should be viewed in terms of vector attributes or as classic attitudinal ideal point. Teas (1993) maintains that the SERVQUAL model, as well as the gap model on which it is based, implicitly assumes vector attributes by specifying a monotonically increasing relationship between P − E and SQ. However, he notes (p. 18) that Zeithaml et al. "suggest expectations 'is similar to the ideal standard in CS/D literature,' Zeithaml et al. (1991, p. 3–4)," which would imply an inverted V-shaped relationship between Perceptions-Expectations and SQ. The issue is further complicated by the fact that a classical ideal point can be conceptualized as a *classical attitudinal model* ideal point or a *feasible ideal point model* (Teas 1993). In the former model, the expectation is equal to the ideal standard; in the latter, the expected performance and ideal performance are not equal. Further, Teas (1994, p. 135) notes that additional possibilities for the interpretation of standards exists, such as "hoped for and adequate service."

A Dynamic Process Model of Service Quality

In a significant departure from the disconfirmation paradigm, Boulding et al. (1993) proposed a dynamic, or iterative, model in which expectations of SQ drive perceptions of SQ, which, in turn, drive future expectations. They distinguished between *will expectations*, which reflect the antici-pated service level, and *should expectations*, which reflect the normative service level. They suggested that each is a function of prior will or should expectations, as well as new information acquired between service encounters and the service level received in the previous service en-counter. However, *should expectations* can only increase, and only if services received exceed prior expectations. Further, *perceived service* is posited to be a function of *both will and should* expectations, new information (e.g., word of mouth and advertising), and delivered service level. Finally, will and should expectations *influence perceptions inversely.* That is, will expectations play an assimilative role and raise perceptions while should expectations serve as a standard against which perceptions are contrasted. Boulding et al. provided empirical evidence that sup-ports these relationships.

A third type of expectation, *ideal expectations* (cf. Teas 1993, 1994), is also delineated but not specifically modeled. In part, this is because ideal expectations are viewed as remaining relatively unchanged and as having only an indirect effect on perceptions through should expectations.

The departure of this model from the disconfirmation paradigm is in two dimensions. The first is the dynamic, iterative nature of the process. The second concerns the *perceptual bias* nature of the comparative process, as opposed to the linear-function assumption of disconfirmation. While not explicitly specified, the Boulding et al. (1993) model implies an *evaluative zone* comprising, if not bounded by, "will" and "should" expectations.

As with CS/D research, SQ research has increasingly moved in the direction of the conceptualization of evaluation in terms of these zones or latitudes. These models, including a more explicit zone model of SQ, the *zone of tolerance* model of Zeithaml, Berry, and Parasuraman (1993), are discussed in the next section.

Zone and Latitude Models of Evaluative Processes

The central feature of zone or latitude models is the proposed existence of a range, zone, or latitude within which objective differences are perceptually equivalent. Thus, they have the com-mon characteristic of positing a nonlinear relationship between a performance (e.g., on a dimen-sion of a service encounter) and the perception or evaluation of that performance, as opposed to the linear relationship typically assumed by the disconfirmation paradigm. While these models are similar, they differ in (1) the number of standards assumed to be operating, (2) the nature of the standards (latitude boundaries or anchors), and (3) the nature of the focal latitude(s) (positive, negative, and/or neutral).

While relatively new to marketing, as a class these models are not new to social scientific inquiry. Their foundations can be found in one or more of the following models and theoreti-cal frameworks.

Behavioral Foundations for Zone and Latitude Models

The Weber-Fechner Law

The most cited framework for the notion that perception of stimuli may occur as categories, in which physically different stimuli are judged to be equivalent or similar, is probably Weber's law (Savage 1970), which suggests that the level of difference that can be perceived between two stimuli is a constant function of the intensity of the first stimulus presented. As modified by Fechner (1966), it implies a zone of indifference, within which changes in stimulus values are perceptually equivalent, and above and below which stimulus values are perceived as greater than and less than the stimulus, respectively. This zone of indifference is called the just-noticeable-difference (jnd).

Adaptation-Level Theory

Whereas the Weber-Fechner law views the zone of indifference and the associated sensation-response to be a function of stimulus intensity, adaptation-level theory (Helson 1959) sees neutrality and sensation-response to be a function of all current and previously experienced stimuli. That is, based on all currently and previously experienced levels of a stimulus, individuals form a pooled area of neutrality, or equilibrium, about which their own scale for that stimulus is formed.

The existence of an AL, which represents an equilibrium, implies a "bipolarity of behavior." That is, stimuli above AL elicit one response (e.g., positive) while stimuli below AL elicit an opposite response (e.g., negative). Thus, AL serves as a frame of reference against which stimuli are judged. Importantly, it represents a *neutral* zone, rather than an *affectively* preferred point, or zone of acceptability or desirability. A special case of this neutral AL, or frame of reference, is "expectancy level."

Prospect Theory

Prospect theory was first proposed by Kahneman and Tversky (1979) as an alternative to expected utility theory as an explanation of decisionmaking under conditions of risk. They proposed an asymmetric, S-shaped value function about a neutral reference point (cf. Helson 1964), which is (1) concave for gains and convex for losses and (2) more steep for gains than losses. That is, (1) the subjective perception of successive, equal amounts of a gain or a loss (e.g., money) decreases, and (2) losing results in more displeasure than an equal gain results in pleasure. Thus, judgments can be affected by the way they are framed in terms of losses or gains.

Kahneman (1991) distinguished between reference points and anchors. Reference points are neutral points such as the AL, whereas anchors are "graded" values of a stimuli that represent the *salient values* in norms or categories and affect evaluation of other stimuli, including the determination of reference points. Since the reference point is a point of sharp transition in the slope of the value function, it might therefore be characterized as point of *contrast*. Kahneman further noted that a multiplicity of reference points might be operative at the same time.

Assimilation/Contrast

Assimilation/contrast theory is probably most closely associated with SJI theory developed by Sherif (e.g., Sherif and Hovland 1953). It suggests that performances close to salient anchors are seen as perceptually equivalent to those anchors (cf. Weber-Fechner law), and performances distant from salient anchors are perceptually displaced further away from those anchors than they are objectively different. This perceptual distortion results in categories or latitudes that serve as a frame of reference for evaluating similar stimuli. Assimilation/contrast effects are discussed further in the context of both CS/D and SJI.

Zone and Latitude Models in Consumer Satisfaction

Several studies have suggested zone or latitude models as an alternative to, or modification of, the disconfirmation model in the study of (dis)satisfaction. Most of these studies have been conceptual rather than empirical. Additionally, latitude-generating processes (e.g., assimilation-contrast effects) have been studied in the context of disconfirmation models without direct reference to latitudes.

Olson and Dover (1979) found that pretrial product expectations constrained posttrial disconfirmations and attributed the constraint to assimilation effects, consistent with both cognitive dissonance (Festinger 1957) and SJI theory. However, consistent with SJI, they noted the low-involvement nature of the judgment task (coffee bitterness) and pointed out the necessity of taking ego-involvement and past experience into account prior to generalization of assimilation-only effects. More directly related to the service encounter, Pieters, Koelemeijer, and Roest (1996) found that expectations influence service-encounter experiences through *forward assimilation,* and experiences influence recall of expectations through *backward assimilation.* This distortion implies a nonlinear relationship between actual and perceived performance, although the researchers make no direct mention of latitudes.

Anderson (1973) examined four theories proposed to account for the disparity between expectations and perceived product performance: cognitive dissonance (assimilation only), contrast-only, generalized negativity (essentially an ideal point model), and combined assimilation-contrast effects (the SJI latitude model). Only the combined assimilation-contrast was found to account for the nonlinear relationship that characterized the perceived discrepancies.

Miller (1977) was probably the first to directly posit the existence of zones or latitudes in the perception of satisfaction. Specifically, he suggested that, instead of viewing satisfaction in terms of points, "it may be helpful to consider 'distributions of possible points,' or 'latitudes,' similar to the concepts used by Sherif" and hypothesized "latitudes of satisfaction," "indifference," and "dissatisfaction," as the perceptual outcomes of satisfaction judgments. He did, however, question if an "area of indifference" was possible. Additionally, Miller suggested the existence of multiple comparison standards: ideal, expected, minimum tolerable, and deserved. However, he did not link these different standards of comparison with the notion of latitudes.

Citing Miller (1977), Woodruff, Cadotte, and Jenkins (1983) elaborated the notion of a "zone of indifference" used in place of a single point of comparison in the disconfirmation model. Like Miller, they distinguished between different standards of comparison but collapsed Miller's four types of standards into "predictive" (expected) and "normative" (deserved, ideal, or minimum tolerable) categories. In practice, norms represent the *pooled* result of past experiences with the product and/or brand (cf. Helson 1964). While *expectations are used in perception, norms are used as the comparison standard* in disconfirmation judgments. However, "perceived performance within some interval around a performance norm is likely to be considered equivalent to the norm" (p. 299). They call this interval the "zone of indifference" and invoke an assimilation explanation. Positive and negative confirmation occur when perceptions are outside the zone of indifference but within the full range of experience-based possible performances. It is not clear what results if the perception of performance is outside of this latter range.

Based on restaurant and lodging complaint and compliment data, Cadotte and Turgeon (1988) speculated about the shapes of the distribution of experienced-based norms and the "zone of indifference" within these distributions. They proposed four types of attributes. *Satisfiers* are attributes that lead to compliments if present but do not usually lead to complaints if absent. *Dissatisfiers* are attributes that are likely to result in complaints when absent but generally do not result in compliments if present. *Criticals* are attributes that have narrow zones of indifference and will usually result in either complaints or compliments. *Neutrals,* by contrast, are characterized by wide zones of tolerance and seldom result in either complaints or compliments.

Building on Woodruff, Cadotte, and Jenkins (1983), Oliver (1988) extended their normative distribution model to account for perceptions outside the experience-based boundaries of the norms. As noted, Oliver delineated three major (dis)confirmation categories: (1) an acceptance region, (2) a plausible disconfirmation that is either gratifying or disappointing, and (3) disconfirmation beyond experience-based norms that is surprising.

Also like Woodruff, Cadotte, and Jenkins (1983), Bleuel (1990) noted that attributes that cause satisfaction are not the same as those that cause dissatisfaction. Additionally, he noted that a zone of uncertainty separates satisfaction and dissatisfaction, and contended that this zone "is the most often overlooked and is certainly the least understood of all the concepts of customer satisfaction" (p. 50).

Hesket et al. (1994) took the concept of latitudes a step further by linking satisfaction and customer loyalty. They proposed that the two measures are related by a nonlinear function in which a zone of indifference (high satisfaction and moderate loyalty) separates a zone of defection (dissatisfaction and low loyalty) and a zone of affection (high satisfaction and high loyalty). The model is based on case studies and not tied to any theoretical framework.

The Zone of Tolerance Model of Service Quality

There are fewer studies suggesting zone or latitude models in the SQ literature than in the CS/D literature. Most are directly or indirectly related to the "zone of tolerance model" of Zeithaml, Berry, and Parasuraman (1993) and Parasuraman, Zeithaml, and Berry (1994), arguably one of the most thoroughly specified, though relatively untested, zone models in marketing.

Zeithaml, Berry, and Parasuraman (1993), in a major modification of their gap model, proposed a dynamic latitude or "zone of tolerance" to replace the single-point conceptualization of the standard normally employed in comparative judgment models. This zone of tolerance is presumed to be bound by "desired service" (upper boundary) and "adequate service" (lower boundary). *Desired service* is defined as "the level of service the customer *hopes to receive*" (p. 6) and represents a combination of what the service *should* and *can be*. *Adequate service* represents the *minimum tolerable* level of service the customer will accept (cf. Miller 1977) and, according to Zeithaml et al., is comparable to *experience-based norms* proposed by Woodruff, Cadotte, and Jenkins (1983). They proposed that this zone expands and contracts, partially as a function of (1) "situational" and "enduring service intensifiers," which represent individual-specific variables; (2) "situational factors," which are specific to and vary with the situation; (3) information provided by others, including the service provider, and brought into the situation; and (4) past experience. Adequate service is seen as being more variable than desired service, and therefore contributing more to the dynamic nature of the zone of tolerance. A partial representation of the zone of tolerance model is shown in Figure 6.1b.

Zeithaml, Berry, and Parasuraman (1993) explicitly distinguished between *consumer satisfaction* and *SQ*. The former is the "gap" between predicted service and perceived service, and the latter is the "gap" between range of expected service and perceived service. Because expected service is based on two comparison standards, SQ can be conceptualized as two "gaps": one between perceived service and *adequate service,* which they call *perceived service adequacy,* and one between perceived service and *desired service,* which they call *perceived service superiority.* It should be clear from this discussion that the zone of tolerance model is an extension of the disconfirmation of expectations paradigm with comparisons between perception and multiple standards representing different constructs (e.g., SQ and consumer satisfaction) and varying conceptualizations (e.g., service adequacy and service superiority) of the same construct.

Parasuraman, Zeithaml, and Berry (1994) tested three alternative methods (and indirectly the zone of tolerance model) for assessing SQ from the perspective of the zone of tolerance model:

- *Three-column format,* in which desired, adequate, and perceived service are rated on side-by-side scales and difference scores are calculated for *Measured Service Adequacy* (MSA) and *Measured Service Superiority* (MSS).
- *Two-column format,* in which MSA and MSS are measured directly (i.e., is your perception greater than or less than the adequate and desired levels, respectively) on adjacent nine-point scales.
- *One-column format,* in which direct measures of MSA and MSS are made sequentially rather than side by side.

SERVQUAL items were used as stimuli. "Minimum service" was substituted for "adequate service" after a pilot test revealed "logical inconsistencies" in responses. Across a variety of service types, the direct, performance-only measure of MSS was superior in predictive validity to either direct MSA measures or the difference scores derived from the three-column format.

Strandvik (1994), using the a priori latitude conceptualization employed by Zeithaml, Berry, and Parasuraman (1993), employed conjoint analysis to investigate the shape of the utility function within the zone of tolerance in a restaurant setting. He operationalized *desired* or excellent service as the "best you have experienced at this type of restaurant" and *adequate* as "barely acceptable" for a restaurant. The *normal,* or expected, level was operationalized as the restaurant where the respondents were interviewed (and had just eaten dinner). The utility functions calculated from the conjoint part-worth estimates showed a consistent pattern of nonlinearity for "food" and "personal service," in which the utility (quality) slopes increased rapidly between adequate and normal but much less rapidly between normal and excellent. These two attributes were also rated as most important to the respondents. By contrast, the slopes of the utility functions for menu and servicescape were linear. Strandvik noted the similarity between these results and the classification of criticals, satisfiers, dissatisfiers, and neutrals by Cadotte and Turgeon (1988). He also noted the similarity between his finding that, for the most important attributes, losses cause more of a negative reaction than gains cause a positive reaction, and the predictions of prospect theory.

Strandvik (1994, p. 153) noted several potential shortcomings with range of the evaluative domain investigated:

> The three points measured were theoretically determined and operationalized to represent the range of customer experience. This leads to a rather large zone of tolerance, where performance very seldom exceeds the excellent level or the adequate level. Another operationalization may give different results. One explanation why the results show this asymmetric shape in the present study is related to these operationalizations.

Further, Strandvik (p. 159) noted, "There may be alternative ways of conceptualizing tolerance zones by using other comparison standards than those in the present study."

Liljander (1995), in a study primarily intended to investigate the relationship between the various standards of comparison proposed in studies of CS/D and SQ, also addressed questions of the width of the zone of tolerance and the relative position of standards used in the Zeithaml, Berry, and Parasuraman (1993) model. She found that standards such as "adequate," "predictive expectations," and various brand and product "norms" were not significantly different from each other but were different from "excellent service." She (p. 119) did, however, distinguish between her operationalization of adequate service, "the lowest level of each item that the customer could *accept and still be satisfied*" or "on the *border of what would satisfy the customer*," and the "minimum tolerable" standard suggested by Miller (1977)—thus, different from Parasuraman,

Zeithaml, and Berry's (1994) operationalization. She also used a ten-point scale anchored by "the worst restaurant I have ever experienced" (1) and "as at an ideal restaurant" (10). Interestingly, the average location of the "desired" level was usually between seven and nine.

The Social Judgment-Involvement Approach

Social judgment-involvement (SJI) theory (e.g., Sherif and Hovland, 1961; Sherif, Sherif, and Nebergall 1965) was originally developed as a theoretical approach to the conceptualization, assessment, and study of attitudes, attitude formation, and attitude change. In a departure from traditional single-point conceptualizations of attitudes, SJI theorists saw attitudes as ranges or evaluative categories, which are used by individuals to define what is acceptable and what is unacceptable. These "latitudes" of acceptability and unacceptability were posited to expand and contract as a joint function of the relationship between the referent and the individual's self-concept and the situational context.

The SJI orientation may be worthy of particular attention in the understanding of the service-encounter evaluation in general, and for zone models in particular, for several reasons. First, the evaluation of the service encounter is, by definition, an attitude phenomenon. Second, SJI is the only approach to the understanding of attitudes that explicitly models attitudes in terms of latitudes, or a set of evaluative categories. Finally, SJI does not make a priori assumptions about the valence of stimuli above and below a given standard or zone, that is, vector attributes versus ideal points.

Psychophysical Foundations of Social Judgment-Involvement

The theoretical and empirical underpinnings of SJI theory are grounded in psychophysical scaling and attitude formation and change research. The prototypical psychophysical experiment for SJI research involves the comparison of a series of weights, first in isolation and then in the presence of an increasingly large reference weight (Sherif, Taub, and Hovland 1958). In isolation, the relative weights of the individual stimuli in the series are normally judged with a high degree of accuracy. However, as heavier reference weights are systematically introduced into the judgment process, the relative weights of the original stimulus series are first skewed toward, and then away from, the reference.

The SJI interpretation is that the perceptual scale used for judgment of heaviness is adjusted as the reference weights are introduced. These displacements are attributed to "assimilation" and "contrast" effects. The reference stimuli are assumed to serve as *anchors* against which other stimuli are judged, and in relation to which the underlying evaluative categories form the individual's reference scale. These reference scales have been shown to stabilize and become internalized with increased experience with the stimuli and to be employed in further, similar judgment tasks performed by the same individuals (Sherif and Hovland 1961).

Psychosocial Reference Scales

The development of psychosocial reference scales is presumed to be relatively isomorphic with the development of psychophysical scales. The classical crossover experiment (from psycho physical to psycho social scaling) centered on the "autokinetic" effect—the apparent movement of a stationary light in a dark room. Sherif (1935) found that, when asked to estimate the range of movement of the light when the judgment of a "confederate" provided an external anchor, subjects tended to displace their judgments of the amount of movement toward the confederates, and to subsequently internalize the resulting reference scale and employ it in further, similar judgment tasks.

For SJI theorists, the development and internalization of psychosocial reference scales are at the heart of their related conceptualization of attitudes. Reference scales are seen as providing stable ties and anchors with the physical and social environment. These stable ties and anchors are represented as attitudes, which are defined as:

> . . . a set of evaluative categories formed toward an object or class of objects as the individual learns, in interaction with others, about his environment, including evaluations of other people. (Sherif, Sherif, and Nebergall 1965, p. 20)

Because these attitudes make up the individual's self-concept and the psychological tendency is presumed to be toward stability, they serve as internal anchors, and, in interaction with other attitudes and with external anchors (situational cues), provide a frame of reference, or reference scales, for the judgment of stimuli (Sherif, Sherif, and Nebergall 1965).

Attitudes as Latitudes

For SJI theorists, the structure of attitudes is modeled as a series of latitudes, or ranges of evaluative judgments of stimuli. The *latitude of acceptance* (LA) consists of the position in the domain of an issue that the individual finds most acceptable, as well as any other acceptable positions (cf. "zone of tolerance"). The *latitude of rejection* (LR) is composed of the position within the domain that the individual finds most objectionable, plus any other positions that the individual finds objectionable. The *latitude of noncommitment* (LNC) comprises all of the positions that the individual finds neither acceptable nor objectionable (cf. AL). A schematic representation of latitudes is shown in Figure 6.1c.

As the attitudes are accessed in the context of appropriate stimulus situations, the associated latitudes are hypothesized to expand or contract as a function of (1) the centrality of the attitude in the individual's ego-attitude hierarchy, mediated by assimilation-contrast effects, and (2) the situational context (cf. Zeithaml, Berry, and Parasuraman 1993). Latitude width is seen as an indicator of *ego-involvement,* which Sherif, Sherif, and Nebergall (1965, p. 65) define as:

> . . . the arousal singly or in combination, of the individual's commitments and stands in the context of appropriate situations, be they interpersonal relations or a judgment task in actual life or an experiment.

That is, ego-involvement is the situational arousal of the central attitudes with which the individual defines his or her self-concept, and represents the affective-motivational component of attitudes.

Social Judgment Methods of Latitude Assessment

Empirical support for the categorization process that represents attitudes usually comes from studies that involve the employment of some variation of two approaches. The first, called the *own categories procedure,* involves participants placing statements that are derived from content analyses of various media accounts concerning a social issue into categories, according to the subject's perception of similarity. The research instructions impose no categorical constraints on the subject. Only after the subjects have sorted all of the statements according to similarity, are they asked to identify which stacks they find acceptable and which they find objectionable. Respondent samples are usually drawn both from groups whose members are known to have strong feelings (pro or con) on the issue and from a general population frame.

SJI researchers (e.g., Sherif and Hovland 1953) have consistently found that individuals in the criterion groups (highly involved) use fewer categories to sort the statements than do average subjects. Further, the number of statements that are judged to be most objectionable by the highly involved subjects is normally disproportionately large in comparison to both the number of statements that they find acceptable and to the number of statements judged most objectionable by the average subjects.

A second method, the *method of ordered alternatives,* is a more direct attempt at capturing the cognitive structure of the underlying attitudinal scales. The method involves asking subjects to indicate latitude categorizations (evaluative) of an ordered set of nine statements ranging from extremely favorable toward one end of an issue continuum, to extremely favorable toward the opposing end. The same heightened threshold of acceptance and lowered threshold of rejection for involved, as opposed to less involved, subjects are normally found (e.g., Elbing 1962; Sherif 1960). The own-categories technique has the advantages of being relatively disguised in purpose and information-rich, but the disadvantage of being difficult to construct, administer, and evaluate. The reverse can be said of the method of ordered alternatives.

A hybrid latitude assessment method, the *imposed categories method* (Sherif and Hovland 1961), restricts the number of categories to a fixed number (usually eleven). It provides most of the information of the own-categories procedure (and difficulty of construction), and also some of the ease of evaluation of the method of ordered alternatives. A summary of latitude assessment instruments is represented in Table 6.1.

Social Judgment-Involvement Theory in Marketing

In addition to the application of SJI theory and/or the investigation of the related assimilation/contrast effects in satisfaction research previously discussed, SJI theory has served as a theoretical foundation for understanding a variety of marketing phenomena. For example, Monroe (1971) used the own-categories procedure of SJI in a partial replication of Sherif's (1961) investigation of reference scales for prices associated with clothing items. He found evidence that buyers have ranges of price acceptability, with prices *both above* and *below* (i.e., objectionably low) the acceptable range *judged to be objectionable.* Likewise, Raju (1977) found that consumers perceived price in three "chunks": unacceptably low, unacceptably high, and acceptable. Kalyanaram and Little (1994) integrated a number of the theories used in latitude research—that is, AL theory, prospect theory, and assimilation/contrast—in their investigation of a "region of indifference" (p. 408) around a reference price, which they equated to "adaptation level." Other latitude-related investigations of price can be found in Kosenko and Rahtz (1988); Lichtenstein, Bloc, and Black (1988); Rao and Sieben (1992); and Sorce and Widrick (1991).

In product class evaluation research, Naryana and Markin (1975) extended Campbell's (1969) notion of "evoked set" to an exhaustive, tripartite classification of "evoked set," "inert set," and "inept set," and found empirical support for the use of this classification schema by consumers. They (p. 3) note the similarity between their classification and "the Sherifs' trichotomy" of latitudes. Divine (1995) later elaborated on the similarities between LA and evoked set in an investigation of the relationship between involvement, "latitude of acceptance for price," "latitude of acceptance for attributes," and consideration set size.

Table 6.1

Social Judgment-Involvement Theory: Summary of Related Instruments

Procedure	Number of categories	Number of statements	Statement sort	Latitude determination
Own-categories procedure	Subject-determined	Varies: approx. 50–60	Yes: by similarity	Yes: after sort
Imposed categories procedures	Fixed: usually 11	Varies: approx. 50–60	Yes: by similarity	Yes: after sort
Method of ordered alternatives	Fixed: usually 9	Same as number of categories	None	Yes: primary task

Emerging Issues in Latitude Studies

From the above discussion, several assumptions underlying latitude models and/or patterns in the investigation of latitude-related phenomena seem to emerge. Several of the more prominent assumptions and patterns are discussed in the following sections. While highlighted separately, most are related.

Exclusive Investigation of the Latitude of Acceptance

Essentially all of the studies in the marketing literature that employ a latitude model assume the existence of a single latitude; that is, what is acceptable. This exclusive focus on acceptability may appear to be so obviously correct as to be unremarkable. However, it is contrary to the underlying theory and findings of SJI researchers, which suggest that not only are there latitudes of rejection and neutrality (noncommitment), but also that the dynamics of evaluation are often driven more by these latter two latitudes than by the LA (also cf. prospect theory). If the underlying model is assumed to be disconfirmation, and if the standard is assumed to have vector attributes (Teas 1993, 1994), this issue may be irrelevant. But as researchers move toward the adoption of latitude models, as appears to be the case, the investigation of the positive, negative, or neutral valence of the portion of evaluative domain that is "not acceptable" (or not satisfactory) becomes critical to understanding the evaluation process.

Correspondence of Zones and Latitudes

Related to the exclusive focus on the latitude of acceptability is the generally implied notion that all theoretical frameworks that support latitude models have a central focus on the same zone, that is, what is acceptable. This assumption does not appear to be well founded. Both AL and the reference point of prospect theory are explicitly neutral, therefore neither acceptable nor objectionable. They cannot be directly comparable to normative expectations such as "desired" service; of the zone of tolerance model, the "most acceptable position" of SJI (see Sherif, Sherif, and Nebergall 1965, p. 238); or "should" expectations used in various models. Similarly, if zones are the points surrounding, but perceptually equivalent to, ALs and reference points, they must also be neutral. In contrast, perceptions distinct from those considered neutral must be either positively or negatively charged.

This assumption that zone models are concerned with the same zone (acceptance) may be a product of the internalization of the disconfirmation paradigm, which, in spite of the theoretical possibility of simple confirmation, usually sees every judgment as either positive or negative. That is, evaluation is a binary variable.

However, when taken together, AL theory, prospect theory, the zone of tolerance model, and the various investigations of latitudes discussed above imply the possibility of at least three zones or latitudes: (1) a range of acceptability, (2) a range of objectionability, and (3) a range of neutrality. Only SJI explicitly models evaluative reference scales as including all three of these latitudes.

Relationship Between Standards and Latitudes

While similar standards are integral to the various latitude models, the role they play in defining latitudes falls into several different patterns. Some models see a standard as an *anchor* around which latitudes are formed, implying some perceptual distortion process such as assimilation, contrast, or both. Other models require no such distortion process; they see standards (often multiple) as serving as the *boundaries* for latitudes. In spite of the fact that SJI is a hybrid model that employs multiple standards and distortion processes, its inclusion in research in the marketing literature is usually limited to the use of a single standard and associated latitude (acceptability) with the implicit assumption that all of the evaluative reference scale outside of this latitude is negative.

Need for New Methods for Mapping Reference Scales

In spite of the tendency in the marketing literature toward the suggestion of latitude or zone models of evaluation, often incorporating multiple standards, there has been little development of assessment techniques that lend themselves to the exploration of (1) the organization of the underlying reference scale used in the evaluation process, potentially including latitudes, (2) the relative position of the multiple standards that have been proposed as anchors or boundaries, and (3) the apparent role of the standards. Most assessment techniques continue to assume disconfirmation processes and are designed to measure the discrepancy between a salient standard (e.g., expectation) and performance, either directly or indirectly. As noted, some have modeled disconfirmation of multiple standards such as expectations and desires, but have assumed a priori a vector-based disconfirmation process (e.g., Spreng and Mackoy 1996). Also as noted, Parasuraman, Zeithaml, and Berry (1994) did investigate alternative scales for assessing their zone of tolerance model of SQ, but the scales they investigated assumed both a disconfirmation model and that the zone of tolerance was bounded by standards that were determined a priori.

As discussed, SJI researchers developed techniques intended to reveal underlying reference scales used in evaluation, but to date, the application of these techniques has been limited to investigation of attitudes in relation to social issues and restricted to a limited number of standards that were of specific interest to SJI theory. With the partial exception of price evaluation as investigated by Sherif (1961) and partially replicated by Monroe (1971), they have not generally been used to investigate the evaluation of marketing stimuli and/or the full range of alternative standards proposed in the marketing literature.

What follows is a first attempt at modification of one of the SJI assessment techniques for revealing consumer references scales (individually or collectively). It is intended to address the specific concerns of CS/D and SQ researchers, especially those proposing the use of latitudes or zones in evaluation. An exploratory, empirical application of the techniques is also reported.

Reference Scale Instrument Development

As discussed, there are three methods generally associated with latitude assessment: own-categories, the method of ordered alternatives, and a hybrid method, imposed categories. Because of the advantages and disadvantages associated with each of these methods—also previously discussed—we used a modified form of own-categories in this study. The modification consists of the provision of eleven categories with the end categories (one and eleven) labeled as the extremes of the dimension under investigation—in the present case, restaurant waitperson friendliness. The instructions stipulate that these eleven categories represent the *maximum* number of categories rather than a required number. The specific instructions are discussed below. The modified own-categories technique requires the generation of approximately fifty statements representing varying levels of the dimension under investigation. These statements were generated and selected as part of a pretest.

Participants

The respondents used in the item-generation and selection process were members of an upper-division marketing class. All responses were provided on a voluntary basis, for which extra credit was awarded. Approximately sixty students participated in the item-generation and development tasks.

Item Generation and Selection

To generate an initial item pool of statements for the own categories procedure, respondents were first asked to provide a list of statements representing experienced or conceivable waitperson behaviors in a restaurant. Each respondent was asked for a minimum of twenty-two statements, two for each point on an eleven-point scale ranging from "extremely unfriendly" to "extremely friendly." The type of restaurant was left undefined. Specific instructions are shown in Appendix 6.1A.

The responses were edited to eliminate duplicates and ensure all statements were written in the present tense and degendered. The result was a pool of 149 statements. The complete list is shown in Appendix 6.1B. Later, these 149 refined statements were put on small cards and returned to the original respondents, along with eleven cards numbered one to eleven and instructions to sort the statements based on the level of unfriendliness or friendliness (see Appendix 6.1C).

Item Selection for Final Sort

Based on a review of SJI literature, there does not appear to be any standard procedure for selection of items for the final instrument. A number of the early studies (e.g., Hovland and Sherif 1952) employed the 114 items from the original pool used by Hinckley (see Sherif, Sherif, and Nebergall 1965) in Thurston scaling. Sherif and Hovland (1953, p. 137) noted "the statements were originally compiled to represent a range (of stands on the issue), with a large number representative of the middle range where variability of judgment is greater. The original items included a fair number which were too ambiguous to use in the final versions of the Hinckley scale, but were of interest for the present study." Sherif (1961) did not state the original source of her stimulus statements but did explain that she had students rate behavioral statements on an eleven-centimeter scale and found the median and interquartile range (Q1 and Q2) scores for each item. She (Sherif 1961, p. 59) then selected fifty items "designed to form an approximately rectilinear distribution for the three classifications 'perfectly acceptable,' 'intermediate,' and 'very unacceptable,'" plus some "new" statements. Reich and Sherif (1963) chose sixty statements from a pretested pool of 120, of which fifteen had been consistently judged as favorable, fifteen consistently judged as unfavorable, and thirty had been rated with high variability (Sherif, Sherif, and Nebergall 1965). Sherif, Sherif and Nebergall (1965, p. 125) did not give specific selection procedures but emphasized the need for " . . . a sufficient number of clear-cut statements at the extremes" and indicated that "a large number of intermediate items should be included, especially items with alternative interpretations (*judged with great variability*) or which are in some respect intermediate."

It should be clear that in one sense the purpose is not to scale items. In fact, what is partly required is to identify statements that *are not reliably scalable,* but are instead ambiguous and subject to displacement—for example, through assimilation-contrast—as a function of perceptual anchors. Therefore, a primary purpose is to identify and select items that would be eliminated because of low reliability if they were being scaled using traditional Thurston (Thurston and Chave 1929) techniques. These are the items that have a high degree of variability in placement. The exception to this "nonscaling" requirement is the need to identify a few items that are consistently rated (i.e., have very low variability) at the extremes. These items serve as anchors of extremity.

Given the above, the following guidelines were used for item selection:

1. A goal of approximately fifty items.
2. Select approximately four items at each extreme with medians close to the extremes (1 or 11) and with the *lowest variability possible.*
3. Select the maximum possible number of items with medians within one position of the midpoint (i.e., 5, 6, or 7) and *high variability.*
4. Select as many items as necessary to reach the target number of statements with medians 2, 3, or 4 and 8, 9, or 10, with *high variability* (keeping the positive and negative items approximately equal in number).
5. Fill in any unrepresented points with items having that median and the *maximum variability possible.*

Arguably, there are a number of reasonable variations of the above criteria that could be used while still following the strategy of first anchoring the extremes and then selecting the remainder of the items with the goal of maximizing the variability. For example, means could be used in lieu of medians for measures of central tendency. However, medians may be preferred to means since they are less influenced by outliers.

These guidelines do not specify a measure of variability. SJI studies typically used the interquartile range. This statistic could be used in the present study. Other candidates are variance (or standard deviation) and range. Additionally, because the overall goal is to select anchors on the basis of nonambiguity or relative certainty and to select nonanchor items on the basis of their relative ambiguity or uncertainty, a measure reflecting the *entropy* in item placement could also be used. A similar measure is the kurtosis (flatness or peakedness) of the distribution of item placement. There is no clearly superior option.

For this study, entropy was used as the measure of relative ambiguity or uncertainty with which an item was judged to be friendly or unfriendly. Arguably, it is a more pure measure of what interquartile range was intended to measure—that is, dispersion after adjusting for outliers. In the case of Thurston scaling, the interquartile range was intended as a measure of ambiguity for the purposes of item elimination. However, a high interquartile range could result from a distribution that is bimodal but flat in the middle, a condition that would reflect ambivalence rather than ambiguity. Kurtosis only measures flatness. Consequently, a flat distribution with a small range (or interquartile range) would produce a low measure of kurtosis, reflecting uncertainty. Entropy, however, may be viewed as a simultaneous measure of flatness and dispersion. As noted by Weisberg (1992):

> Entropy statistics are little used. . . . However, the theoretical basis of these statistics is very strong. Other nominal measures of spread have an ad hoc basis to them, whereas entropy statistics are elegantly based on information theory. A further advantage is that entropy statistics generalize readily to multiple variables, so uncertainty-based measures can be used to determine how much an explanatory variable helps reduce uncertainty as to the dependent-variable category in which a case holds.

The entropy measure in this study is the standardized form

$$S = -k \sum_{i-1}^{1} p \ln p$$

where S is entropy, k is a constant representing the maximum entropy possible (i.e., a statement had equal likelihood of being judged as belonging to each of its categories), and p is the probability that a statement will be judged as belonging to its category. At least in the present study, the items selected as anchors and ambiguous stimuli were extremely similar with respect to alternative indices. The relevant statistical information for each statement is shown in Appendix 6.1D. Based on these above criteria and procedures, fifty-four statements were chosen for use in the modified own-categories instrument (see Appendix 6.1C).

Scenario Definition

To provide a common context in which respondents could imagine themselves for the purpose of evaluating waitperson behaviors, while holding constant variables such as restaurant type, price, food quality, situational criticality, and servicescape, a restaurant service encounter scenario was developed. The scenario was pretested for realism. The scenario used in the primary study was:

> You and a casual acquaintance run into each other and begin to chat. In the course of the conversation, your acquaintance mentions that s/he is hungry; you realize that you are hungry also. On several occasions you have noticed a relatively new family restaurant across the street from where you are. Neither of you has previously been either to this particular restaurant or one with the same name. You suggest that you walk over and try it. Your acquaintance agrees.
> When you enter the restaurant you find that it looks about as you have anticipated, with simple but pleasant atmosphere, a sign asking you to "please wait to be seated," and a combination of booth and table seating with no tablecloths. You can see some of the food that other patrons are eating and observe that it looks acceptably appetizing and is served in an acceptable quantity for a family restaurant. You ask to see a menu and observe that it is

sufficiently varied so that each of you should be able to find something you would like to eat. The prices appear to be in line with the menu variety, the appearance and quantity of the food, and the general appearance and atmosphere of the restaurant. You suggest that you stay and try the restaurant and your friend agrees. The time it takes to be seated is reasonable.

This scenario could of course be varied and used in an experiment to investigate differences in reference scales as a function of various independent variables, such as restaurant type, situational criticality, and so forth.

Sorting Materials

Statement Cards

All statements of waitperson behaviors were printed on 8½" × 11" card stock with four statements across and five deep, resulting in statement cards approximately 43 mm by 69 mm when cut. In addition to the stimulus (waitperson behavior), the words "Statement Card" were printed on top and a small number representing the statement code was printed in parentheses in the bottom right-hand corner to facilitate data entry.

Category Cards

Similar to the printing of statement cards, individual cards were printed with the numbers "1" through "11" in the center and the word "Category Card" at the top. Additionally, the words "Extremely Unfriendly" and Extremely Friendly" were printed on cards numbered 1 and 11 respectively.

Card-Sort Instructions

The purpose of both the original SJI own-categories card-sort instrument and the modified instrument developed here is to provide maximum flexibility of response that allows the respondent to reveal his or her own evaluative reference scale. In the original SJI version, the respondent is asked first to sort the statements into as many or few stacks as appropriate according to their similarity on the dimension under study—in this case waitperson friendliness—and only then to indicate the most acceptable and most objectionable stacks, as well as any other acceptable and objectionable stacks, if any. In this modified version, the same general procedures are followed, but the "most acceptable" and "most objectionable" standards are augmented with other standards—for example, expected, deserved, desired, and minimally tolerable—frequently proposed in the marketing literature as influencing evaluation.

Specifically, the modified own-categories card-sort technique used in this study required the respondents to:

1. Look through all of the waitperson behavior statements.
2. Sort the statements into stacks based on their *similarity* in terms of their level of *friendliness.* The respondents are free to sort the statements into as few as one or as many as eleven stacks, as they feel appropriate.
3. Identify the *one stack* (and only one) that represents each of the following (*Note:* respondents are free to associate any single stack with multiple labels):

   a. The *most acceptable* level of friendliness given the scenario.
   b. The *most objectionable* level of friendliness given the scenario.
   c. The level of friendliness that they would *expect* given the scenario.
   d. The level of friendliness that they would *desire* given the scenario.
   e. The level of friendliness they *deserve* (should receive) given the situation.
   f. The service level that they feel is *minimum tolerable* given the scenario.
4. Identify as many (or as few) of the stacks, in addition to *most acceptable* and *most objectionable,* that represent behaviors that are *also acceptable* and *also objectionable* as the respondent judges appropriate given the situation.

Specific instructions for all of these tasks are provided in Appendix 6.2.

Primary Exploratory Study of Consumer Reference Scales

Sample

The sample consisted of seventy-six upper-division business students at a western U.S. university. Participation was voluntary and respondents were given extra credit for participating in the study. Participation took place outside of regularly scheduled classtime.

Materials

The materials used in this study consisted primarily of the instrument described in the previous section. The statement cards for the modified own-categories card-sort for waitperson friendliness were shuffled, banded with a rubber band, and put into a 10½" × 11¾" clear plastic bag. The category cards were banded together unshuffled and put into the same bag, together with the assembled written scenario and sorting instructions described in the previous section, and some questionnaire items not related to the present study.

Procedures

The respondents were asked to open the plastic bags and take out the materials. They were told that it was very important that they read the rest of the instructions very carefully and to complete all tasks in the exact order indicated by the instructions, and were instructed that if they had any problem understanding or completing any of the tasks to raise their hand and a researcher would assist them. They were then instructed to begin and to work at their own pace. The researcher was present during the entire time that the respondents were completing the required tasks to answer questions. Additionally, he circulated through the classroom to see if it looked as if anyone was having difficulty.

   Most respondents completed all tasks without assistance. A few respondents asked questions about further definitions of the scenario, such as the gender of the waitperson, or about specific waitperson friendliness behaviors. The researcher explained that neither the scenario nor the stimulus materials could be defined beyond the information provided. In a few instances it appeared to the researcher that respondents were having a problem with the required tasks. For example, some respondents were observed putting the materials from the card-sort back into the bag without sorting all of the items. In these cases the researcher intervened to correct the situation. In most instances, these problems occurred because the respondent inadvertently skipped one or

Table 6.2

Average Position of Standards and Latitude Boundaries

Standard/Latitude boundary	Average position
Most acceptable	8.59
Most objectionable	2.46
Expected	7.88
Desired	8.49
Deserved	7.35
Minimum tolerable	5.00
Latitude of acceptance—lower boundary	6.70
Latitude of acceptance—upper boundary	9.53
Latitude of objectionability (lower range)—lower boundary	1.47
Latitude of objectionability (lower range)—upper boundary	3.84
Latitude of objectionability (upper range)—lower boundary	10.56
Latitude of objectionability (upper range)—upper boundary	10.94

more instructions. The average total time to complete all of the tasks was approximately twenty minutes. Most respondents completed the tasks in less than thirty minutes.

Results and Discussion of Exploratory Study

The modified own-categories technique is potentially information rich. Among the measures available for analysis are (1) the number of categories (stacks) used in the sorting task; (2) the magnitude of the latitudes of acceptance, objectionability, and noncommitment, as measured by either the number of stacks included in the latitude (size) or the number of statements (density) included in the latitude; (3) the average position of the boundaries of the latitudes; (4) the average position of the standards (most acceptable, most desirable, expected, etc.); and (5) the relative position of latitude boundaries and the standards to each other.

Potentially, the first four of these lend themselves to dependent measures in experiments in which variables such as type of service (e.g., restaurant type), situational criticality, and prior attitude are systematically manipulated. In the present, exploratory study, the initial interest is in the apparent ability of the instrument to detect the underlying reference scale, the nature of that scale, and some indication of the relative position and apparent role of the various standards suggested in the marketing literature. Consequently, only the average position and relative placement of latitude boundaries and standards are analyzed here. The average position of the latitude boundaries and the standards are shown in Table 6.2 and graphically in Figure 6.2. Several patterns are immediately apparent.

Perhaps the most significant result is the appearance of three latitudes (acceptability, objectionability, and noncommitment). This tripartite latitude structure is particularly noteworthy because it is not demanded by the method. That is, the respondents are free to classify all stacks of statements as either acceptable or objectionable, making noncommitment an empty set. However, consistent with many SJI findings, approximately half of the reference scale is categorized as neither acceptable nor objectionable. Because the LNC is determined residually (i.e., defined by what is not categorized as acceptable or objectionable), it could be argued that it is partially a methodological artifact. However, the consistency with which it appears (within this study and across other studies), together with the fact that the size of the latitude of objectionability has been found to vary with varying levels of involvement, suggests otherwise. Regardless, the method

Figure 6.2   **Average Position of Latitudes and Standards (Friendliness)**

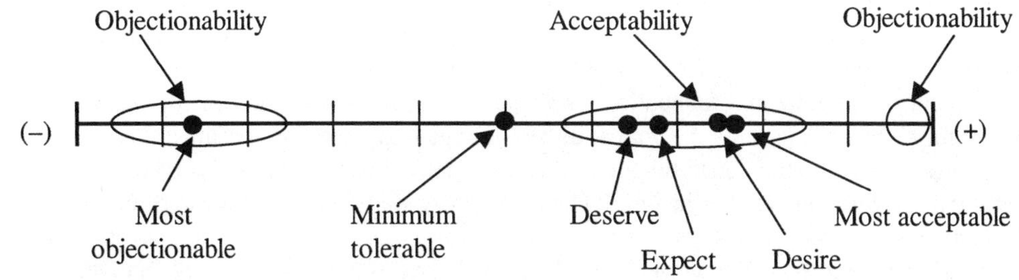

could be modified by asking respondents to specifically indicate the existence of neutrally valenced stacks of statements.

A second, and related, interesting pattern is the existence of part of the latitudes of noncommitment and objectionability above (more friendly than) the LA. Arguably, their existence implies a relatively high degree of discriminant validity that, in turn, argues against the LNC's resulting from response laziness. This may be especially true given the detection of too much friendliness—what might be called "hyperservice"—being objectionable. It is also consistent with both the theory and findings of SJI research.

The detection of hyperservice also seems to imply that positive standards such as "most acceptable" or "most desirable" serve as ideal points rather than having vector attributes as implied by the disconfirmation paradigm. Additional support for the ideal point nature of these standards is the apparent pattern that standards associated with the LA (including "deserved" and "expected") do not serve as latitude boundaries. This is inconsistent with the zone of tolerance model but is consistent with the SJI contention that standards serve as anchors. However, the results do seem to indicate that the LA may be anchored by multiple anchors, consistent with contemporary marketing literature, rather than by a single anchor as posited by SJI.

A further interesting pattern is the apparent relative positions of the various standards in relation to each other. At least in the present context, as noted, the standards of deserved, expected, most acceptable, and most desirable appear to be associated with the LA, with the former two standards and latter two standards roughly equivalent. In all cases, the standards appear to be serving as anchors rather than as latitude boundaries.

Contrary to the zone of tolerance model, the minimally tolerable standard does not appear to be associated with the LA but rather with the LNC. This latter indication is somewhat counterintuitive but may suggest an "AL" role, in which case its apparent role in anchoring the LNC would be consistent with Helson's (1959) findings and could represent an important extension of SJI's original findings. Clearly, all of these patterns require further investigation and the modified own-categories technique employed in this study needs replication and further development.

Conclusion

A review of models of evaluation from the marketing literature dealing with consumer satisfaction and SQ suggests much has been learned about these phenomena. The dominant research paradigm has modeled these processes as a linear function of disconfirmation of expectations. However, as this dominant paradigm has allowed us to learn more, it has also revealed its shortcomings. In fact, there is growing discontentment with the disconfirmation paradigm and beginning indications of convergence on a more complex model that may be characterized by (1) multiple comparison standards, which may (2) have ideal-point properties, and (3) latitudes or zones of acceptance and/or indifference. To date, however, no theoretic foundation has been identified for advancing the emerging model, and few instruments for investigating the model and addressing the many questions associated with it have been suggested.

SJI theory is a theoretical foundation with apparent similarities to the zone or latitude model that seems to be emerging. Its theoretical underpinnings may shed light on the issues associated with consumer evaluation. Additionally it has associated methods for investigating reference scales that may provide further insights. The exploratory study reported here appears to support this contention.

Social judgment theory, however, was developed for a limited range of evaluative stimuli, primarily the contemporary social issues of the 1960s and 1970s. The large body of research that has been undertaken by marketing scholars can potentially advance and extend the work begun by SJI researchers. Hopefully, this review and exploratory study is a step toward bringing those research streams together. Nonetheless, this review also raises at least as many research questions as it answers. Some of the research questions are:

1. What are the relevant standards of comparison?
2. What is the role of these standards; do they have vector attributes or serve as ideal points?
3. Are all latitudes associated with positive and negative evaluation, or do some latitudes represent neutrality?
4. What are the boundaries of latitudes and what is the relationship between standards and latitude boundaries?
5. What effect do such situational cues as price and servicescape have on latitude formation?
6. Does latitude structure change as a function of the level of ego-involvement with the service encounter?
7. What is the relationship between latitudes and postevaluative behavioral intentions and behaviors?
8. What is the impact of service-recovery on latitude structure?
9. Do consumers have different reference scales for brands with which they have experience and/or preference than for brands that are being evaluated for the first time?

It is our hope that others will find our review and the proposed methodology helpful as a framework for addressing these and many other issues related to assisting the marketing discipline to better understand the more complex aspects of consumer satisfaction and SQ.

Acknowledgment

The authors wish to thank Julie Baker, Fred Morgan, and Birud Sindhav for their helpful suggestions while preparing this manuscript.

Appendix 6.1A
Statement Generation Instructions

Your assistance with a marketing research project is requested. Two tasks are involved. The first task is outlined below and is due in one week. The second task will require a resorting of the items developed as part of the first task. It will be assigned later.

Task 1. The purpose of this task is to generate a *large number of statements* concerning the *activities* that you might observe of *service personnel in a restaurant*. It does not matter whether or not you have actually observed the behavior, just that it might occur. The specific types of statements of interest are ones that reflect various levels of *friendliness or unfriendliness*. The type of the restaurant does not matter; it may be fast-food, family, fine-dining, et cetera. It is preferable if the statements could apply to multiple types. Some examples of statements are:

1. The waitperson introduces her/himself by first name.
2. The waitperson does not smile at any time during the meal.
3. The waitperson comments that s/he likes the way that I am dressed.
4. The waitperson says s/he has better things to do than wait for me (us) to make up my (our) mind(s).
5. The waitperson sits down at the table and begins a conversation.

It is important that the statements reflect *a variety of different levels* of friendliness. You should think of an *eleven-point scale* ranging from extremely unfriendly (1) to neutral (6)—that is, neither friendly nor unfriendly—to extremely friendly (11), for example:

1	2	3	4	5	6	7	8	9	10	11
Extremely Unfriendly					Neutral				Extremely Friendly	

You should attempt to write *at least two statements* reflecting acts of service-encounter unfriendliness/friendliness for each of the eleven points on the scale (at least twenty-two total statements—more if possible). Because placement of all items on the scale is entirely subjective, there can be no correct or incorrect placement of items. What is important is that you try to come up with as many statements as possible that represent as many different levels of friendliness and unfriendliness as possible.

You may use any source you desire to come up with the statements. In fact, you are encouraged to use multiple sources. Some possible sources are asking family members, asking friends, paying attention to the actions of service-encounter personnel, or thinking back to previous service encounters.

Some guidelines for statements are:

1. Use the present tense if possible.
2. Keep the language of the statements simple, clear, and direct.
3. Each statement should contain only one complete thought; when possible avoid complex and compound sentences.
4. Remember that you are selecting and rating the statements on the basis of friendliness, not appropriateness—that is, you may rate an act as extremely friendly even though you would find the act inappropriate for service-encounter personnel in most situations.

Appendix 6.1B
Friendliness Statements Item Pool

Number	Statement
(1)	The waitperson apologizes repeatedly for a minor error on your order.
(2)	The waitperson asks your first name.
(3)*	The waitperson asks if you smoke.
(4)	The waitperson begins a conversation with you.
(5)*	The waitperson begins talking to someone else while you are ordering.
(6)	The waitperson clears your meal without asking if you are finished.
(7)*	The waitperson comments, "I've enjoyed serving you tonight."
(8)	The waitperson comments on the food.
(9)*	The waitperson comments that your clothes are out of fashion.
(10)*	The waitperson complains about the problems s/he is having today.
(11)	The waitperson compliments you on your smile.
(12)	The waitperson discusses the weather with you.
(13)	The waitperson does not converse about anything except your order.
(14)	The waitperson does not initiate any conversation.
(15)	The waitperson does not introduce herself (himself).
(16)	The waitperson does not make eye contact with you.
(17)	The waitperson doesn't say anything when s/he brings your meal.
(18)	The waitperson greets you immediately.
(19)	The waitperson hurries.
(20)	The waitperson ignores you.
(21)*	The waitperson introduces you to another waitperson who is a friend of his (hers).
(22)*	The waitperson is very efficient.
(23)	The waitperson is very methodical.
(24)	The waitperson jokes a lot.
(25)	The waitperson jokes about your appearance.
(26)*	The waitperson makes teasing and joking comments.
(27)	The waitperson makes occasional comments about his (her) job.
(28)	The waitperson makes insulting jokes about the other staff.
(29)	The waitperson makes conversation with you.
(30)	The waitperson makes small talk with you every time s/he comes by the table.
(31)	The waitperson never smiles.
(32)	The waitperson offers his (her) own food recommendations without being asked.
(33)	The waitperson provides advice concerning the menu.
(34)	The waitperson recommends his (her) favorite menu item without being asked.
(35)	The waitperson says, "Howdy."
(36)	The waitperson says very little.
(37)	The waitperson seems preoccupied.
(38)*	The waitperson seems especially attracted to your companion.
(39)	The waitperson smiles occasionally.
(40)*	The waitperson swears at you.
(41)*	The waitperson takes your order without smiling.
(42)	The waitperson talks with you constantly.
(43)	The waitperson tells a joke.
(44)	The waitperson will not provide information about the items on the menu.
(45)	The waitperson remains silent unless asked a direct question.
(46)*	The waitperson suggests that there is a better restaurant down the street.
(47)*	The waitperson laughs when s/he accidentally spills a drink on you.
(48)	The waitperson does not smile at all.
(49)	The waitperson says, "If you need anything just holler."
(50)*	The waitperson asks what your plans are for the evening.
(51)	The waitperson stoops down to be at eye level with you when taking your order.
(52)	The waitperson asks you to come back again.
(53)	The waitperson says, "I will be back in a moment."

(54)   The waitperson greets you with a big smile.
(55)*   The manager of the restaurant stops by the table and asks, "How is everything?"
(56)   The waitperson acts like a waitperson can act.
(57)   The waitperson comments that s/he cannot wait to get off work.
(58)   The waitperson asks if you need change.
(59)   The waitperson tells you to "Please come again."
(60)   The waitperson gets upset when you complain about a problem with the food.
(61)*   The waitperson comments s/he really dislikes waiting on you.
(62)   The waitperson takes your order but does not say anything.
(63)   The waitperson asks, "How are you doing today?"
(64)   The waitperson walks you to the door.
(65)*   The waitperson is very quick and efficient.
(66)*   The waitperson comes to the table every five minutes to see if everything is OK.
(67)*   The waitperson points out the least expensive items on the menu.
(68)*   The waitperson (of the opposite sex) flirts with you.
(69)   The waitperson does not thank you for your business.
(70)   The waitperson frowns when you ask for some extra sauce.
(71)*   The waitperson (of the opposite sex) gives you a kiss on the cheek when you leave.
(72)   The waitperson tells you, "Thank you; have a nice day."
(73)   The waitperson comments s/he is having a bad day and will be happy when it is over.
(74)   The waitperson smiles every time s/he comes to your table.
(75)   The waitperson tells you that s/he enjoyed waiting on you.
(76)   The waitperson tells you that s/he would rather be someplace else.
(77)*   The waitperson (of the opposite sex) hugs you when you leave.
(78)   The waitperson slams the food down in front of you.
(79)   The waitperson thanks you for coming in.
(80)*   The waitperson comments that your dress is inappropriate.
(81)*   The waitperson asks when your birthday is.
(82)   The waitperson comments on the time it takes you to order.
(83)   The waitperson comments that s/he just bought the same shirt you are wearing.
(84)   The waitperson asks if you would like some dessert.
(85)*   The waitperson suggests you may not like what you are ordering.
(86)*   The waitperson comments that s/he likes the way you are dressed.
(87)   The waitperson is obviously busy but looks up and says, "I'll be with you in a moment."
(88)*   The waitperson tells you about a lot of personal problems s/he has been having.
(89)*   The waitperson tells you that you made his (her) night very pleasant.
(90)   The waitperson waits quietly while you make up your mind.
(91)   The waitperson argues that if your meal is wrong, then you must have ordered incorrectly.
(92)   The waitperson explains things on the menu without being asked.
(93)   The waitperson hears you discussing a movie and tells you about several movies you
         must see.
(94)   The waitperson notices that you did not eat everything and asks if something is wrong.
(95)   The waitperson tells you s/he does not have time to wait on you.
(96)   The waitperson offers to replace any of your food if you do not like it.
(97)*   The waitperson writes a personal note of thanks on the check.
(98)*   The waitperson comes to your table once during your meal.
(99)   The waitperson says that what you ordered is one of his (her) favorites.
(100)*   The waitperson says, "What you are ordering is not on the menu!"
(101)   The waitperson pays more attention to other customers than to you.
(102)*   The waitperson asks a lot of personal questions.
(103)*   The waitperson gives you his (her) phone number and asks you to call.
(104)   The waitperson answers all of your questions patiently.
(105)   The waitperson helps you with your seat.
(106)   The waitperson shows you to your seat.
(107)   The waitperson frowns when s/he sees more customers entering the restaurant.
(108)*   The waitperson tells you that you should order from the light menu.
(109)   The waitperson tells you about the specials of the day.

(continued)

Appendix 6.1B *(continued)*

Number	Statement
(110)	The waitperson doesn't come to your table very often.
(111)*	The waitperson sits down at the table and talks with you.
(112)*	The waitperson stands next to your table and talks to you throughout your meal.
(113)*	The waitperson stands next to your table and watches you eat.
(114)	The waitperson asks how you like the restaurant.
(115)	The waitperson complains to you about the management.
(116)	The waitperson does not ask how the meal was once you are finished eating.
(117)	The waitperson explains the specials of the day.
(118)	The waitperson keeps you informed about the amount of time that you will be waiting.
(119)	After you pay for your meal, the waitperson says, "Thanks."
(120)	Having heard your first name mentioned, the waitperson uses it to address you.
(121)	The waitperson does not welcome you to the restaurant.
(122)	When you make a minor change to your order, the waitperson sighs.
(123)	The waitperson seems impatient for you to make a decision.
(124)	The waitperson seems in a hurry to get your order and move on to the next customer.
(125)*	The waitperson touches you when talking to you.
(126)	The waitperson speaks in a harsh tone.
(127)	The waitperson does not regularly check up on you during the meal.
(128)*	The waitperson tells you to hurry up and order.
(129)	When you enter the restaurant the waitperson looks at you but says nothing.
(130)	After your food is ready, the waitperson asks if you need anything else.
(131)	After you make your selection, the waitperson suggests that you have an additional item.
(132)*	The waitperson says, "What do you want?"
(133)	The waitperson asks if the food was OK.
(134)*	The waitperson explains that s/he went to a great party last night and has a terrible hangover.
(135)*	The waitperson tells you that you were wonderful customers.
(136)*	The waitperson says, "Let me know when you have made up your mind."
(137)*	The waitperson brings you some food you did not order and does not charge you.
(138)	The waitperson does not look at you while you order or ask questions.
(139)*	The waitperson gives you a dessert you did not order and insists, "You must try this."
(140)	When you leave, the waitperson thanks you for coming.
(141)	The waitperson says, "It's about time you made up your mind."
(142)	The waitperson says, "Others are waiting; you must hurry up."
(143)	The waitperson says, "Hi, how are you doing?"
(144)	The waitperson shakes your hand when you leave.
(145)	The waitperson suggests a place for you to spend the evening.
(146)	The waitperson argues with you about your order.
(147)	The waitperson does not reply to your statement about the weather.
(148)	The waitperson does not respond to your joking comments.
(149)	The waitperson tells you to enjoy your meal.

Note: (* = used in final instrument)

Appendix 6.1C
Instructions for Initial Statement Screening Sort

You should have an envelope that contains the following items:

1. A set of eleven cards numbered 1–11,
2. A set of cards with statements printed on them,
3. Some rubber bands,
4. A card with some questions on it.

Please complete the following tasks without assistance from anyone else.

1. Take out the set of numbered cards from the envelope. Put the card with a 1 on it at your extreme left and spread out the rest of the cards in order (1–11) from left to right.
2. Take out the cards with statements printed on them and *look through them* to get an idea of the kind of statements with which you will be working. Each statement is a brief description of the behavior of a waitperson in a restaurant. Ignore the small number after the statement; it does not relate to your task.
3. Your primary task is to sort the statements in terms of the degree of FRIENDLINESS represented by the behavior (you should ignore whether you consider the behavior to be appropriate or inappropriate). You do this sorting by placing the statements on the numbered cards as follows.
   a. If you find any statements representing behaviors that you consider to be EXTREMELY UNFRIENDLY, you should place them on the card numbered 1.
   b. If you find any statements representing behaviors that you consider to be EXTREMELY FRIENDLY, you should place them on the card numbered 11.
   c. Place all other statements on the cards numbered 2–10 according to the degree of unfriendliness (2–5) or friendliness (10–7) represented by the behavior, with statements of behaviors that are neither friendly nor unfriendly placed on the card numbered 6.

You should try *to place statements on all of the eleven numbered cards,* if appropriate. However, you are not required to use all eleven categories. You may move statements around as much as you wish.

IT IS *VERY IMPORTANT* TO REMEMBER THAT YOU ARE SORTING THE STATEMENTS ACCORDING TO THE *DEGREE OF FRIENDLINESS* THAT EACH BEHAVIOR REPRESENTS, *NOT* WHETHER YOU VIEW THE BEHAVIOR TO BE *APPROPRIATE OR INAPPROPRIATE.*

Appendix 6.1D

Selected Statistics for Original Item Pool

State	n	M	SD	Quartile 3	Median	Quartile 1	Range	IQR	Selected–IQR	Entropy	Standard entropy	Kurtosis	Selected–entropy
001	41	7.83	2.13	9.00	8.00	7.00	10.00	2.00	—	1.97	.82	1.3783	9.00
002	40	7.18	2.19	9.00	7.50	6.00	8.00	3.00	9	1.79	.75	4.8147	6.00
003	41	5.63	1.26	6.00	6.00	6.00	7.00	.00	—	1.02	.42	1.5878	—
004	39	8.56	1.17	9.00	8.00	8.00	4.00	1.00	—	1.40	.58	.4003	—
005	39	2.43	1.33	4.00	2.00	1.00	4.00	3.00	3	1.48	.62	1.0174	—
006	39	3.28	1.52	4.00	3.00	2.00	5.00	2.00	—	1.73	.72	.8574	3.00
007	40	9.40	1.08	10.00	9.50	8.00	3.00	2.00	9	.91	.38	1.2754	11.00
008	40	6.60	1.50	7.50	6.00	6.00	9.00	1.50	—	1.52	.63	2.2462	—
009	41	1.41	.67	2.00	1.00	1.00	2.00	1.00	1	.82	.34	.6774	1.00
010	41	3.95	1.90	5.00	4.00	3.00	10.00	2.00	3	1.74	.72	3.4522	—
011	40	9.13	1.22	10.00	9.00	8.00	5.00	2.00	—	1.21	.50	.2951	—
012	41	7.07	.88	8.00	7.00	6.00	3.00	2.00	—	1.03	.43	.2049	—
013	41	5.07	.93	6.00	5.00	5.00	3.00	1.00	—	1.18	.49	.2293	—
014	40	4.70	.94	5.00	5.00	4.00	3.00	1.00	—	1.29	.54	.6641	—
015	40	4.30	1.30	5.00	4.50	3.00	4.00	2.00	—	1.56	.65	.9050	—
016	41	4.10	1.10	5.00	4.00	4.00	4.00	1.00	—	1.36	.57	.0307	—
017	39	3.90	1.37	5.00	4.00	3.00	5.00	2.00	—	1.66	.69	.6091	—
018	41	8.63	1.48	9.00	9.00	7.00	5.00	2.00	—	1.87	.78	.8615	9.00
019	37	5.58	1.66	6.00	6.00	5.00	7.00	1.00	—	1.75	.73	.2840	6.00
020	41	2.34	1.26	3.00	2.00	1.00	4.00	2.00	—	1.49	.62	.5472	—
021	40	7.05	2.42	9.00	8.00	5.50	10.00	3.50	9	1.63	.68	.4558	—
022	41	8.22	1.74	10.00	8.00	6.00	6.00	4.00	9	1.49	.62	1.1222	—
023	41	6.73	1.47	7.00	6.00	6.00	6.00	1.00	—	1.36	.57	.1818	—
024	41	6.95	2.46	9.00	8.00	6.00	10.00	3.00	—	2.14	.89	.0697	9.00
025	39	1.79	1.38	2.00	1.00	1.00	7.00	1.00	—	1.14	.48	10.0842	—
026	39	4.49	2.59	7.00	4.00	2.00	8.00	5.00	3	1.94	.81	1.3257	3.00
027	41	4.98	1.35	6.00	5.00	4.00	6.00	2.00	—	1.55	.65	.3704	—
028	41	2.66	1.39	4.00	3.00	1.00	5.00	3.00	3	1.62	.67	.6995	—
029	41	8.32	1.24	9.00	8.00	7.00	5.00	2.00	—	1.30	.54	.1833	—
030	40	7.70	1.79	9.00	8.00	7.00	6.00	2.00	—	1.76	.73	.6652	—
031	41	3.39	1.20	4.00	4.00	3.00	4.00	1.00	—	1.52	.63	.7334	—
032	41	7.17	1.20	8.00	7.00	6.00	5.00	2.00	—	1.29	.54	.1157	—
033	40	7.83	1.30	9.00	8.00	7.00	6.00	2.00	—	1.89	.79	.0199	—
034	41	7.98	1.37	9.00	8.00	7.00	5.00	2.00	—	1.49	.62	.5580	—

035	40	6.75	1.98	8.00	7.00	6.00	10.00	2.00		1.72	.72	1.1682	—
036	41	4.39	1.12	5.00	4.00	4.00	4.00	1.00		1.46	.61	.5515	—
037	41	4.51	1.34	5.00	5.00	4.00	6.00	1.00	3	1.58	.66	.9262	3.00
038	41	3.22	2.16	5.00	3.00	1.00	9.00	4.00		1.76	.73	.6060	—
039	37	6.14	1.46	7.00	1.00	6.00	7.00	1.00	1	1.46	.61	2.0964	1.00
040	40	1.23	.73	1.00	1.00	1.00	3.00	1.00		.43	.18	10.0910	—
041	39	4.03	1.11	5.00	4.00	3.00	5.00	2.00	6	1.46	.61	1.2362	6.00
042	40	6.73	2.59	9.00	7.00	5.00	10.00	4.00		2.23	.93	.8299	—
043	40	7.78	1.49	8.50	8.00	7.00	7.00	1.50		1.50	.63	.4904	—
044	38	2.71	1.04	3.00	3.00	2.00	4.00	1.00	6	1.42	.59	.2622	6.00
045	41	4.73	1.38	6.00	5.00	4.00	6.00	2.00	6	1.62	.67	1.0913	3.00
046	41	4.68	2.34	6.00	5.00	3.00	8.00	3.00	3	2.01	.84	.9633	—
047	39	2.51	1.50	4.00	2.00	1.00	5.00	3.00		1.60	.67	.2317	6.00
048	41	3.32	1.33	4.00	4.00	2.00	5.00	2.00	6	1.60	.67	.7552	—
049	40	6.63	2.14	8.00	7.00	5.50	9.00	2.50		1.95	.81	1.4450	—
050	40	7.50	1.66	9.00	7.00	6.00	7.00	3.00		1.75	.73	.5953	6.00
051	40	7.88	2.01	9.50	8.00	7.00	10.00	2.50		1.27	.53	3.7686	—
052	40	8.28	1.30	9.00	8.00	7.00	5.00	2.00	6	1.76	.73	.3429	—
053	40	6.40	1.32	7.00	6.00	6.00	8.00	2.00		1.25	.52	6.7528	—
054	41	9.07	1.40	10.00	9.00	8.00	5.00	2.00	9	1.56	.65	.8377	9.00
055	39	9.44	1.43	11.00	9.00	8.00	5.00	3.00		1.43	.59	.6703	—
056	40	6.45	1.08	7.00	6.00	6.00	5.00	1.00		1.11	.46	2.7031	—
057	41	4.05	1.64	5.00	4.00	3.00	6.00	2.00		1.81	.76	1.0109	3.00
058	40	6.10	2.22	7.00	6.00	5.50	9.00	1.50		1.76	.73	.4130	6.00
059	40	8.10	1.68	9.00	8.00	7.00	10.00	2.00		1.50	.63	7.1697	—
060	41	2.44	1.23	3.00	2.00	2.00	6.00	1.00	1	1.42	.59	3.3049	1.00
061	40	1.25	.74	1.00	1.00	1.00	4.00	.00		.55	.23	17.2765	—
062	39	4.82	1.43	5.00	5.00	4.00	9.00	1.00		1.46	.61	4.5430	—
063	41	7.98	1.23	9.00	8.00	7.00	5.00	2.00		1.71	.71	.6131	—
064	41	7.78	1.12	8.00	7.00	7.00	10.00	1.00		1.04	.44	.8495	—
065	41	8.76	1.96	10.00	9.00	8.00	6.00	2.00	9	1.29	.54	4.9000	9.00
066	40	8.03	1.80	10.00	8.00	6.00	10.00	4.00	9	1.37	.57	1.4064	6.00
067	38	8.34	2.41	10.00	9.00	7.00	10.00	3.00	6	1.68	.70	1.9027	9.00
068	38	5.53	2.35	7.00	6.00	4.00	9.00	3.00	9	1.95	.81	.5234	—
069	40	7.45	3.08	10.00	8.00	6.00	10.00	4.00		1.94	.81	.1113	3.00
070	39	3.87	1.40	5.00	4.00	3.00	7.00	2.00	9	1.60	.67	1.2758	9.00
	41	2.54	1.23	3.00	2.00	2.00	4.00	1.00		1.52	.63	.7355	3.00
			.80	11.00	10.00	5.00	10.00	6.00	9	1.60	.67	1.1052	9.00
					7.00	7.00	6.00	3.00		1.31	.54	.4403	—

(continued)

Appendix 6.1D *(continued)*

State	n	M	SD	Quartile 3	Median	Quartile 1	Range	IQR	Selected-IQR	Entropy	Standard entropy	Kurtosis	Selected-entropy
074	41	4.29	1.62	5.00	4.00	3.00	7.00	2.00	—	1.84	.77	.3512	3.00
075	39	9.05	1.21	10.00	9.00	8.00	4.00	2.00	—	1.02	.43	1.0800	—
076	41	8.98	1.42	10.00	9.00	8.00	6.00	2.00	—	1.28	.53	.2597	—
077	38	3.21	1.40	4.00	3.00	2.00	5.00	2.00	—	1.66	.69	.5932	9.00
078	41	7.98	3.72	11.00	10.00	6.00	10.00	5.00	9	1.47	.61	.6557	9.00
079	41	1.73	1.16	2.00	1.00	1.00	5.00	1.00	—	1.15	.48	4.5530	—
080	38	8.13	1.28	9.00	8.00	7.00	5.00	2.00	—	1.45	.60	.0282	—
081	41	1.63	.92	2.00	1.00	1.00	3.00	1.00	1	1.05	.44	.3917	1.00
082	39	7.36	2.07	9.00	7.00	6.00	10.00	3.00	6	1.70	.71	1.3468	—
083	40	3.43	1.95	4.00	3.00	2.00	8.00	2.00	—	1.68	.70	1.8274	—
084	41	7.66	1.91	9.00	8.00	7.00	9.00	2.00	—	1.92	.80	.7114	—
085	40	7.03	1.14	8.00	7.00	6.00	5.00	2.00	—	1.13	.47	2.3444	6.00
086	41	5.66	1.91	7.00	6.00	4.00	8.00	3.00	6	1.88	.78	.0310	6.00
087	41	9.34	1.41	10.00	10.00	9.00	6.00	1.00	11	1.02	.42	1.9190	11.00
088	40	8.10	1.55	9.00	8.00	7.00	7.00	2.00	—	1.41	.59	.2046	—
089	41	4.27	2.11	5.00	4.00	3.00	9.00	2.00	3	1.98	.83	.3892	3.00
090	40	9.75	1.03	11.00	10.00	9.00	4.00	2.00	11	.98	.41	.1806	11.00
091	39	7.26	1.35	8.00	7.00	6.00	5.00	2.00	—	1.43	.59	.3132	—
092	41	1.78	1.19	2.00	1.00	1.00	6.00	1.00	—	1.14	.47	8.0598	—
093	40	7.43	1.52	8.00	8.00	6.00	6.00	2.00	—	1.51	.63	.4068	—
094	39	7.64	2.23	9.00	8.00	7.00	9.00	2.00	—	1.49	.62	1.1722	—
095	41	7.10	1.69	8.00	7.00	6.00	9.00	2.00	—	1.59	.66	3.2853	—
096	40	1.90	1.06	3.00	1.50	1.00	3.00	2.00	—	1.22	.51	.7895	—
097	41	8.80	1.66	10.00	9.00	8.00	10.00	2.00	—	1.16	.48	11.5124	—
098	41	9.20	1.50	10.00	10.00	8.00	5.00	2.00	11	1.23	.51	.7538	9.00
099	40	4.20	2.02	5.50	4.00	2.00	9.00	3.50	3	1.79	.75	.6531	—
100	39	8.49	1.35	9.00	8.00	8.00	5.00	1.00	3	1.52	.63	.5394	3.00
101	40	3.08	1.91	4.00	3.00	1.00	7.00	3.00	—	1.77	.74	.4069	—
102	41	2.83	1.14	4.00	3.00	2.00	4.00	2.00	—	1.39	.58	.8714	—
103	40	5.18	2.98	7.50	5.00	2.00	10.00	5.50	6	1.99	.83	1.0458	6.00
104	41	7.54	3.56	11.00	8.00	5.00	10.00	6.00	9	1.89	.79	.8254	—
105	41	8.73	1.64	10.00	9.00	8.00	8.00	2.00	—	1.29	.54	2.2359	—
106	38	8.84	1.37	10.00	9.00	8.00	4.00	2.00	—	1.43	.60	1.0962	—
107	41	6.93	1.33	7.00	7.00	6.00	7.00	1.00	—	1.25	.52	2.1465	—
108	40	3.18	1.20	4.00	3.00	2.00	4.00	2.00	—	1.52	.63	.0823	—
109	40	2.68	2.06	4.00	2.00	1.00	7.00	3.00	3	1.50	.63	.2830	—

ID														
110	40	7.00	1.28	7.00	7.00	6.00	4.00	1.00	—	1.12	.47	.3974	—	—
111	40	3.88	1.38	5.00	4.00	3.00	6.00	2.00	—	1.65	.69	.6426	—	—
112	40	8.33	2.75	11.00	9.00	7.00	10.00	4.00	9	1.71	.72	.8689	9.00	9.00
113	41	5.90	3.27	9.00	5.00	3.00	10.00	6.00	6	2.14	.89	.1266	6.00	6.00
114	40	3.10	1.88	4.50	3.00	1.00	7.00	3.50	3	1.77	.74	.4414	3.00	3.00
115	40	7.83	1.20	8.00	8.00	7.00	5.00	1.00	—	1.12	.47	1.9060	—	—
116	39	3.69	1.59	5.00	4.00	3.00	5.00	2.00	—	1.55	.65	.7022	—	—
117	41	4.51	1.50	5.00	4.00	4.00	8.00	1.00	—	1.52	.64	3.0873	—	—
118	39	7.36	1.39	8.00	7.00	6.00	4.00	2.00	—	1.06	.44	.3417	—	—
119	38	7.66	1.36	9.00	8.00	7.00	6.00	2.00	—	1.67	.70	.2386	—	—
120	40	8.00	1.81	9.00	8.00	7.00	9.00	2.00	—	1.56	.65	2.2410	—	9.00
121	41	7.85	2.07	9.00	8.00	7.00	10.00	2.00	—	1.94	.81	2.1499	9.00	—
122	41	3.56	1.43	5.00	4.00	3.00	5.00	2.00	—	1.59	.66	.7291	—	—
123	40	2.70	1.30	4.00	3.00	2.00	4.00	2.00	—	1.57	.65	1.0540	—	—
124	40	3.40	1.26	4.00	3.00	3.00	7.00	1.00	—	1.45	.60	3.7630	—	—
125	41	3.37	1.32	4.00	3.00	2.00	6.00	2.00	6	1.64	.68	.2338	—	6.00
126	41	7.00	2.67	9.00	7.00	5.00	10.00	4.00	—	2.10	.88	.2885	6.00	3.00
127	38	2.58	1.52	3.00	2.00	1.00	7.00	2.00	—	1.58	.66	3.4146	3.00	—
128	39	4.23	1.39	5.00	5.00	4.00	7.00	1.00	3	1.64	.68	.9491	—	—
129	41	3.80	1.23	5.00	4.00	3.00	6.00	2.00	—	1.55	.65	.2516	—	—
130	41	2.05	1.59	3.00	2.00	1.00	9.00	2.00	—	1.18	.49	15.6510	—	—
131	41	3.93	1.46	5.00	4.00	3.00	8.00	2.00	6	1.49	.62	3.0231	6.00	—
132	40	8.10	1.30	9.00	8.00	7.00	5.00	2.00	3	1.51	.63	.8992	3.00	6.00
133	39	6.08	1.83	8.00	6.00	5.00	7.00	3.00	—	1.70	.71	.1361	—	3.00
134	39	2.67	1.64	4.00	2.00	1.00	6.00	3.00	6	1.70	.71	.1068	6.00	—
135	41	7.37	1.28	8.00	7.00	7.00	7.00	1.00	3	1.76	.73	2.0790	3.00	6.00
136	41	4.29	2.02	6.00	8.00	2.00	7.00	4.00	6	1.97	.82	1.1371	6.00	11.00
137	41	9.85	1.39	11.00	10.00	9.00	6.00	2.00	11	.95	.40	3.6809	11.00	6.00
138	40	6.13	2.42	8.00	6.00	5.00	9.00	3.00	6	1.88	.78	.5982	6.00	—
139	39	8.26	2.45	10.00	9.00	7.00	5.00	3.00	9	1.41	.59	2.5788	9.00	—
140	39	3.85	1.65	5.00	4.00	3.00	7.00	2.00	—	1.62	.67	1.4672	—	6.00
141	41	6.24	3.33	9.00	6.00	3.00	10.00	6.00	6	2.09	.87	1.4491	6.00	—
142	38	8.42	1.22	9.00	8.50	7.00	5.00	2.00	—	1.36	.57	.9173	—	—
143	39	1.77	1.13	2.00	1.00	1.00	5.00	1.00	—	1.14	.48	5.0816	—	—
144	41	1.76	.97	2.00	2.00	7.00	4.00	1.00	—	1.15	.48	2.5331	—	—
145	40	8.05	1.30	9.00	8.00	9.00	5.00	2.00	—	1.40	.58	.1798	—	—
146	41	8.54	1.57	10.00	9.00	8.00	7.00	2.00	—	1.39	.58	.6943	—	—
147	41	7.76	1.53	9.00	8.00	7.00	7.00	2.00	—	1.76	.73	.2983	—	—
148	40	1.98	1.05	6.00	2.00	1.00	4.00	2.00	—	1.30	.54	.2686	—	—
149	40	3.85	1.17	5.00	4.00	3.00	5.00	2.00	—	1.42	.59	.8595	—	—
150	40	4.43	1.30	5.00	4.00	3.50	6.00	1.50	—	1.58	.66	.0783	—	—
151	39	7.77	1.16	8.00	7.00	7.00	5.00	1.00	—	1.18	.49	1.7440	—	—

Appendix 6.2
Card-Sort Instructions

**PLEASE DO NOT GO ON TO THE NEXT PAGE
UNTIL YOU HAVE FINISHED ALL OF THE INSTRUCTIONS BELOW**

You should have an envelope that contains the following items.

1. A set of eleven "CATEGORY" cards numbered 1–11,
2. A set of "STATEMENT" cards with times (in minutes) printed on them,
3. Some rubber bands.

While imagining yourself in the situation presented, please complete and check off the following tasks:

___ 1. Take the set of CATEGORY cards out of the envelope. Put the card with a 1 on it at your extreme left and spread out the rest of the cards in order (1–11) from left to right, like this:

1   2   3   4   5   6   7   8   9   10   11
Extremely Unfriendly   Extremely Friendly

___ 2. Take out the STATEMENT cards. Each card is a statement of the **WAITPERSON BEHAVIOR** in the restaurant described in the situation. Look through them to get an idea of the kind of statements with which you will be working. Ignore the small number after the time; it is not related to your task.

___ 3. Your task is to sort *all* of the STATEMENT cards in terms of the degree of FRIENDLINESS AND UNFRIENDLINESS of the waitperson *in the context of the situation presented to you.* You do this sorting by placing the STATEMENT cards behind the CATEGORY cards (1–11) as follows:

___ a.   If you find any behaviors that you consider to be **EXTREMELY TOO UNFRIENDLY** given the situation, you should place them behind the card numbered 1. *You are not required to use this category if no statement(s) fit(s) its description.*

___ b.   If you find any behaviors that you consider to be **EXTREMELY TOO FRIENDLY** given the situation, you should place them behind the card numbered 11. *You are not required to use this category if no statement(s) fit(s) its description.*

___ c.   Place all other STATEMENT cards behind the CATEGORY cards according to the degree to which you feel they represent serving times that are similarly UNFRIENDLY or FRIENDLY given the situation presented to you.

NOTE: You are not required to use all of the categories: you should USE AS FEW OR AS MANY (up to eleven) OF THE CATEGORIES as you feel appropriate so that statements that belong together are in the same stack. You may move statements around as much as you wish.

___ 4. After you have sorted all of the statements to your satisfaction, put the CATEGORY cards on top.

WHEN YOU HAVE FINISHED ALL OF THE ABOVE

PLEASE GO TO THE NEXT PAGE
PLEASE DO NOT GO ON TO THE NEXT PAGE
UNTIL YOU HAVE FINISHED ALL OF THE TASKS BELOW

Mark the <u>CATEGORY cards</u> according to the following instructions. *It may be necessary to make more than one mark on a CATEGORY card*; you may make as many marks on each category as you find appropriate.

1.   __ A.   Select the *one stack* of STATEMENT cards that represents the waitperson behavior(s) that you find most acceptable, given the situation presented. Put two checks (✓ ✓) on the associated CATEGORY card.
   __ B.   If there is <u>another stack or stacks</u> that represent waitperson behavior(s) that you also find acceptable, put a <u>single check </u>(✓) on the associated CATEGORY card(s). Mark as *many or as few* as you feel appropriate.

2.   __ A.   Select the <u>one stack</u> of STATEMENT cards that represents the waitperson behavior(s) that you find most objectionable, given the situation presented. Put <u>two Xs</u> (XX) on the associated CATEGORY card.
   __ B.   If there is <u>another stack or stacks</u> that represent(s) waitperson behavior(s) that you <u>also find objectionable</u>, put a <u>single X</u> (X) on the associated CATEGORY card(s). Mark as *many or as few* as you feel appropriate.

For the following instructions (3–6) mark only one CATEGORY card.

__ 3. Place an "E" on the CATEGORY card of the *one stack* representing the waitperson behavior(s) *you would EXPECT* given the situation.

__ 4. Place a "D" on the CATEGORY card of the *one stack* representing the waitperson behavior(s) *you would DESIRE* given the situation.

__ 5. Place an "MT" on the CATEGORY card of the *one stack* representing the waitperson behavior(s) *you would consider the MINIMUM TOLERABLE* given the situation.

__ 6. Place an "S" on the CATEGORY card of the *one stack* representing the waitperson behavior(s) *you would feel you would DESERVE* given the situation.

WHEN YOU HAVE FINISHED THE ABOVE PLEASE <u>PLACE A RUBBER BAND</u>
<u>AROUND EACH STACK</u>, <u>PUT THE STACKS IN THE ENVELOPE</u>,
AND THEN <u>GO TO THE NEXT PAGE</u>

References

Anderson, R.E. (1973), "Consumer Dissatisfaction: The Effect of Disconfirmed Expectancy on Perceived Product Performance," *Journal of Marketing Research*, 10 (February), 38–44.

Bitner, Mary Jo and Amy R. Hubbert (1994), "Encounter Satisfaction Versus Overall Satisfaction Versus Quality," in *Service Quality: New Dimensions in Theory and Practice*, R.T. Rust and R.L. Oliver, eds. Thousand Oaks, CA: Sage.

Bleuel, Bill (1990), "Customer Dissatisfaction and the Zone of Uncertainty," *Journal of Services Marketing*, 4 (Winter), 49–52.

Bolton, R.N. and J.H. Drew (1991), "A Multistage Model of Customers' Assessments of Service Quality and Value," *Journal of Consumer Research*, 17 (March), 375–84.

Boulding, William, Ajay Kalra, Richard Staelin, and Valerie Zeithaml (1993), "A Dynamic Process Model of Service Quality: From Expectations to Behavioral Intentions," *Journal of Marketing Research*, 15 (February), 7–21.

Cadotte, Ernest R. and Normand Turgeon (1988), "Key Factors in Guest Satisfaction," *The Cornell Hotel and Restaurant Administration Quarterly*, 28 (4), 44–51.

Campbell, B.M. (1969), "The Existence of Evoked Set and Determinants of Its Magnitude in Brand Choice Behavior," doctoral dissertation, Columbia University.

Cardoza, Richard N. (1965), "An Experimental Study of Customer Effort, Expectation, and Satisfaction," *Journal of Marketing Research*, 2 (August), 244–49.

Carlsmith, Elliott and J. Merrill Aronson (1963), "Some Hedonic Consequences of the Confirmation and Disconfirmation of Expectancies," *Journal of Abnormal and Social Psychology*, 66 (2), 151–56.

Carman, James M. (1990), "Consumer Perceptions of Service Quality: An Assessment of the SERVQUAL Dimensions," *Journal of Retailing*, 66 (1), 33–55.

Chase, Richard B. and David E. Bowen (1991), "Service Quality and the Service Delivery System: A Diagnostic Framework," in *Service Quality: Multidisciplinary and Multinational Perspectives,* S.W. Brown, E. Gummesson, B. Edvardson, and B. Gustavsson, eds. Lexington, MA: D.C. Heath.

Cronin, T.J. and S.A. Taylor (1992), "Measuring Service Quality: A Re-examination and Extension," *Journal of Marketing*, 56 (July), 55–68.

Dabholkar, Pratibha, A., C. Davis Shepard, and Doyle I. Thorpe (2000), "A Comprehensive Framework for Service Quality: An Investigation of Critical Conceptual and Measurement Issues through a Longitudinal Study," *Journal of Retailing*, 76 (Summer), 139–73.

Day, Ralph L. (1976), "Toward a Process Model of Consumer Satisfaction," in *Conceptualization and Measurement of Consumer Satisfaction and Dissatisfaction*, H. Keith Hunt, ed. Cambridge, MA: National Science Foundation.

Divine, Richard L. (1995), "The Influence of Price on the Relationship Between Involvement and Consideration Set Size," *Marketing Letters*, 6 (4), 309–19.

Elbing, A.O. (1962), "An Experimental Investigation of the Influence of Reference Group Identification on Role Playing as Applied to Business," doctoral dissertation, University of Washington.

Fechner, G.T. (1966), *Elements of Psychophysics.* Volume 1. Helmut E. Adler, trans. New York: Holt, Reinhart, and Winston.

Festinger, Leon (1957), *A Theory of Cognitive Dissonance.* Stanford CA: Stanford University Press.

Fishbein, M. and Icek Ajzen (1975), *Belief, Attitude, Intention, and Behavior: An Introduction to Theory and Research.* Reading, MA: Addison-Wesley.

Gronroos, Christian (1982), "Strategic Management and Marketing in the Service Sector," Research Report No. 8. Helsinki: Swedish School of Economics and Business Administration.

Helson, Harry (1959), "Adaptation Level Theory," in *Psychology: A Study of a Science*, Sigmund Koch, ed. New York: McGraw-Hill.

———— (1964), *Adaptation-Level Theory: An Experimental and Systematic Approach to Behavior.* New York: Harper and Row.

Hesket, J.L., T.O. Jones, G.W. Loveman, W.E. Sasser, and L.A. Schlesinger (1994), "Putting the Service-Profit Chain to Work," *Harvard Business Review*, (March/April), 165–74.

Hovland, C.I. and M. Sherif (1952), "Judgmental Phenomena and Scales of Attitude Assessment: Item Displacement in Thurston Scale," *Journal of Abnormal and Social Psychology*, 47, 822–32.

Kahneman, Daniel (1991), "Reference Points, Anchors, and Mixed Feelings," *Organizational Behavior and Human Decision Processes*, 51, 296–312.

Kahneman, Daniel and A. Tversky (1979), "Prospect Theory: An Analysis of Decision Making Under Risk," *Econometrica*, 47, 263–91.

Kalyanaram, Gurumurthy and John D.C. Little (1994), "An Empirical Analysis of Latitude of Price Acceptance in Consumer Package Goods," *Journal of Consumer Research*, 21 (December), 408–18.

Kosenko, Rustan and Don Rahtz (1988), "Buyer Market Price Knowledge Influence on Acceptable Price Range and Price Limits," *Advances in Consumer Research*, 15, 328–33.

LaTour, Stephen A. and Nancy Peat (1979), "Conceptual and Methodological Issues in Consumer Satisfaction Research," in *Advances in Consumer Research*, 6, 431–37.

Lichtenstein, Donald, Peter H. Bloch, and William C. Black (1988), "Correlates of Price Acceptability," *Journal of Consumer Research*, 15 (September), 243–52.

Liljander, Veronica (1995), *Comparison Standards in Perceived Service Quality*. Helsinki: Swedish School of Economics and Business Administration.

Miller, John A. (1977), "Studying Satisfaction, Modifying Models, Eliciting Expectations, Posing Problems, and Making Meaningful Measurements," in *Conceptualization and Measurement of Consumer Satisfaction and Dissatisfaction*, Keith Hunt, ed. Cambridge, MA: Marketing Science Institute.

Monroe, Kent (1971), "Measuring Price Thresholds by Psychophysics and Latitudes of Acceptance," *Journal of Marketing Research*, 8 (November), 460–64.

Naryana, C.L. and R.J. Markin (1975), "Consumer Behavior and Product Performance: An Alternative Conceptualization," *Journal of Marketing*, 39 (October), 1–6.

Oliver, Richard L. (1977), "Effect of Expectation and Disconfirmation on Postexposure Product Evaluations: An Alternative Explanation," *Journal of Applied Psychology*, 62 (August), 480–86.

——— (1980), "Theoretical Bases of Consumer Satisfaction Research: Review, Critique, and Future Direction," in *Theoretical Developments in Marketing*, J.R. Lamb and Patrick M. Dunne, eds. Chicago: American Marketing Association.

——— (1981), "Measurement and Evaluation of Satisfaction Processes in Retail Settings," *Journal of Retailing*, 57 (3), 25–48.

——— (1988), "Processing of the Satisfaction Response in Consumption: A Suggested Framework and Research Agenda," *Journal of Consumer Satisfaction, Dissatisfaction, and Complaining Behavior*, 2, 1–16.

Olshavsky, Richard W. and John A. Miller (1972), "Consumer Expectations, Product Performance, and Perceived Product Quality," *Journal of Marketing Research*, 9 (February), 19–21.

Olson, Jerry and Jerry Dover (1976), "Effects of Expectation Creation and Disconfirmation on Belief Elements of Cognitive Structure," in *Advances in Consumer Research*, B. Anderson, ed. 3, 168–75. Urban, IL: Association for Consumer Research.

——— and ——— (1979), "Disconfirmation of Consumer Expectations Through Product Trial," *Journal of Applied Psychology*, 64 (2), 179–89.

Page, Thomas J. and Richard A. Spreng (2002), "Difference Scores Versus Direct Effects in Service Quality Measurement," *Journal of Service Research*, 4 (February), 184–92.

Parasuraman, A., Leonard Berry, and Valerie Zeithaml (1991), "Refinement and Reassessment of the SERVQUAL Scale," *Journal of Retailing*, 77 (Winter), 420–50.

———, ———, and ——— (1994), "A Reassessment of Expectations as a Comparative Standard in Measuring Service Quality: Implications for Future Research," *Journal of Marketing*, 58 (January), 111–24.

Parasuraman, A., Valerie Zeithaml, and Leonard Berry (1985), "A Conceptual Model of Service Quality and Its Implications for Future Research," *Journal of Marketing*, 49 (Fall), 41–50.

———, ———, and ——— (1988), "SERVQUAL: A Multiple-Item Scale for Measuring Consumer Perceptions of Service Quality," *Journal of Retailing*, 64 (Spring), 12–40.

———, ———, and ——— (1994), "Alternative Scales for Measuring Service Quality: A Comparative Assessment Based on Psychometric and Diagnostic Criteria," *Journal of Retailing*, 70 (3), 201–30.

Peter, J. Paul, Gilbert A. Churchill Jr., and Tom J. Brown (1993), "Caution in the Use of Difference Scores in Consumer Research," *Journal of Consumer Research*, 19 (March), 655–62.

Pieters, Rik, Kitty Koelemeijer, and Henk Roest (1996), "Assimilation Processes in Service Satisfaction Formation," *International Journal of Service Industry Management*, 6 (3), 17–33.

Prakash, Ved (1984), "Validity and Reliability of Expectations Paradigm as a Determinant of Consumer Satisfaction," *Journal of the Academy of Marketing Science*, 12 (Fall), 63–76.

Raju, P.S. (1977), "Product Familiarity, Brand Name, and Price Influences on Product Evaluation," *Advances in Consumer Research*, 9, 64–71.

Rao, Akshay R. and Wanda Sieben (1992), "The Effect of Prior Knowledge on Price Acceptability and the Type of Information Examined," *Journal of Consumer Research*, 19 (September), 256–70.

Reich, J. and M. Sherif (1963), *Ego-Involvement as a Factor in Attitude Assessment by the Own Categories Technique*. Norman: Institute of Group Relations, University of Oklahoma.

Savage, C. Wade (1970), *The Measurement of Sensation: A Critique of Perceptual Psychophysics*. Los Angeles: University of California Press.

Sherif, Carolyn W. (1961), "Established Reference Scales and Series Effects in Social Judgment," unpublished doctoral dissertation, Austin, University of Texas.

Sherif, Carolyn W., M. Sherif, and R.E. Nebergall (1965), *Attitude and Attitude Change: The Social Judgment-Involvement Approach*. Philadelphia: Saunders.

Sherif, M. (1935), "A Study of Some Social Factors in Perceptions," *Archives of Psychology*, 27, 1–60.

———— (1960), "Some Needed Concepts in the Study of Social Attitudes," in *The Psychology of Ego-Involvements, Social Attitudes, and Identifications*, M. Sherif and H. Cantril, eds. .New York: Wiley.

Sherif, M. and Carl Hovland (1953), "Judgmental Phenomena and Scales of Attitude Measurement: Placement of Items with Individual Choice of Number of Categories," *Journal of Abnormal and Social Psychology*, 48, 135–41.

———— and ———— (1961), *Social Judgment: Assimilation and Contrast Effects in Communication and Attitude Change*. New Haven: Yale University Press.

Sherif, M., D. Taub, and Carl Hovland (1958), "Assimilation and Contrast Effects of Anchoring Stimuli on Judgments," *Journal of Experimental Psychology*, 55, 150–55.

Shostack, G.L. (1985), "Planning the Service Encounter," in *The Service Encounter: Managing Employee/ Customer Interaction in Service Businesses*, J.A. Czepiel, M.R. Soloman, and C.F. Surprenant, eds., 243–45. Lexington: MA: Lexington Books.

Sorce, Patrick and Stanley M. Widrick (1991), "Individual Differences in Latitude of Acceptable Prices," *Advances in Consumer Research*, 18, 802–805.

Spector, Aaron J. (1956), "Expectations, Fulfillment, and Morale," *Journal of Abnormal and Social Psychology*, 52 (January), 51–56.

Spreng, Richard A. and Robert D. Mackoy (1996), "An Empirical Examination of a Model of Perceived Quality and Satisfaction," *Journal of Retailing*, 72 (2), 201–14.

Strandvik, Tore (1994), *Tolerance Zones in Perceived Service Quality*. Helsinki: Swedish School of Economics and Business Administration.

Swan, John E. and Linda J. Combs (1976), "Product Performance and Consumer Satisfaction: A New Concept," *Journal of Marketing*, 40 (April), 25–33.

Swan, John E. and I. Fredrick Trawick (1980), "Satisfaction Related to Predicted vs. Desired Expectations," in *Refining Concepts and Measures of Consumer Satisfaction, Dissatisfaction, and Complaining Behavior*, H. Keith Hunt and Ralf L. Day, eds. Bloomington: Indiana University Press, 17–24.

Teas, K.R. (1993), "Expectations, Performance, and Consumers' Perceptions of Quality," *Journal of Marketing*, 57 (October), 18–34.

———— (1994), "Expectations as a Comparison Standard in Measuring Service Quality: An Assessment of a Reassessment," *Journal of Marketing*, 58 (January), 132–39.

Thurston, L.L. and E.J. Chave (1929), *The Measurement of Attitude: A Psychophysical Method and Some Experiments with a Scale for Measuring Attitude toward the Church*. Chicago: University of Chicago Press.

Vargo, Stephen L. and Robert F. Lusch (2004), "The Four Service Marketing Myths: Remnant of a Manufacturing Model," *Journal of Service Research* (May), 224–35.

Weisberg, Herbert F. (1992), *Central Tendency and Variability*. Newbury Park, CA: Sage.

Woodruff, R.B., E.R. Cadotte, and R.L. Jenkins (1983), "Modeling Consumer Satisfaction Processes Using Experience-Based Norms," *Journal of Marketing Research*, 10 (August), 296–304.

Zeithaml, V.A., L.L. Berry, and A.V. Parasuraman (1993), "The Nature and Determinants of Customer Expectations of Service," *Journal of the Academy of Marketing Science*, 21 (1), 1–12.

CHAPTER 7

CORRESPONDENCE ANALYSIS

Methodological Perspectives, Issues, and Applications

NARESH K. MALHOTRA, BETSY RUSH CHARLES, AND CAN USLAY

Abstract

The literature focusing on the methodological perspectives, issues, and applications related to correspondence analysis (CA) is reviewed. Starting with a historical note, the key features of CA are described and the principles and requirements governing CA are identified. In addition, the equivalent approaches to CA are discussed, the methods for scaling of points along the principal axes are examined, and the various diagnostic tools are described. Special attention is given to the interpretation of solutions. The appropriateness of homogeneity analysis is discussed. The article ends with a list of creative applications and the technique's limitations.

Introduction

The mathematical principles for relating categories in contingency tables originated with Karl Pearson in 1905 (de Leeuw 1983; Lancaster 1966) and were refined by R.A. Fisher (1940). The next year, Louis Guttman (1941) independently developed optimal (or dual) scaling for creating the perfect scale. Chikio Hayashi (1950) applied dual scaling to a Japanese language manual. Jean-Paul Benzécri (1969) created a geometric interpretation of dual scaling called "l'analyse factorielle des correspondancies." Greenacre, a student of Benzécri, translated Benzécri's work into English in 1978 (Lebart, Morineau, and Warwick 1984). According to Greenacre and Hastie (1987), French statisticians have elevated correspondence analysis (CA) to a jack-of-all-trades technique of data analysis. "CA is such a widely used approach, at least in France, that every attempt to challenge it is difficult but stimulating" (Caussinus 1986, p. 274).

While French statisticians were developing CA, American and British statisticians were developing loglinear and logit models (Fienberg and Meyer 1983). Generally speaking, American research practice focuses on testing hypotheses with quantitative data, whereas European research practice focuses on seeing relationships with qualitative data to understand behavior. However, both research perspectives are required for accurate decisions. Exploratory research describes relationships among factors relevant to the decision, whereas confirmatory research selects the best decision given the factors. Because CA describes relationships rather than predicts quantities, it is most useful in the exploratory stage of decisionmaking.

We find a good deal of confusion about CA in the literature. In part, the confusion arises because different names are used for the same techniques by different people and in different fields. Other names for CA have included "optimal scaling," "reciprocal averaging," "optimal scoring," "dual scaling," "homogeneity analysis," and "quantification method." Correspondence analysis has been invented independently by researchers in different fields. Scholars in different fields had a tendency of not reading each other's work, so that developments in one field were little known to researchers in different fields. Furthermore, as solutions are obtainable from a large number of different computational approaches, researchers using different approaches may reason they are using different techniques (Weller and Romney 1990). Conflicting perspectives on CA and related approaches have sparked public debates in research publications and conferences (e.g., Carroll, Green, and Schaffer 1989; Goodman 1986; Greenacre 1989).

A series of four international conferences have been organized on CA in Europe thus far. The first of these conferences was held in 1991 in Cologne, Germany, and led to the publication of *Correspondence Analysis in the Social Sciences,* edited by Greenacre and Blasius (1994). The second conference was on the wider topic of visualization (also held in Cologne) in 1995, and resulted in *Visualization of Categorical Data,* edited by Blasius and Greenacre (1998). The last of these conferences to date (Correspondence Analysis and Related Methods—CARME 2003) was held in Barcelona, Spain, under the leadership of Michael Greenacre and colleagues in 2003, the year that marked the thirtieth anniversary of Benzécri's (1973) highly influential work (www.econ.upf.es/carme/).

The purpose of this article is to integrate differing perspectives, to resolve issues surrounding CA, and to crystallize knowledge in this burgeoning field. Attention is devoted to different applications of CA in extant literature to underline and communicate its potential in the social sciences a la Greenacre and Blasius (1994). We use the following questions as an outline and review relevant literature pertinent to answering them.

1. What is CA?
2. What are the principles?
3. What are the requirements?
4. What approaches are equivalent?
5. Which scaling method is best?
6. What diagnostic tools are available?
7. How should solutions be interpreted?
8. When is homogeneity analysis appropriate?
9. What are some of the applications?
10. What are some of the limitations?

What Is Correspondence Analysis?

Correspondence analysis has several key features. The approach: (1) describes relationships among categories, (2) summarizes multivariate data, (3) reconciles row and column percentages, (4) displays differences from expectations with a perceptual map, (5) reveals dimensions of perceptions, (6) defines metric distances among points, (7) plots the points in the same space, and, (8) thus, simplifies the interpretation of data matrices. These features are described further.

Describes Relationships Among Categories

The objective of CA and equivalent approaches is to best summarize and represent relationships among categories in a data matrix by their proximity on a perceptual map. Correspondence analysis is "a way of analyzing the structure of dependencies in a contingency table" (Saporta 1975, p. 322) so that patterns reveal themselves a priori (Benzécri 1969, 1973). Correspondence analysis describes two-way associations but does not predict one-way causality. For example, it positions brands relative to their attributes and attributes relative to the brands so that each set of points is profiled relative to the other set of points.

Summarizes Multivariate Data

Guttman readily observed that "categorical data need multivariate techniques" (1950, p. 81). Correspondence analysis is a multivariate technique for categorical data for several reasons. Since several dimensions (principal components) describe the data, the data is multidimensional (Saporta 1975). Correspondence analysis lowers the dimensionality of data and scales them in a manner similar to our intuitive interpretation of physical space (Greenacre and Underhill 1982). In contrast to nonmetric methods of multidimensional scaling (MDS) that summarize the rank order of distances between pairs of points, CA and other metric MDS methods summarize the actual values of interrelationships among all points in the solution (Heiser and Meulman 1983, p. 140). "The usefulness of a technique like CA is that the gain in interpretability far exceeds the loss in information" (Greenacre 1984, p. 7). Another reason is that CA can superimpose supplemental (passive) categories on the solution.

Reconciles Row and Column Percentages

Correspondence analysis may be described as a three-stage procedure. Stage one reconciles row and column percentages. At this stage, the data matrix is transformed (or standardized) by premultiplying the data with the square root of the inverse of the row sum matrix, and postmultiplying the data with the square root of the inverse of the column sum matrix. This process of dividing each cell in the matrix by the square root (geometric mean) of the corresponding row and column totals has been called proximity analysis.

Displays Differences from Expectations

The second stage summarizes the transformed matrix of row and column profiles with generalized singular value decomposition. The solution is an array of the relative frequency deviations of points from the origin (the expected value or centroid of the points). In contrast to regression-like approaches that minimize least squares distance orthogonally to the *axis* of the dependent variable, CA minimizes least squares distance orthogonally to the *centroid* of the residual distances among the points (Greenacre 1984, pp. 37–41). This process is conceptually similar to subtracting out the chi-squared expected cell values from the observed cell values (Weller and Romney 1990, p. 16). Because the main effects of both the row and column categories are removed by the transformation, the first eigenvalue (or singular value) of the solution is one, a trivial solution in which all points are positioned at the origin. This eigenvalue serves to center the solution at the origin so the nontrivial points have a weighted mean of zero.

Reveals Dimensions of Perceptions

The maximum number of dimensions is one less than the rank of the matrix because the trivial solution is ignored. The two largest nontrivial eigenvalues report the variance explained by the x and y axes. Since each subsequent axis best explains the remaining variance in the relationships among the points, it reveals uncorrelated (or orthogonal) dimensions of the respondents' perceptions. The axes in CA are not factors, but rather composite variables emerging from the analysis. They are simply mathematical constructs that are useful for graphical display (Gittins 1990, p. 180). Thus, in some applications it may not be necessary to name or superimpose the axes on the solution.

Defines Distances Among Points

In stage two, the eigenvalues define the distance and the eigenvectors define the direction of row and column profiles relative to the centroid (or origin). Thus, CA defines profiles in space as points, rather than as vectors. If we visualize any two points and the origin as a triangle, we have defined two sides of the triangle as the distance of each point to the origin and the angle between these two sides of the triangle as the angle of the points at the origin. According to the Pythagorean theorem, defining two sides and one angle of a triangle defines the third side of the triangle (i.e., the distance between the points). In summary, CA maximizes the distance from the centroid and among points.

Plots Points in the Same Space

In the third stage, singular value decomposition of the transformed matrix yields the optimal solution, the eigenvalues and eigenvectors that scale the row and column points in the same space. The row and column vectors are rescaled by the square root of the corresponding total to obtain "optimal scores." For data in a typical two-dimensional contingency table, both the row variables and the column variables are represented in the same geometric space. Numerical scores are assigned to the rows and columns of a data matrix so as to maximize their interrelationships. The scores are in corresponding units, allowing all the variables to be plotted in the same space for ease of interpretation. It is because of the geometric correspondence of the two sets of points in position and inertia that we can merge the two displays into one joint display (Hoffman and Franke 1986, p. 219). "The placing of both the row and the column variables explicitly in the same space is one of the important advantages of CA and is a great aid in interpretation of the data" (Weller and Romney 1990, pp. 58, 73). Cases (supplementary points) as well as variables (supplementary variables) that were not included in the original analysis may also be displayed in biplots from CA (Gabriel 1995; Graffelman and Aluja-Banet 2003).

Simplifies Interpretation

A CA map is interpreted in the same way as our intuitive interpretation of physical space. Correspondence analysis scales the space in weighted (normalized) Euclidean (or chi-squared metric) distance. The square of the unweighed Euclidean distance between a row and column point is the sum of the squared difference between their observed and expected joint occurrences divided by the marginal of either the corresponding row or column point. For example, dividing by the row marginals removes the main effect of the row points (e.g., brands), leaving the main effect of the column points (e.g., attributes). Thus, the solution describes a one-way relationship of the column points to the row points (i.e., the attributes to the brands). Weighted Euclidean distance removes the main effects of both row and column points by dividing the Euclidean distance by the square root of the other marginal, leaving only the interaction effect between the row and column points as follows:

$$d_c^2(j,j') = \sum_{i=1}^{I} \frac{f_{++}}{f_{i+}}(\frac{f_{ij}}{f_{+j}} - \frac{f_{ij'}}{f_{+j}})^2; \quad d_r^2(i,i') = \sum_{j=1}^{J} \frac{f_{++}}{f_{+j}}(\frac{f_{ij}}{f_{i+}} - \frac{f_{ij'}}{f_{i+}})^2$$

where $d_c^2(j,j')$ and $d_r^2(i,i')$ are the squared distances between two column points and row points, respectively, f_{++} is the total number of responses, f_{i+} and f_{+j} are the row and column marginals respectively, and f_{ij} is a cell value.

What Are the Principles?

The basic principles employed in CA are: the principle of distributional equivalency (PDE), the principle of equivalent partitioning (PEP), and the principle of internal consistency (PIC).

1. The PDE of chi-squared distance means that the results will be invariant irrespective of how the variables were originally coded (Benzécri 1973; Greenacre 1984, p. 35). Thus, the categories can be collapsed or subdivided without changing the meaning of the solution. This universal principle is based on the symmetry of relations that exist with nominal data (Carroll, Green, and Schaffer 1986, 1989).

2. The PEP means that "proportional rows (or columns) have identical optimal weights. Rows and columns simultaneously can be partitioned into proportional vectors without altering their optimal weights" (Nishisato and Gaul 1990, p. 355). It should be noted that Nishisato's PEP is the same as PDE; he just gave it another name. This principle refers to the duality of CA, the ability to calculate the optimal scores of row and column points in terms of one another.

3. The PIC means that "optimal weights are determined so as to minimize the within-row (within-column) variation and to maximize the between-row (between-column) variation of a data matrix" (Guttman 1953; Nishisato and Gaul 1990, p. 355). The principle of internal consistency is applicable to MCA rather than simple CA, whereas PDE and PEP are applicable in general.

What Are the Requirements?

The requirements for CA are not stringent. The technique can handle nominal data, mixed-level data, or "pick-any" data. Also, it does not require a strict representation of the sample and reveals the range of responses, as discussed in the following.

Nominal Data

Correspondence analysis and equivalent techniques analyze nominal data and can handle any level of cross-tabulated data. In contrast, other MDS approaches require ordinal or metric data. Thus, in CA, respondents can describe objects more directly, rather than rating or ranking them. This results in simplified questionnaires with some compelling benefits. These questionnaires can reduce the time commitment of the respondent, raise a respondent's level of interest, more naturally reflect a respondent's cognitive process, and potentially result in higher data quality than that obtained by traditional questionnaires based on rating scales (Whitlark 1989, p. 3).

Mixed-Level Data

Correspondence analysis also handles mixed-level data if the following precautions are observed. If groups in the matrix are disjoint (or unassociated), the groups should be analyzed separately. For rank-order data, the preferred choice should be assigned the largest number because the data must be in the form of "similarities" rather than "dissimilarities." The data of a square matrix must include the diagonals. Attribute rating scales can be summarized as the mean (or median) score of each object on each attribute if the data is normally distributed. Since most data does not satisfy this assumption, "top box" scores usually summarize the data better than mean (or median) scores.

Pick-Any Data

Pick-any data contains multiple mentions or missing data. Multiple mentions occur whenever a respondent reports more than one answer to a question, whereas missing data occurs whenever a respondent does not answer a question. Other MDS approaches cannot neatly handle pick-any data, because they require forced-choice questions and familiarity with all brands, although these approaches can accommodate missing data. These approaches also set mean rejection to zero, when it could mean "not considered, not chosen, or rejection" (Holbrook, Moore, and Winer 1982). "The pick-any format of Levine's procedure resolves some of these problems" (Cooper 1983, p. 444) because it does not "place 'structural dependencies' on the number or format of the choices and non-choices of a respondent" (DeSarbo and Hoffman 1987). Dual scaling has a structural dependency because it scales the solution by the total number of responses. In contrast, Levine's centroid approach does not, because it scales the solution by row and column marginals. Noma's (1982) reconstitution of order zero also defines zeros as nonchoice (de Leeuw and Heijden 1988).

Sample

Correspondence analysis does not require a large random sample to fulfill the assumptions of classical multivariate techniques. Muehsam (1989) demonstrates that CA obtains the same results as classical techniques even when the underlying assumptions required for the classical procedures are violated. Correspondence analysis simultaneously combines the R-mode and Q-mode techniques "without assumptions concerning the distribution of variables nor the structure of the phenomenon under study" (Madsen 1988, p. 14). As stated by Greenacre (1984, p. 182), a contingency table does not require as strict a representation of the sample as do percentages or mean estimation. Obviously, a sample where certain aspects of the parent population are not represented cannot give projectable results, even if the configurations obtained are stable. Perhaps the only full-fledged assumption is that the data elements be nonnegative.

What Approaches Are Equivalent?

Karl Pearson and his assistant Yule first measured association in contingency tables in 1905 at the Galton Laboratory (de Leeuw 1983; Lancaster 1966) using discriminant analysis to maximize the canonical correlation between row and column scores. The same approach was used by Hotelling (1933) and called reciprocal averages by Horst (1935) at Proctor and Gamble. The other equivalent approaches are based on analysis of variance (ANOVA) (optimal or dual scaling), principal components (factor) analysis, generalized canonical analysis (homogeneity or multiple correspondence analysis [MCA]), and Levine's centroid (pick-any) approach. These approaches and their equivalence are discussed next.

Reciprocal Averaging

Fisher (1940) called Pearson's approach "reciprocal averaging" because it iteratively applies discriminant analysis to replace column values with the average of the row values and vice versa until stability is reached. The solution is the eigenvectors of the nontrivial eigenvalues of either of the following equivalent nonsymmetric matrices:

Solution for column categories:
$$\frac{1}{p}D^{-1}X'X$$

Normalization:
$$\Psi = \frac{1}{\sqrt{\lambda}}\frac{1}{p}X\Phi$$

Solution for row categories:
$$\frac{1}{p}XD^{-1}X'$$

Normalization:
$$\Phi = \frac{1}{\sqrt{\lambda}}D^{-1}X'\Psi$$

where p is the number of categories, D is a diagonal matrix of the row and column marginals, X is the data matrix, and λ is the relevant eigenvalue. Φ nd Ψ represent the coordinates of column points and row points on the relevant axis. Each eigenvalue indicates the relative length, significance, and percentage of variance (or relationships) among active categories explained by an orthogonal axis, and each eigenvector indicates the coordinates of a category on an axis. The scaling of row and column categories does not correspond, so the coordinates of the column categories must be transformed when using the first matrix, and the coordinates of the row categories must be transformed when using the second matrix. After the coordinates are transformed, the row and column categories are positioned uniformly on the correspondence map. Mosier (1946), Baker (1960), and Lingos (1964) wrote early programs using reciprocal averaging but lost interest in this approach when more efficient approaches, such as the following, were developed.

Analysis of Variance Approach (Optimal or Dual Scaling)

The ANOVA approach was proposed by Hotelling (1933) and demonstrates that the optimal scale values for both the row and column categories maximize their homogeneity. Guttman developed optimal scaling in 1941 to refine the one-dimensional Binet-Simon scale during the war effort (Saporta 1975). The solution to the ANOVA approach is reached when the square of the correlation ratio is maximized and when the resulting coordinates for the column categories are transformed as shown previously. The solution maximizes the homogeneity both within the row categories and within the column categories.

$$\eta^2 = \frac{\Phi'X'X\Phi}{p\Phi'D\Phi}$$

where the optimal correlation ratio η^2 is equal to the eigenvalue λ. This approach decomposes and transforms the same asymmetric matrices as in reciprocal averaging. Bock (1960) and Lingos (1963) wrote early programs for this approach, which Nishisato called "dual scaling" (1980, 1994). Nishisato and Gaul (1988) considered forced classification as one of the most useful options available in dual scaling. Dual scaling and CA provide identical solutions after the data is transformed by "doubling" the respondents (Greenacre and Torres 1999; Torres and Greenacre 2002).

Principal Components Analysis Approach

Another derivative of Pearson's approach is the principal components (factor) analysis approach developed by Burt (Horst et al. 1941). Guttman (1953) explains that his optimal scaling approach and Burt's factorial analysis approach developed independently because the war broke down communication between the Americans and the Europeans. "Guttman observed that the two systems are identical in principal component weights and scores. The centroid formula is an extension to quantitative variables of the usual formula for investigating association in the case of qualitative attributes" (Burt 1953, pp. 5–11).

Building on Burt's (1950, 1953) factor analytic approach, Jean-Paul Benzécri rediscovered optimal scaling in 1969 and applied it geometrically to Chinese linguistics. The *Centre International de Statistique et d'Informatique Appliquees* programmed his factor analytic approach as SPAD, a Statistical Package for the Analysis of Data. The French school includes Benzécri (1969); Lebart, Morineau, and Tabard (1977); Cailliez and Pages (1976); Cazes et al. (1977); and Deville and Saporta (1983). Other developers of principal component analysis (PCA) of qualitative data are Tenenhaus (1977); Young, Takane, and de Leeuw (1978); and Torgerson (1958). CA can be considered a dual generalized PCA (Greenacre 1984; Greenacre and Torres 1999). This geometric approach finds low-dimensional subspaces closest to row and column profiles. The solution maximizes the variance of the scaled variables by deriving the eigenvalues of the symmetric matrix:

$$\frac{1}{p} D^{-1/2} X' X D^{-1/2}$$

The normalized scaling of the row and column categories is respectively obtained through the following transformations:

$$\Phi^h = \sqrt{f_{++p} D^{-1/2} \lambda_h} \qquad \Psi^h = \frac{\frac{1}{p} X \Phi^h}{\sqrt{\lambda_h}}$$

where h refers to the relevant axis resulting in the maximum eigenvector solution. CA is advantageous over PCA since it can represent rows and columns in a joint space on a graphical display. The joint graphical displays are also referred to as biplots (Gower and Hand 1996; Greenacre 1992). Cheung (1994) also reported that CA fared well against PCA, and that there was little or no loss of information resulting from categorizing continuous data.

Generalized Canonical Analysis (Homogeneity Analysis or MCA)

Generalized canonical correlation analysis was developed by Carroll (1968); McKeon (1966); Masson (1974); Bouroche, Saporta, and Tenenhaus (1975); Leclerc (1980); de Leeuw (1982); and Gifi (1990) (*Note:* "Gifi" is a pseudonym for de Leeuw and his department of Data Theory). Its purpose is to correlate row and column categories in a binary indicator (or Burt) matrix of objects by responses. This matrix disaggregates a contingency table so that each response (column category) of each object (row category) is dichotomously coded as a zero or one. MCA has more dimensions than CA because the matrix is much larger. MCA can be considered as a PCA using nominal variables (Wels-Lips, van der Ven, and Pieters 1998). Categories of variables that tend to co-occur are located close to each other whereas unrelated variables are located farther from each other, and the interpretation of the solution is based on the factor loadings as in PCA (Wels-Lips, van der Ven, and Pieters 1998). The singular values for the same dimensions of MCA and CA are related for the two variable case as follows:

$$\lambda_c^2 = (2\lambda_I^2 - 1)^2$$

where λ_c is the singular value from the decomposition analysis of the contingency table and λ_I is the singular value from the decomposition analysis of the indicator matrix. The optimal scores are the same as those reported for the corresponding unweighted scores for the same data. The weights are the expected frequencies assuming the categories are independent (Greenacre 1988, p. 459). This approach uses weighted least-squares lower-rank approximation of a contingency table. The solution maximizes the sum of the correlation between the scaling of row and column categories as follows:

$$\frac{1}{f_{++p}} \sum_{n=1}^{m} (\psi_h)' X D^{-1} X' \psi_h$$

where n and m are the number of row and column categories, respectively. Canonical CA has been shown to be equivalent to Fisher's linear discriminant analysis (LDA) (Zhu 2001). Zhu and Hastie (2003) use a nonparametric generalization of Fisher's LDA in order to increase the flexibility of constrained ordination modeling, thereby enabling the use of asymmetric and multimodal response functions.

Levine's Centroid (Pick-Any) Approach

In contrast to previous approaches, Levine's centroid, or pick-any, approach (Holbrook, Moore, and Winer 1982; Levine 1979) allows multiple responses to questions and also allows missing data. This approach solves for the eigenvectors of the nontrivial eigenvalues of the following symmetric matrix:

$$D^{-1}E$$

$$E = \begin{pmatrix} \Phi_n & X \\ X' & \Phi_m \end{pmatrix} \qquad d_{ii} = \sum_{j=1}^{n+m} e_{ij}$$

where E is a symmetric matrix of dimensions $n + m$, X is an $n \times m$ matrix of cell values, Φ_n and Φ_m are $n \times n$ and $m \times m$ null matrices, and D is a diagonal matrix of order $n + m$. No transformation is necessary since matrix E treats the row and column points equally. Thus, Levine's centroid approach projects row and column points in the same space and explicitly defines distances between points. This approach is appropriate for analyzing binary indicator (or Burt) matrices, pick-any data, and contingency tables. As in the other approaches, Levine's centroid approach scales the solution in weighted Euclidean (or chi-squared) metric distance (Goodnow 1988; Noma 1982).

Equivalence of the Various Approaches

Tenenhaus and Young (1985) demonstrate that reciprocal averaging, ANOVA (optimal or dual scaling), principal components (factor) analysis, and canonical correlation (homogeneity or MCA) are mathematically equivalent approaches to CA. There are five different derivations of the method: singular value decomposition, eigen analysis, least squares, the multivariate general linear model, and minimization of a Euclidean distance (Weller and Romney 1990, p. 14). Goodnow (1988) and Whitlark (1989) demonstrate that Levine's centroid approach is mathematically equivalent to the ANOVA approach (dual scaling). In fact, Levine's centroid method (1979) also can be viewed as a special case of CA where a different type of normalization is employed (DeSarbo and Hoffman 1987, p. 41). These mathematically equivalent approaches use different terminology to refer to the same concepts. For example, optimal scores, row or column scores, canonical scores or variates, factor loadings or scores, and coordinates are equivalent. They are rescalings by weights (singular values or canonical correlations) of the eigenvalues (row or column latent vectors) on the dimensions (factors or components) (Weller and Romney 1990, p. 15). Goodman (1996) introduced a general method for the analysis of nonindependence between rows and columns incorporating methods of CA, arguing that Pearson, Yule, and Fisher's methods are special cases of the generalized approach.

Which Scaling Method Is Best?

The main difference among the mathematically equivalent approaches is the scaling of the points along the principal axes (Greenacre 1981,1984). The scaling methods used are: principal coordinates (PRN); standard coordinates (STD); Carroll, Green, Schaffer profile metric (CGS); and the asymmetric method used by van der Heijden and de Leeuw (VHL). These methods are discussed along with their reliability and validity and the scaling used in some popular software. Software that can perform CA is readily available and modules were developed for widely used statistical packages (i.e., BMDP, SAS, and SPSS) by the early 1990s (Greenacre and Blasius 1994).

The Principal Coordinates Method

Reciprocal averaging and PCA use the principal coordinates (PRN) method that scales row and column points in separate spaces relative to the variance explained by the axes, the principal inertia, as shown below:

$$\Psi = R^{-1/2} P\lambda; \quad \Phi = C^{-1/2} Q\lambda$$

where R is a diagonal matrix of row marginals, C is a diagonal matrix of column marginals, and P and Q are the eigenvector matrix and the inverted eigenvector matrix, respectively, and λ is the relevant eigenvalue. In PRN CA, the temptation is to interpret between-set (row-to-column) distances in the symmetric plot, but no such interpretation is, in fact, intended or valid. Distances between points within the same cloud are defined in terms of the relevant chi-square distance, while the between-cloud correspondence is governed by the barycentric nature of the transition formula (Greenacre 1984, p. 65).

The Standard Coordinates Method

The ANOVA (optimal or dual scaling) and Levine's centroid approaches use the standard coordinates (STD) method (Whitlark 1989, p. 133). According to Weller and Romney (1990, p. 16), these optimal or canonical scores are those most frequently quoted in the literature. Points displayed in STD are representations of vertex points, or unit profiles, and define the extreme corners of the multidimensional display (Greenacre 1984). The scaling formulae are:

$$\Psi = R^{-1/2} P; \ \Phi = C^{-1/2} Q$$

In the STD approach, the weight for each value is its row or column mass. Because these sum to one for both row and column points, the approach scales the axes equally to create a square map regardless of the variance explained by the axes. It is important to remember that they are unweighted and thus assume that each dimension is equally important; that is, they are weighted the same (Greenacre 1981, 1984).

The Carroll, Green, and Schaffer Profile Metric Method

The Carroll, Green, Schaffer (CGS) profile metric method uses MCA to summarize a binary indicator (or Burt) matrix as follows.

$$\Psi = R^{-1/2} P(\lambda+1)^{1/2}; \ \Phi = C^{-1/2} Q(\lambda+1)^{1/2}$$

where 1 is an identity matrix. The rationale for this proposal was that the table acquired equal status in the indicator matrix as a single set of categories and that all chi-squared distances were then interpretable within this set. Some scholars disagree with this rationale, contending that adding the identity matrix stretches the y axis, and the CGS approach distorts both within-set and between-set distances (Greenacre 1989).

The van der Heijden and de Leeuw Method

The asymmetric method, VHL, used by van der Heijden and de Leeuw (1985, 1989) scales either row or column points as PRN and the other points as STD. The formulae used are:

$$\psi = R^{-1/2} P\lambda; \Phi = C^{-1/2}Q$$

The asymmetric method clusters the principal coordinate points nearer the origin as the size of the eigenvalues (or principal inertias) decreases. When the principal inertias or eigenvalues are low, the PRN will be much smaller than the display in STD (Greenacre 1984, p. 94). Nishisato (1998) emphasizes that the asymmetric approach should be used to recover the ranks in dual scaling of rank order data.

Didoublement

Hoffman and Franke (1986) recommend the French technique of "didoublement," in which the data include the complement of each category, such as the top and bottom box scores. Didoublement displays the range of the responses. In order to standardize their dispersion, Escoufier (1979) proposes that continuous variables be coded as $y+ = (1+z)/2$ and $y- = (1-z)/2$ where z is a standardized variable with a mean of zero and variance of one (Greenacre and Hastie 1987).

Greenacre (2002) introduces the ratio map, which can be used to analyze contingency tables and compositional data. Ratio maps are essentially row and column weighed logratio biplots (Aitchison and Greenacre 2002; Greenacre 2002). With the potentially problematic exception of difficulty in handling zero frequencies, the potential of the ratio maps looks promising because it "leads to a method of visualization that has both subcompositional coherence and distributional equivalence" (Greenacre 2002, p. 5).

Reliability and Validity

Although all approaches are reliable, only the PRN method is valid for solutions with unequal eigenvalues and with higher dimensions. The agreement between attribute-to-brand distances estimated by PRN CA and attribute-to-brand scale values do not deteriorate as more dimensions are added to the solution. They provide a good overall prediction of attribute-to-brand scale values. The other approaches in declining order of validity are asymmetric scaling, CGS profile metric, and STD. These solutions are only valid when the first two axes each explain about half of the variance (Whitlark 1989, p. 142).

Standard and Advanced Software

Relevant program modules are available from SPSS, BMDP, SAS, Statistica, Systat, and several other sources (Lebart, Morineau, and Warwick 1984; Smith 1988). Hoffman (1991) reviewed five specialized programs for CA (Dual3, MapWise, PC-MDS: CORAN, PC-MDS: CORRESP, and SimCA). Her review evaluates the machine requirements, language, documentation, data requirements, and graphics, but not their accuracy. Most commercial software for CA rescale PRN solutions to generate square maps that are equivalent to STD, the least valid scaling method. Greenacre and Hastie (1987) recommend that such maps be interpreted with vectors. "The factor-analytic style of interpretation strictly along principal axes, as described by Greenacre and Hastie (1987), is valid for all scalings . . . In this style of interpretation the relative position of one of the sets is used to name the principal axis, following which the position of the other set along this axis is interpreted alone" (Greenacre and Hastie 1987, p. 10).

Dual3 (Nishisato and Nishisato 1990) and MapWise (Goodnow 1988; Pelton, Tudor, and Goodnow 1991) plot row and column points in the same space using the STD method. These programs then rescale the solution using the PRN method as recommended by Weller and Romney (1990).

Other software useful for analyses and/or visualization of correspondence include: 3WAYPACK (Kroonenberg 1996); ADDAD (1983); AMADO (Risson et al. 1994); ANACONDA, TOSCANA, and JOSICA (Wolff and Gabler 1998); CORA (Fehlen 1998); EyeLID (Le Roux and Rouanet 1998); GOLDminer (Magidson 1998); LACORD (Rost 1990); S-Plus (Becker, Chambers, and Wilks 1988; cf. Blasius and Greenacre 1998); Lisp-Stat (Bond and Michailides 1997); and Excel (Lipkovich and Smith 2002).

Several other techniques are related to CA. Greenacre (1986) proposes a multidimensional unfolding approach that optimally summarizes the position of each point in space and converges the row and column configurations. TABMAP positions objects with PRN CA and attributes with MDS in order to better define between-set distances (Whitlark 1989). Generalized Canonical Correlation (GENCOR) merges perceptual mapping solutions (Green and Carroll

1988). Nominal MDS, called forced classification (Takane 1987), defines the principal component that maximizes the discrimination of categories by repeating an item in the data (Nishisato and Nishisato 1990, p. 355).

What Diagnostic Tools Are Available?

Many diagnostic tools have developed with the maturing of CA. These tools can assist in determining external validity, goodness of fit, statistical significance, the optimal number of axes, outliers, point stability, contribution to the axes, the perfect scale, and optimal coding of ordinal data.

External Validity

Where available, the validity of the CA map may be tested by comparing it with an external criterion. For example, the validity of CA may be tested by relating U.S. cities on a correspondence map with data on their geographic distances (Malhotra and Bartels 2002). Each city is listed as both row and column (supplemental) category to prove that the proximity of both row and column categories describes their correlation with all other categories. Malhotra and Bartels (2002) used ten representative U.S. cities. The resulting spatial map highly resembled the geographical map and explained 96 percent of the variance among the cities. The U.S. map is more recognizable if the cities in both the rows and columns represent all regions of the country. To verify this point, we used MapWise software to analyze the proximity (similarity) of twenty-one representative U.S. cities, each entered as an active and passive category. The perceptual map was significant, explained 98 percent of the variance, and closely approximated a geographic map. This indicated that MapWise accurately relates both active and passive points (also see Pelton, Tudor, and Goodnow 1991). Therefore, we recommend validating other CA programs by reconstructing a geographic map.

It is also desirable to run CA by using different approaches (computer programs) to see if similar results are obtained. In all cases the eigenvalues, the percentage of variance explained, and the configuration of the map should be examined. Even though the solutions obtained from the different approaches are mathematically equivalent, some maps may be rotated and the coordinates multiplied by a different scalar.

Goodness of Fit

The goodness of fit can be assessed by reconstructing the data and comparing it to the observed data. Reconstructing the data is based on the following mathematical relationship between CA and chi-square.

$$\frac{\chi^2}{n} = \sum \lambda_i^2$$

The sum of the squared canonical correlations (eigenvalues or squared singular values) is equivalent to the degree of association present in the data (Weller and Romney 1990, pp. 64–65). Each cell value in the original data matrix can be reconstructed by summing the components for each axis.

$$f_{ij} = \frac{f_{i+} * f_{+j}}{f_{++}}(1) + \frac{f_{i+} * f_{+j}}{f_{++}} \lambda_1 \, x_1 \, y_1 + \ldots + \frac{f_{i+} * f_{+j}}{f_{++}} \lambda_h \, x_h \, y_h$$

where f_{ij} is the cell value, f_{i+} is the row marginal, f_{+j} is the column marginal, f_{++} is the grand total, λ is the singular value, x's and y's are the coordinates of the row and intersecting column categories, and h is the number of dimensions. Each nontrivial axis summarizes the difference between the observed and expected cell values. If the reconstructed and observed cell values are not significantly different, the goodness of fit between the solution and data is considered to be highly satisfactory.

Statistical Significance

Pearson (1913) states that a bivariate normal distribution can be assumed if the contingency table has at least ten cells (Lancaster 1966). A significant solution approximates that obtained from a bivariate normal distribution. Significance is a more inferentially oriented statistic than the percent of variance explained by the axes. By maximizing the explained variance relative to the total variance, a significant solution "best distinguishes" relationships among active categories. Even solutions that are not significant maximize explained variance, that is, best describe correlations among categories given the distribution of responses. Nishisato (1980, p. 569) recommends Bock's adaptation (1960) of Bartlett's chi-square to test a solution for significance. This significance test requires a true contingency table to meet the assumption of multinominal sampling (Greenacre and Underhill 1982, p. 207). A significance test is not appropriate if the data has multiple mentions or missing data. Since the data need not be independent, the same respondents can describe each brand (Whitlark 1989).

Significance Tests for Axes and Maps

The eigenvalue of an axis determines the significance of an axis, whereas the sum of the eigenvalues of two axes determines the significance of a map. The chi-square for an axis and map is calculated as follows:

Axis:
$$\chi^2 = [f_{++} - 1 - 1/2(n+m-1)]Log_e(1 - \lambda_h^2)$$

$$df = n + m - 1 - 2h$$

where f_{++} is the total number of responses in the table, n the number of rows, and and m the number of columns, and h is the number of dimensions.

Map:
$$\chi^2 = [f_{++} - 1 - 1/2(n+m-1)]\sum_{h=2} Log_e(1 - \lambda_h^2)$$

$$df = (n-2)(m-2)$$

The critical chi-square depends on the degrees of freedom and desired level of significance. If the calculated chi-square value is larger than the critical chi-square value, the axis or map best distinguishes relationships among the active categories. Another approach is testing the rotational stability of each axis through bootstrapping (Escoufier and Junca 1986, p. 280). This method creates clouds of points by analyzing subsamples of the data, superimposing the solutions, and drawing ellipses around the clouds of points. For example, if the ellipses (confidence area) resulting from bootstrapping contain 80 percent of the points, we can be 80 percent confident of the results (Heiser and Meulman 1983, pp. 163–64). CA has been shown to be a robust method and its results are remarkably stable even if the data are perturbed (Lebart, Morineau, and Tabard 1977, p.169).

Significance of Association

Testing the significance of association of a contingency table and of a CA solution is conceptually similar. Total inertia measures the spread of points around the origin, the centroid of expectations, using Pearson's mean-square contingency coefficient (Gower and Digby 1980, p. 35). If the points are significantly distant from the origin, we can reject the null hypothesis that the array is no different from expectations (Pearson 1913). Muehsam (1989) proposes various distance measures and a test of symmetry and deviations from the underlying assumptions in factorial ANOVA experiments.

The Optimal Number of Axes

The preceding formulae can determine the optimal number of axes. For example, one axis is optimal if the observed data and data reconstructed by summing the trivial and first components are not significantly different (Weller and Romney 1990, pp. 65–66). According to Bock's adaptation of Bartlett's chi-square, an axis should be included in the optimal solution if it is significant. If the first axis is not significant, the corresponding scoring scheme is still the best one can obtain. According to Jolliffe (1986), the rules with relatively sound statistical foundations seemed to offer little advantage, if any, over the simpler approaches. He suggests that the optimal number of axes should explain 70 to 100 percent of the total variance. Another simple approach is plotting the eigenvalues relative to the axes and retaining those axes prior to the "elbow" in the plot. The overriding consideration is the sophistication of the researcher.

Outliers

Correspondence analysis tends to position a category with many responses near the origin, the centroid of the categories, because it tends to have large joint occurrences with many categories. Similarly, CA tends to position a small category near a border because it tends to have small joint occurrences with many categories. Categories that are too small for stability are outliers and should be excluded from the solution. Hoffman and Franke (1986, p. 225) recommended superimposing unstable points on the solution as a passive category. All passive (supplemental) categories are stable because they are not weighted in the solution. Heiser and Meulman (1983, p. 163) recommended omitting the most eccentric 10 percent of points from the computation.

On the other hand, Greenacre and Blasius (1997) suggested overcoming the problem of the influence of diagonal entries in a square matrix by centering it. The operation results in spatial maps of one symmetric and one skew-symmetric matrix (Greenacre 2000). Both the percentage of variance explained and interpretability of the solution were enhanced with the centering approach in the context of social mobility (Greenacre and Blasius 1997).

Point Stability

We recommend comparing proximity and CA solutions of the same data. In essence, proximity analysis reconciles row and column percentages by dividing each cell value by the product of the square root of the row and column marginals. Then, CA weighs the proximity analysis solution to best summarize relationships among the active categories. Active categories that contribute substantially to the solution have a large weight, whereas those that contribute little to the solution have a small weight. Lightly weighted categories have relatively few responses and/or responses that are not consistent with the other responses. If a point is nearer to a border of a CA solution than a proximity analysis solution, the point is unstable and should be removed from the analysis.

Contribution to the Axes

If the researcher wants the axes displayed on the solution, the contribution of points to the axes implies their meaning. The distance of a point from the origin weighted by its marginal approximates its contribution to an axis (de Leeuw and van der Heijden 1988, p. 227). If the ellipse (confidence area) surrounding a point includes the origin, the point is not important in interpreting the axes. This method is very insensitive to the presence of outliers, which is an appreciable advantage (Greenacre 1984).

The Perfect Scale

Only one axis is needed when the data are linear (or ordinal) because subsequent axes do not provide further information (Guttman 1953). When one axis is sufficient, "the classical 'horseshoe' effect often shows up in CA and also in other forms of multivariate analysis" (Carroll, Green, and Schaffer 1989, p. 498). It can be proved mathematically that when a single natural gradient exists in the data, the later axes may be approximate polynomials of the first (Hill 1974; Madsen 1988). For example, Guttman used the horseshoe effect to evaluate the Binet-Simon scale. He describes the perfect scale as one in which each item is always a perfect linear function of all the principal components taken simultaneously. Furthermore, the second principal component is a perfect horseshoe–shaped function of the first one, and the third principal component is a curve with line bends (e.g., a cubic parabola) if the data have continuity. Since they are orthogonal to each other (and have zero means), the linear correlation between any two principal components is always zero, but the curvilinear correlation of each with the first component is perfect. In this sense, the further principal components beyond the first add no new information, although they provide a psychological frame of reference for ordinal data. The second component is intensity, and the third and fourth are closure and involution, respectively (Guttman 1953).

Optimal Coding of Ordinal Data

Fuzzy coding can smooth out the horseshoe effect using basis-splines. In shipbuilding, "spline" refers to an elastic strip of wood that goes through fixed points called drecks. In mathematics, "spline" refers to an arbitrary mathematical function that allocates ordinal data across boundaries of categories (knots). For example, crisp coding allocates each observation to one category with a 0-degree B-spline. Trapezoidal coding allocates each observation to two categories with a 1-degree B-spline, and polynomial coding allocates each observation to three categories with a 2- degree B-spline. B-splines are essentially polynomials with their degree referring to the polynomial degree (the highest coefficient in the polynomial) as opposed to its order. The optimal B-spline function quickly converges to crisp coding and generates a smooth curve. For continuous data, knots should be uniform, frequent, and group at least five data points in each category (de Leeuw 1988).

How Should Solutions Be Interpreted?

Key issues are related to the definition, evaluation, and interpretation of within-set and between-set distances.

Within-Set Distance

Whitlark (1989) and Greenacre (1989) define true distances between row points as row percentages and true distances between column points as column percentages. They tested the correlation between true and observed within-set (row-to-row or column-to-column) distances in solutions obtained by various approaches. Both Whitlark (1989) and Greenacre (1989) concluded that PRN CA yields within-set distances that can be meaningfully interpreted. Its solutions "yield inter-brand distances that reflect brand differences as perceived by the market . . . Hence, interbrand distances estimated by CA can be interpreted directly, not unlike interbrand distances estimated by other MDS algorithms" (Whitlark 1989, p. 87). The sign for the variable coordinates can change depending on the choice of software, yet the relative position of variables with respect to the center of the factor is constant and useful in interpreting the solution (cf. Martinez and Polo 1999).

Asymmetric Between-Set Distance

True between-set (row-to-column or column-to-row) distance is more difficult to define than within-set (row-to-row or column-to-column) distance. A relevant between-set distance should be directly related to the row-column association in the table and should also include some form of standardization to allow comparisons among all between-set distances (Greenacre 1984). Whitlark (1989) defines the true between-set distance as the joint occurrence of a row and column point expressed as a row percent divided by the square root of the column's weight as follows:

$$d_c^2(j,j') = \sum_{i=1}^{I}(S_{ij} - S_{ij}')^2, S_{ij} = \sqrt{\frac{f_{++}}{f_{i+}} * \frac{f_{ij}}{f_{+j}}}$$

With this definition of true between-set distance, Whitlark found that the correlation between true and observed distances for principal coordinate CA ranged from .74 to .84 for his data. Hence, Whitlark concluded that "attribute-to-brand distances produced by a CA are not meaningful and can result in misinterpretation of data" (1989, p. ii).

Symmetric Between-Set Distance

Whitlark's measure of true between-set distance does not allow comparisons among all between-set distances because it is asymmetric. We recommend the following symmetric definition of true between-set distance obtained by dividing each joint occurrence by the product of the row marginal and the column marginal:

$$d_c^2(j,j') = \sum_{i=1}^{r}(S_{ij} - S_{ij}'); \quad S_{ij} = \frac{f_{ij}}{f_{i+}^* f_{+j}}$$

We selected MapWise to test between-set distances, because MapWise scales the solution as recommended by Weller and Romney (1990). Approaches that do not transform one set of points relative to the other set of points "allow the meaningful interpretation of both within-set and between-set interpoint distances when the axes are scaled relative to the percent of variance explained by the axes" (Whitlark 1989, p. 93). We found that the correlation between true and observed distances was .89 for Greenacre's data (1984, p. 160) and at least .89 for Whitlark's data (1989).

Our experience in validating CA using inter-city data reveals that the correlation between true and observed between-set distances is directly related to the exhaustiveness of the row and column categories included in the analysis. For example, if Kansas City is the most western of the row cities and San Francisco is the most western of column cities, CA positions Kansas City near San Francisco. We speculate that if all competitive brands and all relevant attributes were included in the analysis, the correlation between true and observed between-set distances would approach perfection. Thus, we propose that between-set distances can be meaningfully interpreted when the row and column categories are exhaustive and the solution scales the axes by the percent of explained variance, but even then great caution should be exercised.

When Is Homogeneity Analysis Appropriate?

"Surprisingly enough, the discretization of numerical variables is very efficient and does not lead to a loss of information" (Gifi 1990; Masson 1974). Resulting solutions have low dimensionality, least squares fit, and parameter estimates available to sensible interpretation (Gittins 1990). However, caution should be exercised in using homogeneity analysis as it violates assumptions of multivariate normality and linearity, and can generate unstable and inaccurate solutions.

Types of Homogeneity Analysis

Data in contingency tables that are discretized as a binary indicator (or Burt) matrix can be summarized by many types of homogeneity analyses. MCA analyzes objects as rows and attributes as columns. Composite CA analyzes attributes as rows and objects as columns. Conditional CA employs a separate (simple) CA for each category of a third variable. Partial CA partitions the effects of a third variable similar to partial canonical correlation analysis. These types of homogeneity analysis are available in the homogeneity analysis (HOMALS) module (van der Burg, de Leeuw, and Verdegaal 1988; van Rijckevorsel and de Leeuw 1979) of OVERALLS (Young 1981).

Similarity to Correspondence Analysis

Although homogeneity analysis derives more singular values (eigenvalues) than CA because the matrix is larger, they are related for the same axes as:

$$\lambda_c^2 = (2\lambda_I^2 - 1)^2$$

where λc represents the eigenvalues from CA and λ_I represents the eigenvalues obtained by analyzing a binary indicator matrix with homogeneity analysis. The optimal scores are the same as those reported for the corresponding unweighted scores for the same data. We disagree with Weller and Romney (1990) in the flexibility of homogeneity analysis. They state (1990, p. 85), "The number of categories per variable need not be the same so that the variables with two, three, or four or more categories can be in the indicator matrix." We note that the principle of distributional equivalency (PDE) applies only to categories of the same variable. PDE does not apply to a Burt matrix, which combines categories of different variables. We recommend that the number of categories per variable be equal (or equally weighted) so they have an equal impact on the solution.

Departure from Assumptions

Homogeneity analysis requires multivariate normality and linear data distribution (Gittins 1990, p. 180). "Any departure from linearity or regularity is likely to be reflected in the results obtained, and, indeed, may well dominate them" (Kent 1986, p. 273). Because mixed-level data tend to be Poisson rather than normally distributed, mixed-level data do not fulfill a requirement of PCA (Madsen 1988, p. 23). The approach is a "misspecified model, where we 'pretend' the discrete data follow a multivariate normal distribution" (Kent 1986, p. 273).

Point Stability

The major disadvantage of homogeneity analysis is underassessment of variation explained by a principal axis (Greenacre 1988, p. 466). Since the axes tend to explain relatively little variance and to be unstable, homogeneity analysis may yield uninterpretable maps (Kaciak and Louviere 1990). The solutions involve many steps, may be degenerate, and are difficult to interpret (Gittins 1990). Accordingly, unless sample size is large relative to the total number of (indicator) variables, overfitting occurs, with consequent instability of estimated quantities. As de Leeuw and van Rijckevorsel (1988) warn, it is necessary to investigate the stability of the results.

Evaluation

Although homogeneity analysis can theoretically summarize single numerical to multiple nominal data, the approach may not be appropriate for continuous variables or variables with many possible values. "Further, as with classical multivariate methods generally, quantification techniques deal only with bivariate associations; higher-order interactions are ignored" (Gittins 1990, pp. 177–78). Homogeneity analysis does not superimpose passive categories on the solution. While de Leeuw and van Rijckevorsel's (1988, p. 55) conclusion that "[h]omogeneity analysis is a dangerous technique" seems too harsh, we do recommend caution in using this approach.

What Are Some of the Applications?

Researchers have found uses for CA in accounting, archeology, biomedical research, ecology, education, genetics, geology, health economics, linguistics, literary research, management, marketing, medicine, philosophy, political science, psychiatry, psychology, and sociology among other areas. Correspondence analysis has been useful in developing indexes (e.g., Cortinovis, Vella, and Ndiku 1993), scales (e.g., Reed 2002), frameworks (e.g., McCort 1994), and theory (e.g., Lubbe and Remenyi 1999) among its diverse set of applications.

The applications of CA within marketing have been equally rich and diverse. On the marketing

Table 7.1

Sample Empirical Uses of (Multiple) Correspondence Analysis (in reverse chronological order)

	Concept	Context	Description of study
1.	Competitive positioning	Product positioning for a multinational U.S. corporation in the Dominican Republic	Malhotra and Bartels (2002) used nonattribute based CA to mitigate cultural bias (self-reference criterion) in perceptual mapping and demonstrated the validity of the approach in comparison to MDS.
2.	Scale development	Workplace morale	Reed (2002) developed a scale to measure workplace morale from individual level multivariate data collected from a large sample of workplaces. The study has implications for measuring sales force and channel members' satisfaction.
3.	Collaboration profiling	University–industry relations in life sciences in Europe and the United States	Owen-Smith and colleagues (2002) studied the organizational and scientific profiles of the U.S. and European public research systems. The results implied that the division of labor for innovation in Europe is more focused around regional specializations and less diverse than those in the United States.
4.	Positioning	Web sites in the telecommunications industry	Berthon and colleagues (2001) examined fifteen Web sites and seven attributes to derive clusters on a spatial map.
5.	Image and positioning	Higher education institutions in the UK and South Africa	Ivy (2001) identified the unique positioning of old and new higher education institutions in the UK vs those in South Africa; also see Cheung (1994).
6.	Patronage behavior and product/service purchase patterns	Shopping malls	Yavas (2001) examined the relative importance of a set of patronage motives: when consumers choose a place to shop; shoppers' purchase patterns of a set of products; and inter and intra similarities/dissimilarities among motives and product purchase patterns.
7.	Attitudes toward employment	Married women's employment over the life course in twenty-three industrialized countries	Treas and Widmer's (2000) analysis revealed three distinct attitude patterns. These were "work-oriented," "family accommodating," and "motherhood-centered."
8.	Theory development	IT investments	Lubbe and Remenyi (1999) performed CA on case study data as one of their steps in developing a theory of IT investment (evaluation and benefit identification).
9.	Determinants of purchase influence	Family purchase decisionmaking	Martinez and Polo (1999) reported that joint decisionmaking took precedence for young couples, and when the wife worked, whereas the husband dominated the purchase decisions if the wife did not work or if the couple had been married for a long time; also see Green et al. (1983).

10. Labor profiling	Immigrants to Canada between 1945 and 1961	Mata and Pendakur (1999) studied the age-education cohorts of immigrants to Canada and the employment patterns over four census periods. Immigrants without high levels of education tended to be self-employed more often and this phenomenon became more dominant with increased length of stay.
11. Determining functional power	Power of marketing department within firms	Workman and Webb (1999) used the functional background of the CEO as a proxy for the power of the marketing department in a firm and examined business type, resource allocations, and strategic orientations. They found that classification of firms as business-to-consumer and business-to-business was the single best indicator of the marketing function's power.
12. Extraction of profiles	Memorable gift-giving and receiving profiles across gender	Areni, Kiecker, and Palan (1998) reported distinct gift-giving and receiving profiles for men and women. Four out of five female profiles included gift-receiving, whereas two out of three male profiles were associated with gift-giving as the most memorable experience.
13. Attitudes	Perceptions of the European currency	Meier and Kerchler (1998) grouped attitudes of Austrians toward the single European currency into five categories (from strong opponents to strong supporters). Belief in a stronger European identity and perceived threat to the Austrian identity were found to be associated with opposition and support to the Euro, respectively.
14. Critical incident classification	Service industries	Wels-Lips, van der Ven, and Pieters (1998) examined the generic dimensions underlying the classification of critical incidents in six service industries. MCA revealed two generic dimensions: service system (negative incidents) vs. service people (positive incidents), and customer initiative vs. employee initiative.
15. Classification of strategic variables	Barriers to adoption of total quality management	Ngai and Cheng (1997) created a perceptual map of barriers to TQM implementation and grouped them as managerial and organizational barriers.
16. Service positioning	Fast-food outlets in the United States and Canada	Kara, Kaynak, and Kucukemiroğlu (1996) examined ten fast-food chains on eleven attributes and reported differences based on country for age groups and purchase frequency.
17. Image assessment	Banking industry	Yavas and Shemwell (1996) studied the images of U.S. banks in comparison to competitors and extracted several strategic options, such as being first in new services and association with traditional bank attributes.

(continued)

Table 7.1 (continued)

Concept	Context	Description of study
18. Measurement of functional spinoffs	Marketing channels	Atwong and Rosenbloom (1995) concluded that functional spin-offs could be quantified through the use of CA. They presented a map that revealed the spin-off patterns of twelve marketing functions. The research had implications for forecasting structural changes and strategic integration decisions.
19. Competitive positioning	1,000 physicians and their perceptions of eight tertiary hospitals on nine attributes	Javalgi, Joseph, and Gombeski (1995) identified the niche positions and opportunities for the hospitals in their data set.
20. Transaction cost economics	Idiosyncratic investments	Lohtia, Brooks, and Krapfel (1995) identified six dimensions and six types of idiosyncratic investments and used CA to examine their relationships. They also reported that all six types but only three of the six dimensions of idiosyncratic investments had been empirically nvestigated thus far.
21. Framework development	Relationship marketing strategy	McCort (1994) derived from Rogers' interpersonal theory to develop a framework consisting of accessibility, accountability, commitment, enhancement, and positive regard. He verified the applicability of the framework with nonprofit organization data.
22. Service quality gap analysis	IT services in a management college	Remenyi and Money (1994) reported differences between the IT service performance evaluations. Academics and research associates were particularly displeased with the services as opposed to other users, and there were disagreements between the IT staff and users over what were the important problems.
23. Classification of telephone	Call-intercept characteristics and the type of respondent contacted	Strutton and Pelton (1994) reported that while contacts varying the number of times callbacks enabled reaching specific demographics, varying the time of day and the day of the week did not have significant impact on who was contacted.
24. Development of a socio-economic index	Health data in developing countries	Cortinovis, Vella, and Ndiku (1993) constructed a socioeconomic index for conceiving, implementing, and monitoring health interventions.
25. Graphic display of information	One vs. two variable charts	Loslever and Bourlon (1993) compared the perceptions of different business charts.

27. Risk evaluation	Car insurance in Belgium	Beirlant and colleagues (1992) examined the distributional properties of the customer portfolio along with relevant factors and mechanisms governing large claims.
28. Use and role of money in gift-giving	Christmas gift perceptions of under-graduates in the UK	Burgoyne and Routh (1991) reported that gifts should communicate the level of status and intimacy between the parties. Money did not communicate intimacy and its message regarding status was not perceived well.
29. Effectiveness of export promotion	Forty-five states of the United States	Goodnow and Goodnow (1990) related export promotion activities to the level of exports. Export promotion budgets were found to be linearly related to export levels. States seemed to collect more data as their budgets increased. States with smaller budgets were internal oriented, whereas states with larger budgets focused on external activities.
30. Country images and market segmentation	Tourism potential of Singapore vs. the Pacific Rim	The segmentation study by Calantone and colleagues (1989) did not reveal a more attractive alternative to Singapore. However, the tourists from the United States and Japan had significantly different perceptions.
31. Strategic positioning	Automobile industry in the UK	Meade (1987) utilized CA to compare companies and model ranges on a spatial map along with other methods.
32. Image study	1. Adjectives that describe celebrities; 2. Categories that apply to banks vs. savings and loan associations on product and institutional dimensions.	Mullet (1987) mapped the objects, attributes, changing images, and multiple dimensions.

management side, these have included market segmentation (e.g., Calantone et al. 1989); brand positioning (e.g., Berthon et al. 2001); image identification, tracking, and assessment (e.g., Ivy 2001; Yavas and Shemwell 1996); product/service positioning (e.g., Javalgi, Joseph, and Gombeski 1995); channel decisions (e.g., Atwong and Rosenbloom 1995); sales promotion and advertising (establishing objectives and evaluating effectiveness), pricing patterns, international marketing (e.g., Goodnow and Goodnow 1990; Shimp, Samiee, and Madden 1993); and other tactical and strategic issues.

Correspondence analysis also presents promising applications for consumer behaviorists as can be readily evidenced by its utilization in a wide range of social sciences. This potential of CA is underutilized in marketing. CA could particularly aid ethnographic researchers and complement qualitative research efforts as an exploratory/descriptive technique. On the consumer behavior side, research using (M)CA has included patronage behavior and purchase patterns (e.g., Yavas 2001), family purchase decisionmaking (e.g., Martinez and Polo 1999), extraction of consumer profiles (e.g., Areni, Kiecker, and Palan 1998), attitudes and cognitions (e.g., Meier and Kerchler 1998), and critical service encounters (Wels-Lips, van der Ven, and Pieters 1998) among others.

Correspondence analysis also improves the quality of surveys by detecting errors in data. Applications we have developed include the following: identifying purchase motives by chaining brands-features-benefits-values, superimposing attributes on a culturally unbiased solution, and using scenario analysis to set advertising objectives. Greenacre (2003) employed PCA to examine matched matrices, that is, analysis of matrices with identical row and column variables as in time-series data. Whereas loglinear analysis answers questions about the interaction between variables on the "variable level," Correspondence analysis answers questions on the "category level" (van der Heijden and de Leeuw 1985, p. 436). Correspondence analysis can "circumvent the 'cumbersome job' of interpreting a large number of loglinear interaction parameters" (van der Heijden and Worsley 1988, p. 287). For example, the row column association model restricts interactions between two variables to display the residual interactions with a third variable. Kaciak and Louviere (1990) have illustrated the application of MCA to multiple-choice experiment data. Such applications suggest that MCA can be used for new ways of market segmentation and for the development and specification of consumer choice models. We present, in Table 7.1, a sample of CA and MCA applications from extant literature to demonstrate the diverse and innovative applications of the technique. It should be noted that in many instances, it is best to use CA as a supplement/complement to other multivariate techniques due to its exploratory nature.

What Are Some of the Limitations?

It should be realized that CA has several limitations. It is limited to describing joint occurrences in cross-tabulated data. Correspondence analysis requires that at least three row and three column categories be cross-tabulated. It is recommended that the expected cell size of all categories be at least five. This approach cannot visualize percentages because it merges row and column percentages. It cannot predict a dependent variable or reveal causality because CA associates categories of variables. The underlying dimensions cannot be identified, except subjectively, because CA relates categories to one another, rather than to axes or vectors. Furthermore, the number of dimensions is determined subjectively.

For Euclidean metric distances, the active categories cannot include both top and bottom box scores (didoublement), and the axes must be scaled by the square root of the variance they explain. Although CA is not limited to linear metric data and large random samples, measures of central tendency and homogeneity analysis (MCA) require normally distributed responses, linearity

Figure 7.1   **Schematic Representation of a Sample of Important CA Works in English**

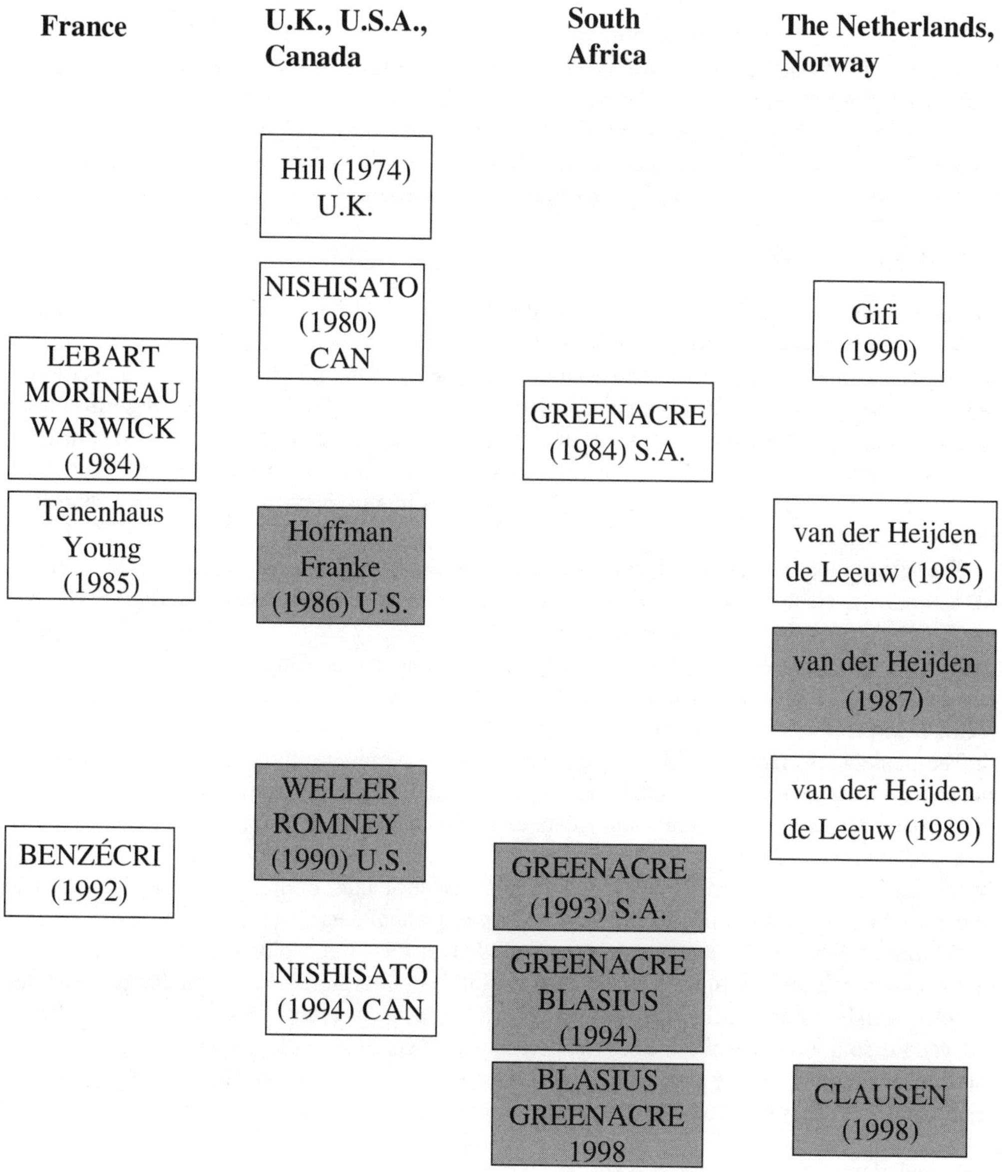

France	U.K., U.S.A., Canada	South Africa	The Netherlands, Norway

Hill (1974)
U.K.

NISHISATO
(1980)
CAN

LEBART
MORINEAU
WARWICK
(1984)

Gifi
(1990)

GREENACRE
(1984) S.A.

Tenenhaus
Young
(1985)

Hoffman
Franke
(1986) U.S.

van der Heijden
de Leeuw (1985)

van der Heijden
(1987)

WELLER
ROMNEY
(1990) U.S.

van der Heijden
de Leeuw (1989)

BENZÉCRI
(1992)

GREENACRE
(1993) S.A.

NISHISATO
(1994) CAN

GREENACRE
BLASIUS
(1994)

BLASIUS
GREENACRE
1998

CLAUSEN
(1998)

Note: Adopted and extended from Clausen (1998, p. 7). Small letters refer to articles; capital letters refer to books; shaded boxes represent less technical texts.

and metric data. Homogeneity analysis also requires that the number of levels for each variable be equal or equally weighted.

Significance testing is not appropriate for measures of central tendency, homogeneity analysis, pick-any data, percentages, or utility values. CA is a descriptive method that is more useful for exploratory research than it is for hypothesis testing. Despite the claims by some authors, the issue of interpreting between-set distances has yet to be resolved satisfactorily.

A noncomprehensive schematic representation of important works (in English) that treat CA methodology in detail is presented in Figure 7.1. The readers are kindly referred to these writings for further information on CA, its applications and limitations.

Summary and Conclusions

Correspondence analysis best summarizes multivariate relationships within and between row and column points of a data matrix by their physical closeness on a perceptual map. Stage one removes the main effect of the row and column totals, leaving the interaction of row and column points. Stage two decomposes the standardized data matrix into a solution that describes how interaction differs from expectations, the origin of the perceptual map. The two largest nontrivial eigenvalues in the solution indicate the variance (or relationships) in the data explained by the x and y axes. The third stage positions row and column points in the same space to best represent their relationships.

The various approaches called reciprocal averages, ANOVA (optimal or dual scaling), principal components (factor) analysis, generalized canonical analysis (homogeneity analysis or MCA), and Levine's centroid (pick-any) approach are mathematically equivalent. However, they differ in the scaling of the points along the principal axes. Although all scaling methods are reliable, the corresponding validity declines in the following order: PRN, the asymmetric method used by VHL, CGS profile metric, and STD.

The perceptual mapping of joint occurrence by CA requires only a representative sample, rather than a large, random sample, and cross-tabulated similarity data, rather than ordinal or metric data. The approach permits quick data collection and analyzes mixed-level data, pick-any data, and symmetric matrices. Many diagnostic tools are available for evaluating external validity, model fit, statistical significance, the optimal number of axes, outliers, point stability, contribution to the axes, and scaling and optimal coding of ordinal data.

Whitlark (1989) and Greenacre (1989) conclude that PRN CA yields within-set (row-to-row or column-to-column) distances that can be meaningfully interpreted. We warn that between-set distances can be meaningfully interpreted only when the row and column categories are exhaustive and the solution scales the axes by the percentage of variance explained by the axes, but even then great caution should be exercised. In conclusion, the major benefit of CA is that the approach simultaneously analyzes mixed-level variables without implying causality.

Acknowledgment

The authors would like to thank Michael J. Greenacre for his useful comments on a previous version of this article.

References

ADDAD (1983), *Reference Manual.* Paris: Association pour le Développement at la Diffussion De l'Analyse des Données.

Aitchison, J. and M.C. Greenacre (2002), "Biplots of Compositional Data," *Journal of the Royal Statistics Society*, Series C, Applied Statistics, 51 (4), 375–92.

Areni, C.S., P. Kiecker, and K.M. Palan (1998), "Is It Better to Give Than to Receive? Exploring Gender Differences in the Meaning of Memorable Gifts," *Psychology & Marketing*, 15 (1), 81–110.

Atwong, C.T. and B. Rosenbloom (1995), "A Spatial Approach to Measuring Functional Spin-offs in Marketing Channels," *Journal of Marketing Theory and Practice*, 3 (Fall), 58–73.

Baker, F.B. (1960), "Univac Scientific Computer Program for Scaling of Psychological Inventories by the Method of Reciprocal Averages CPA 22," *Behavioral Science*, 5, 268–69.

Becker, R., J.M. Chambers, and A.R. Wilks (1988), *The New S Language. A Programming Environment for Data Analysis and Graphics.* Pacific Grove, CA: Wadsworth.

Beirlant J., V. Deneaux, A.M. De Meyer, and M.J. Gooyaerts (1992), "Statistical Risk Evaluation Applied to (Belgian) Car Insurance," *Insurance, Mathematics and Economics*, 10 (January), 289–303.

Benzécri, J.P. (1969), "Statistical Analysis as a Tool to Make Patterns Emerge from Data," in *Methodologies of Pattern Recognition*, S. Watanabe, ed. New York: Academic, 35–74.

——— (1973), *L'analyse des Données: T. W, L'analyse des Correspondances* [Data Analysis: T.2, Correspondence Analysis]. Paris: Dunod.

——— (1992), *Correspondence Analysis Handbook.* New York: Dekker.

Berthon, P., L. Pitt, M. Ewing, B. Ramaseshan, and N. Jayaratna (2001), "Positioning in Cyberspace: Evaluating Telecom Web Sites Using Correspondence Analysis," *Information Resources Management Journal*, 14, (January–March), 13–21.

Blasius, J. and M. Greenacre (1998), "Preface," in *Visualization of Categorical Data*, Jörg Blasius and Michael J. Greenacre, eds. San Diego: Academic.

Bock, R.D. (1960), *Methods and Applications of Optimal Scaling.* Chapel Hill, NC: L.L. Thurstone Psychometric Laboratory, Report No. 25.

Bond, J. and G. Michailides (1997), "Interactive Correspondence Analysis in a Dynamic Object-Oriented Environment," *Journal of Statistical Software*, 2, 8. [www.jstatsoft.org/v02/i08/jss.pdf]

Bouroche, J.M., G. Saporta, and M. Tenenhaus (1975), "Generalized Canonical Analysis of Qualitative Data," U.S.–Japan seminar.

Burgoyne, C.B. and D.A. Routh (1991), "Constraints on the Use of Money as a Gift at Christmas: The Role of Status and Intimacy," *Journal of Economic Psychology*, 12 (March), 47–70.

Burt, C. (1950), "The Factorial Analysis of Qualitative Data," *British Journal of Psychology*, 3, 166–85.

——— (1953), "Scale Analysis and Factor Analysis," *The British Journal of Statistical Psychology*, 6 (May), 5–23.

Cailliez, F. and J.P. Pages (1976), *Introduction a L'analyse des 'Donnees* [Introduction to Data Analysis]. Paris: Smash.

Calantone, R.J., C.A. di Benedetto, A. Hakam, and D.C. Bojanic (1989), "Multiple Multinational Tourism Positioning Using Correspondence Analysis," *Journal of Travel Research*, 28 (Fall), 25–33.

Carroll, J.D. (1968), "A Generalization of Canonical Correlation Analysis to Three or More Sets of Variables," *Proceeding of the 76th Convention of the American Psychological Association*, 3, 227–28.

Carroll, J.D., P.E. Green, and C.M. Schaffer (1986), "Interpoint Distance Comparisons in CA," *Journal of Marketing Research*, 23 (August), 271–80.

———, ———, and ——— (1989), "Reply to Greenacre's Commentary on the Carroll-Green-Schaffer Scaling of Two-Way Correspondence Analysis Solutions," *Journal of Marketing Research*, 26 (August), 366–68.

Caussinus, H. (1986), "Discussion of Goodman, Leo A., 'Some Useful Extensions of the Usual Correspondence Analysis Approach and the Usual Log-Linear Models Approach in the Analysis of Contingency Tables,'" *International Statistical Review*, 54 (3), 243–309.

Cazes, P., A. Boumerder, S. Bonnefous, and J.P. Pages (1977), "Codage et analyse des tableaux logiques, Introduction a la practique des variables qualitatives," *Cahier du Bureau Universitaire de Recherche Operationnelle*, Serie Recherche, Cahier No. 27.

Cheung, Y.L. (1994), "Categorical Criteria Values: Correspondence Analysis," *Omega*, 22 (July), 371–81.

Clausen, S.E. (1998), *Applied Correspondence Analysis: An Introduction* (Sage University Papers Series on Quantitative Applications in the Social Sciences, series no. 07–121). Thousand Oaks, CA: Sage.

Cooper, L.G. (1983). "A Review of Multidimensional Scaling in Marketing Research," *Applied Psychological Measurement*, 7 (4), 427–50.

Cortinovis, I., V. Vella, and J. Ndiku (1993), "Construction of a Socio-economic Index to Facilitate Analysis of Health Data in Developing Countries," *Social Science and Medicine*, 36 (8), 1087.

de Leeuw, J. (1982), "Generalized Eigenvalue Problems with Positive Semi-Definite Matrices," *Psychometrika*, 47, 87–93.

———— (1983), "On the Prehistory of Correspondence Analysis," *Statistica Neerlandica*, 37, 161–64.

———— (1988), "Fuzzy Coding and B-Splines," in *Component and Correspondence Analysis: Dimension Reduction by Functional Approximation*, Jan L.A. van Rijckevorsel and Jan de Leeuw, eds. Chichester, UK: Wiley.

de Leeuw, J. and P.O.M. van der Heijden (1988), "Correspondence Analysis of Incomplete Contingency Tables," *Psychometrika*, 53 (June), 223–33.

de Leeuw, J. and J.L.A. van Rijckevorsel (1988), "Beyond Homogeneity Analysis," in *Component and Correspondence Analysis: Dimension Reduction by Functional Approximation*, Jan L.A. van Rijckevorsel and Jan de Leeuw, eds. Chichester, England: Wiley.

DeSarbo, W.S. and D.L. Hoffman (1987), "Constructing MDS Joint Spaces from Binary Choice Data: A Multidimensional Unfolding Threshold Model for Marketing Research," *Journal of Marketing Research*, 4, 40–54.

Deville J.C. and G. Saporta (1983), "Correspondence Analysis with an Extension Towards Nominal Time Series," *Journal of Econometrics*, 22, 169–89.

Escoufier, Y. (1979), "Une represtation des variables dans l'analyse des correspondances multiples" [Representation of variables in multiple correspondence analysis], *Revue de Statistique Appliquee*, 27, 37–47.

Escoufier, Y. and S. Junca (1986), "Discussion of Goodman, Leo A., 'Some Useful Extensions of the Usual Correspondence Analysis Approach and the Usual Log-Linear Models Approach in the Analysis of Contingency Tables,' " *International Statistical Review*, 54 (December), 279–83.

Fehlen, F. (1998), "The Cloud of Candidates. Exploring the Political Field," in *Visualization of Categorical Data*, Jörg Blasius and Michael J. Greenacre, eds. San Diego: Academic.

Fienberg, S.E. and M.M. Meyer (1983), "Loglinear Models and Categorical Data Analysis with Psychometric and Econometric Applications," *Journal of Econometrics*, 22, 191–214.

Fisher, R.A. (1940), "The Precision of Discriminant Functions," *Annuals of Eugenics* 10 (December), 422–29, cited in Michael J. Greenacre, *Theory and Applications of CA*. London: Academic.

Gabriel, K.R. (1995), "Biplot Display of Multivariate Categorical Data, with Comments on Multiple Correspondence Analysis," in *Recent Advances in Descriptive Multivariate Analysis*, W.J. Krzanowski, ed. Oxford, UK: Clarendon Press.

Gifi, A. (1990), *Non-Linear Multivariate Analysis*. New York: Wiley.

Gittins, R. (1990), "Review of Abby Israels, Eigenvalue Techniques for Qualitative Data," *Psychometrika*, 55 (March), 177–81.

Goodman, L.A. (1986), "Some Useful Extensions of the Usual Correspondence Analysis Approach and the Usual Log-Linear Models Approach in the Analysis of Contingency Tables," *International Statistical Review*, 54 (3), 243–70.

———— (1996), "A Single General Method for the Analysis of Cross-Classified Data: Reconciliation and Synthesis of Some Methods of Pearson, Yule, and Fisher, and Also Some Methods of Correspondence Analysis and Association Analysis," *Journal of the American Statistical Association*, 91 (March), 408.

Goodnow, J.D. and W.E. Goodnow (1990), "Self-Assessment by State Export Promotion Agencies: A Status Report," *International Marketing Review*, 7 (3), 18–31.

Goodnow, W.E. (1988), "MapWise," Version 2.02. Clarendon Hills, IL: Market ACTION Research Software Inc.

Gower, J.C. and P.G.N. Digby (1980), "Looking at Multivariate Data," in *Interpreting Multivariate Data*, Vic Barnett, ed. Chichester, UK: Wiley.

Gower, J.C. and D.J. Hand (1996), *Biplots*. London: Chapman and Hall.

Graffelman, J., and T. Aluja-Banet (2003), "Optimal Representation of Supplementary Variables in Biplots from Principal Component Analysis and Correspondence Analysis," *Biometrical Journal*, 45 (4), 491–509.

Green, P.E. and J.D. Carroll (1988), "A Simple Procedure for Finding a Composite of Several Multidimensional Scaling Solutions," *Journal of the Academy of Marketing Science,* 16 (Spring), 25–35.

Green, R.T., J.P. Leonardi, J.L. Chandon, I.C.M. Cunningham, B. Verhage, and A. Strazzieri (1983), "Societal Development and Family Purchasing Roles," *Journal of Consumer Research*, 9 (March), 436–42.

Greenacre, M.J. (1981), "Practical CA," in *Interpreting Multivariate Data*, Vic Barnett, ed. Chichester, UK: Wiley.

———— (1984), *Theory and Applications of CA*. London: Academic.

———— (1986), "An Alternating Least-Squares Algorithm to Perform Multidimensional Unfolding," *Psychometrika*, 51 (2), 241–50.

———— (1988), "Correspondence Analysis of Multivariate Categorical Data by Weighted Least-Squares," *Biometrika*, 75 (3), 457–67.

———— (1989), "The Carroll-Green-Schaffer Scaling in CA: A Theoretical and Empirical Appraisal," *Journal of Marketing Research*, 16 (August), 358–65.

———— (1992), "Biplots in Correspondence Analysis," *Journal of Applied Statistics*, 20, 251–69.

———— (1993), *Correspondence Analysis in Practice.* London: Academic.

———— (2000), "Correspondence Analysis of Square Asymmetric Matrices," *Applied Statistics*, 49, 297–310.

———— (2002), "Ratio Maps and Correspondence Analysis," working paper No. 598, Department of Economics and Business, Pompeu Fabra University, Spain.

———— (2003), "Singular Value Decomposition of Matched Matrices," *Journal of Applied Statistics*, 30, 1101–13.

Greenacre, M.J. and J. Blasius (1994), "Preface," in *Correspondence Analysis in the Social Sciences*, Michael J. Greenacre and Jörg Blasius, eds. London: Academic.

———— and ———— (1997), "Correspondence Analysis of Square Tables, with an Application to Social Mobility," in *Classification and Knowledge Organization*, R. Klar and O. Opitz, eds. Berlin: Springer Verlag, 573–80.

Greenacre, M.J. and T. Hastie (1987), "The Geometric Interpretation of Correspondence Analysis," *American Statistical Association*, 82 (398), 437–47.

Greenacre, M.J. and A. Torres (1999), "Dual Scaling of Dominance Data and Its Relationship to Correspondence Analysis," working paper No. 430, Department of Economics and Business, Pompeu Fabra University, Spain.

Greenacre, M.J. and L.G. Underhill (1982), "Scaling a Data Matrix in Low-Dimensional Euclidean Space," in *Topics in Applied Multivariate Analysis*, D.M. Hawkins, ed., Cambridge, UK: Cambridge University Press, 183–268.

Guttman, L. (1941), "The Quantification of a Class of Attributes: A Theory and Method of Scale Construction," in *The Prediction of Personal Adjustment*, P. Horst et al., eds. New York: Social Science Research Council, 319–48.

———— (1950), "The Relation of Scalorgram Analysis to Other Techniques," in *Measurement and Prediction*, S.A. Stouffer et al., eds. Princeton, NJ: Princeton University Press.

———— (1953), "A Note on Sir Cyril Burt's 'Factorial Analysis of Qualitative Data,'" *The British Journal of Statistical Psychology*, 6 (May), 1–4.

Hayashi, C. (1950), "On the Quantification of Qualitative Data from the Mathematico-Statistical Point of View," *Annals of the Institute of Statistical Mathematics*, 2 (1), 35–47.

Heiser, W.J. and J. Meulman (1983), "Analyzing Rectangular Tables by Joint and Constrained Multidimensional Scaling," *Journal of Econometrics*, 22, 139–67.

Hill, M.O. (1974), "Correspondence Analysis: A Neglected Multivariate Method," *Applied Statistics*, 23 (3), 340.

Hoffman, D.L. (1991), "Review of Four Correspondence Analysis Programs for the IBM PC," *The American Statistician*, 45 (November), 305–11.

Hoffman, D.L. and G.R. Franke (1986), "Correspondence Analysis: Graphical Representation of Categorical Data in Marketing Research," *Journal of Marketing Research*, 10 (August), 213–27.

Holbrook, M.B., W.L. Moore, and R.S. Winer (1982), "Constructing Joint Spaces from Pick-Any Data: A New Tool for Consumer Analysis," *Journal of Consumer Research*, 9 (June), 99–105.

Horst, P. (1935), "Measuring Complex Attitudes," *Journal of Social Psychology*, 6, 369–74.

Horst, P. et al., eds. (1941), *The Prediction of Personal Adjustment.* New York: Social Science Research Council, 319–48.

Hotelling, H. (1933), "Analysis of a Complex of Statistical Variables into Principal Components," *Journal of Educational Psychology*, 24, 417–41, 498–520.

Ivy, J. (2001), "Higher Education Institution Image: A Correspondence Analysis Approach," *The International Journal of Educational Management*, 15 (6), 276–82.

Javalgi, R.G., W.B. Joseph, and W.R. Gombeski, Jr. (1995), "Positioning Your Service to Target Key Buying Influences: The Case of Referring Physicians and Hospitals," *The Journal of Services Marketing*, 9 (5), 42–52.

Jolliffe, I.T. (1986), *Principal Component Analysis.* New York: Springer-Verlag.

Kaciak, E. and J. Louviere (1990), "Multiple Correspondence Analysis of Multiple Choice Experiment Data," *Journal of Marketing Research*, 27 (November), 455–65.

Kara, A., E. Kaynak, and O. Kucukemiroğlu (1996), "Positioning of Fast-Food Outlets in Two Regions of North America: A Comparative Study Using Correspondence Analysis," *Journal of Professional Services Marketing*, 14 (2), 99–119.

Kent, J.T., (1986),"Discussion of Goodman, Leo A., 'Some Useful Extensions of the Usual Correspondence Analysis Approach and the Usual Log-Linear Models Approach in the Analysis of Contingency Tables,'" *International Statistical Review*, 54, 3 (December), 273–74.

Kroonenberg, P.M. (1996), *3WAYPACK User's Manual*. Leiden, The Netherlands: Department of Education, Leiden University.

Lancaster, H.O. (1966), "Kolmogorov's Remark on the Hotelling Canonical Correlations," *Biometrika*, 53, 585–88.

Lebart, L., A. Morineau, and N. Tabard (1977), *Techniques de la Description Statistique: Methodes et Logiciels pour l'Analzse des Grands Tableaux*. Paris: Dunod.

Lebart, L., A. Morineau, and K.M. Warwick (1984), *Multivariate Descriptive Statistical Analysis: CA and Related Techniques for Large Matrices*. New York: Wiley.

Leclerc, A. (1980), "Quelques Proprietes Optimales en Analyse de Donnees, in Terme de Correlation entre Variables," *Mathematique et Sciences Humaines*, 18, 51–67.

Le Roux B., and H. Rouanet (1998), "Interpreting Axes in Multiple Correspondence Analysis: Method of the Contributions of Points and Deviations," in *Visualization of Categorical Data*, Jörg Blasius and Michael J. Greenacre, eds. San Diego: Academic. (EyeLID demo version available at: ftp.math-info.univ-paris5.fr/pub/MathPsy/EyeLID.)

Levine, J.H. (1979), "Joint Space Analysis of 'Pick-Any' Data: Analysis of Choices from an Unconstrained Set of Alternatives," *Psychometrika*, 44 (March), 85–92.

Lingos, J.C. (1963), "Multivariate Analysis of Contingencies: An IBM 7090 Program for Analyzing Metric/Non-Metric or Linear/Non-Linear Data," *Computational Report*, 2, 1–24, University of Michigan Computing Center.

——— (1964), "Simultaneous Linear Regression: An IBM 7090 Program for Analyzing Metric/Non-Metric or Linear/Non-Linear Data," *Behavioral Science*, 9, 87–88.

Lipkovich, I. and E.P. Smith (2002), "Biplot and Singular Value Decomposition Macros for Excel," *Journal of Statistical Software*, 7, 5. [www.jstatsoft.org/v07/i05/BIPLOT_paper_6_6_02.pdf]

Lohtia, R., C.M. Brooks, and R.E. Krapfel (1994), "What Constitutes a Transaction-specific Asset? An Examination of the Dimensions and Types," *Journal of Business Research*, 30, 3 (July), 261–71.

Loslever, P. and F. Bourlon (1993), "Graphic Display of Information: How Do Individuals Judge One and Two Variable Charts?" *Journal of Information Science*, 19 (1), 81–85.

Lubbe, S. and D. Remenyi (1999), "Management of Information Technology Evaluation—The Development of a Managerial Thesis," *Logistics Information Management*, 12 (1/2), 145.

Madsen, T. (1988), "Multivariate Statistics and Archaeology," in *Multivariate Archaeology: Numerical Approaches in Scandinavian Archaeology*, Torsten Madsen, ed. Jutland Archaeological Society Publications XXI. Aarhus, Denmark: Aarhus University Press.

Magidson, J. (1998), "Using New General Ordinal Logit Displays to Visualize the Effects in Categorical Outcome Data," in *Visualization of Categorical Data*, Jörg Blasius and Michael J. Greenacre, eds. San Diego: Academic.

Malhotra, N.K. and B.C. Bartels (2002), "Overcoming the Attribute Prespecification Bias in International Marketing Research by Using Non-attribute Based Correspondence Analysis," *International Marketing Review*, 19 (1), 65–79.

Martinez, E. and Y. Polo (1999), "Determining Factors in Family Purchasing Behaviour: An Empirical Investigation," *The Journal of Consumer Marketing*, 16 (5), 461.

Masson, M. (1974), "Processus Lineaires et Analyse des Donnees Non Lineaire," These d'Etat, Universite Paris VI.

Mata, F. and R. Pendakur (1999), "Immigration, Labor Force Integration and the Pursuit of Self-Employment," *The International Migration Review*, 33, 2 (Summer), 378–402.

McCort, D.J. (1994), "A Framework for Evaluating the Relational Extent of a Relationship Marketing Strategy: The Case of Nonprofit Organizations," *Journal of Direct Marketing*, 8 (Spring), 53–66.

McKeon, J.J. (1966), "Canonical Analysis: Some Relations Between Canonical Correlation, Factor Analysis, Discriminant Function Analysis and Scaling Theory," *Psychometric Monograph*, No. 13.

Meade, N. (1987), "Strategic Positioning in the UK Car Market," *European Journal of Marketing*, 21 (5), 43–57.

Meier, K. and K. Erich (1998), "Social Representations of the Euro in Austria," *Journal of Economic Psychology*, 19 (6), 755–75.

Mosier, C. I. (1946), "Machine Methods in Scaling by Reciprocal Averages." Endicott, NY: IBC, Proceedings, Research Forum, 35–39.

Muehsam, M.J. (1989), "Application of Correspondence Analysis to Classical Statistical Procedures (Outlier Detection)," University Microfilms ADG90–15553, Texas A&M University.

Mullet, G.M. (1987), "Correspondence Analysis: A New Tool for Image Studies," *Journal of Professional Services Marketing*, 2, 3 (Spring), 41–62.

Ngai, E.W.T. and T.C.E. Cheng (1997), "Identifying Potential Barriers to Total Quality Management Using Principal Component Analysis and Correspondence Analysis," *The International Journal of Quality & Reliability Management*, 14 (4), 391.

Nishisato, S. (1980), *Analysis of Categorical Data: Dual Scaling and Its Applications.* Toronto: University of Toronto Press.

——— (1994), *Elements of Dual Scaling: An Introduction to Practical Data Analysis.* Hillsdale, NJ: Lawrence Erlbaum Associates.

——— (1998), "Graphing Is Believing: Interpretable Graphs for Dual Scaling," in *Visualization of Categorical Data*, Jörg Blasius and Michael J. Greenacre, eds. San Diego: Academic.

Nishisato, S. and W. Gaul (1988), "Marketing Data Analysis by Dual Scaling," *International Journal of Research in Marketing*, 5 (3), 151–71.

——— and ——— (1990), "An Approach to Marketing Data Analysis: The Forced Classification Procedure of Dual Scaling," *Journal of Marketing Research*, 27 (August), 354–60.

Nishisato, S. and I. Nishisato (1990), *Dual3*, Version 3.2. Ontario, Canada: MicroStats.

Noma, E. (1982), "The Simultaneous Scaling of Cited and Citing Articles in a Common Space," *Scientometrics*, 4, 205–31.

Owen-Smith, J., M. Riccaboni, F. Pammolli, and W.W. Powell (2002), "A Comparison of U.S. and European University-Industry Relations in the Life Sciences," *Management Science*, 48 (January), 24–43.

Pearson, K. (1913), "On the Measurement of the Influence of 'Broad Categories' on Correlation," *Biometrika*, 9, 116–39.

Pelton, L.E., K.R. Tudor, and B. Goodnow (1991), "MapWise Version 2.03—Perceptual Mapping Software for Correspondence Analysis; Comments," *Journal of the Academy of Marketing Science*, 19 (Fall), 383–90.

Reed, K. (2002), "The Use of Correspondence Analysis to Develop a Scale to Measure Workplace Morale from Multi-level Data," *Social Indicators Research*, 57, 3 (March), 339.

Remenyi, D.S.J. and A.H. Money (1994), "Service Quality and Correspondence Analysis in Determining Problems with the Effective Use of Computer Services," *European Journal of Information Systems*, 3 (January), 2–13.

Risson, A., P. Rolland, J. Bertin, and J.H. Chauchat (1994), "AMADO: Analyse Graphique d'une MAtrice de DOnnées, guide de l'utilisateur du logiciel" (AMADO User Guide). Saint-Mandé, France: CISIA.

Rost, J. (1990), *LACORD. Latent Class Analysis for Ordinal Variables. A FORTRAN Program* (2nd ed.). Kiel, Germany: IPN, University of Kiel.

Saporta, G. (1975), "Liaison entre Plusieurs Ensembles de Variables et Codage de Donnees Qualitatives," These de 3e cycle, Universite Paris VI.

Shimp, T.A., S. Samiee, and T.J. Madden (1993), "Countries and Their Products: A Cognitive Structure Perspective," *Journal of the Academy of Marketing Science*, 21 (Fall), 323–31.

Smith, Scott M. (1988), *PC-MDS: Multidimensional Scaling and Conjoint Analysis.* Provo, UT: Brigham Young University.

SPSS (1989), *Categories.* New York: McGraw-Hill.

Strutton, D. and L.E. Pelton (1994), "A Multiple Correspondence Analysis of Telephone Contact Rates," *The Mid-Atlantic Journal of Business*, 30 (March), 27–40.

Takane, Y. (1987), "Analysis of Contingency Tables by Ideal Point Discriminant Analysis," *Psychometrika*, 53 (4), 493–513.

Tenenhaus, M. (1977), "Analyse en Composantes Principales d'un Ensemble de Variables Nominales ou Numeriques," *R.S.A.*, 25 (2).

Tenenhaus, M. and F.W. Young (1985), "An Analysis and Synthesis of MCA, Optimal Scaling, Dual Scaling, Homogeneity Analysis and Other Methods for Quantifying Categorical Multivariate Data," *Psychometrika*, 50, 91–119.

Torgerson, W.S. (1958), *Theory and Methods of Scaling*. New York: Wiley.

Torres, A. and M.J. Greenacre (2002), "Dual Scaling and Correspondence Analysis of Preferences, Paired Comparisons and Ratings," *International Journal of Research in Marketing*, 19 (December), 401.

Treas, J. and E.D. Widmer (2000), "Married Women's Employment over the Life Course: Attitudes in Cross-National Perspective," *Social Forces*, 78 (June), 1409–36.

van der Burg, E., J. de Leeuw, and R. Verdegaal (1988), "Homogeneity Analysis with k Sets of Variables: An Alternating Least Squares Method with Optimal Scaling Features," *Psychometrika*, 53 (June), 177–97.

van der Heijden, P.G.M. (1987), *Correspondence Analysis of Longitudinal Categorical Data*. Leiden, the Netherlands: DSWO Press.

van der Heijden, P.G.M. and J. de Leeuw (1985), "Correspondence Analysis used Complementary to Loglinear Analysis," *Psychometrika*, 50 (December), 429–47.

——— and ——— (1989), "Correspondence Analysis, with Special Attention to the Analysis of Panel Data and Event History Data," in *Sociological Methodology*, C.C. Clogg, ed. Oxford: Blackwell, 43–87.

van der Heijden, P.G.M. and K.J. Worsley (1988), "Comment on 'Correspondence Analysis Used Complementary to Loglinear Analysis,'" *Psychometrika*, 53 (May), 287–91.

van Rijckevorsel, J. and J. de Leeuw (1979), "An Outline to PRINCALS," University of Leiden, The Netherlands.

Weller, S.C. and A.K. Romney (1990), *Metric Scaling: Correspondence Analysis*. Newbury Park, CA: Sage.

Wels-Lips, I., M. ven der Ven, and R. Pieters (1998), "Critical Services Dimensions: An Empirical Investigation Across Six Industries," *International Journal of Service Industry Management*, 9 (3), 286.

Whitlark, D.B. (1989), "Mapping Brand Association Data," University Microfilms ADG90–23481, Colgate Darden Graduate School of Business Administration, University of Virginia.

Wolff, K.E. and S. Gabler (1998), "Comparisons of Visualizations in Formal Concept Analysis and Correspondence Analysis," in *Visualization of Categorical Data*, Jörg Blasius and Michael J. Greenacre, eds. San Diego: Academic.

Workman, J.P., Jr., and K.L. Webb (1999), "Variations in the Power of Marketing between Consumer and Industrial Firms," *Journal of Business-to-Business Marketing*, 6 (2), 1.

Yavas, U. (2001), "Patronage Motives and Product Purchase Patterns: A Correspondence Analysis," *Marketing Intelligence and Planning*, 19 (2), 97.

Yavas, U. and D.J. Shemwell (1996), "Bank Image: Exposition and Illustration of Correspondence Analysis," *The International Journal of Bank Marketing*, 14 (1), 15.

Young, F.W. (1981), "Quantitative Analysis of Qualitative Data," *Psychometrika*, 46 (December), 357–88.

Young, F.W., Y.Y. Takane, and J. de Leeuw (1978), "The Principal Components of Mixed Measurement Level Data: An Alternating Least Squares Method," *Psychometrika*, 43, 279–81.

Zhu, M. (2001), "Feature Extraction and Dimension Reduction with Applications to Classification and the Analysis of Co-occurrence Data," doctoral dissertation, Stanford University.

Zhu, M. and T.J. Hastie (2003), "Feature Extraction for Nonparametric Discriminant Analysis," *Journal of Computational and Graphical Statistics*, 12, 101–20.

ABOUT THE EDITOR AND CONTRIBUTORS

Sundar G. Bharadwaj is Caldwell Research Fellow and Associate Professor of Marketing at Goizueta Business School, Emory University.

Betsy Rush Charles is Associate Professor of Marketing at Bethune–Cookman College.

Morris B. Holbrook is the W.T. Dillard Professor of Marketing, Graduate School of Business, Columbia University.

Shelby D. Hunt is the Jerry S. Rawls and P. W. Horn Professor of Marketing at Rawls College of Business, Texas Tech University.

Allison R. Johnson is a doctoral candidate in the Department of Marketing in the Marshall School of Business at the University of Southern California.

Robert F. Lusch is Department Head and Professor at the University of Arizona.

Naresh K. Malhotra is Regents' Professor in the Department of Marketing, College of Management, Georgia Institute of Technology.

Kent B. Monroe is the J.M. Jones Professor of Marketing, Department of Business Administration, University of Illinois.

Robert M. Morgan is Associate Professor of Marketing and J. Reese Phifer Faculty Fellow at Culverhouse College of Commerce, University of Alabama.

David W. Stewart is the Robert E. Brooker Professor of Marketing and Deputy Dean in the Marshall School of Business at the University of Southern California.

Can Uslay is a Marketing Ph.D. candidate at the College of Management, Georgia Institute of Technology.

Rajan Varadarajan is Distinguished Professor of Marketing and Ford Chair in Marketing and E-Commerce at Mays Business School, Texas A&M University.

Stephen L. Vargo is Visiting Professor of Marketing at the Robert H. Smith School of Business, University of Maryland.

Lan Xia is Assistant Professor of Marketing at Bentley College.

INDEX

319